"When Christ confronted Saul on the road to Damascus he asked a penetrating question: 'Why are you persecuting me?' This simple question made it clear that when one of Christ's followers is hurting, He hurts too. I believe that few things grieve the heart of God more than when His children suffer abuse. In this practical yet profound book, June offers hope, help, and healing."

SHEILA WALSH
Author, *Beautiful Things Happen When a Woman Trusts God*

"I've known June Hunt for more than 20 years. She is an exceptionally thorough and biblical counselor whose work I enthusiastically recommend. Over the years, I have referred many of the abuse victims I've worked with to June, and they have benefitted greatly from her teaching on the subject...which, now, is reflected masterfully in a single volume."

CAROLYN BEST
Abuse Victim Counselor
Exchanged Life Ministries, Texas

"There's no better person to help a victim than one who has been victimized, and who is now victorious. Whether you're living with abuse—or helping someone who is—*How to Rise Above Abuse* provides biblical hope and practical help for permanent healing."

DR. ROBERT S. MCGEE
Author, *The Search for Significance*

"Those who have lived with abuse often find it difficult to recognize that they have indeed been abused. June carefully turns on the light for wounded and battered minds and hearts, inviting them to step into the truth and find healing and freedom."

DR. DIANE LANGBERG
Psychologist
Author, *Counseling Survivors of Sexual Abuse*

"This I personally know—even if you've been victimized, you don't need to live with a victim mentality. Page after page of *How to Rise Above Abuse* reveals how to renew your mind and move triumphantly beyond the pain of your past."

DORIE VAN STONE
Author, *No Place to Cry: The Hurt and Healing of Sexual Abuse*
and *Dorie: The Girl Nobody Loved*

HOW TO RISE ABOVE ABUSE

JUNE HUNT

HARVEST HOUSE PUBLISHERS

EUGENE, OREGON

Cover by Garborg Design Works, Savage, Minnesota

Cover photos © iStockphoto / larryye, rtyreel

Disclaimer

Dear Reader,

Be aware that some victims of abuse could experience difficulty reading certain portions of this book because the words might trigger an emotional reaction due to past trauma. Therefore, caution needs to be taken by those who have not processed the pain of past abuse.

Our prayer is that the truths within these pages will encourage you to move toward emotional and spiritual healing.

Yours in the Lord's hope,
June

HOW TO RISE ABOVE ABUSE
Copyright © 2010 by Hope for the Heart, Inc.
Published by Harvest House Publishers
Eugene, Oregon 97402
www.harvesthousepublishers.com

Library of Congress Cataloging-in-Publication Data
Hunt, June.
  How to rise above abuse / June Hunt.
      p. cm. — (Counseling through the Bible series)
  Includes bibliographical references.
  ISBN 978-0-7369-2333-0 (pbk.)
    1. Adult child sexual abuse victims—Religious life. 2. Psychological abuse victims—Religious life. 3. Abused wives—Religious life. 4. Child sexual abuse—Religious aspects—Christianity.
  5. Psychological abuse—Religious aspects—Christianity. 6. Wife abuse—Religious aspects—Christianity. I Title.
    BV4596.A25H96 2010
    248.8'6—dc22
                                                                                              2010012644

Printed in the United States of America

10 11 12 13 14 15 16 17 18 / LB-SK/ 10 9 8 7 6 5 4 3 2 1

This book is fittingly dedicated to my "sister-in-love," whom I admire beyond words, for she has helped countless women and children rise above the storm clouds of abuse.

Nancy Ann Hunt is the kind of volunteer/board member/organizer every executive director dreams about—but few wake up to find. She is, indeed, their "dream come true."

Through Nancy Ann's tireless service on the board of the Genesis Women's Shelter—a sanctuary for victims of domestic abuse—she has been used by God to give help to the helpless…and hope to those who feel hopeless. At this haven of refuge, women and children find a place where hands are not used for hitting and a place where hearts begin their healing.

Because people love being around Nancy Ann, with her delightful humor and extraordinary thoughtfulness, she has enjoyed great success in mobilizing volunteers and leaders alike…and has inspired people to give to the lifesaving ministry of CONTACT. Through this 24-hour crisis line, adults and teenagers—many suicidal—receive real help: resources, education, and emergency assistance. Victims of violence, runaway teens, and others in crisis receive free cab rides to hospitals and *safe* shelters.

How well I remember first learning about New Friends, New Life, a marvelous Christian ministry that reaches out to women involved in sexually oriented trades—women who were almost always the victims of childhood sexual abuse, and who, as many as one-third, were the victims of sex trafficking.

Typically these prostitutes and exotic dancers fear they cannot earn a living in any other profession. However, this ministry equips them to enter safe, dignified, and conventional careers. In the early years, the devoted board members struggled to leverage their modest resources. Then came Nancy Ann—full of creativity, encouragement, and commitment! As a result, public awareness and support began to flow—like overflowing baskets of loaves and fishes.

Notice what Proverbs 31:8 says: "Speak up for those who cannot speak for themselves." Well, Nancy Ann has indeed spoken up—both *passionately* and *compassionately*—using her enormous influence on behalf of victims who would otherwise have no voice. Only in heaven will we get a glimpse of the wounded throngs who—because of her life—have been able to lift off, take flight, and *rise above abuse.*

Acknowledgments

Just as a lone, wounded bird is more vulnerable to further harm, healing from the pain of abuse doesn't occur in isolation. Real healing is completed and even celebrated in an atmosphere of caring people. The same could be said of the creation of this book on abuse. Members of our Hope for the Heart family contributed their best efforts so that every page could "take wing." Thus with great pleasure, I gratefully acknowledge the "caring flock" who made this book possible:

From the "early nest":

Beth Stapleton, June Page, and *Kay Deakins,* who helped launch the earliest versions of the five *Biblical Counseling Keys* contained in this volume.

From the "current nest":

Barbara Spruill and *Carolyn White,* who helped the project climb with cohesion and clarity in each chapter, and who brought our excessively soaring word count back to earth. And *Jill Prohaska,* who glided through the introduction and sidebars with grace.

Angie White, our conscientious project coordinator, whose chirping kept our flock flying forward. And *Elizabeth Cunningham,* who swooped in with last-minute assistance.

Connie Steindorf and *Jeanne Sloan,* who pecked away at countless drafts to key, research, and proof all revisions.

Titus O'Bryant, who meticulously researched every footnote and endnote to make sure they would truly "all fly."

Bea Garner, Karen Williams, and *Laura Lyn Benoit,* who hovered over the manuscript to proof with perfect precision.

And our trusty Harvest House editor extraordinaire, *Steve Miller,* whose steady support enabled this book to soar to new heights.

CONTENTS

WIFE ABUSE

INTRODUCTION

Have you ever been shocked by what shocks another person? I have, and I'll never forget the feeling of disbelief. It was the early 1990s. I had just interviewed a victim of domestic violence to gather firsthand information for my teaching on the topic of wife abuse.

That afternoon I was sitting with June (oddly enough, my coworker's name!), both of us listening intently to the interview of this precious woman sharing about her tragic marriage filled with verbal, emotional, and physical abuse. After the interview, June and I began to discuss how we would use her story to help others. Then June—almost in disbelief—"dropped the bomb."

"I can't understand why any woman would stay in an abusive marriage! If my husband had ever hit me, I guarantee he'd never do it again!"

My eyes widened as I looked at June to see if she was serious. She was. Quickly it became clear to me: She was stunned that anyone would tolerate abuse. Then it immediately became clear to June that I too was shocked… *by her shock*!

The fact June was so perplexed helped me realize that she had not come from an abusive background. She didn't understand what it was like to feel utterly powerless in the presence of cruelty, completely helpless to escape evil, with no boundary for her protection and no strategy to force a change.

In contrast, I understood powerlessness all too well. Growing up in a home where my father's abusive treatment was the "norm," I learned that questioning authority resulted in my banishment, that stuffing my feelings helped numb the pain, and that "walking on eggshells" helped preserve the peace. Basically, I became a peace-at-any-price person.

WAS PEACE AT ANY PRICE THE WAY OF CHRIST?

Many people think that peace at any price is the Christian way to live.

"After all," they could reason, "Jesus is called the Prince of Peace. He said, 'My peace I give you'[1] and 'Blessed are the peacemakers.'[2] Even the apostle Paul said, 'If it is possible, as far as it depends on you, live at peace with everyone.'"[3]

In light of all these biblical passages, wasn't Jesus a peace-at-any-price person? By no means! Instead, He countered this common misconception by declaring, "I did not come to bring peace, but a sword."[4]

Jesus confronted what was wrong. He cut straight to the heart with *truth*—because truth sets us free![5] At times the sword of truth is necessary to confront what is wrong to establish what is right. The Bible says, "Give up your violence and oppression and do what is just and right" (Ezekiel 45:9).

Abused people need to know the truth. And this is absolutely true: God *never* calls anyone to endure abuse for the sake of peace at any price. For the millions of people presently suffering abuse, this truth can evoke powerful change and literally set them free. In fact, the truths spoken by the Lord are so powerful that the Bible describes them as "living and active, sharper than any double-edged sword" (Hebrews 4:12).

So what about the issue of *peace*? Let me speak to you as if you are personally in an abusive predicament and you want peace.

- First, God wants you to know that He *sees* what's happening to you—the abuse you're experiencing—and He *cares*. He longs for you to turn to Him for help, and He plans to give you His peace.

- Second, realize His peace surpasses all understanding. His peace protects you when dark rain clouds pour. How does this happen? When we receive Jesus Christ as our personal Lord and Savior, by giving Him control of our lives, He gives us inner peace. Because He is the Prince of Peace, *He will be peace for you.*

- Third, God's will is *not* for you to become a peace-at-all-costs person. Having the peace of Christ inside you is entirely different from being a peace-at-any-price person.

For a long time, I didn't know that fact. When people became angry with me, I tried to do whatever was necessary to keep them from *staying* angry.

The "whatever" included shutting down emotionally, not saying a word, lying about the situation, and caving in to pressure even when I knew that was wrong. And sadly, when the "whatever" occurred, I thought, *Well, at least I'm being loyal.* Today I would call that a *misplaced loyalty* because I wasn't, first and foremost, being loyal to the Lord.

PEOPLE-PLEASING—MY SURVIVAL STRATEGY

I grew up in a dysfunctional family, but at the time, I didn't know that term. But this I did know: I was told to make certain statements—and answer certain questions—with words that weren't true. (By the way, teaching a child to lie classifies as *verbal abuse*.)

In reality, my mother, brother, two sisters, and myself were a family "on the side." My father had two families (actually three) going at the same time. It was bizarre. At that time, I didn't have a friend. How could I trust anyone with my awkward, embarrassing life? Be assured, I kept *all* the secrets—*I did not tell a soul.*

Eventually my father married my mother, but still…many years passed by before I *ever* spoke of it.

In my home growing up, dad (who was double my mom's age) was the dictator, the *only* decision maker. In his mind, his decisions were the only ones that mattered. He had complete control.

I hated my dad's anger. Because I grew up in an angry home, I was scared of angry people. As a result, "people-pleasing" became my survival strategy. I was so fearful of anyone's anger that I became the classic people pleaser. If someone said, "Jump!" I would say, "How high?"

After I entrusted my life to Christ, I slowly gained a stability I had never possessed before. Over the years, the Lord began healing me from my painful past. With wisdom from God's Word and the help of caring Christians, I began to see myself, my problems, and even the difficult people in my life more and more through God's eyes.

Later there came an amazing "exchange": Gradually, God began replacing my brokenness with a resolve to reach out to others. I saw wounded souls around me with their broken wings, struggling to make it through life in the same way I had struggled. Then I realized I could give others the comforting compassion that God had given me. The Bible says it well: "The Father of compassion…comforts us in all our troubles, so that we can comfort those in any trouble with the comfort we ourselves have received from God."[6]

The Hope for Healthy Change

My overriding desire to give *biblical hope and practical help* to others led me to found Hope for the Heart in 1986—now a worldwide biblical counseling ministry. Since then, I've had the undeserved privilege of presenting *God's truth for today's problems* before many different kinds of audiences.

Through my own journey of unspoken personal pain, I've made this fascinating observation: As I've taught on various topics of abuse—verbal and emotional abuse, victimization, child abuse, wife abuse, rape, and spiritual abuse—I've come to understand that, like straw in a bird's nest, *issues involving abuse are delicately intertwined.*

Understandably, sexually abused children are also victims of *emotional abuse.* Without effective intervention, they grow up with a *victim mentality.* Because adults with a victim mentality *feel* powerless even when they are not, they become more vulnerable to other kinds of abuse, such as physical, sexual, and spiritual abuse.

If you grew up in a home where verbal and emotional abuse were the norm, in the absence of inner healing, you've probably experienced other kinds of victimization as well as difficulty maintaining boundaries. You may have tried to get your legitimate needs for love, significance, and security met through illegitimate sources, such as living for the approval of people. This sets you up to repeatedly entrust your heart to those who do not seek your highest good, making it easier for victimizers to victimize you.

Likewise, if your boundaries were once trampled, typically you're an easier target today for a manipulator or a spiritual abuser who uses methods of mind control. In my years of counseling, I've observed that such intertwining is all too common. Sadly, wounded birds are prime targets for predators… unless someone comes to help and heal their broken wings.

And that is God's specialty. The Bible says while most people look "at the outward appearance, God looks at the heart."[7] He sees each damaged wing, each wounded heart, each despondent spirit that He designed to soar. And because He is the Great Physician, He knows how to be your Healer.

If in your past you've felt broken, please don't settle for staying broken! Just as a splint will hold a wounded wing steady, allow God's wisdom to hold you steady. And please be patient—healing takes time, tenderness, and truth. If you have suffered any form of abuse, I encourage you to take all the time that is necessary to learn *how to rise above abuse.*

So, what do you need to know? God has much to say about abuse—

however, these thoughts are not organized topically in the Bible. Therefore, at our ministry called Hope for the Heart, we mine the Scriptures to discover "What has God said about *this* topic?" Then we *identify* all the verses related to the problem, *organize* the verses within four categories (definitions, characteristics, causes, and solutions), and *present* action steps that help put those principles to work in real life.

This is what our *Biblical Counseling Library* is all about. Each of the 100 topics in our *Biblical Counseling Library* (five of which are examined in this book), present *God's truth for today's problems.* But why prioritize *truth?* Long ago, I learned that we need to line up our thinking with God's thinking because *a changed mind produces a changed heart, and a changed heart produces a changed life.* That's the ultimate end: that we all experience a changed life through Christ and become all He created us to be.

As you read the following pages, nothing would give me greater joy than *for you* to find the *biblical hope and practical help* needed to rise above the storm clouds of your past so that you can soar to unimagined new heights. But that's not all. Realize that your abuse doesn't have to remain *pointless.* It can become full of *purpose*—the Lord can powerfully use it to bring healing and to help other hurting people begin to soar. Therefore, my sincere prayer is that you will be greatly used by God to help others feel *His* wind beneath their wings.

Yours in the Lord's hope,
June Hunt

CHILDHOOD SEXUAL ABUSE

CHILDHOOD SEXUAL ABUSE

The Secret Storm

"There she is...Miss America..."[1] She graced the Atlantic City runway with statuesque beauty and charm. The familiar song wafts throughout the auditorium—and into the hearts and homes of millions of adoring television viewers.

"There she is...your ideal..." So goes the second line of the song, signifying that this 20-year-old embodied all a young American woman could hope to be.

Straight-A student, swim champ, gifted musician—yet with the winsome appeal of "the girl next door"—Marilyn Van Derbur was crowned Miss America. After reigning for a year with whirlwind spotlight appearances, she graduated from college Phi Beta Kappa and embarked on a highly visible speaking career.

As the epitome of self-confidence and composure, this host of 23 television specials served a major corporation for 16 years as their only female guest lecturer. Years later, Marilyn stepped up to a very different podium, this time to deliver a very different message: "Tonight, I break my silence...It means speaking the unspeakable word."[2] She revealed, "From the time I was five until I was eighteen and moved away to college, my father sexually violated me."[3]

As a motivational speaker, Marilyn had a new motivation—a passion to help other victims break their silence, salvage their lives, and be made whole. The description of her hidden horror has helped other victims reveal their terror and survive their shame. Still there are many victims in the midst of their own secret storm who inwardly cry…

> *"My heart is in anguish within me;*
> *the terrors of death assail me.*
> *Fear and trembling have beset me;*
> *horror has overwhelmed me"*
> (Psalm 55:4-5).

I. Definitions of Childhood Sexual Abuse

Francis Van Derbur beamed with fatherly pride as his youngest daughter was crowned Miss America. Before the world he boasted, "She's been a lovely girl all her life."[4]

But this loyal father-role was all a façade…for "Van," as he was called, had in no way been a virtuous father, but rather a perverted victimizer. He believed he *owned* his wife and four daughters—he considered them his property—therefore, this millionaire socialite felt entitled to do anything he wanted with them…*anything.*[5]

A former mayor of Denver, Colorado, described Van as "a figure in the state's history."[6] Meanwhile, Marilyn and her family knew him as demeaning, demanding, and demoralizing. Their innermost cry echoed that of the psalmist:

> *"Turn your ear to me, come quickly to my rescue;*
> *be my rock of refuge, a strong fortress to save me"*
> (Psalm 31:2).

A. What Constitutes Childhood Sexual Abuse?

The sound of the garage door going up at night sent a surging stream of anxiety through Marilyn like nothing else. As a child, she lay in bed and waited…*and waited*…often for hours, wondering when she would hear the quiet scuffle of gray felt slippers approaching her room…then slowly her father's fingers turning the doorknob. As soon as the large figure in the white terry cloth robe emerged, Marilyn squeezed her eyes shut—pretending to be asleep.[7]

And for 13 years, Marilyn recalls, "I pretended not to know what he was doing."[8] But every muscle tightened as the hands of her father swept over her body. Marilyn was only five years old when the devastating abuse and deceit began. And how many other children like Marilyn feel the heartbreak of these words today?

> *"No one is near to comfort me,*
> *no one to restore my spirit"*
> (LAMENTATIONS 1:16).

- **Abuse** is mistreatment: using something or someone in an inappropriate manner.[9]
  — *Abuse* results in emotional, mental, spiritual, and physical harm. In the Old Testament, the Hebrew word for abuse is *alal*, which can mean "to treat severely, harshly, or cruelly, to defile."[10]
  — *Abuse* is intentional, not accidental.

The Bible does not shy away from acknowledging the reality of abuse:

> *"They raped her and abused her throughout the night,*
> *and at dawn they let her go"*
> (JUDGES 19:25).

- **Sexual abuse** of a child is any physical, visual, or verbal interaction with a minor by an older child or adult whose purpose is sexual stimulation or sexual satisfaction.
  — *Sexual abuse victims* are boys and girls under the age of 18* who have suffered one or many experiences of sexual abuse.
  — *Sexual abuse of a child* is almost always committed by someone the child knows or with whom the child has frequent contact.[11]

family member	neighbor
family friend	coach
babysitter	church leader

---

* The age at which a child is considered a minor or underage will vary from country to country.

teacher	older friend
doctor	playmate's older sibling
institutional worker	daycare worker
mother's live-in boyfriend or transient suitor	

Such familiarity sets the stage for a child to be all the more vulnerable to a victimizer. The Bible is not silent about the deceitful schemes of such a victimizer…

Biblical Claim

"He lies in wait like a lion in cover;
he lies in wait to catch the helpless;
he catches the helpless
and drags them off in his net"
(PSALM 10:9).

B. What Is Incest?

Marilyn would lie stiff as a board, but night after night her father would overpower her, force himself upon her, violate her body, invade her mind, lacerate her soul and spirit. *Nothing would dissuade him.* Marilyn would open wide the windows of her room to let cold air into the room—he still came in. She took a little sign from a train that read, "Please go 'way and let me sleep" and hung it on her doorknob—he still came in. She pretended she was having her period—he still came in. She wouldn't bathe—he still came in.

Like Job, Marilyn found no safe haven from the terrors she experienced.

"Terrors overwhelm me;
my dignity is driven away as by the wind,
my safety vanishes like a cloud"
(JOB 30:15).

- **Incest** is sexual interaction with a child or an adolescent by a person who is a member of the child's family—any blood relative, adoptive relative, or relative by marriage or remarriage. [12]
  — *Incest* usually progresses from subtle touching to sexual fondling and then typically to more extensive sexual activity. [13]

— *Incestuous relationships* usually continue over a long period of time.[14]

- **Incest** occurs primarily in the following relationships (in order of predominance):

  — *For a girl*, her father or stepfather, grandfather, uncle or male cousin, older brother, half brother, brother-in-law, mother, or other female relative.

  — *For a boy*, his father or stepfather, grandfather, uncle or male cousin, older brother, half-brother, brother-in-law, sister, mother, or other female relative.

Biblical Censure

The Bible is not silent about the act of incest…

> *"No one is to approach any close relative*
> *to have sexual relations.*
> *I am the LORD"*
> (LEVITICUS 18:6).

(Read Leviticus 18:6-18.)

C. What Is the Difference Between Molestation and Rape?

Even though children have a natural inclination to trust their parents, Marilyn knew that what was happening to her had nothing to do with fatherly love. In fact, it was *rape*. All the heinous acts committed against her were "about control and winning."[15]

"Whether I was awake with an intense alertness, or awakened by his hands touching me, my body was as electrified as if a huge, growling bear were standing over my bed just ready to pounce on me. Just the waiting brought on feelings of inexpressible dread, of the need to be hyper-alert, ready for battle, ready for the bear, the warriors with huge knives, my father."[16]

Marilyn could have echoed the words of Job:

> *"When I think about this,*
> *I am terrified; trembling seizes my body"*
> (JOB 21:6).

- **Molestation** is unlawful sexual contact.[17]
    - *Molestation* is usually not sexual penetration.
    - *Molestation* often continues over a period of time.
- **Rape** is both a forceful and nonforceful act resulting in some form of sexual penetration.
    - *Rape* is defined by many law enforcement agencies as forced sexual penetration regardless of age, relationship, or duration.
    - *Rape* can be a onetime event or repeated incidents over a period of time.
- **Molestation** and **rape** consist of illegal sexual contact.
    - *Molestation* and *rape* are words sometimes used in place of the word *incest*, even when the perpetrator is a family member.
    - *Molestation* and *rape* are committed primarily by people the child knows.

Biblical Consequence

The Bible is not silent about the seriousness of rape…

> *"If out in the country a man happens to meet a girl*
> *pledged to be married and rapes her,*
> *only the man who has done this shall die.*
> *Do nothing to the girl;*
> *she has committed no sin deserving death"*
> (Deuteronomy 22:25-26).

D. What Is the Scope of Childhood Sexual Abuse?

The only way Marilyn could fight back was to *mentally* and *emotionally* deny what she was *physically* experiencing. "I would fight with every ounce of my being to not feel anything he was doing…Every pore, every muscle, every cell of my being had fought from opposite ends…it feels good…I *hate* the feelings [sic]."[18]

Marilyn became torn—*tormented*—like so many childhood sexual abuse victims, all of whom can relate to the words of the psalmist:

"The troubles of my heart have multiplied;
free me from my anguish"
(Psalm 25:17).

Checklist for Childhood Sexual Abuse

INDIRECT SEXUAL ABUSE

As a child, did you experience...?

☐ Voyeurism — Being stared at while undressing, bathing, or urinating

☐ Exhibitionism — Being exposed to the intentional, inappropriate nudity of someone much older

☐ Lewdness — Being made to listen to sexual talk or watch sex acts

☐ Pornography — Being shown sexual pictures, magazines, videos, or movies

☐ Child pornography — Being made to pose for sexual photographs, videos, or movies

☐ Masturbation — Being made to engage in self-stimulation of sexual parts while another person observes

☐ Psychological abuse — Being teased/ridiculed about private body parts, subjected to sexual name-calling, or made to feel like a sex object

DIRECT SEXUAL ABUSE

As a child, did you experience...?

☐ Fondling — Being touched, stroked, or caressed in sexually sensitive areas, bathed in a way that felt sexually intrusive, or made to touch the sexual parts of another person

☐	Intimate kissing	Being kissed in a sexual way
☐	Oral sex	Being made to perform oral genital contact
☐	Penetration/rape	Being forced into unwanted sexual intercourse or anal sex
☐	Child prostitution	Being made to perform sex acts for money
☐	Sadism	Being subjected to the painful use of objects on sexual parts
☐	Satanic ritual abuse	Being forced to suffer systematic acts of sadistic sexual abuse in ceremonies exalting Satan or evil

Biblical Commitment

The Bible promises justice and hope…

> *"What the wicked dreads will overtake him;*
> *what the righteous desire will be granted.*
> *When the storm has swept by, the wicked are gone,*
> *but the righteous stand firm forever"*
> (PROVERBS 10:24-25).

E. Who Are the Victims?

The secret is so shaming—the savagery of childhood sexual abuse so crippling—that you tell *no one*, according to Marilyn. And the family dynamic in the Van Derbur household only fueled the frenzied hush. "Telling on others" was taboo among the sisters because the one who reported a misdeed received a harsher punishment than the one who did something wrong.

And then there was the fact that Marilyn's oldest sister had been sent off to boarding school for being defiant and rebellious. The same would likely happen to Marilyn if she said anything. Therefore, the trauma of the sexual abuse caused Marilyn to dissociate. She "split" and became two different people—to repress what was happening night after night.[19]

A "day child" emerged…"happy, sparkly…highly moral."[20] But then there

was the "night child," often found curled up on her bed in a fetal position...
waiting...only to have her perpetrator pry her arms and legs apart.[21] Together,
the day child and the night child exemplified the truth of this proverb:

> *"Even in laughter the heart may ache,*
> *and joy may end in grief"*
> (Proverbs 14:13).

- **Child victims** of sexual abuse are any boys or girls who have
  suffered a single instance or many instances of sexual abuse.
  — *Children,* in legal terms, are referred to as minors.
  — *Children* (minors) are defined, in the United States, as persons under the age of 18.[22]
- **Child victims** have no choice about being abused and no ability to stop the abuse unless they are *trained to resist*.
  — *Victims* are defenseless against the resulting emotional pain.
  — *Victims* feel overwhelmed, powerless, and totally alone.

Biblical Comfort

The Bible describes God's concern for victims...

> *"You, O God, do see trouble and grief;*
> *you consider it to take it in hand.*
> *The victim commits himself to you...*
> *You hear, O Lord, the desire of the afflicted;*
> *you encourage them, and you listen to their cry"*
> (Psalm 10:14,17).

F. Who Are the Victimizers?

He was considered a pillar of the community in Denver. Marilyn's mother
considered him an Adonis, the Greek god. And she was the picture of the
submissive wife—to a fault.[23]

Van rose to prominence in the business community after he married and
purchased his wife's family company. Not only was he a founding trustee of
the Denver Civic Center and a board member of the Denver Center for the

Performing Arts, but this father of four daughters was ironically president of the Denver Area Boy Scouts Council.[24]

Just as Marilyn became two people—day child and night child—Francis Van Derbur was a friendly philanthropist by day and a family perpetrator by night. His daytime giving stood in sharp contrast to his nighttime groping. How well his life mirrored this scriptural contrast:

> *"The good man brings good things*
> *out of the good stored up in him,*
> *and the evil man brings evil things out of the evil stored up in him"*
> (Matthew 12:35).

Perpetrators

Adult Seducers of Children

- **Family Members** (familial perpetrators)
  - Are most frequently fathers and stepfathers
  - Prefer sex with children who are merely available and vulnerable—that is, their own children
- **Pedophiles** (preferential perpetrators)[25]
  - Are considerably older than their victims and demonstrate a preference for prepubescent children while having little or no sexual interest in their own peers
  - Primarily victimize nonfamily members (averaging 90 victims, whereas familial pedophiles abuse an average of two victims)
- **Predators** (chance perpetrators)
  - Do not have a true preference for children, but will have sex with a child just because the child is available or in order to seek revenge
  - Feel angry, bored, or powerless and thus set out in search of anyone to violate sexually, with children often being accessible and easy prey

Child/Adolescent Perpetrators of Children

- **Minors** who sexually violate younger or less powerful children
  - Are typically victims of sexual abuse themselves who learn to abuse other children in the same way they have been or are presently being abused
  - Comprise the most underreported group of child abusers

Adult Rapists of Children

- **Cruel victimizers** who commit violent sexual acts against children
  - Usually significantly older than their victims
  - The most dangerous of child abusers, but typically do not rape a particular child more than once

Biblical Condemnation

The Bible reveals the intent of a victimizer...

> *"A malicious man disguises himself with his lips,*
> *but in his heart he harbors deceit.*
> *Though his speech is charming, do not believe him,*
> *for seven abominations fill his heart.*
> *His malice may be concealed by deception,*
> *but his wickedness will be exposed in the assembly"*
> (Proverbs 26:24-26).

G. Who Are the Nonprotective Parents?

Where was Marilyn's mother when all this abuse was happening? "Silence is the voice of complicity," the saying goes. And her silence was cloaked in a pretense she would protect—no matter the cost.

Marilyn's mother wanted the world to believe she had the perfect family, and from the outside, they appeared to be just that—attractive, wealthy, and accomplished. She herself was the picture of charm, always optimistic and active in the civic theater and other organizations. Raised in a highly regarded Denver family, she was determined to forever remain esteemed by the other millionaire socialites. [26]

So desperate was Marilyn's mother to disguise the family dysfunction that once when she was hospitalized, she ordered flowers from the gift shop so she could tell everybody they were from Van. He, on the other hand, had flatly told her years before that if she were ever incapacitated, he wouldn't care for her. [27]

So…let's look at the real question: Why don't the "nonoffending parents" of sexually abused children protect their vulnerable young ones? Why do they further victimize their innocent children by failing to shield them, guard them, shelter them? Don't they realize the ever-present, all-knowing God sees and holds them accountable? Proverbs 24:12 poses these questions:

> *"If you say, 'But we knew nothing about this,'*
> *does not he who weighs the heart perceive it?*
> *Does not he who guards your life know it?*
> *Will he not repay each person according to what he has done?"*

Typically, nonprotective parents can be divided into four categories. Those within the first three categories reject their most basic parental role: to protect their offspring. Not only do they permit their children to be abused, but also they appear to favor the guilty over the innocent—the abuser over the abused. Surprisingly, abused children feel more anger toward the nonoffending parent for failing to protect them than toward the abuser for abusing them.

The four categories are:

#1 Passive Parents

— Give silent consent to sexual abuse by ignoring it

— Usually feel powerless to protect themselves or their children

— Victimize their children by withholding both physical protection and emotional support

#2 Preoccupied Parents

— Don't know about the abuse because they have excessively immersed themselves in their own personal lives

— Put their time and energy into solving their own emotional problems and satisfying their own unmet needs

— Overlook the observable signs of a child in distress due to their lack of sensitivity and discernment

#3 Prideful Parents

— Highly value outward appearances, and thus adamantly insist their family life is the ideal

— Refuse to believe sexual abuse could exist within their picture-perfect home

— Will not take their child's word that such a travesty as sexual abuse has occurred

Biblical Chastisement

The Bible chastises protectors of the guilty and those who fail to protect the innocent...

> *"It is not good to be partial to the wicked*
> *or to deprive the innocent of justice"*
> (PROVERBS 18:5).

A fourth category of nonprotecting parents is clearly distinct from the others. While most nonoffending parents believe they are in *this* group, sadly, only a minority truly belong to it—those who deeply love their children yet who also trust the untrustworthy. They presume that their children are safe when, in reality, they are in danger. They miss the signs of abuse because they assume there is no reason to look for such signs.

#4 Positive Parents

— Have a positive influence on their children but cannot see signs of abuse because the perpetrator is highly skilled at hiding the abuse

— Look for and guard against other dangers to their children but fully trust those closest to them

— Do protect if made aware of the abuse, no matter who the abuser might be

These positive parents need to pray diligently for wisdom because Jesus said, "Wisdom is proved right by all her children" (Luke 7:35).

H. What Is the Typical Course of Childhood Sexual Abuse?

Terror tied Marilyn's tongue, keeping her from telling about the sexual abuse her father inflicted on her and the harsh discipline he imposed on all of his daughters. When Marilyn was five years old, Van once held her by the ankles over a second-floor banister. It wasn't about fun, she recalls—it was about power. As a further reminder, there was a switch (a slender whip or rod) atop every door frame in the house—a handy tool for making sure the Van Derbur girls "toed the line."

"My father was the master. You did it his way, always."[28]

Back rubs...that's how Van explained his absence from his wife's bedroom and his presence in Marilyn's. "Just trying to help her get to sleep," he would say. And Marilyn's mother would drift off to sleep, persisting in her delusional fantasy of family perfection.[29]

As with Van, childhood sexual abuse doesn't typically occur as a onetime, isolated incident. Rather, it's more common for the perpetrator to have a premeditated plan that results in repeated abuse. While the details in each case are different, perpetrators tend to follow this pattern of behavior: First they *seduce,* then they *stimulate,* then they *silence,* and then they *suppress* the child. Once suppressed, the child loses all hope.

The following could easily reflect the feeling of never-ending sorrow:

> *"How long must I wrestle with my thoughts*
> *and every day have sorrow in my heart?*
> *How long will my enemy triumph over me?"*
> (Psalm 13:2).

- **Seduction**—The perpetrator emotionally entices and leads the child astray by...[30]

  — Developing intimacy and a warped sense of loyalty through granting special privileges

  — Building trust progressively with ulterior motives

  — Becoming an attentive "friend" with appealing hobbies or interests

— Showing preferential treatment by playing games or by giving money, gifts, bribes, or rewards

- **Stimulation**—The perpetrator physically prepares the child for sexual activity by...

  — Giving the child what appears to be appropriate, affirming, warm touches through playful wrestling, hugs, back rubs, and other such activity

  — Using frequent physical contact to gradually desensitize the child to a progression toward increasingly inappropriate touch and sexual contact that introduces sexual activity as being fun or special

  — Increasing the amount of physical encroachment, which is not enjoyable to the child (but nonetheless permitted by the child) and takes advantage of natural sexual curiosity

  — Escalating toward sexual stimulation that is likely both painful and pleasurable (as the child's body naturally responds to sexual stimulation) and results in conflicted feelings and a guilty conscience (although the guilt belongs to the abuser alone!)

- **Silence**—The perpetrator methodically moves to ensure the child's silence by...

  — Using intimidation and fear-inducing threats of stopping the relationship or harming the child or the child's family members, friends, or pets

  — Accusing the child of disloyalty if their "special secret" is shared with anyone

  — Creating a quagmire of ambivalent feelings in the child such as love and hate, pleasure and shame, tenderness and terror

  — Countering the child's feelings of rage at the reality of being *in* the relationship with rage at the possibility of *losing* the relationship

- **Suppression**—The perpetrator stealthily subdues the child by...

  — Ensuring no one rescues the child from the abusive relationship, causing the child to feel doubly betrayed

— Destroying any hope the child might have of ever being rescued by anyone, including God

— Leaving the child feeling that he or she has no choice but to bow to the power of the perpetrator and slip quietly into acceptance of the inevitable abuse that leads to emotional enslavement

— Causing hopelessness to reign within the child, suppressing the child's soul and snuffing out the light within the child's spirit

The child concludes that *love* has a hidden hook in it and *trust* is no longer a viable option. The perceptions are that nothing of value is freely given and that all good gifts carry hidden price tags too high to pay. This destruction of trust can impair a child's ability to trust God when it comes time to seek healing.

Biblical Caution

The Bible describes such self-centered abusers in the following way...

> *"There is no fear of God before his eyes.*
> *For in his own eyes he flatters himself*
> *too much to detect or hate his sin.*
> *The words of his mouth are wicked and deceitful;*
> *he has ceased to be wise and to do good.*
> *Even on his bed he plots evil;*
> *he commits himself to a sinful course*
> *and does not reject what is wrong"*
> (Psalm 36:1-4).

=========== Incest and False Guilt ===========

QUESTION: "I feel guilty about the sexual acts my father performed on me over the years. Why didn't I stop him?"

ANSWER: Victims of sexual sin are typically plagued with feelings of guilt—even when those acts were initiated by the perpetrator and not the victim. You didn't "cause" the abuse to occur! When someone's sin spills acid onto you, you cannot escape the impact—and you *can* feel contaminated.

The fact is, however, you did not seduce your father. Obviously you weren't *trained* to stop a sexual perpetrator, especially not your father. Take to heart these key points:

- Your father initiated the sexual acts upon you—you had no choice. As a child, you were not physically, mentally, or emotionally strong enough to overpower or stop him.

- Because he was the adult, he knew exactly what he was doing and bears full responsibility for his perversion.

- All professionals in this field would testify that you are in no way to blame for your father's choices. Although grown children typically feel guilty over such past offenses, you need to discern false guilt from true guilt.

Perpetrators are experts at making their victims feel like willing participants—leading them to feel guilty for what is actually the perpetrator's wrongdoing. This results in false guilt. When that happens, you need to seek and discover what lies you were manipulated into believing and replace those lies with biblical truth.

> *"Let the wise listen and add to their learning,*
> *and let the discerning get guidance"*
> (PROVERBS 1:5).

I. What Common Challenge Faces Survivors of Child Abuse?

It is truly reprehensible that Marilyn's mother turned a blind eye to what was happening in Marilyn's bedroom virtually every night. Marilyn recalls the time she first realized her mother knew what was going on. One night she heard the sounds made by her mother's dress slippers on the hard-surfaced steps outside Marilyn's closed bedroom door. There they lay—Marilyn and her father—in her bed. At the sound of her mother's footsteps, he immediately stopped, unable to continue his assault.

Her rescuer was no more than six feet away, and the hope of blessed help filled the little girl's heart. Finally...it would end! Like a fearless mama bear, her protective mother would reach in and snatch her cub from the sinister wolf. In silence, perfectly still, she and her father waited. Then the sound of her mother's footsteps reversed their course. Her mother walked back into her make-believe world in which nothing was wrong.[31]

> There was never any doubt in my mind, after that night, that she knew. She walked away from me, back into her perfect world— a world in which she was admired, respected, and charming. I knew she would never come back and for the hundreds and hundreds of nights to come she never did...[32]

Children like Marilyn cannot change their parents; however, they can change their powerless responses in adulthood by *choosing not to stay powerless*. If you were abused as a child, your challenge—along with that of every victim—is to move from victim to victor, from sufferer to survivor, from emotional cripple to overcomer. By giving your life to the Lord, you can experience Jesus' healing power.

> *"In this world you will have trouble.*
> *But take heart! I have overcome the world"*
> (JOHN 16:33).

- **Victims**
  - *Continue to feel like victims* into adulthood, living with a "victim mentality"—still feeling powerless and therefore acting powerless
  - *Relive their past* by moving from one abusive relationship to another
  - *Live in denial* and refuse to face the dark, hidden secret of the past
  - *Possess no knowledge* of how to find help and healing, and have little hope of receiving either

- **Survivors**
  - *Realize the need for facing the past* in order to heal from the past
  - *Work hard to identify and resolve false guilt,* shame, anger, and an unforgiving heart

— *Honestly deal with debilitating issues* such as personal sin and repentance, loneliness and grief

— *Commit to gaining mental, emotional, psychological, and spiritual healing*

- **Conquerors**

  — *Live victoriously over the past,* no longer in bondage to painful memories

  — *Develop an intimate relationship with Christ,* giving Him control of everything

  — *Grow in self-worth* and the capacity to experience authentic love and intimacy with others

  — *Experience the desire and reality of reaching out and ministering to others*

Biblical Challenge

The Bible reveals our hope for victory...

> *"In all these things we are more than conquerors through him who loved us"*
> (ROMANS 8:37).

Emotionally Stuck Victims

QUESTION: "Why do many victims seem emotionally stuck?"

ANSWER: The abuse experienced by children usually interrupts their ability to progress to the next stage of emotional growth. It takes some degree of normalcy, safety, and a healthy home environment for children to develop properly, reach expected goals, and mature.

After the abuse is successfully processed, emotional healing takes place and developmental goals can be attained. Until that happens, victims are likely to respond emotionally to life as children rather than adults. The ultimate aim is to experience lasting healing—to move from being a victim to being a victor—and be able to say...

"When I was a child, I talked like a child,
I thought like a child, I reasoned like a child.
When I became [an adult], I put childish ways behind me"
(1 Corinthians 13:11).

II. Characteristics of Childhood Sexual Abuse

Marilyn wrote:

> Until I was 24, the day child had no conscious knowledge of the night child. During the day, no embarrassing or angry glances ever passed between my father and me. I had no rage toward him at all, because I had no conscious knowledge of what he was doing to me. Anyone who knew me would say I was the happiest child. I believed I was happy. Still, incest colored every aspect of my life.[33]

After years of being victimized, Marilyn won her first battle in the long war to salvage her split soul. As a college student, Marilyn came home for Christmas break. When she went into her parents' bedroom to say good night, her father pulled her down to himself.

"I pushed away from him with such anger," she recounts.[34] But it was unmistakably the "day child" who reacted, because it would be years later—not until the age of 24—that Marilyn's memories of incest would begin to surface. And after that wintry, cold Colorado night, Van never touched Marilyn again.

Though sexual abuse differs from victim to victim, Marilyn mirrored the experience of many other victims. They disconnect themselves from their feelings in order to survive. "Memory loss" may be God's way of protecting their young hearts from this paralyzing fact: *Those who should have been their protectors were their perpetrators!*

Thank God, He is Jehovah Rapha, "the God who heals." He knows when to bring to the surface repressed memories, and He knows how to bring complete healing to each and every heart. He says,

"I am the Lord, who heals you"
(Exodus 15:26).

A. What Are the Emotional Signs of Abuse?[35]

Marilyn's sexual betrayal permeated her body, soul, and spirit, wounding and scarring every aspect of her being even into late adulthood. But healing eventually came…through the keen perception of the church youth minister she met at age 15. It was this godly man who discovered the "night child" buried deep in Marilyn's soul and helped surface her horrific secrets. His influence cannot be overstated. "As clearly as if he had swum out to rescue me from a strong riptide pulling me out to sea, D.D. Harvey would save my life."[36]

The powerful impact of her father's incestuous behavior led Marilyn to describe herself as "walking anxiety." In elementary school and beyond, Marilyn felt a compelling need to perform, to excel, to be perfect at everything she did—yet she was filled with dread. Despite deep angst and inner fear, somehow she always managed to look confident and composed on the outside—leaving others clueless about her inner agony.

Meanwhile, any reference to anything sexual would shake her to the core. During a sorority initiation, she broke into heaving, convulsive sobs when asked, "What is digitational intercourse?" (answer: holding hands). And, "What is osculation?" (answer: kissing).[37]

Years later Marilyn would spontaneously break into sobs when she saw photos of herself in advertising campaigns. Though at the time she was unaware of why she did so, it was because she thought she looked seductive—and "incest victims never want to look seductive."[38]

More uncontrollable fits of sobbing came when Marilyn's daughter, Jennifer, turned five years old—the age at which Marilyn's abuse began. And when Jennifer entered puberty, Marilyn became "totally dysfunctional," suffering from acute anxiety and shutting down emotionally. A devastating irony about all this is that at age 47, Marilyn was named Outstanding Woman Speaker in America. When her two worlds collided, Marilyn emotionally collapsed.[39]

> *"My face is red with weeping, deep shadows ring my eyes"*
> (JOB 16:16).

Typically, a victim experiences some of the following *emotional symptoms*:

- Afraid of authority figures
- Anxiety or panic attacks
- Apathy
- Avoidance of intimacy
- Confused sexual identity

- Frequent crying
- Depression
- Emotional withdrawal, introversion
- Excessive need for love and attention
- False guilt
- Fear of going to bed, nightmares, or other sleep disturbances
- Hysteria
- Inability to concentrate
- Low feelings of self-worth
- Mistrust
- Neurotic disorders (obsessions/compulsions)
- Pseudomature (adultlike) behavior
- Regression to an earlier phase of development (babylike)
- Self-consciousness and insecurity
- Shame
- Unexplained mood changes
- Unpredictable anger, aggression, rage

Children who grow up in abusive families learn early to distance themselves from the pain—inwardly through denial and outwardly through addictions. Eventually, however, these coping mechanisms break down, and they are left to face their raw pain.

All child victims of any type of abuse know the angst of anxiety much too well. However, when victims come to know Jesus personally and intimately, they come to know His comfort and feel His compassion. Only then can they feel perfect peace and genuine joy in their souls.

> *"When anxiety was great within me,*
> *your consolation brought joy to my soul"*
> (PSALM 94:19).

B. What Are the Physical Signs of Abuse?

One recognizable physical sign of abuse surfaced when Marilyn was in fifth grade—through an embarrassing incident during gym class. The gym teacher asked everyone to bend over and touch their toes. Marilyn couldn't even reach to the middle of her calves—her body was so tight and rigid. Humiliated, she was then singled out as the teacher began pushing on her back, forcing a meeting between fingers and toes.[40] "I could never allow my body to 'let go' because that would mean to submit, to feel, to respond, to lose, to be wholly and reprehensibly bad."[41]

Marilyn also suffered from chronic constipation since childhood due to tightening her buttocks so hard that nothing from the outside could get in, and to keep everything on the inside from getting out.

Signs of sexual abuse can appear much later in life. Accompanying Marilyn's bouts of sobbing after her daughter turned age five were bouts of paralysis, for which doctors had no physical explanation…because none existed. Marilyn's paralysis did not originate in her body, but in her anguished soul. These Scripture passages speak of such agonizing anguish:[42]

"My soul is in anguish.
How long, O LORD, how long?"
(PSALM 6:3).

"My pain is not relieved…it does not go away"
(JOB 16:6).

Most victims display some of the following more obvious signs of physical abuse:

- Abdominal pain
- Bed-wetting/change in toilet habits
- Complaints of sickness
- Dissociative identity disorder (mind splitting into different parts)
- Failure to accomplish simple tasks
- Frequent headaches
- Genital itching/yeast or bladder infections
- Habit disorders (severe biting, thumb-sucking, rocking)
- Masturbation, excessive or in public
- Memory loss
- Obsessive washing and cleaning
- Pain when urinating
- Premarital pregnancy
- Sad facial expressions/ frequent crying
- Self-injury (cutters, burners)
- Sitting/walking difficulties
- Suicidal gestures

- Torn, stained, blood-spotted underpants
- Undernourished appearance
- Vaginal/rectal pain, swelling, bruises, bleeding
- Vaginal/penile discharge
- Venereal disease

Note: If a child experiences any of these physical problems, consult a health care professional immediately.

Every child victim can identify with the painful words Job spoke as he suffered:

> *"Night pierces my bones;*
> *my gnawing pains never rest"*
> (JOB 30:17).

C. What Are the Social Signs of Childhood Sexual Abuse?

Marilyn believes in love at first sight; it happened to her. But rather than cling to the love of her life, she fled from him—for nine years—and hadn't the faintest idea why.

Marilyn first laid her eyes on Larry Atler as a sophomore in high school while he was conversing with his fellow seniors. They began dating, and as their courtship developed, so did Marilyn's fears. Larry might find out she wasn't the moral, upstanding young woman he thought she was, and she couldn't bear for him to know "the truth." "I was a bad, bad, bad person, unworthy of anyone."[43] She broke off the relationship and married someone else, a bond that lasted only three months.

It was Marilyn's former youth minister, D.D. Harvey, who later urged her to contact Larry. The grueling healing process from childhood sexual abuse would occur with her soul mate by her side. He would be the person through whom God would express His love to Marilyn—the person who would accurately define love to her.

> *"Love is patient, love is kind…*
> *It is not self-seeking…*
> *It always protects, always trusts,*
> *always hopes, always perseveres.*
> *Love never fails"*
> (1 CORINTHIANS 13:4-5,7-8).

Victims of childhood sexual abuse usually have difficulty developing healthy habits and relationships, exhibiting several of the following social signs of abuse:

- Abnormal expression of sexuality in writing, drawing, or playing
- Alcohol and/or drug abuse
- Antisocial behavior, defiance, problems with authority and rules
- Assumes a parental role
- Avoids specific people or situations
- Defensive reaction to touch
- Dependent, clinging behavior
- Distrust of sleepovers
- Early arrival/late departure from school or another safe place
- Eating disorders
- Excessive compliance (inability to set personal boundaries)
- Exclusive relationship with an older person
- Extreme modesty, reluctant to change clothes in front of others
- Fear of saying *no* to adults
- Poor peer relationships
- Premature sexual knowledge or behavior
- Promiscuity or seductive behavior toward older males
- Makes attempts to run away
- Secretive behavior
- Sexual abuse of another child
- Sudden drop in school performance or other activities

All child victims struggle with not understanding their needs and not knowing how to meet those needs. When wounded "children" of all ages become aware of these God-given needs, they may be drawn to the Lord. Regardless of the past, He is the One who will satisfy their needs and strengthen their lives.

> *"The Lord will guide you always;*
> *he will satisfy your needs in a sun-scorched land*
> *and will strengthen your frame.*
> *You will be like a well-watered garden,*
> *like a spring whose waters never fail"*
> (Isaiah 58:11).

Promiscuity and Sexual Abuse

QUESTION: "Will a victim of early childhood sexual abuse have problems with promiscuity?"

ANSWER: Children respond to sexual abuse in varied ways depending on their temperament, personality makeup, and environment—all of which influence the way they interpret and process abuse.

- Sexualized children may believe they have value *only as sex objects*.
- They may equate sex with love and often become promiscuous.
- It is not that they *enjoy being sexually active*, but they have come to believe sex is the only thing they have to offer someone.
- They may believe that sex is the only means by which they can give and receive the feeling of love.

The premature arousal of a child's sexual desires leads to destruction of sexual boundaries. Longing to feel loved, many but not all child victims harden their hearts to God and turn to sexual promiscuity. With a distrust of the Lord, they can easily "look for love in all the wrong places."

D. What Are the Spiritual Signs of Abuse?

Marilyn's mother read her Bible every night and knelt beside her bed to pray to a "heavenly Father." Yet she allowed her daughter's earthly father to commit sexual abuse night after night after night. Understandably, Marilyn never prayed as a child or young adult—she believed the "Father" to whom her mother always prayed wasn't protecting her anyway. "It would be many years before I understood why I didn't want another father—certainly not a more powerful one."[44]

It's not unusual for victims to vent their anger toward God for allowing the abuse they experienced. Like so many other victims of incest, Marilyn's knowledge of a "heavenly Father" was skewed. Because Marilyn had transferred the characteristics of her earthly father to the "heavenly Father" her mother prayed to, Marilyn's image of God was severely distorted.[45]

However, Jesus came to show us what the heavenly Father is really like. And His tender care and compassion for children were so great that He gave this stern warning:

"Whoever causes the downfall
of one of these little ones who believe in Me—
it would be better for him if a heavy millstone were hung around his neck
and he were drowned in the depths of the sea!"
(Matthew 18:6 hcsb).

Sadly, children who are victimized generally struggle with some of the following obstacles to their spiritual growth:

- Are afraid of an intimate relationship with God
- Are ignorant of the true character of God
- Carry false guilt before God
- Don't grasp the grace of God
- Doubt the existence of God
- Fear the anger of God
- Feel painfully rejected by God
- Feel unworthy before God
- Harbor bitterness toward God
- Never experience the love of God
- Possess a warped view of God
- Project the abuser's attributes upon God
- Try to earn the approval of God

Unfortunately, all too often children live out in their adulthood what they experienced in their childhood. That is why abused children need to experience God's love through godly people. Children learn more from what is *shown* to them than from what is *told* to them. Without intervention, children who grow up lacking true and accurate knowledge of God are headed for destruction as adults. The Lord says it plainly:

"My people are destroyed from lack of knowledge"
(Hosea 4:6).

God and Independent Choice

Question: "I prayed for God to stop the abuse. Why didn't He?"

Answer: God did not create a "puppet state" where—by the flick of His finger or by pulling this string or that—everyone must move the way He wants.

God has given every person free will, or independent choice. And at times we are *all* victims of the wrong choices of others.

While no one possesses a "divine umbrella" to protect them from the storms of life, know that the Lord will walk with you through the rough waters. He will comfort and guide you; He will strengthen and sustain you. He will even use the storms to deepen your relationship with Him. The Lord promises,

> *"When you pass through the waters, I will be with you;*
> *and when you pass through the rivers, they will not sweep over you.*
> *When you walk through the fire, you will not be burned;*
> *the flames will not set you ablaze"*
> (ISAIAH 43:2).

E. What Characterizes the Male Victim of Childhood Sexual Abuse?

Daughters like Marilyn are not the only ones who fall prey to predatory fathers. Sons are also vulnerable to the sin of sexual abuse. Evil is not a respecter of persons, no matter their gender or age. All children are at risk of being abused by those who practice sexual perversion.

Likewise, all children—both male and female—are at risk of becoming an abuser of other weaker, more vulnerable children. Sadly, sin produces sin, causing the transfer of abuse from victim to victim to victim. The book of Proverbs frequently addresses "my son," warning him of a perverse man.

> *"Who goes about with a corrupt mouth, who winks with his eye,*
> *signals with his feet and motions with his fingers,*
> *who plots evil with deceit in his heart—*
> *he always stirs up dissension"*
> (PROVERBS 6:12-14).

- **A male *child* victim** of sexual abuse is generally between the ages of 4 to 11 and is more likely than a female child victim...
  — To be victimized by someone outside the family who is a stranger or authority figure such as a camp counselor, church leader, schoolteacher, or sports coach
  — To be victimized in conjunction with other children
  — To come from impoverished and single-parent families
  — To be a victim of physical abuse

— To have the abuse reported to the police rather than to a hospital or child protective agency

- **A male *adolescent* victim** of sexual abuse by a male perpetrator is generally 17 years of age and…

  — Is commonly raped outdoors in remote areas or automobiles

  — Is usually heterosexual, as is his perpetrator

  — Is more likely than a female victim to be gang raped, raped by a stranger, forced to engage in multiple types of sexual acts, threatened with weapons, and to have serious physical injuries

  — Is unlikely to acknowledge his victimization

  — Is forced to deal with the experience of sexual role inversion and a pervasive mythology revolving around "loss of manhood" and homosexuality

How fitting are the words of the psalmist, how accurately they portray the victimizer and his victims:

> *"The wicked man hunts down the weak,*
> *who are caught in the schemes he devises…*
> *His victims are crushed, they collapse;*
> *they fall under his strength"*
> (Psalm 10:2,10).

III. Causes of Childhood Sexual Abuse

The sexual abuse committed by Francis Van Derbur was contemptible—and out of control. The day finally came when Marilyn shared the shameful secret with her oldest sister, Gwen. Immediately, she saw the blood drain from her sister's face.

"Oh…oh my God" Gwen lamented. "I thought I was the only one!" Marilyn, too, had thought she was the only one—the only victim of his warped affection.[46]

What kind of father could betray his own daughters? What kind of depravity would steal the innocence of someone's childhood? "My father was a handsome, intelligent man…But there was another—secret—side to him."[47]

Marilyn's words reveal the pervasive deceptiveness of sin. Evil isn't confined to the back alleys of life. It can secretly live in the heart of anyone!

"There is deceit in the hearts of those who plot evil,
but joy for those who promote peace"
(Proverbs 12:20).

A. What Is the Setup for an Abuser?

Francis Van Derbur was not a religious man, but he acted as if he had God-given authority to dominate and rule.

While his wife told the world she had the perfect marriage, Van frequently told her to "shut up"—further belittling her with comments like, "You lose so many opportunities to be quiet." And if she didn't like things around the Van Derbur household, Van had one word for her: *leave.* "I don't need anyone" was Van's mantra as he abused his family emotionally, physically, and sexually.[48]

The vast majority of abusers were themselves victims of abuse. This fact reveals that certain sins can be generational. That which is modeled before children is too often repeated years later. This does not excuse abuse. Regardless of how evil penetrates our lives, God eventually holds us all accountable for our behavior. But be assured, God's redemptive power can break any family stronghold.

This general principle is seen in the Bible with regard to an evil father (King Manasseh) who was succeeded by his evil son (King Amon). However, Amon's son broke the despicable pattern of evil. He did only what was right in the eyes of God.

"He [Amon] did evil in the eyes of the Lord,
as his father Manasseh had done...
Josiah his [Amon's] son succeeded him as king...
He did what was right in the eyes of the Lord...
not turning aside to the right or to the left"
(2 Kings 21:20,26; 22:2).

The Profile of Child Abusers[49]

A—Alcohol or drug abuse—use drugs to lower their inhibitions

B—BACKGROUND **of abuse**—have experienced emotional deprivation and/or childhood trauma

U—UNRESOLVED **anger**—feel they have been victims all their lives

S—SEXUAL **addiction to pornography**—want to act out the perversion they have seen

E—EMOTIONAL **immaturity**—use children to receive comfort and to bolster their low sense of self-worth

R—RIGID, **religious background**—attend church religiously and/or espouse moralistic beliefs and traditional roles

S—STEPFAMILIES **or family problems**—have greater difficulty communicating with their wives than with their daughters

Justification of Abuse

QUESTION: "What kind of perverted thinking 'justifies' the victimization of a child by any male family member?"[50]

ANSWER: These perpetrators basically believe that God intended for men to dominate women, and children, in turn, should unquestionably bow to their male authority. Not only do many of them believe that women are morally inferior to men and thus must not have any say over what a man does, they also believe that children are inherently evil and must be treated sternly.

They wrongly believe that no one in the family can act independently and that suffering is a "Christian virtue." Therefore, Christians must immediately forgive those who sin against them and never hold them accountable in the future. In addition, they believe the family must be preserved at all costs. However, the Bible presents the problem of perversion as an issue of the *heart*:

> *"Out of men's hearts,*
> *come evil thoughts, sexual immorality...*
> *adultery...deceit, lewdness"*
> (MARK 7:21-22).

B. Why Do Perpetrators Abuse Children?
As stunned as Marilyn was when she learned that her sister was also an

incest victim, she was also shocked by a letter she received many years later from an abuse victim who said she had been sexually violated by Van "about 20 times in 1983," *when Van was 75 years old.*[51] Marilyn's mind began to reel when she read the letter. Were there countless others who had suffered at the hands of her father? How many other lives had been devastated by his debauchery?

It took a fatal heart attack to stop his lewd, insatiable lust…to stop this sick, sexual predator who was always on the prowl.

Perpetrators are master manipulators of their own minds. Through perverted reasoning they rationalize and justify their sexual advances. Yet the Bible says,

> *"There is a way that seems right to a man,*
> *but in the end it leads to death"*
> (PROVERBS 14:12).

Perpetrators…

- Feel powerless and have a desperate need to control someone.[52]
- See their sexual actions as a solution to their problems.
- Use children to bolster their sense of significance.
- Fear their daughters' sexual development.
- Want to take care of their daughters' innermost, intimate needs.
- Use sex to feel loved.
- Have difficulty forming healthy adult relationships.
- Rationalize and justify their actions:
    — "My wife is cold and indifferent…It's her fault."
    — "It's my duty to provide sex education for her [the victim]."
    — "I view sex as loving and gentle."
    — "It's better for me to prepare her than for someone else to do so."
    — "It is only play, not intercourse."
    — "I can't control my impulses."
    — "I need something to relieve my stress."
    — "She is seducing me."

No excuse for sexually abusing anyone—especially a child—can hold up under the scrutiny of God:

> *"All a man's ways seem innocent to him,*
> *but motives are weighed by the LORD"*
> (PROVERBS 16:2).

C. Why Are Victims Chosen?

Power and perversion put Van on the prowl, looking for victims who would cower beneath his seeming omnipotence. He cared nothing about the trauma and heartache he left behind. At age 40, when Marilyn confronted him about what he had done to her, she cringed with disdain at her father's empty words: "If I had known what it would do to you, I never would have done it."[53] She didn't believe it then, and she doesn't believe it now—especially after receiving the lamentable letter that her father had abused *outside* the family as well. "It was an egregious lie," Marilyn flatly states.[54]

Abusers typically look for specific things in their potential victims that indicate susceptibility to being abused. In this sense, victims don't become victims by chance but by the choice of the victimizer:

> *"He [the victimizer] lies in wait near the villages;*
> *from ambush…watching in secret for his victims"*
> (PSALM 10:8).

The Profile of Victims

V—VULNERABLE—open to attack, susceptible to injury, weak, defenseless, at risk, helpless

I—INSECURE—anxious, timid, lacking confidence, self-doubting, apprehensive, ill at ease

C—COMPLIANT—acquiescent, obedient, submissive, amenable, accommodating, yielding

T—TRUSTING—gullible, credulous, naïve, unquestioning, susceptible, unthinking

I—INTIMIDATED—frightened, scared, unsettled, panicky, nervous, worried

M—**MANIPULATED**—influenced, controlled, maneuvered, used, managed, persuaded

S—**SUPPRESSED**—contained, concealed, held back, stifled, restrained, bottled up

D. Why Don't Children Tell?

For years D.D. Harvey had felt that something was wrong with Marilyn but couldn't put his finger on why. Over time, the pieces of the puzzle slowly...eventually...started falling into place. One day this former youth minister—whom Marilyn greatly esteemed—arranged a visit with her.

With no warm-up, no small talk, D.D. looked Marilyn squarely in the eyes and uttered two words: "father...bedroom."[55] Marilyn broke down into deep, gut-wrenching sobs, and finally at the point of exhaustion she managed to whisper back, "Don't...tell...anyone."[56]

Compassionately, D.D. steered Marilyn onto the road to recovery, which, in turn, enabled her to tell *everyone* about her tumultuous journey. She spoke out in the hopes of helping other victims and their families. Victims of child abuse need to hear truth over and over and over. That is why victims who still grapple with fear will benefit greatly by reading this scripture repeatedly:

> *"God has not given us a spirit of fear,*
> *but of power and of love and of a sound mind"*
> (2 TIMOTHY 1:7 NKJV).

For a number of reasons, most abused children never share "the secret" of their abuse. And if they do, it's usually many years after the abuse took place. Typically they feel they must protect their perpetrators—or at least the secret—because...[57]

- They feel immense shame and guilt—*false guilt*—and assume it's all their fault.

- They fear going to jail.

- They feel love for and loyalty toward the abuser.

- They fear the one they tell will respond with disbelief, denial, or disgust.

- They feel no need to tell because the trauma caused dissociation, resulting in no memory of abuse.
- They fear the abuser's authority and power.
- They feel threatened by the abuser.
- They fear what will happen to the abuser.
- They feel obligated to the abuser.
- They fear no one will love them anymore.
- They fear being taken away from their family.
- They feel no one cares because no one asks!

Denial of Abuse Contradicted by Behavior

QUESTION: "What can I do if I suspect my child has been sexually abused but she repeatedly denies it?"

ANSWER: Regardless of her denial, if you suspect abuse has occurred or is presently occurring:

- Take your daughter to the doctor for a checkup.
- Privately explain to the doctor that your purpose for bringing your daughter in is to find out whether sexual activity is presently occurring or has previously occurred.
- Describe the signs you have seen in your daughter that led you to form your opinion and request to be present during her exam.
- Retrace your daughter's recent activities and write a list of all the people she has been around and which ones may have had opportunity to violate her without anyone else knowing.
- Go through the list of people one by one with your daughter, asking which ones she enjoys spending time with and would want to spend more time with in the future.
- Observe which people your daughter verbally says no to and especially which ones she nonverbally says no to.
- Be diligent to watch your daughter closely and to keep her safe

around each person you now have any reason to suspect might be abusing her.

Remember the protective words of Jesus:

> *"When a strong man, fully armed, guards his own house,*
> *his possessions are safe"*
> (LUKE 11:21).

As long as the child is afraid of the abuser, the child is kept captive. However, the truth of this scripture will set the captive free:

> *"Fear of man will prove to be a snare,*
> *but whoever trusts in the LORD is kept safe"*
> (PROVERBS 29:25).

The Guilt Game

After sexually abusing a child, victimizers fear being found out, so they shift the blame for the abuse to the victim by unloading a truckload of guilt. This strategy is known as the perverted guilt game.

Most games are fun, and most games require some level of strategy. In the case of child abuse, perpetrators use one of the most powerful strategies in existence—guilt. In fact, most perpetrators possess an expertise at playing the guilt game—a game of deceit. For victims, this game is not fun—it is cruel. The Bible says,

> *"The words of his mouth are wicked and deceitful;*
> *he has ceased to be wise and to do good"*
> (PSALM 36:3).

- "If you share our secret, it will break my heart."
- "If you share our secret, Mother's feelings will be hurt."
- "If you share our secret, they won't let me see you again."
- "If you share our secret, Mommy won't understand and will leave us."
- "If you share our secret, your mother will divorce me."

- "If you share our secret, our family will be destroyed."
- "If you share our secret, no one will believe you. I'll say you started it."
- "If you share our secret, I'll tell them you wanted it. It's your fault."
- "If you share our secret, I won't love you anymore."
- "If you share our secret, I'll kill you. I'll kill myself."

Never try to protect the perpetrator.
And never, ever blame the victim—
the guilt lies solely in the hands of the victimizer.

E. Why Should Victims Tell?

Unhealed victims of childhood sexual abuse walk around in darkness with unsettled fear. They begin to heal as truth is brought into the light. As they yield the pain of their past to the Lord, He will reveal what is hidden in the shadows...and what is necessary to be shared. Job 12:22 says, "He reveals the deep things of darkness and brings deep shadows into the light."

Victims should share the secret...

- To protect other children from being abused by the perpetrator
- To break the power "the secret" holds over them as victims
- To enable skilled professionals to identify the lies victims believe as a result of being abused—lies about themselves, God, and others—and replace each lie with the truth
- To stop victims from living a lie in order to cover up the truth
- To enable victims to face the facts, process the pain, and work toward becoming an overcomer
- To free each victim of false guilt and unwarranted shame
- To encourage other victims to reveal they are being abused
- To give the victim a sense of personal power
- To open the door for victims to receive support from others
- To break the power of darkness with the light of truth

Victims *should tell* because truth is paramount to Jesus, who said,

> *"You will know the truth, and the truth will set you free"*
> (John 8:32).

F. What Are the Root Causes of Childhood Sexual Abuse?

The root causes of perpetrations of childhood sexual abuse run so deep that without the transforming power of Jesus Christ in a person's life, statistics show that most abusers *never stop*. Marilyn explains, "They don't look like monsters. No one suspects that the charismatic gymnastics coach, or the gentle priest, or the fun grandfather is a sexual predator."[58]

Sadly, repeat abusers tend to be either "family members or highly regarded people in positions of trust."[59] But abusers never are worthy of trust. Unless they experience a changed life through Christ, every one of them will receive the judgment of God, according to Scripture:

> *"Woe to those who plan iniquity,*
> *to those who plot evil on their beds!*
> *At morning's light they carry it out*
> *because it is in their power to do it"*
> (Micah 2:1).

The Abuser

To understand the emotional makeup of a child abuser, we must keep in mind every person's three God-given inner needs for love, significance, and security.[60] Victimizers typically struggle with an overwhelming sense of insignificance. They will do whatever is necessary to obtain a sense of power and significance.

As children, they had no control; as adults, they abuse children in order to be in control. Their sexual dominance makes them feel significant, even superior. They like having these feelings of power replace their feelings of insignificance or having no control over their circumstances.

Wrong Belief of the Abuser

"Having sex with a child meets my needs. I have the right to get my needs met, and this gives me a sense of power and significance and relieves the intense stress and anger I feel."

Right Belief for the Abuser

"I don't need to exert power over a child to get my needs met. My need for significance is already met because God chose to create me, and He has a plan and purpose for me. By giving Jesus control of my life, I can see children as His precious creations and desire to protect every child at all costs."

Jesus specifically said, "I tell you the truth, whatever you did for one of the least of these...you did for me" (Matthew 25:40).

The Abused

Even small children instinctively recognize inappropriate behavior. A young child's great needs for love and security are immensely threatened by fear of disapproval and rejection. Young, sensitive hearts feel that "keeping the secret" is the safest way to be loved and accepted. Children who live in terror of their abusers feel that keeping the secret is the only way to stay safe.

Wrong Belief of the Abused

"I can't stop what's going on, and I can't tell anyone—I've got to keep it a secret. God must really hate me because I'm so bad. I know it's my fault. I am so dirty...I can never be clean again."

Right Belief for the Abused

"What is happening to me is bad, but I myself am not bad. This abuse is not my fault. Telling the truth to someone I can trust is good because it may help prevent the bad from happening again. Jesus loves all children, and He loves me. I'm trusting in Him to make me clean and to take care of me."

"Guard my life and rescue me; let me not be put to shame, for I take refuge in you...wash me, and I will be whiter than snow" (Psalm 25:20; 51:7).

How Can I Be Fully and Finally Free?

God's heart is grieved when any one of His precious creations is abused. He loves you and knows how to set you free physically, mentally, emotionally, and yes, even spiritually.

There are four spiritual truths you need to know—see the appendix on pages 411-13.

IV. Steps to Solution

Marilyn described it as "the *second* day of the rest of my life."[61] And it involved the secret—her personal secret storm.

On May 9, 1991, the secret Marilyn had struggled for years to bury deep within her soul surfaced in a way she never would have expected. Until that day, D.D. Harvey "knew"…and her beloved Larry "knew." But now anyone reading the daily newspaper would discover the detestable secret, the disgusting shame, the sordid dysfunction within one of Denver's most prominent families. When the news broke, the *Denver Post* devoted numerous pages to detailing the personal stories that disclosed the twisted perversion forced upon the city's pride and joy, the former Miss America.[62]

Just as Marilyn's childhood was divided between the "day child" and the "night child," her life as a middle-aged adult would "be split into 'before May 8' and 'after May 8'"[63] Marilyn now had a new platform—not as a beauty queen, but as an incest survivor—and she had a new message: to bring hope and healing to families shattered by the secret storm of childhood sexual abuse.

Many sufferers like Marilyn have learned from their painful experiences that

> *"the Lord is close to the brokenhearted*
> *and saves those who are crushed in spirit"*
> (Psalm 34:18).

A. A Key Verse to Memorize

As Marilyn and all other victims of childhood sexual abuse know, fear and stark terror reign in their hearts. They find it very difficult to trust others. Safety, not happiness, is their goal. Always on the defense, they are preoccupied with spotting signs of danger and planning ways of escape, ways to save themselves. Because of those around them who have been untrustworthy, their greatest need is to find security in the One who is completely trustworthy—the Lord. The Bible says,

> *"Be strong and courageous.*
> *Do not be afraid or terrified because of them,*
> *for the Lord your God goes with you;*
> *he will never leave you nor forsake you"*
> (Deuteronomy 31:6).

B. A Key Passage to Read and Reread

Everyone needs to know who is trustworthy and who is not. Those who have been victimized have great difficulty in the area of trust. In fact, some victims come to the conclusion, "There is no one I can trust." The heart cry of every victim of child abuse—of every victim of violation—can be found in Psalm 55.

=========================== *Psalm 55* ===========================

MY PRAYER FOR DEVELOPING TRUST

God, I appeal to You . . . . verse 1

I am troubled and distraught . . . . verse 2

I suffer at the voice and the stares of my victimizer . . . . verse 3

My heart is in anguish, and I am terrified . . . . verse 4

Fear and horror have overwhelmed me . . . . verse 5

How I long to escape far from the tempest and storm! . . . . verses 6-8

I see the violence and strife . . . . verse 9

I know the malice and abuse . . . . verse 10

I hear the threats and lies . . . . verse 11

I feel absolutely betrayed . . . . verses 12-14

Deal with my betrayer as his evil demands . . . . verse 15

I call upon You, and You save me . . . . verse 16

I am distressed, and You hear me . . . . verse 17

I am opposed, and You ransom me . . . . verse 18

You know all about my abuser and will punish him . . . . verse 19

My betrayer attacks those close to him . . . . verse 20

He is a smooth talker whose words can't be trusted . . . . verse 21

I cast my cares on You, Lord, for You will sustain me . . . . verse 22

You won't let me fall . . . . verse 22

You will bring judgment upon my betrayer . . . . verse 23

I choose to put my trust in You! . . . . verse 23

C. How to Apply the Do's and Don'ts of Awareness

From the very first day that full family disclosure appeared in the *Denver Post*, Marilyn's story spread like wildfire. People emerged from all walks of life saying one of two things: "I too am a survivor of incest" or "I too am a survivor of childhood sexual abuse." The phones would not stop ringing.

One of the first public attempts to help other survivors was the giving of a $250,000 grant made by the Van Derbur family to Denver's Kempe National Center for the Prevention and Treatment of Child Abuse and Neglect.[64] The center had many programs, but up until this time no treatment had been offered for adults who had been sexually abused as children.

When it comes to abuse of any kind, too many people become like an ostrich. They stick their head in the sands of denial. Although it is tremendously difficult to do so, facing the truth that child abuse has taken place is the first step to healing. Take comfort in the fact that

"when justice is done,
it brings joy to the righteous but terror to evildoers"
(Proverbs 21:15).

When it comes to facing the truth about child sexual abuse, know these Do's and Don'ts:

Do's[65]

— *Do* be aware that child abuse is illegal, a crime that must be reported.

— *Do* be aware that children are usually abused by people they know.

— *Do* be aware that children seldom lie about abuse.

— *Do* be aware that most often physical abuse is violent, but sexual abuse is usually not violent.

— *Do* be aware that children may deny or change their stories because of fear.

— *Do* be aware that sexual abuse is progressive and will get worse if not stopped.

Don'ts

— *Don't* be in denial, no matter how difficult it is to believe the child.

— *Don't* assume that if it happened only once, it is not serious.

— *Don't* minimize the abuse.

— *Don't* let the offender go without confrontation.

— *Don't* blame other family members.

— *Don't* keep abuse a "family secret."

Realize...

> *"The heart of the discerning acquires knowledge;*
> *the ears of the wise seek it out"*
> (PROVERBS 18:15).

Babysitters and Perpetrators

QUESTION: "How can we protect our children from being sexually abused by babysitters?"

ANSWER: Most parents don't realize that children in need of childcare are highly vulnerable to sexual violation.

- First, talk to your children: "Don't let anyone touch your private parts or the parts covered by your bathing suit."
- Then, talk to the babysitter/childcare worker: "We're glad you will care for our children, who are very dear to us. We want you to know that we've trained them to not let anyone touch the parts of their bodies covered by their bathing suits. And if anyone does try, they must tell us. If our children tell you about any inappropriate touching—anything sexual either now or in the future—we expect you to share that information with us. Please help us keep our children safe. Thank you for being loving toward our children."[66]

It's wonderful that the love chapter in the Bible says,

> *"[Love] always protects"*
> (1 CORINTHIANS 13:7).

D. How to Respond to Childhood Sexual Abuse

Nothing penetrates the core of a child's inner being like sexual abuse. Its long tentacles reach deep within the child, wrapping around the young heart and choking and killing innocence and trust. For many, the terror is so overwhelming that no part of the soul is able to escape its evil presence.

The impact of the abuse inflicted upon Marilyn Van Derbur continued to corrode her personal dignity and pervert her perception of others even after the abuse ended. She, as well as other victims, can truly identify with the heart cry of Proverbs 25:20: "Like one who takes away a garment on a cold day, or like vinegar poured on soda, is one who sings songs to a heavy heart."

To handle the hundreds upon hundreds of cries for help, Marilyn quickly established a survivor's network that offered counseling and support.[67]

Marilyn then accepted countless speaking engagements to help increase abuse awareness and to provide healing for adult survivors. Today, many victims-turned-victors are sharing their stories of hope and, as a result, many others are—for the first time—facing the future with hope.

The Bible says,

> *"There is surely a future hope for you,*
> *and your hope will not be cut off"*
> (Proverbs 23:18).

- **If You Suspect Child Abuse…**
  - Contact Child Protective Services and other child advocacy programs to verify or share your suspicions and to plan a course of action. (Remember, many states in the United States have laws that require the reporting of suspected child abuse.)
  - Contact a family attorney.
  - Contact a shelter for women and children.
  - Contact a pastor or spiritual leader and a professional child abuse counselor.
  - Contact the local police or a law enforcement agency.
  - Contact the local district attorney's office.

The Bible says,

> *"A wise man has great power,*
> *and a man of knowledge increases strength;*
> *for waging war you need guidance,*
> *and for victory many advisers"*
> (Proverbs 24:5-6).

- **If a Child Discloses Abuse...**

  — Stay calm.

  — Take time to sensitively answer any questions from the child.

  — Be available to the child at all times.

  — Stay with the child. Leave the child only with another adult whom both you and the child trust.

  — Respect the privacy of the child from those who have no need to know her story.

  — Make no promises you can't keep, such as, "Your mom won't be angry" or "He won't get into trouble."

  — Explain that law enforcement agencies must be informed, and then describe what will happen next.

  — Be prepared to provide protection, arrange for a medical exam, and obtain professional counseling.

Follow the scriptural admonition to

> *"encourage the timid,*
> *help the weak, be patient with everyone"*
> (1 Thessalonians 5:14).

- **If You See Questionable Marks on a Child's Body...**

  — Take the child to a pediatrician or the local hospital emergency room for immediate examination and documentation.

  — Relate why you suspect possible child abuse and state that a child abuse case should be turned over to a caseworker.

  — Ask for a copy of the medical report in writing and for copies of photographs if they are taken. (An attorney can subpoena them.)

  — Keep a paper trail of all contacts you make: calls, reports, and photographs.

  — If a caseworker's file disappears, supply duplicates of your copies of photographs and reports.

— Follow up with caseworkers on a regular basis, asking about the status of the case and how you can be of assistance.

— If the local services are not responsive, appeal to higher authorities by contacting a state or federal agency.

Follow the biblical mandate to

> *"submit yourselves for the Lord's sake*
> *to every authority instituted among men…*
> *who are sent by him to punish those who do wrong*
> *and to commend those who do right"*
> (1 PETER 2:13-14).

E. How to Surface the Secret

"Has anyone ever touched you in an uncomfortable way?"[68] This is the most important question a parent or guardian can ask a child, according to Marilyn. Why? Because *children don't tell*, believing that they are to blame or that no one will believe them—or even worse, that no one will love or help them. Older boys and girls can struggle even more with guilt, fearing questions like, Why didn't you fight back, leave, or run away?

No matter the initial answer to your question, further conversation and more assurances will be needed. Why? Because most violated children do not immediately answer *yes*. Children watch your reaction—subconsciously testing you—and if you express immense relief over a "no touch" answer, they may never tell you at all. *They don't want Mom and Dad to have to deal with this.*[69]

The better follow-up response is this: "If you ever do want to come and tell me something, just remember that we can always work things through together. Most kids don't tell because they feel ashamed. There is never anything to be ashamed of. I love you so much. There is nothing that could ever change that."[70]

Not telling leaves victims of childhood sexual abuse in bondage to "the secret." Revealing the truth is the only strategy for breaking the power of that secret. The key to opening the hearts of victims is to give them loving care and the tender compassion of Christ.

> *"The LORD is good, a refuge in times of trouble.*
> *He cares for those who trust in him"*
> (NAHUM 1:7).

As you seek to surface the secret...[71]

- Pray for supernatural wisdom from God.

- Provide a safe atmosphere, away from upsetting people and places.

- Ask, "Have you been experiencing something uncomfortable or confusing?"
  "Has anyone ever touched you in a way that made you uncomfortable?"

- Listen carefully, repeat what is said, and ask, "Did I get it right?"

- Be cautious about asking "leading questions," such as, "Did he do _____ to you?"

- Let authorities with expertise in childhood sexual abuse ask most of the questions in order to determine the truth.

- Communicate that you believe the child.

- Acknowledge that the offender is wrong.

- Give assurance that the child is not to blame.

- Confirm that telling is the right thing to do.

- Don't reach out with physical affection unless you ask permission: "Would you like for me to hold your hand?" Or, "Can I give you a hug?" Even if the answer is yes, if you sense hesitation, slowly withdraw.

- Provide a safe atmosphere by displaying genuine love and compassion.

Remember...

> *"The purposes of a [child's] heart are deep waters,*
> *but a [person] of understanding draws them out"*
> (PROVERBS 20:5).

F. How to Give Children Permission to Say "No!"

As a child, Marilyn Van Derbur excelled in scholastics and sports...but no one told her that she had the *right* to say no to something wrong. Giving children permission to say no teaches them that they have the right of control over their own bodies and helps them establish safe, personal boundaries.

It should be *their choice* as to whether and by whom they want to be touched or kissed.[72]

Instilling this concept of *protective power* in children doesn't display disrespect for others, but rather builds a healthy sense of self-respect. And its implications include recognizing that others have the right to establish the same healthy boundaries. Yet millions of children are violated every day because they believe their only options are to say, "Yes" or to remain totally silent, which may be taken as consent while their hearts are yelling, "No!" Sadly, they do not realize...

> *"the grace of God that brings salvation...*
> *teaches us to say 'No' to ungodliness"*
> (Titus 2:11-12).

Many children do not know they have permission to take action to protect themselves. They don't realize what is happening, and they become too frightened to react quickly. Because most children are taught to obey authority figures, they need to be empowered to protect themselves from any authority figure who would hurt them.

Protection Power

The following statements can instill confidence and build assertiveness in a young heart and help a child to resist inappropriate sexual advances:

- "God loves you and made your body with a special plan and purpose."
- "If you are asked to do something you think is wrong, say, 'No!' even to an older relative or friend of the family. Then come tell me whether saying, 'No!' worked or not." (Role-play saying "No!" in a firm, assertive voice.)
- "Your body belongs to you, and you decide who touches it."
- "The parts of your body covered by a bathing suit are private."
- "Never allow anyone to touch your private parts, unless it is for medical reasons and a parent is present."
- "If someone tries to touch your private parts, scream and run to a safe place."

- "If someone touches your private parts and says that it's okay, that person is wrong! If that happens, you must tell me or someone you trust."

- "If a person does not stop touching you, say, 'I'll tell if you don't stop!' Then tell me or someone else when it is safe for you to do so."

- "If someone threatens you, do not be afraid. Tell on that person anyway."

- "If you are asked to keep the touching a secret, tell on that person anyway."

- "If you report that you were touched in a wrong way and the person you tell this to doesn't believe you, keep telling no matter how embarrassed you feel. Keep telling about what happened until someone believes you."

- "Pray that you will find a safe adult whom you can trust to help you (someone who is not a member of your family)."

This verse is perfect to share with any child:

> *"If sinners entice you, do not give in to them"*
> (Proverbs 1:10).

G. How to Warn Parents

Marilyn Van Derbur has described the trauma many sexually abused children face when they go to a doctor's office. Even the simplest procedure—like swabbing for a throat culture—can cause nauseating flashbacks, emotional trauma, and physical reactions that may result even in a child's running away.

Therefore, "stepping up to the plate"—warning others about past abusers in positions of authority—can save many children immense grief for years to come and in ways perhaps never imagined.

Some people feel uncomfortable—as though they're being a tattletale—revealing the sexual abuse others have committed. However, if you know that a child abuser is about to be put in a position of authority over children, *for the children's sake* you must share what you know—even if your warning is dismissed. All responsible adults have a heart to protect children. If you take action based on the golden rule, you just may save a child's life:

> *"In everything,*
> *do to others what you would have them do to you"*
> (Matthew 7:12).

Warning Parents About Perpetrators

Question: "As a child, I was sexually abused by an older relative. Now he is planning to marry a woman with young children. Should I express my concern?"

Answer: Yes, absolutely! Although you may be accused of vindictiveness, digging up dirt, stirring up trouble, or other such things, you must speak up on behalf of the vulnerable children.

When you express your concern, approach your relative in a calm, non-attacking manner and say,

- "I sincerely thank you for talking with me."
- "Something has been concerning me. I've prayed about this and need to ask you several questions."
- Optional: "I'm not here to make you feel uncomfortable or to attack you."
- "I just need to ask: How have you dealt with your sexual behavior toward me when I was ___ years old?"
- "Have you received counseling for the past sexual abuse you committed? When? Where? With whom? What did you learn?"
  - If you are not satisfied with his responses, express your heartfelt concern for the physical and emotional protection of his fiancée's children.
  - Explain your moral obligation to talk with the children's mother. After all, they are her children.
  - Ask the fiancée, "Are you aware of the childhood sexual abuse committed by [relative's name] in the past?"
  - If the answer is no, then say, "I feel morally obligated to share a painful memory with you."
  - After you have briefly described what happened, communicate to her, "If he has not received adequate help through

counseling to understand both his inappropriate thinking and behavior, and if he has not learned to honor appropriate boundaries with children, there is reason to have great concern for your children."

In seeking to protect children, remember...

> *"A truthful witness saves lives,*
> *but a false witness is deceitful"*
> (Proverbs 14:25).

H. How to Share the Heart of God

Childhood sexual abuse brainwashes its victims into believing that they are unlovable, or that they will no longer be loved if people find out what happened. What they perceive to be *conditional* love buries their secret all the more.

Unconditional love was the healing balm Marilyn Van Derbur needed to begin moving toward wholeness. Marilyn was blessed beyond measure to have unconditional love poured into her heart and soul by a persistent youth minister, a compassionate husband, and a loving daughter—all gifts from God.[73] (Although such gifts are helpful, recovery is possible for any victim even without such gifts.) Children who have experienced the trauma of sexual abuse need not only a physical haven of safety, but also an emotional haven for the wounded heart. Tell them about God's unconditional love, and then live as an example of His unconditional love. Help children run into the arms of Jesus to receive His emotional support and security.

> *"He [Jesus] took the children in his arms,*
> *put his hands on them and blessed them"*
> (Mark 10:16).

===== **Assurances That Will Help Children** =====

As you seek to help children receive the unconditional, grace-filled love of God, ask them to repeat the following assurances every single day:

- "Nothing can ever cause me to lose God's love."

"I have loved you with an everlasting love;
I have drawn you with loving-kindness"
(JEREMIAH 31:3).

• "Even if someone in my family rejects me, God still accepts me."

"Though my father and mother forsake me,
the LORD will receive me"
(PSALM 27:10).

• "I will tell God what I really feel, and He will understand."

"Cast all your anxiety on him
because he cares for you"
(1 PETER 5:7).

• "When I come to God for help, He will heal my hurts."

"O LORD my God, I called to you
for help and you healed me"
(PSALM 30:2).

• "I will let Jesus live in my heart, and I will be a brand-new person."

"If anyone is in Christ, he is a new creation;
the old has gone, the new has come!"
(2 CORINTHIANS 5:17).

• "God has a wonderful plan for my life."

"'I know the plans I have for you,' declares the LORD,
'plans to prosper you and not to harm you,
plans to give you hope and a future'"
(JEREMIAH 29:11).

I. How to Sow Seeds of Safety

Wise parents, grandparents, teachers, and others who work with children know the importance of early training for the children's personal safety. The best defense against sexual abuse is prevention.[74]

Tell children they have God-given worth. Your words will cultivate the soil of a young heart and sow seeds of safety that will in turn produce self-confidence and self-protection.

> *"Listen, my son, to your father's instruction*
> *and do not forsake your mother's teaching"*
> (Proverbs 1:8)

- **Tell children…**[75]

  — *Don't go* to a public place without first memorizing our [the parents'] names, phone numbers, and address or without having that information written on a card in your pocket.

  — *Don't go* outside your yard or leave a playground without permission.

  — *Don't go* wandering around looking for your parents if you get separated in a public place. Go to a security guard, checkout counter, or the lost and found for help.

  — *Don't go* near anyone following you, especially if they are in a car or even walking or on a bicycle.

  — *Don't go* with anyone who asks for your help to look for a lost pet (a common trick).

  — *Don't go* near the car of someone who asks for directions.

  — *Don't go* with people who tell you that someone in your family is in trouble and that they were sent to get you.

  — *Don't go* near parked cars, alleys, or dark doorways—always stay in plain view of crowds of people.

  — *Don't go* to extracurricular school activities or walk to or from school alone.

- **Teach children…**

  — *Don't hesitate* to call 9-1-1 if someone is lurking around your house or trying to get inside.

  — *Don't talk* to someone you don't know, no matter how nice the person may look.

  — *Don't accept* a ride home or get into a car to go anywhere with anyone, even if it's someone you know, unless you have your parents' permission.

— *Don't ride* your bike alone, and never walk alone at night.

— *Don't keep* special secrets with older people, and if someone asks you to keep something secret, tell your parents or another adult you can trust.

— *Don't allow* older strangers to play in your games.

— *Don't open* the door when you are home alone.

— *Don't let* a stranger take your picture.

— *Don't hesitate* to scream as loud as you can, "Help, this man/woman is trying to take me" or "Help, this is not my father/mother." Scream and keep screaming.

The Bible gives vivid warnings about

"men whose words are perverse,
who leave the straight paths to walk in dark ways,
who delight in doing wrong and rejoice in the perverseness of evil,
whose paths are crooked and who are devious in their ways"
(PROVERBS 2:12-15).

THE BACKYARD CAPTIVE: THE JAYCEE LEE DUGARD STORY[76]

In August 2009, I was stunned to read the true story of a young girl held captive for years. Imagine the scene...

Like growing mounds of ant hills, the mounds of garbage grew wider throughout the backyard. The stench of human waste overpowered the sweet smell of mimosa trees.

Four tents, five sheds, and an outdoor toilet and shower dotted the half-acre lot. Strewn across the rotting refuse were artifacts of shattered innocence: dirt-covered tricycles, dingy-haired Barbie dolls, dilapidated swings. A "Welcome" sign hung outside one of the sheds...but it should have read "Run for Your Life." Yet for some reason, Jaycee Dugard never did.

Abducted in 1991 at age 11, missing for 18 years, and found alive at age 29, Jaycee had been concealed in the Antioch, California, hideaway. But she wasn't alone. Two daughters born to her during her captivity—15-year-old Starlit and 11-year-old Angel—were also subjected to the squalor.

Jaycee's nightmare began while walking to a school bus stop in South Lake Tahoe, California. Suddenly, a gray sedan pulled up beside her and a middle-aged couple dragged her into the car…then sped away. It was a "random hit." To captors Phillip and Nancy Garrido, Jaycee was a perfect stranger and a perfect target for their perverted plans.

Jaycee's stepfather was only a few hundred yards away when he heard his daughter's chilling screams and witnessed her brazen abduction. He mounted his bicycle and tried to catch the fleeing car—but to no avail. Jaycee vanished and became the powerless victim of seemingly endless sexual abuse.

Renamed *Allissa* by Garrido, Jaycee would never attend another day of school or step foot in a doctor's office or a hospital while in captivity. Starlit and Angel, fathered by Garrido, believed Jaycee was their older sister and had no idea she was their mother.

Although the news headlines remained focused on Jaycee, she was not Garrido's first kidnapping and rape victim. He had served 11 years of a 50-year sentence for the 1976 kidnapping and rape of a casino worker. Garrido, a registered sex offender, had a long history of violence and troubled behavior connected to LSD use in high school.

Garrido's immorality didn't stop him from becoming a self-proclaimed prophet of God. Believing himself to be a powerful messenger from above, Garrido became "minister" to his church congregation of four—his "family." But his pursuit for more proselytes led to the rescue of Jaycee and her daughters.

On August 25, 2009, Garrido visited the U.C. Berkeley campus—bringing Starlit and Angel along with him—to obtain a permit for an "evangelism" event. The university's special events manager was alarmed at the girls' nonresponsive, robotic behavior.

After a background check on Garrido revealed his criminal record, the university's security staff contacted Garrido's parole officer, who summoned him to his office the very next day. When Garrido arrived with his entire "family," 29-year-old Jaycee was led into another room for questioning, and she told officials her entire story.

The greatest mystery surrounding Jaycee's case is why she didn't run away as an adult. Why wasn't there a single attempt to escape—especially in view of her private journal, which chronicled a deep longing to be free? On July 5, 2004, she wrote, "It feels like I'm sinking...This is supposed to be my life to do with what I like...but once again he has taken it away. How many times is he allowed to take it away from me? I'm afraid he doesn't see how the things he says makes me a prisoner."[77] In spite of the forced abduction, rape, and imprisonment, Jaycee evidently developed what is known as Stockholm syndrome, in which captives form a sympathetic bond with their captors out of a sense of total dependence.

Phillip Garrido postured himself as a loving, protective father when in reality he was a heartless perpetrator of childhood sexual abuse. His parental role was a perversion, a deviant departure from all God intends fathers to represent and uphold for their families.

- *Fathers are to morally guide* their children, to be a compass for them and lead them to do what is right in God's sight. Garrido instead conceived his children in the most immoral of circumstances—by raping a kidnapped prisoner and robbing her of her innocence.

- *Fathers are to amply provide* for their children, ensuring that their physical, emotional, and spiritual needs are met. Garrido instead subjected his "family" to inhumane living conditions, failing to provide for their most basic physical, emotional, and spiritual needs.

- *Fathers are to painstakingly protect* and guard their children from the sinful snares of the world and preserve their childhood innocence. Garrido instead opened the floodgates to sin, and the "protective guards" he placed around his daughters left them isolated as well as socially and emotionally impaired.

- Finally, *fathers are to lavishly love* with the very same love modeled by God the Father Himself. God's love is pure, overflowing, sacrificial. It is never self-seeking; it always seeks the very best interests of His children. Our relationship with our heavenly Father is characterized by intimacy—so much so that we come to Him as *Abba*, our "Daddy," who draws us to Him with tender endearment.[78]

If you have struggled with the deep wounds of childhood sexual abuse, always remember: Unlike human fathers, our heavenly Father's unconditional love toward His children is perfect, sincere (1 Corinthians 13:4), sacrificial (1 John 3:16), and secure (Jeremiah 31:3).

> *"How great is the love the Father has lavished on us,*
> *that we should be called children of God!"*
>
> (1 JOHN 3:1).

J. How to Change the Cycle of Abuse for the Abuser

When Francis Van Derbur went to his grave in 1984, there had been no hint of repentance, no evidence of change, no sense of sorrow over his sexual perversions.[79]

And in the end, Marilyn's mother accepted that abuse had occurred, but denied ever knowing what was happening night after night in Marilyn's bedroom. When Marilyn had previously told her what had gone on—with deep, heaving sobs punctuating a lifetime of pain—her mother sat calmly in her chair, arms folded, and coldly stated, "I don't believe you. It's in your fantasy."[80]

The Bible makes God's position absolutely plain:

> *"Godly sorrow brings repentance*
> *that leads to salvation and leaves no regret,*
> *but worldly sorrow brings death"*
>
> (2 CORINTHIANS 7:10).

Wartime Goals for Male Perpetrators

Christ not only offers healing to the child victims and adult survivors of childhood sexual abuse, but to the perpetrators as well. The cycle of the sins of the father being visited upon the children from one generation to another can and must be changed to a cycle of love and forgiveness being passed from generation to generation. To do this, war must be declared against this enemy of our children. Many say that child abusers can never change. However, if the violator is completely repentant and willing, through the power of God, any behavior can be changed. Any heart can be changed. Any life can be changed. God has said,

> *"I am the LORD, the God of all mankind.*
> *Is anything too hard for me?"*
> (JEREMIAH 32:27).

W—WORK on understanding the relationship between *emotions, thoughts, beliefs,* and *behaviors:*

- How you became a sex offender
- How your wrong thinking maintains your behavior
- How you can stop offending

> *"Do not conform any longer to the pattern of this world,*
> *but be transformed by the renewing of your mind.*
> *Then you will be able to test and approve what God's will is—*
> *his good, pleasing and perfect will"*
> (ROMANS 12:2).

A—ADDRESS the following areas:

- Denial
- Sexual assault cycle
- Relapse prevention plan

> *"Rid yourselves of all the offenses you have committed,*
> *and get a new heart and a new spirit...*
> *Clothe yourselves with the Lord Jesus Christ,*
> *and do not think about how to gratify the desires of the sinful nature"*
> (EZEKIEL 18:31; ROMANS 13:14).

R—REACH the following requirements:

16 Steps to Transformation

— Accept full responsibility for your offensive behaviors.

— Understand all facets of your *denial.*

— Comprehend your *sexual abuse cycles.*

— Demonstrate the ability to break those cycles.

— Learn new coping strategies to manage your deviant sexual arousal.

— Develop an effective *relapse prevention plan.*

— Develop an awareness of the social implications of sexual abuse.

— Participate in *skills training* to improve the quality of your inter-personal relationships.

— Discuss your life history in a trustworthy group.

— Disclose any other *victimization* or sexually inappropriate behavior.

— Gain insight into how your offenses affected your victims.

— Develop *empathy* for the pain you have caused.

— Participate in *family therapy* when family members are available.

— Ensure that the family is supportive of newly learned behavior.

— Transform your thinking patterns by memorizing Scripture.

— Join a spiritual accountability group and Bible study group.

"With regard to your former way of life…
put off your old self,
which is being corrupted by its deceitful desires…
be made new in the attitude of your minds;
and…put on the new self,
created to be like God in true righteousness and holiness"
(Ephesians 4:22-24).

If you have been sexually inappropriate with others, we strongly encourage you to obtain the practical resource *Sexual Addiction: The Way Out of the Web,* published by Hope for the Heart.

K. How to Dismantle the Damage

For years, former Miss America Marilyn Van Derbur had no memory of her father's incestuous relationship with her. Like many victims of trauma, she buried her painful memories under layers of disbelief and denial. Later, when Marilyn's daughter reached the same age she was when her abuse began, Marilyn began to experience anxiety attacks and chest pains. Seeing her young daughter at that age triggered memories of her past abuse.[81]

This experience is common for many incest survivors. If this is true for you, trust in God's timing. He knows when and how to bring truth to the surface and healing to your wounded heart.

> *"'I will restore you to health*
> *and heal your wounds,' declares the LORD"*
> (JEREMIAH 30:17).

How to Deal with Denial

— Desire complete honesty with yourself and with others.

— Decide to believe the truth: You were not responsible for the abuse.

— Through journaling each day, face the personal damage to your heart.

— Deal with any unresolved anger.

— Allow yourself to grieve over your loss of innocence.

> *"Teach me your way, O LORD,*
> *and I will walk in your truth"*
> (PSALM 86:11).

How to Have a Pure Heart

— Acknowledge your desire to change.

— Admit your excessive desire to be in control and your strategies for self-protection.

— Recognize that living in fear and shame means that you are not fully trusting God.

— Experience genuine sorrow over any known sin in your life.

— See your need for the Savior and rely on Him alone.

"I acknowledged my sin to you and did not cover up my iniquity.
I said, 'I will confess my transgressions to the LORD'—
and you forgave the guilt of my sin"
(PSALM 32:5).

How to Grow in Your Love for Others

— Desire to grow in the character of Christ.

— Rely on Christ within you to do what you cannot do.

— Choose to forgive your offender. (See "How Can I Forgive?" on page 272.)

— Reach out to others—especially to those who are victims.

— Walk each day in prayer and Bible study.

— Choose to trust God with your future.

"There is no fear in love.
But perfect love drives out fear,
because fear has to do with punishment.
The one who fears is not made perfect in love"
(1 JOHN 4:18).

"We love because he first loved us"
(1 JOHN 4:19).

Marilyn would tell you that her one-year reign as Miss America in 1958 pales in comparison to the greatest accomplishment of her life—surviving 13 years of incest! But Marilyn didn't just survive. She overcame.

Likewise, many other victims now live victoriously. No longer insecure, they know their source of security. They no longer feel helpless, and their hearts are filled with hope.

"You will be secure, because there is hope;
you will look about you and take your rest in safety"
(JOB 11:18).

> In child abuse, the "secret"—knowing the child won't
> tell—is the perpetrator's most powerful weapon. God's strategy
> is to surface the secret…for the *truth* is what sets us *free*.

Childhood Sexual Abuse—Answers in God's Word

QUESTION: "Does having a new life in Christ have any effect on my old life and the abusive things that happened to me as a child?"

ANSWER: "If anyone is in Christ, he is a new creation; the old has gone, the new has come!" (2 Corinthians 5:17).

QUESTION: "Can I trust anyone to truly love me after being forsaken by my own father and mother?"

ANSWER: "Though my father and mother forsake me, the LORD will receive me" (Psalm 27:10).

QUESTION: "Is there someone whose faithfulness will provide love and compassion to keep me from being consumed by my painful past?"

ANSWER: "Because of the LORD's great love we are not consumed, for his compassions never fail. They are new every morning; great is your faithfulness" (Lamentations 3:22-23).

QUESTION: "How can I overcome my past, which has been like a desert wasteland?"

ANSWER: "Forget the former things; do not dwell on the past. See, I am doing a new thing! Now it springs up; do you not perceive it? I am making a way in the desert and streams in the wasteland" (Isaiah 43:18-19).

QUESTION: "Is it possible to put behind me the thoughts and ways I had as a child and am still experiencing even now as an adult?"

ANSWER: "When I was a child, I talked like a child, I thought like a child, I reasoned like a child. When I became [an adult], I put childish ways behind me" (1 Corinthians 13:11).

QUESTION: "How can I justify being kind, compassionate, and forgiving toward those who have grievously sinned against me?"

ANSWER: "Be kind and compassionate to one another, forgiving each other, just as in Christ God forgave you" (Ephesians 4:32).

QUESTION: "If I forgive my perpetrators without taking revenge, who will avenge me and repay them in order to deliver justice on my behalf?"

ANSWER: "Do not take revenge, my friends, but leave room for God's wrath, for it is written: 'It is mine to avenge; I will repay,' says the Lord" (Romans 12:19).

QUESTION: "How can I have hope and look forward to future plans when my past was so filled with harm?"

ANSWER: "'I know the plans I have for you,' declares the LORD, 'plans to prosper you and not to harm you, plans to give you hope and a future'" (Jeremiah 29:11).

QUESTION: "My spirit was crushed as a child; now I feel brokenhearted. Where is the Lord in this?"

ANSWER: "The LORD is close to the brokenhearted and saves those who are crushed in spirit" (Psalm 34:18).

QUESTION: "Who can help bring healing to my hurting heart?"

ANSWER: "O LORD my God, I called to you for help and you healed me" (Psalm 30:2).

SPIRITUAL ABUSE
Religion at Its Worst 79

SPIRITUAL ABUSE
Religion at Its Worst

Think about it. Who in our society offends us the most? Isn't it the robbers, the killers, the rapists, the flagrant *lawbreakers*?

Now think about Jesus. Who in His society offended Him the most? Wasn't it the Pharisees, the religious leaders of the day... the legalistic *law keepers*? Didn't they upset Him the most?

But why the Pharisees? After all, they went to the temple, paid tithes, read the Word, kept the law, prayed the prayers. So, why the prominent law keepers?

The answer is clear. Although they were representatives of the house of God, they did not represent the heart of God. Christ called them hypocrites. And He made it plain: They would be rewarded here on earth, but not in heaven.

Jesus said,

> *"When you pray, do not be like the hypocrites,*
> *for they love to pray standing in the synagogues*
> *and on the street corners to be seen by men.*
> *I tell you the truth,*
> *they have received their reward in full"*
> (MATTHEW 6:5).

I. DEFINITIONS OF SPIRITUAL ABUSE

The Pharisees couldn't believe their eyes when they saw the disciples' hands. The dirty, unwashed hands were such a contrast to their own pristine palms. These religious leaders strove to be the picture of perfection externally. They criticized the followers of Jesus, who lifted their food to their mouths with "unclean" hands—ceremoniously defiled hands that had not been washed according to their customs. The Pharisees said, in essence, "Beware…your unclean hands soil any hope of righteousness." But Jesus corrected them and said it was the Pharisees' *unclean hearts* that stained their so-called righteousness:

> *"What goes into a man's mouth does not make him 'unclean,'*
> *but what comes out of his mouth, that is what makes him 'unclean'"*
> (Matthew 15:11).

A. What Is Spiritual Abuse?

The practice of spiritual abuse has persisted ever since the serpent distorted and outright lied about God's words to Adam and Eve in the Garden of Eden. In doing so, the serpent managed to create doubt in their minds regarding the character of God and His relationship to those He had created. The result, of course, was that Adam and Eve found the thought of becoming like God more appealing than the thought of remaining dependent upon God. That led them to trust Satan's words rather than God's, and their descendants have struggled with this same problem ever since.[1] The serpent said to Eve,

> *"Did God really say,*
> *'You must not eat from any tree in the garden?'…*
> *'You will not surely die…*
> *For God knows that when you eat of it your eyes will be opened,*
> *and you will be like God, knowing good and evil'"*
> (Genesis 3:1,4-5).

The serpent contradicted God's word and seduced the first couple into taking the fatal bite.

Though the practice is age-old, the term *spiritual abuse* is relatively new. The following definitions explain how spiritual leaders can misuse their position:

- **Spiritual abuse** is the *mistreatment* of a person by *someone in a position of spiritual authority* and results in diminishing that person's spiritual vitality and growth.[2]
- **Spiritual abuse** is the use of *religious words or acts to manipulate someone* for personal gain or to achieve a personal agenda, thereby harming that person's walk with God.

- **Spiritual abuse** is often broadly defined as *any misuse of Scripture whereby truth is twisted* and which may or may not result in harming a person's relationship with God. The victim in this case may not be an individual, but *truth itself.* In his second letter to the Corinthians, Paul said, "We do not use deception, nor do we distort the word of God. On the contrary, by setting forth the truth plainly we commend ourselves to every man's conscience in the sight of God" (2 Corinthians 4:2).

- **Spiritual abuse** is *putting confidence in your position of authority* and your *perceived right to use those under your influence* to accomplish your personal agenda. However, God alone has the right, wisdom, and power to accomplish His plans and purposes for those He has created.

> *"To the elders among you,*
> *I appeal as a fellow elder, a witness of Christ's sufferings*
> *and one who also will share in the glory to be revealed:*
> *Be shepherds of God's flock that is under your care,*
> *serving as overseers...not because you must, but because you are willing,*
> *as God wants you to be; not greedy for money,*
> *but eager to serve; not lording it over those entrusted to you,*
> *but being examples to the flock"*
> (1 PETER 5:1-3).

The Heart of Spiritual Abuse

QUESTION: "What is at the heart of spiritual abuse?"

ANSWER: At the core of spiritual abuse is excessive control of others. Spiritual abuse is acting "spiritual" to benefit oneself by using self-centered efforts to control others.

> A—**Acting** spiritual to
> B—**Benefit** oneself by
> U—**Using**
> S—**Self-centered**
> E—**Efforts** to control others

Examples:

- The pastor who uses guilt or greed to compel attendance, financial giving, or service
- The spiritual leader who takes emotional or sexual advantage of a counselee in the name of comfort or compassion
- The religious people who accuse those who disagree with them of being rebellious against God
- The parent, spouse, or ministry head who demands absolute, unquestioned obedience from family members or ministry staff—no matter what, whether reasonable or not, whether biblical or not

"Jesus said to them,
'The kings of the Gentiles lord it over them;
and those who exercise authority over them call themselves Benefactors'"
(LUKE 22:25).

Spiritual Abuse Is Not...

ADMINISTERING CHURCH DISCIPLINE

God commanded the church to administer church discipline for the purpose of correcting and restoring sinning Christians to fellowship with the Lord and with the church. Because the focus of church discipline is not on punishment, it must be administered prayerfully and in love. Another purpose of church discipline is to help maintain the church's purity in belief and practice.

Example: The apostle Paul instructed the believers in the church at Corinth to discipline a sexually immoral man by removing him from their midst. "Your boasting is not good. Don't you know that a little yeast [sin] works through the whole batch of dough [church]? Get rid of the old yeast that you may be a new batch without yeast...as you really are. For Christ, our Passover lamb, has been sacrificed" (1 Corinthians 5:6-7).

REJECTING A PERSON'S INCORRECT THEOLOGICAL BELIEFS

The church must evaluate those who teach the Bible to other church members. The church, as the "pillar and foundation of the truth," must reject incorrect interpretations and false teaching, just as Christ rejected the self-made righteousness and erroneous teachings of the Pharisees.

Example: The apostle Paul does not hesitate to identify those who would subvert the message of truth as being like those who opposed truth in the past. "Just as Jannes and Jambres opposed Moses, so also these men oppose the truth—men of depraved minds, who, as far as the faith is concerned, are rejected" (2 Timothy 3:8).

B. What Is Legalism?

"Do this…Don't do that…Do this…Don't do that."

What was the purpose of the Old Testament law—especially since we are not bound by it today? Simply stated, the hundreds upon hundreds of rules and regulations making up the law reveal a supreme standard of holiness—a standard no human being can keep. The law was never intended to leave God's people discouraged and in despair, but to first show them that they were sinners and then to lead them to a Savior who would not only pay the penalty for their sins and forgive their sins, but give them power over sin and give them eternal life.

In other words, no one can keep the law perfectly, so no one can ever be saved by the law. The requirement of the law (perfection) shows that we all need God's mercy and grace, which is found in Jesus alone. However, between the time God gave the law and the time Jesus came, the religious leaders so distorted and mishandled the law that it came to be viewed as the way to become righteous before God, making it a type of savior in and of itself.

According to this "distorted" law, the outward practice of do's and don'ts defined people as righteous—and woefully neglected the issues of the heart. Then, when the true Savior came, the religious leaders failed to recognize Him and condemned those who did. Jesus adamantly opposed the religious legalism of His day and the spiritual abuse His people suffered at the hands of those who had been entrusted with the law. The apostle Paul said,

"Since they did not know the righteousness that comes from God
and sought to establish their own,
they did not submit to God's righteousness.
Christ is the end of the law
so that there may be righteousness for everyone who believes…

> *Clearly no one is justified before God by the law, because,*
> *'The righteous will live by faith'"*
> (ROMANS 10:3-4; GALATIANS 3:11).

Whereas the general motive behind most spiritual abuse is power, the primary tool by which this power is gained is legalism.[3]

What Legalism Is

The following statements provide a comprehensive definition of legalism:

- **Legalism** is a system of *living by the law* in order to make spiritual progress and earn God's blessing. The word *legalism* comes from the Latin word *legalis*, which means "law."[4]
- **Legalism** is strict adherence to a code of do's and don'ts as a means of earning the approval of God.[5]
- **Legalism** is a misuse of the law, resulting in a *wrong* way of trying to appear *right*.
- **Legalism** is any attempt to gain or maintain God's favor by human effort.

Unfortunately, the people of Israel were guilty of practicing legalism:

> *"Israel, who pursued a law of righteousness,*
> *has not attained it. Why not?*
> *Because they pursued it not by faith*
> *but as if it were by works"*
> (ROMANS 9:31-32).

========= Heart of Legalism =========

QUESTION: "What is at the heart of legalism?"

ANSWER: At the core of legalism is a works mentality that looks to your own efforts to gain the acceptance of the Lord.

L—**Looking** to your own

E—**Efforts** to

G—**Gain** the

A—Acceptance of the

L—Lord

Examples:

- The congregation that judges another congregation because of their manner of dress, style of worship, or the Bible translation they use
- The spiritual leader who looks down on some in the congregation, perceiving them to be spiritually immature and inferior
- The religious people who put confidence in "the flesh," which means living out of their own resources and their perceived achievement of a self-imposed standard of righteousness that causes them to despise others and to develop a prideful spirit

However, God alone knows the heart of a person. Only He can judge motives. The Bible says,

> *"All a man's ways seem innocent to him,*
> *but motives are weighed by the LORD"*
> (PROVERBS 16:2).

What Legalism Is Not

ESTABLISHING RULES AND REGULATIONS

Every organization, including churches, schools, businesses, and even homes, has rules and regulations. These are necessary for the organization to function properly.

Example: The apostle Paul instructed the church in Corinth about how the people should conduct their religious meetings: "Two or three prophets should speak, and the others should weigh carefully what is said. And if a revelation comes to someone who is sitting down, the first speaker should stop. For you can all prophesy in turn so that everyone may be instructed and encouraged. The spirits of prophets are subject to the control of prophets. For God is not a God of disorder but of peace" (1 Corinthians 14:29-33).

SUBMITTING TO AUTHORITY

God established authority figures in the church, home, and government for our good. These individuals are to meet the needs of those under their authority and provide them with leadership, guidance, protection, and accountability.

Example: The writer of the book of Hebrews explained the function of authority and how Christians are to relate to their leaders: "Obey your leaders and submit to their authority. They keep watch over you as men who must give an account. Obey them so that their work will be a joy, not a burden, for that would be of no advantage to you" (Hebrews 13:17).

HAVING PERSONAL STANDARDS FOR CHRISTIAN LIVING

Within the boundaries of biblical absolutes, God gives us the responsibility to choose how we will live our Christian lives. The choices we make throughout the day as to how we will present ourselves to others and how we will conduct ourselves around others reflect our standards. *Making choices* to live by biblical standards is not legalism, even if the choices we make are more conservative or restrictive than the choices of others.

Example: Through Joshua, God gave the Israelites the choice as to whether they would serve Him or not: "Choose for yourselves this day whom you will serve…But as for me and my household, we will serve the LORD" (Joshua 24:15).

The Unfortunate Fame of Eufame MacLayne

Unbelievable…inconceivable…absolutely unthinkable! When I first heard this story, I had to ask, "How could this possibly happen?"

The horrific incident took place in 1591 after Scottish noblewoman Eufame MacLayne, a lady of rank and refinement, became pregnant with twins. Her concerned midwife provided an herb to ease the painful delivery of the twins. But when church leaders learned she had taken the herb, they believed she had violated the law of God, showing deliberate contempt for the truth of Scripture. Thus, Eufame was condemned to die.

The church leaders reasoned that after Adam and Eve had sinned, God issued judgments, and specifically to the woman He pronounced, "I will greatly increase your pains in childbearing" (Genesis 3:16). Because Eufame had sought relief from agonizing labor pains, the church leaders deemed her act as sin and declared that what she had done was worthy of death. (Yet nowhere in Scripture are women forbidden to take herbs or medicine during childbirth.)

When the official crown bailiff arrived at Eufame's home, she clung tightly to her twins…but they were pulled from her. Eufame was forcibly dragged to Castle Hill in Edinburgh, where she was to be burned at the stake. Chains were wrapped around her kneeling body, and in less than an hour ashes were "all that remained of Eufame MacLayne."[6]

Her murder was a tragic case of woefully misguided spiritual leaders who failed to consider the whole counsel of God and therefore committed spiritual abuse. Rather than gleaning wisdom from the Bible as a whole, one isolated Scripture text became the foundation for a distorted and dangerous theology.

Sadly, for hundreds of years and in many countries this one Scripture passage—read in isolation—was used erroneously to verbally attack, severely punish, and kill countless people, including physicians seeking only to alleviate the pain of childbirth. In my research on this matter, I came across the following fascinating account.

As late as 1847, British physician Sir James Simpson—who discovered the anesthetic properties of chloroform—was denounced mercilessly for trying to circumvent God's Genesis chapter 3 judgment on women who suffer pain during childbirth. Interestingly, his greatest defense for using anesthesia was found in the preceding chapter—Genesis 2. He reminded his opponents about the written "record of the first surgical operation ever performed and that text proves that the Maker of the universe, before he took the rib from Adam's side for the creation of Eve, caused a deep sleep to fall upon him."[7]

Fortunately, Dr. Simpson was well-grounded in both theology and logic. Theologically, he knew the Genesis account of God's judgment extended not just to women, but to men as well—for survival, man's labor would require "painful toil" and "the sweat of your brow" (Genesis 3:17-19). He answered his critics' accusations of heresy with this irrefutable reasoning: Based on God's curse in Genesis 3, if a woman sinned each time she eased her labor pains by using medicine, "then a man sinned each time he eased his labor by using an ox, a plow, or even fertilizer to enrich the soil."[8] Thus he countered that any effort to eliminate the pain of labor for men was as much an avoidance of the Lord's curse as was alleviating the pain of labor for women through an anesthetic.

With this sound logical and biblical defense, Dr. Simpson finally silenced all the critics.

Christians and the Law

QUESTION: "Is there no law for Christians to live by?"[9]

ANSWER: The Bible says that under the New Covenant, God will put His law in the minds and the hearts of every Christian. In addition, everyone has an internal law that is not the law of Moses but rather the Lord's personal law for each of us. According to Romans 2:14-15, "When Gentiles, who do not have the law, do by nature things required by the law, they are a law for themselves, even though they do not have the law, since they show that the requirements of the law are written on their hearts, their consciences also bearing witness, and their thoughts now accusing, now even defending them."

Because Christ indwells every true believer, we who are Christians naturally have both His will and His supernatural power to do His will:

> *"'This is the covenant I will make with them*
> *after that time,' says the Lord.*
> *'I will put my laws in their hearts,*
> *and I will write them on their minds'"*
> (HEBREWS 10:16).

- **He prompts** you to desire and to do His will.

> *"It is God who works in you to will*
> *and to act according to his good purpose"*
> (PHILIPPIANS 2:13).

- **He provides** you with the power to do what He calls you to do.

> *"The one who calls you is faithful and he will do it"*
> (1 THESSALONIANS 5:24).

C. What Is the Difference Between Law and Grace?

They were at it again, trying to trip up the Teacher.

The religious leaders of the day rejected the teaching and ministry of Jesus and were doggedly determined to disgrace Him publicly by asking complicated, manipulative questions. He silenced them each and every time with perfect wisdom, but still they persisted.

Early one morning in the temple courts, during the quiet of dawn, Jesus sat down to teach. While He spoke, commotion broke out. The Pharisees brought a woman before Jesus and made her stand in front of the crowd in utter humiliation, claiming she was caught in the very act of adultery. It was an opportune moment, the Pharisees connived, to "catch" Jesus once and for all and curtail His ministry. They would do anything—and use anyone—to satiate their sinful quest.

And so they asked Him: "Teacher, this woman was caught in the act of adultery. In the Law Moses commanded us to stone such women. Now what do you say?" (John 8:4-5).

The difference between law and grace was about to be displayed. While the Pharisees kept firing away with questions, Jesus was silent. He bent down and wrote on the ground with His finger. Then He stood up and replied, "If any one of you is without sin, let him be the first to throw a stone at her" (John 8:7).

Wisdom spoke and silenced once again His adversaries. And one by one, the people left the temple courts. When Jesus and the accused woman were the only ones who remained, again grace was dispensed. Jesus told her He did not condemn her, and He exhorted her to repent and pursue righteousness. He said,

"Go now and leave your life of sin"
(John 8:11).

D. What Questions Concerning the Law Cause Confusion?

They were spiritual leaders devoid of the Spirit. They claimed to esteem the law of Moses, but they desecrated it daily by their pride and hypocrisy. The Pharisees, Israel's supposed spiritual shepherds, frustrated their flock by requiring them to follow man-made traditions they themselves didn't keep.

Jesus taught a new and different way to please God in the power of the Spirit, to engage the heart, mind, and will in obeying God's commands. But the Pharisees would have none of it. Their rejection—their rebellion against the very God they claimed to serve—prompted harsh rebuke from Jesus Himself.

> *"Woe to you, blind guides!...*
> *Woe to you, teachers of the law and Pharisees, you hypocrites!*
> *You clean the outside of the cup and dish,*
> *but inside they are full of greed and self-indulgence.*
> *Blind Pharisee! First clean the inside of the cup and dish,*
> *and then the outside also will be clean"*
> (Matthew 23:16,25-26).

Right or Wrong?

Question: "Is the law wrong?"

Answer: No. The law is the revelation of God's perfect standard of righteousness. The Bible says,

> *"The law is holy,*
> *and the commandment is holy,*
> *righteous and good"*
> (Romans 7:12).

Abolished Law?

Question: "According to Scripture, was the law abolished?"

Answer: No, Jesus didn't abolish the law. He fulfilled it. That means the standard still exists. The law reflects God's perfect standard of righteousness, a standard we cannot keep because we're sinners. That is why salvation is by grace alone.

> *"Do not think that I have come to abolish the Law or the Prophets;*
> *I have not come to abolish them but to fulfill them"*
> (Matthew 5:17).

The Law Fulfilled

Question: "What does 'Jesus fulfilled it' mean?"

ANSWER: The law was a covenant, an agreement, a contract. Just as a builder is under a contract to build a house, once the house is complete, the contract is fulfilled. The builder does not continue to work at building the house any longer. Likewise, Jesus fulfilled the requirements of the contract (the law) through His teaching and actions. He accomplished what we could never do by our own efforts. Then the Law Keeper became the sacrifice for us, the lawbreakers. The Bible says,

> *"Christ is the end of the law so that there may be*
> *righteousness for everyone who believes"*
> (ROMANS 10:4).

Legalism and Obedience

QUESTION: "What is the difference between legalism and biblical obedience?"

ANSWER: Legalism is conforming outwardly to God's or man's standard for righteous behavior while ignoring God's standard for righteous attitudes, convictions, values, and thoughts. Biblical obedience is conforming outwardly to God's righteous standard while being conformed inwardly to the character of Christ through the enabling grace of God.

- **In legalism,** the resource is self-effort and the motive is self-promotion. Legalism results in pride and approaching God on the basis of your performance.

- **In obedience,** the resource is the Spirit of God and the motive is to glorify God. Obedience results in humility and approaching God on the basis of Christ's performance.

In Christ Jesus, God has fulfilled His promise:

> *"I will give you a new heart and put a new spirit in you;*
> *I will remove from you your heart of stone*
> *and give you a heart of flesh. And I will put my Spirit in you*
> *and move you to follow my decrees and be careful to keep my laws"*
> (EZEKIEL 36:26-27).

II. Characteristics of Spiritual Abuse

They came from opposite sides of the tracks. One was refined, respected, and revered—after all, he was a Pharisee. He had an "in" with God. The other was despised, disdained, and dejected—after all, he was a tax collector. He was a spiritual "outcast."

Both the Pharisee and tax collector said a prayer to God. The Pharisee stood up and said, "God, I thank you that I am not like other men—robbers, evildoers, adulterers—or even like this tax collector. I fast twice a week and give a tenth of all I get" (Luke 18:11-12). So went the prayer of the Pharisee.

By contrast, the tax collector stood at a distance. He wouldn't even look up to heaven. He beat his chest and poured out his heart, "God, have mercy on me, a sinner" (verse 13).

Jesus spoke this parable to those who trust in their own righteousness, who exercise spiritual snobbery toward any who don't "measure up." He said it was the tax collector, and not the Pharisee, who "went home justified before God" (verse 14). The tax collector expressed a humble dependency upon God, which resulted in the forgiveness of his sins. Jesus then said,

> *"Everyone who exalts himself will be humbled,*
> *and he who humbles himself will be exalted"*
> (Luke 18:14).

A. What Characterizes Spiritually Abusive Leaders?

While some religious groups are free of abuse, others are occasionally abusive, and still others are intensely abusive. The people especially vulnerable to systemic spiritual abuse belong to groups where all the power is at the top and average members are subject to the dictates of those over them. Therefore, the structure of a religious organization is of paramount importance in identifying the probability that spiritual abuse occurs. The apostle Peter reflected the heart of humility vital for every spiritual leader when he said,

> *"To the elders among you,*
> *I appeal as a fellow elder, a witness of Christ's sufferings*
> *and one who also will share in the glory to be revealed:*
> *Be shepherds of God's flock that is under your care, serving as overseers—not*
> *because you must, but because you are willing, as God wants you to be;*

not greedy for money, but eager to serve;
not lording it over those entrusted to you,
but being examples to the flock"
(1 PETER 5:1-3).

The Traits of Spiritually Abusive Leaders

Spiritually abusive leaders are…

AUTHORITARIAN[10]

— Implying that God communicates with His people only through a hierarchy of power

— Claiming to have been called and established by God Himself

— Boasting that the leaders speak for God and expecting followers to support and obey them without question

But the Bible says, "Whoever exalts himself will be humbled, and whoever humbles himself will be exalted" (Matthew 23:12).

IMAGE-CONSCIOUS[11]

— Seeking to present an image of perfect righteousness

— Misrepresenting their personal history to wrongly portray a special relationship to God

— Minimizing or covering up their mistakes and character flaws

But the Bible says, "Woe to you, teachers of the law and Pharisees, you hypocrites! You are like whitewashed tombs, which look beautiful on the outside but on the inside are full of dead men's bones and everything unclean" (Matthew 23:27).

SUPPRESSIVE OF CRITICISM

— Determining all issues at the top level of the organization and demanding compliance by the members

— Curtailing individual thinking by saying such individuality leads to division and doubts about God

— Maintaining that those who question or seek to correct

anything about the organization are actually challenging God's authority

But the Bible says, "A rebuke impresses a man of discernment more than a hundred lashes a fool...Whoever loves discipline loves knowledge, but he who hates correction is stupid" (Proverbs 17:10; 12:1).

PERFECTIONISTIC[12]

— Demanding flawless obedience

— Condemning failure of any type or magnitude

— Promoting pride, elitism, and arrogance

But the Bible says, "Pride goes before destruction, a haughty spirit before a fall" (Proverbs 16:18).

UNBALANCED

— Flaunting their distinctiveness to validate their claim that they have a "special" relationship with God

— Carrying biblical law to the extreme

— Majoring on the minor issues

But the Bible says, "Woe to you Pharisees, because you give God a tenth of your mint, rue and all other kinds of garden herbs, but you neglect justice and the love of God. You should have practiced the latter without leaving the former undone" (Luke 11:42).

COERCIVE[13]

— Using any tactic available to get followers to disregard their own logic and do what the leader demands

— Demanding submission by claiming that the messages they receive come directly from God

— Deluding members by presenting themselves as the only ones who can properly interpret God's Word to the people

But the Bible says, "They want to be teachers of the law, but they do not know what they are talking about or what they so confidently affirm" (1 Timothy 1:7).

INTIMIDATING[14]

— Threatening members routinely with punishment or excommunication in order to gain compliance

— Holding the possibility of eternal condemnation over the heads of followers in order to force submission

— Predicting financial ruin or physical calamity for disobedient members in order to assure obedience

But the Bible says, "Woe to the shepherds...who only take care of themselves! Should not shepherds take care of the flock? You eat the curds, clothe yourselves with the wool and slaughter the choice animals, but you do not take care of the flock" (Ezekiel 34:2-3).

TERRORIZING[15]

— Imparting fear, shame, self-doubt, identity confusion, and guilt to members

— Blaming problems within the organization on the sinfulness of the congregation

— Overemphasizing the problems of followers and presenting strict obedience as the only solution

But the Bible says, "You have not strengthened the weak or healed the sick or bound up the injured. You have not brought back the strays or searched for the lost. You have ruled them harshly and brutally" (Ezekiel 34:4).

CONDEMNING[16]

— Heaping condemnation on outsiders and anyone who leaves the congregation

— Teaching that followers will join the ranks of the condemned if they deviate from the teachings of the leaders

— Blaming individual members for failures within the organization

But the Bible says, "How can you say to your brother, 'Let me take the speck out of your eye,' when all the time there is a plank in your own eye?" (Matthew 7:4).

Discriminating[17]

— Promoting church hierarchy

— Responding to people according to their titles and roles

— Instructing average members that their needs are less important than the needs of the leaders

But the Bible says, "Beware of the teachers of the law. They like to walk around in flowing robes and love to be greeted in the marketplaces and have the most important seats in the synagogues and the places of honor at banquets" (Luke 20:46).

Legalistic[18]

— Communicating that approval and acceptance are based on performance and position within the organization

— Burdening the people with excessive demands supposedly given by God directly to the leaders

— Expecting members to make extreme sacrifices of money, time, and energy for the sake of the organization

But the Bible says, "Woe to those who make unjust laws, to those who issue oppressive decrees" (Isaiah 10:1).

Isolating[19]

— Defining relationships outside the congregation as negative and destructive

— Presenting the outside world as a place of egregious sin and temptation without any redeeming qualities

— Encouraging members to minimize or discontinue contact with family, friends, and the outside world

But the Bible says, "If anyone does not provide for his relatives, and especially for his immediate family, he has denied the faith and is worse than an unbeliever" (1 Timothy 5:8).

The Legalism of Spiritually Abusive Leaders

Legalism is basically an attitude in which God is seen as quick to judge. He is viewed as a stern taskmaster and a judgmental judge and arbiter of punishment. With regard to legalism, the attitude toward oneself is a misplaced confidence that leads to frustration, failure, and self-condemnation. And the attitude toward others is prideful exclusivity that produces frustration, fear, and resentment in others.

In Philippians 3:6, the apostle Paul spoke of his former "legalistic righteousness" as "faultless" when he persecuted the early church and caused fear in believers.

> *"Saul began to destroy the church. Going from house to house,*
> *he dragged off men and women and put them in prison"*
> (ACTS 8:3).

As with all types of abuse, certain circumstances are more conducive than others for a spiritual wolf to take advantage of unsuspecting sheep. If you suspect spiritual abuse might be occurring, check to see whether the following traits apply to the specific spiritual leader in mind:

- *Authoritarian:* demanding unquestioned obedience
- *Controlling:* invading aspects of life better left to the individual
- *Performance driven:* emphasizing external rather than internal qualities
- *Hypocritical:* employing a veneer of spirituality to cover carnal motives
- *Rigid:* devising elaborate, extrabiblical guidelines for members to follow
- *Deceitful:* twisting the truth of the Word to fit certain opinions and desires

Remember these words from the book of wisdom:

> *"A simple man believes anything,*
> *but a prudent man gives thought to his steps"*
> (PROVERBS 14:15).

The Hated "Heretic": The John Huss Story

I've tried to imagine what it must have been like: A solitary stake in the ground...his hands tightly bound...his neck closely chained to the stake...a mixture of wood and hay stacked around him. When the religious leader signaled to light the fire, the kindling burst into flames.

So went another alleged heretic—destroyed, discarded, dead. And what was his horrible heresy, the high crime worthy of death?

Czech reformer John Huss preached against the moral depravity running rampant through the church hierarchy. He also exposed the corrupt relationship between the church leaders and political rulers, who cooperated to sell indulgences (which the church claimed could forgive sins) in order to amass wealth and finance crusades. Huss dared to challenge the church edict that called for executing anyone caught with a non-Latin Bible. He recognized Jesus Christ as his ultimate spiritual authority, not the pope.

Unscrupulous bishops used Romans 6:6 to persecute Huss—"that the body of sin might be done away with." However, the point of this scripture was to promote not physical death, but rather the fact that as true Christians, we are dead to sin's power—we don't have to sin because we have a new life in Christ. Unfortunately, spiritual abusers are experts at twisting Scripture.

Huss suffered severe spiritual abuse through harsh imprisonment, malicious slander, and cruel intimidation as numerous attempts were made to force him to recant his "heretical" doctrines. His tormentors used many ugly illustrations to paint a portrait of Huss as a heretic: "a rotten piece of flesh, the little spark, which unless checked turns to a great flame and burns up the house, the creeping cancer, the scabby member of the flock."[20]

Before tying Huss to the stake, church bishops committed his soul to the devil and placed on his head a paper cap that stretched 18 inches high and portrayed three devils mutilating his soul with pitchforks. A single Latin word was etched on the humiliating headdress—a word that translates to *Heretic*.[21]

Finally on July 6, 1415, as John Huss was being anchored to his execution station, wood and hay were piled all around him up to his chin. Even so, he was determined to make a final proclamation:

"In the same truth of the gospel which I have written, taught and preached...I am ready to die today."[22] As the flames leaped upward and danced about his face, Huss began to sing a hymn.

The news of what had happened at the stake that fateful day spread like wildfire across Europe and further confirmed Huss' place in history as a forerunner of the Protestant Reformation. Huss' spiritual abusers could not stamp out the religious reforms that had already begun to blaze a trail toward new spiritual leadership and direction.

These religious leaders kept trying to set a devious trap for John Huss much like the Pharisees of Jesus' day—the supposed good shepherds of God's people who instead manipulated God's Word to protect and promote their man-made traditions. Jesus' stinging rebuke to the Pharisees in Matthew 15:6-9 is an indictment that describes perfectly the many religious leaders down through the centuries who have spiritually abused their flocks: "You nullify the word of God for the sake of your tradition. You hypocrites! Isaiah was right when he prophesied about you: 'These people honor me with their lips, but their hearts are far from me. They worship me in vain; their teachings are but rules taught by men.'"

B. What Characterizes Spiritually Abusive Groups?

Separating from a spiritually abusive group can be grueling because the members often use fear and shame to keep one another from leaving. Regardless of the difficulty, if you are in such a group, the Bible says you must leave. Your spiritual life depends on it!

"If anyone teaches otherwise and does not consent to wholesome words,
even the words of our Lord Jesus Christ,
and to the doctrine which accords with godliness, he is proud,
knowing nothing, but is obsessed with disputes and arguments over words,
from which come envy, strife, reviling, evil suspicions...
From such withdraw yourself"
(1 TIMOTHY 6:3-5 NKJV).

Ask yourself the following questions to determine whether a group is abusive and/or spiritually deceptive:

____ Do they exalt someone as an *irrefutable authority* in the group?

____ Do they discourage my *questions*?

____ Do they demand my *absolute allegiance*?

____ Do they have a long list of *rules* related to dress, hairstyle, or activities?

____ Do they *judge* those who do not keep their list of rules?

____ Do they consider themselves the *only true church*?

____ Do they insist on making my major *life decisions* for me?

____ Do they consider *those who leave* their group apostates, backsliders, or doomed?

____ Do they *shame* people publicly?

For every abuse that your church has committed, repeat the following out loud:

"It was inappropriate for my church to (_name abuse_). I renounce this practice/position and announce my allegiance to God and to His Word."

Pray the following prayer of King David every day to reaffirm your reliance on God to guard and protect you:

> *"You are my rock and my fortress,*
> *for the sake of your name lead and guide me.*
> *Free me from the trap that is set for me,*
> *for you are my refuge"*
> (PSALM 31:3-4).

C. What Are the Symptoms of Spiritual Abuse?

Diseases have accompanying symptoms such as fever and specific aches and pains. The symptoms are not the problem, but rather are the result of the real problem, which is the disease itself. Likewise, legalism produces symptoms that some people mistake for the real problem.

Ultimately, legalistic abusers burden their victims with responsibilities and keep them so busy that they have difficulty processing any liberating truth. They become stricken with a disabling apathy toward gaining deeper knowledge and are intellectually put to sleep as they are constantly told what to believe. Because they cannot adequately think for themselves, they become depersonalized, unable to function as God intended. For these reasons, Jesus sternly addressed the legalistic abusers of His day:

> *"You experts in the law, woe to you,*
> *because you load people down with burdens they can hardly carry,*
> *and you yourselves will not lift one finger to help them…*
> *Woe to you experts in the law, because you have taken away the key to knowledge.*
> *You yourselves have not entered, and you have hindered those who were entering"*
> (LUKE 11:46,52).

As you read the following symptoms, check to see whether you are a victim of a legalistic abuser.[23]

Low Self-worth
— Do you think you must accept abuse?
— Do you think you must accept blame?
— Do you think you must accept condemnation?

Inordinate Fear
— Do you fear disapproval or condemnation?
— Do you fear authority figures?
— Do you fear conflict?

Excessive Guilt
— Do you feel like a failure?
— Do you feel a sense of shame?
— Do you feel a heaviness of heart?

Unresolved Anger
— Do you feel frustrated over not being perfect?
— Do you feel angry for not keeping all the rules?
— Do you feel you are losing patience with yourself and others?

Limited Transparency
— Do you think you must put up a false front to hide the real you?

— Do you think if others really knew you, they would reject you?

— Do you think closeness with others is to be avoided?

Troubled Relationships

— Do you have difficulty saying *no*?

— Do you feel you are not forgiven?

— Do you continually compare yourself with others and keep them at a distance?

High Self-sufficiency

— Do you try to earn love by performing well?

— Do you try to do everything perfectly so as not to be rejected?

— Do you try to stay in control so you can feel a sense of significance?

Misplaced Priorities

— Do you prioritize the externals, such as complying with rules and regulations?

— Do you have difficulty setting boundaries?

— Do you place more importance on outward actions than on inward needs?

It is imperative that you remember…

> *"The LORD said to Samuel,*
> *'Do not consider his appearance or his height,*
> *for I have rejected him.*
> *The LORD does not look at the things man looks at.*
> *Man looks at the outward appearance,*
> *but the LORD looks at the heart'"*
> (1 SAMUEL 16:7).

III. CAUSES OF SPIRITUAL ABUSE

What are the beliefs behind legalism? Trying to maintain God's acceptance is a full-time job for legalists. Thinking of God as their judge is more real an image in their minds than seeing God as a father who grants blessings to His children. But God's Word tells us that we are accepted by God through our acceptance of Christ, not through our human efforts. Christians will not experience God's judgment, for Christ experienced judgment on their behalf at Calvary. The Bible says,

> *"Christ was sacrificed once to take away the sins of many people;*
> *and he will appear a second time, not to bear sin,*
> *but to bring salvation to those who are waiting for him"*
> (Hebrews 9:28).

A. Why Do People Become Trapped in Legalism?

For many reasons people are susceptible to and then become snared by legalistic or spiritually abusive people. Some of those reasons include...

They Have Legalistic Parents

THE INFLUENCE

- *Legalism in the home* either trains children to perform well in order to please or drives children to rebel against the rigidity and hypocrisy found in legalists.
- *Children with legalistic authority figures* tend to view God as harsh, demanding, unmerciful, and unforgiving—a perception that breeds fear-driven compliance.

THE RESULTS

- *Legalism does not create* a climate of love for God based on His love for us. Nor does it encourage a heart inclined to please Him by living according to His Word.
- *Children thrive on being raised in a Christian home* by loving, godly parents—parents who accurately reflect God as a compassionate father who comforts us in our difficulties, disciplines us in love, and mercifully meets our needs.

The Bible says, "Praise be to the God and Father of our Lord Jesus Christ, the Father of compassion and the God of all comfort, who comforts us in all our troubles…Every good and perfect gift is from above, coming down from the Father of the heavenly lights, who does not change like shifting shadows" (2 Corinthians 1:3-4; James 1:17).

They Feel Insignificant and Unacceptable to God

THE INFLUENCE

- *Legalism provides an "exact ruler"* based on the extremely high standards of the legalistic leaders—an objective way to measure where you stand with God and where you fail to measure up.
- *Legalism provides discipline.* Perfectionists become model disciples in a legalistic environment where acceptance is based solely on performance.

THE RESULTS

- *Legalism tends to increase guilt* rather than relieve it. Further, it fails to provide assurance of salvation.
- *Rather than demonstrating humility* before God, legalists become either prideful or so discouraged they give up on God altogether.

The Bible says, "God opposes the proud but gives grace to the humble" (1 Peter 5:5).

They Are Pressured by Others

THE INFLUENCE

- *Legalists feel entitled.* They present themselves as having spiritual authority and therefore entitled to receive immediate agreement and unquestioned compliance.
- *Legalistic peers condemn those who disagree* and accept those who agree with them, creating immense pressure for conformity.

THE RESULTS

- *Legalism cannot make all people think,* feel, reason, or believe the same way, nor can it provide God's rest, which comes from knowing that He loves and accepts us all just as we are.

- *Christians need to share their spiritual struggles* so that they can pray for one another and grow in God's grace together. Doing so will help create deep bonds of Christian love and intimate relationships.

The Bible says, "Confess your sins to each other and pray for each other so that you may be healed. The prayer of a righteous man is powerful and effective" (James 5:16).

They Belong to a Legalistic Church That Lacks Grace

THE INFLUENCE

- *Legalism emphasizes "doing"*—witnessing, discipling, teaching, attending all required activities, and whatever else is expected.
- *Legalistic activity flows out of a need to perform* for God in the hopes of meeting His requirements for righteousness and to gain His approval.

THE RESULTS

- *Legalism cannot give people the spiritual security* that comes only from being assured of God's forgiveness and unconditional love and acceptance.
- *Legalism produces actions done with wrong motives.* Genuine Christian activity flows out of love for God and the grace of God.

The Bible says, "God is able to make all grace abound to you, so that in all things at all times, having all that you need, you will abound in every good work" (2 Corinthians 9:8).

B. Why Are the Abused Drawn to Spiritual Abusers?

Victims of spiritual abuse typically feel that they need to work to please God or they need to be punished by God for displeasing Him. The guilt they feel can be based on *true* guilt for their actual, unconfessed sin. More often, however, they have *false* guilt over actual sin that has already been forgiven... or false guilt for imagined sin. This type of person has usually experienced a series of abusive relationships, often beginning with excessively rigid parents or authority figures.

The crowds who followed Jesus had been brought up believing that their righteous works would save them. "They asked him, 'What must we do to do the works God requires?' Jesus answered, 'The work of God is this: to believe in the one he has sent'" (John 6:28-29).

People in spiritually abusive churches often...

- **Grow up being abused or manipulated** by someone they loved
  - Unjustly and severely disciplined for minor or imagined infractions
  - Coerced into complying with wishes of parents

- **Are neglected** by or inappropriately controlled by one or both parents
  - Ignored or made to feel insignificant
  - Held responsible for meeting the emotional needs of parents

- **Are systematically shamed** or put down
  - Humiliated in front of others or made to feel like a bad person
  - Called degrading names or constantly criticized

- **Come from demanding homes**
  - Unable to please parents
  - Expected always to excel and never to make mistakes

- **View God as a tyrant** who imposes impossible standards
  - Perceive God to be a watchdog who is eager to punish every bad thought or action, no matter how small or insignificant
  - Feel that God has unrealistic expectations and that He is impossible to please

- **Obsess about blame and guilt**
  - Constantly focus on personal faults and failures
  - Live with persistent feelings of self-reproach and regret

- **Cannot accept grace and forgiveness**
  - Persuaded that personal accountability and payment for sin cannot be transferred to another
  - Driven by a strong need to suffer personally and pay for wrongdoings

- **Have low sense of self-worth**
  - Convinced that they have little or no value
  - Feel inferior to others and undeserving

Those who are enslaved to a mind-set that keeps them captive in a cycle of abuse need to heed the words of the apostle Paul:

> *"See to it that no one takes you captive*
> *through hollow and deceptive philosophy,*
> *which depends on human tradition and the basic principles*
> *of this world rather than on Christ"*
> (COLOSSIANS 2:8).

C. What Wrong Thinking Has Kept You in Bondage?

Identifying the Wrong Thought Patterns

If you have found yourself in a spiritually abusive relationship, you can be sure that certain situations made you susceptible to it and kept you in it. Discovering what those situations are will prove helpful as you seek to walk in freedom.

In order to identify the thought patterns that led you into the abusive relationship, you need to evaluate your wrong thinking. Then you can change your thoughts, which will change your choices, which will change your actions, which will change your life![24] As was the case for Job, what you think about will determine how you feel, and that, in turn, will direct your decision making.

> *"When I think about this, I am terrified;*
> *trembling seizes my body"*
> (JOB 21:6).

Asking the Right Questions

Put a check mark next to the questions that apply to you:

__ Do I think I should not hold spiritual authorities accountable for their actions?

__ Do I think it is wrong for me to ask questions in church?

__ Do I think I am too sinful or unspiritual to read the Bible for myself?

__ Do I think I must obey a list of unwritten rules?

__ Do I think it is okay for me to be judgmental?

__ Do I think God wants to burden me with excessive guilt?

__ Do I think I should be shamed because of my sin?

__ Do I think I cannot or should not make decisions for myself?

__ Do I think I deserve to feel guilty for leaving the church?

__ Do I think I should go back to the abusive church?

__ Do I think I am too sinful for God to ever forgive me?

__ Do I think I am unworthy of God's love even though Jesus died for me?

The apostle Paul gave this warning:

> *"Watch out for those who cause divisions*
> *and put obstacles in your way that are contrary*
> *to the teaching you have learned.*
> *Keep away from them"*
> (ROMANS 16:17).

D. Why Does God Allow Spiritual Abuse?

This question, phrased in different ways, is asked in every country and every culture: How can a loving, all-powerful God permit abuse? But even further, why would He permit *spiritual abuse*?

• When God created Adam and Eve, He gave them free will. This means they were not programmed like robots to do His will. They were given the opportunity to make choices. Their freedom allowed them the possibility of going against God's will—even to the extent of abusing someone else.

- Having free will not only means having the *opportunity to choose* wrong, but also the *ability to do* wrong. This is exactly what the original couple did: They chose to exercise their free will by doing what was against God's will. In this way sin entered the human race.

- Free will allows a person to decide between different options without external pressure or force. God causes no one to sin—such "causing" would make God the author of evil and make Him a malevolent God, which He can never be.

- God made spiritual abuse *possible* only by giving human beings free will, but human beings make spiritual abuse *actual* by choosing to sin. Ultimately, God *allows* sin, but human beings *cause* sin by the choices they make.

Although God allows spiritual abuse, He hates it! Those who are godly will hate it also. Proverbs 8:13 says, "To fear the LORD is to hate evil; I hate pride and arrogance, evil behavior and perverse speech." Know that God will execute His justice toward those who sin against Him and spiritually wound His followers. The Bible clearly states,

> *"Do not take revenge, my friends,*
> *but leave room for God's wrath, for it is written:*
> *'It is mine to avenge; I will repay,' says the Lord"*
> (ROMANS 12:19).

E. What Is the Root Cause of Spiritual Abuse?

Isn't it interesting how shifting the blame to God—or someone else—is much easier than taking personal responsibility for our wrong choices? Everyone is born with three inner needs—the needs for love, significance, and security.[25] In abusers, the attempts to meet these three inner needs in illegitimate ways creates a false sense of significance. And in victims who accept abuse, the abusers' attempts create a false sense of security. Those inner needs seem to be met—at least for the moment. But those feelings don't last. The Bible says there is only one way to meet those needs:

"My God will meet all your needs
according to his glorious riches in Christ Jesus"
(PHILIPPIANS 4:19).

A Wrong View of Authority

WRONG BELIEF OF THE ABUSER

"God has given me special authority that sets me above others and entitles me to special treatment. I have more authority, and I know God's will better than others. Therefore, I deserve to have obedience from others. My way is God's way; I should not be questioned. My will is His will; I should not be denied."

A verse frequently quoted by spiritual abusers is Psalm 105:15: "Do not touch my anointed ones; do my prophets no harm."

RIGHT BELIEF FOR THE ABUSER

"As the Lord's appointed undershepherd, I am to protect and provide for the flock of God with a heart totally committed to Him and His holy Word. I am to love God and serve His people with my whole heart, and I am to live a life worthy of His calling. As God's shepherd, I am to lay my life down for His sheep just as He laid down His life for me and for them."

The beloved apostle John stated this clearly and succinctly: "This is how we know what love is: Jesus Christ laid down his life for us. And we ought to lay down our lives for our brothers" (1 John 3:16).

A Wrong View of God's Acceptance

WRONG BELIEF OF THE ABUSED

"God's acceptance of me is dependent on my keeping His laws as revealed by His special messengers. That is the only way I can earn His approval."

The devoted apostle Paul addressed this faulty belief clearly and definitively when he wrote, "Are you so foolish? After beginning with the Spirit, are you now trying to attain your goal by human effort?" (Galatians 3:3).

RIGHT BELIEF FOR THE ABUSED

"God's law shows me my sin and leads me to Christ, who alone can save me from sin. Because my faith is in Christ, not in the law, I am free in Christ. The Spirit of Christ, who lives in me, gives me the desire and the power to overcome sin in my life and to live in a way that pleases Him."

As the Bible says, "The law was put in charge to lead us to Christ that we might be justified by faith. Now that faith has come, we are no longer under the supervision of the law" (Galatians 3:24-25).

F. How Can You Be Set Free?

It was nighttime. Why *wouldn't* he come during the night hour under the cover of darkness? Why *wouldn't* he fear upsetting his fellow religious Pharisees? In truth, he was not like most of the Pharisees: prideful, pompous, and puffed up. This humble seeker of truth truly respected Jesus as a teacher. But what he had just heard from Jesus didn't make sense. Nicodemus, a Pharisee, a member of the Sanhedrin, tried to make sense of the absurd statement made by Jesus: "I tell you the truth, no one can see the kingdom of God unless he is born again" (John 3:3).

Born again? Nicodemus asked, "How can a man be born when he is old?…Surely he cannot enter a second time into his mother's womb to be born!" (John 3:4). Patiently, Jesus explained that this birth far exceeded any physical birth. Then He emphatically stated, "You must be born again" (John 3:7), literally meaning "born from above."

Jesus left Nicodemus no other option. Likewise, He leaves us no other option. It's not enough for us to be physically alive. We also need to be spiritually alive. If we want to hear the counsel of God, we can't be spiritually dead. We must be spiritually alive; we must be born again. We must be born of the Spirit!

To find out what it means to be born of the Spirit, see the appendix on pages 409–411.

IV. Steps to Solution

They're on the prowl! With smooth stealth they circle quietly, looking intently for the right time to close in on the unguarded. Crouching down, they watch to discover the ones most vulnerable, to detect which sheep are weak and defenseless. And when the time is right, they quickly pounce on their prey. How were they able to go unnoticed until it was too late? These wolves wore sheep's clothing. They wore woolly masks and mingled among the woolly sheep. Yet in reality they were ravenous wolves. Jesus warned about them when He said,

> *"Watch out for false prophets.*
> *They come to you in sheep's clothing,*
> *but inwardly they are ferocious wolves"*
> (Matthew 7:15).

A. A Key Verse to Memorize

Open your heart to God, and He will guide you to right living—not through rigid commands or the use of power, but through the help of the Holy Spirit, who indwells all believers. As a Christian, you are completely accepted as His child! Live in the liberty of His love and trust Him to work in you and to change you into the person He created you to be.

> *"It is for freedom that Christ has set us free.*
> *Stand firm, then, and do not let yourselves*
> *be burdened again by a yoke of slavery"*
> (GALATIANS 5:1).

B. A Key Passage to Read and Reread

"Who has bewitched you?" exclaimed the apostle Paul (Galatians 3:1). He was alarmed that his fellow Christians were being enticed by false teachers. These legalistic "law keepers" insisted to new believers that they must submit to the old laws because they were *necessary* for salvation—and *necessary* for staying in right standing in the church.

Upon hearing this, Paul felt passionately compelled to reemphasize the fact that the gospel of salvation comes through *faith alone*. He emphatically refuted the teaching that any legal requirements were necessary to merit the salvation of God and reaffirmed that we receive the Spirit of God *only through faith* in the Lord Jesus Christ. Paul's urgings are equally relevant to us today.

═══════════ *Live by Faith, Not by the Law* ═══════════

GALATIANS 3:1-14—A PARAPHRASE

Don't be foolish! Don't be duped into believing that
keeping the *law* will save you.   verse 1

Ask yourself whether you received the Holy Spirit
by keeping the *law* or by placing *faith* in the
message you heard about in the gospel.   verse 2

Don't be shortsighted! After beginning your life relying
in *faith* on the Spirit's ability, don't think that you
gain success by relying on your human ability to
keep the *law*.   verse 3

Have all your painful experiences under the *law* been for nothing?	verse 4
Stop and think! Is God working in your life because you have obeyed the *law* or because you have placed your *faith* in Jesus Christ?	verse 5
Think about Abraham—God declared him righteous because of his *faith*.	verse 6
Therefore, all who live by *faith* are the true children of Abraham.	verse 7
The Scriptures prophesied how even the Gentiles would be saved through their *faith* as God had announced to Abraham, "All nations will be blessed through you."	verse 8
Therefore, those who have *faith* are blessed, along with Abraham, who is called "the man of faith."	verse 9
If you rely on keeping the *law,* you are doomed because keeping the *law* is impossible!	verse 10
No one is saved in God's sight by keeping the *law.* The righteous live by *faith*.	verse 11
The *law* is not a matter of *faith*, but a measuring stick of "doing."	verse 12
Christ has saved us from the curse of the *law* by becoming the curse Himself.	verse 13
God's purpose is plain. The blessing given to Abraham can also reach the Gentiles through Jesus Christ, but it comes only by *faith*—*faith* alone!	verse 14

C. How to Know Whether You Are Spiritually Abusive

While some people may be aware of their abusive behavior, many refuse to acknowledge it and respond to allegations with defensiveness and denial. If someone has ever suggested that you might be spiritually abusive toward others, you may need to do some self-examination to check whether that may be true.

> *"Surely you desire truth in the inner parts;*
> *you teach me wisdom in the inmost place"*
> (PSALM 51:6).

In addition, if you suspect someone else has the potential of being abusive, you can check that possibility as you test yourself by taking...

The Self-test

___Am I self-sufficient?

"Do I think I am right in God's sight because I am self-disciplined... because I use the right words and do the right works? Do I go about doing things focused solely on my ability to get the job done rather than on God's ability?" Realize that Paul said, "If, in fact, Abraham was justified by works, he had something to boast about—but not before God" (Romans 4:2).

___Am I self-serving?

"Do I do good things for the wrong reasons? If I am absolutely honest, do I desire to please myself more than I desire to please God?" Realize that Jesus said, "When you give to the needy, do not announce it with trumpets, as the hypocrites do in the synagogues and on the streets, to be honored by men. I tell you the truth, they have received their reward in full" (Matthew 6:2).

___Am I self-righteous?

"Do I take great pride in all of my righteous deeds, yet forget to give total credit to God for giving me the ability to do what I do?" (In truth, I take the credit that should be given to God and others.) "When God looks at me, does He at times see me as hypocritical and overly pious, trying to present myself as holier than others?" Realize that Jesus said, "Be careful not to do your 'acts of righteousness' before men, to be seen by them. If you do, you will have no reward from your Father in heaven" (Matthew 6:1).

___Am I self-focused?

"Am I more focused on what I have done well than on what others have done well? Am I taking credit for accomplishments that I should credit to God?" Realize that Paul said, "Not that we are competent in ourselves to claim anything for ourselves, but our competence comes from God" (2 Corinthians 3:5).

___Am I self-promoting?

"Do I work at trying to promote myself, or do I let God promote what He finds good in me…if He chooses to? Do I try to manipulate circumstances so that people will focus on me?" Realize that the book of wisdom says, "Let another praise you, and not your own mouth; someone else, and not your own lips" (Proverbs 27:2).

___Am I self-protective?

"Do I let others know the real me, or do I put up barriers to keep others at a safe distance? Do I admit that I struggle with certain problems in my life, or do I put up a false front?" Realize that Jesus said, "On the outside you appear to people as righteous but on the inside you are full of hypocrisy and wickedness" (Matthew 23:28).

___Am I self-important?

"Do I feel important because I religiously follow traditions, man-made rules, and standards?" Realize that Paul said, "Formerly, when you did not know God, you were slaves to those who by nature are not gods. But now that you know God—or rather are known by God—how is it that you are turning back to those weak and miserable principles? Do you wish to be enslaved by them all over again? You are observing special days and months and seasons and years! I fear for you, that somehow I have wasted my efforts on you" (Galatians 4:8-11).

___Am I self-centered?

"Am I touchy, judgmental, unloving, intolerant, or condemning of others? Do I find it hard to accept another person whose thinking is different from mine?" Realize what Jesus said: "At that time Jesus went through the grainfields on the Sabbath. His disciples were hungry and began to pick some heads of grain and eat them. When the Pharisees saw this, they said to him, 'Look! Your disciples are doing what is unlawful on the Sabbath.' He answered…'If you had known what these words mean, "I desire mercy, not sacrifice," you would not have condemned the innocent. For the Son of Man is Lord of the Sabbath'" (Matthew 12:1-2,7-8).

D. How to Differentiate Between True Sins and Man-made Sins

One of the problems Jesus had with the Pharisees is that they added to God's laws by making up laws of their own and then making them equal to God's laws. The result was that the people were burdened with literally thousands of nitpicky things to remember to do or not to do in order to be right with God.

They were so busy thinking about their actions that they had no time to think about their God or to grow in a personal, intimate relationship with Him—no time to focus on His love, grace, mercy, glory, character, goodness, provision, compassion, blessings, or specific plan and purpose for them.

They were unable to distinguish between what man considered a sin and what God considered a sin. That is why Jesus' Sermon on the Mount was revolutionary for them. It opened up the heart of God to them so they might see the spirit of the law in order that they might interpret the law. We need to understand this today as well. Jesus said,

> *"I tell you that unless your righteousness surpasses that*
> *of the Pharisees and the teachers of the law,*
> *you will certainly not enter the kingdom of heaven.*
> *You have heard that it was said to the people long ago…*
> *But I tell you…*
> *You have heard that it was said…*
> *But I tell you…*
> *Again, you have heard…*
> *But I tell you…*
> *You have heard that it was said…*
> *But I tell you…*
> *You have heard that it was said…*
> *But I tell you…"*
> (MATTHEW 5:20-22,27-28,33-34,38-39,43-44).

As you seek to look into the heart of God and distinguish what He considers sin from what man considers sin, you need to…

Ask Specific Questions
— Is it stated as a sin in God's Word?

"How can a young man keep his way pure?
By living according to your word"
(Psalm 119:9).

— Is it in keeping with following Christ's example?

"Do nothing out of selfish ambition or vain conceit,
but in humility consider others better than yourselves…
Your attitude should be the same as that of Christ Jesus"
(Philippians 2:3,5).

— Is it glorifying to God?

"Whether you eat or drink or whatever you do,
do it all for the glory of God"
(1 Corinthians 10:31).

— Is it a barrier to a Christian brother?

"Let us stop passing judgment on one another.
Instead, make up your mind not to put any stumbling block
or obstacle in your brother's way. As one who is in the Lord Jesus,
I am fully convinced that no food is unclean in itself.
But if anyone regards something as unclean,
then for him it is unclean. If your brother is distressed because
of what you eat, you are no longer acting in love.
Do not by your eating destroy your brother for whom Christ died…
It is better not to eat meat or drink wine or to do anything else
that will cause your brother to fall"
(Romans 14:13-15,21).

Be Fully Convinced in Your Own Mind

— If Scripture doesn't clearly address an issue, look for biblical
principles that will help you determine whether or not you
should take part in an activity.

"All Scripture is God-breathed and is useful

for teaching, rebuking, correcting and training in righteousness,
so that the man of God may be thoroughly equipped
for every good work"
(2 TIMOTHY 3:16-17).

— Bring questionable matters before the Lord in prayer, asking Him to give you personal convictions about those matters or activities.

"'Everything is permissible for me' [a popular saying]…
but not everything is beneficial. [Paul is saying]
'Everything is permissible for me'—
but I will not be mastered by anything"
(1 CORINTHIANS 6:12).

— Realize that the Lord may convict you about something that He doesn't convict someone else about, or vice versa.

"Each of us will give an account of himself to God"
(ROMANS 14:12).

— Don't condemn someone for choosing not to participate with you in something that you think is perfectly acceptable.

"As one who is in the Lord Jesus, I am fully convinced
that no food is unclean in itself. But if anyone regards
something as unclean, then for him it is unclean"
(ROMANS 14:14).

Use Proven Principles of Decision Making

— Learn the difference between spiritual commands and social convictions. Make sure you know whether the Bible prohibits a certain action or if that action is just culturally unacceptable to certain people.

"They worship me in vain;
their teachings are but rules taught by men"
(MATTHEW 15:9).

— Cultivate your convictions. Study the Scriptures and pray that the Lord would show you His heart on certain issues. Write down your convictions on paper and explain why you believe what you believe.

> *"Do your best to present yourself to God as one approved,*
> *a workman who does not need to be ashamed and*
> *who correctly handles the word of truth"*
> (2 TIMOTHY 2:15).

— Limit your liberty out of love. If something is allowable for you but would cause someone else to sin, you are to refrain from that activity. *If your behavior merely offends someone but would not cause the person to sin, you are not dealing with a weaker brother but possibly a legalist.*

> *"Let us stop passing judgment on one another.*
> *Instead, make up your mind not to put any stumbling block*
> *or obstacle in your brother's way"*
> (ROMANS 14:13).

— Let the Holy Spirit do His job. Allow the Lord to establish His convictions in your heart. And don't try to be someone else's conscience; let the Convictor convict and the Counselor counsel.

> *"When [the Holy Spirit] comes, he will convict the world of guilt*
> *in regard to sin and righteousness and judgment"*
> (JOHN 16:8).

Honoring Spiritually Abusive Parents

QUESTION: "What recourse does a son or daughter have with a spiritually abusive parent? How can you confront and honor a parent at the same time?"

ANSWER: Our heavenly Father is surely greatly saddened when an earthly father misuses His Word to hurt the heart and shatter the soul of one of His children. It is a blow to the very heart of God and a misrepresentation of His character. But how precious to God is the heart of a child who, as an adult or a minor, desires to right a parental wrong in a loving and God-honoring way.

The key to honoring someone is dealing with that person in truth without a hint of hypocrisy. Jesus confronted the spiritual "fathers" of Israel by challenging them with truth. You dishonor someone when you withhold a needed confrontation that God could use to bring conviction and change. Here are some ways an adult child can approach an abusive parent:

- "I want you to know I love you, and I want to always act in a way that pleases God and honors you. Therefore, I cannot in good conscience allow you to continue speaking to me in a way that is displeasing to God and puts you in a position of incurring His discipline. God's Word commands us to both encourage and speak kindly to one another, and to refrain from association with someone who is easily angered."

- "Out of honor to both you and God, I must temporarily leave your presence when you speak to me in a way that violates God's will for me and for you."

- "I want to have a wonderful, God-honoring relationship with you, so I pray that you will choose to honor Him by speaking to me in a way that pleases Him and encourages me."

- "In the future, I will take any disrespectful language directed toward me to mean that you do not wish to remain in my presence, and I will then leave until another time when we can enjoy each other's company."

A child who lives at home and is dependent on an abusive parent might find these approaches helpful:

- "I love you and I believe you love me, but it really hurts me when you say ugly things to me."

- "Please ask God to help you not get so angry with me and instead, be nicer to me."

Because a child cannot easily walk away from a parent, the following self-talk might help him or her to ward off the fiery arrows of harsh, harmful speech:

- "Dad is not thinking correctly right now, and his words are not true."
- "God loves me and wants me to believe what He says about me."
- "Lord, I ask you to protect my heart from these hurtful words."
- "Jesus loves me and gave His life for me."
- "Jesus is inside me, and He will help me."
- "God, please forgive Daddy, convict him of his sin, and help him to be more like You."

The apostle Paul wrote the following to the church at Thessalonica, and it applies to us as well:

> *"If anyone does not obey our instruction in this letter,*
> *take special note of him.*
> *Do not associate with him,*
> *in order that he may feel ashamed"*
> (2 Thessalonians 3:14).

E. How to Apply Guidelines in Spiritually Abusive Situations

Blind guides, hypocrites, snakes, and sons of hell—that's what Jesus called the Pharisees. He could see past their pretension and pomposity, stating plainly, "Everything they do is done for men to see" (Matthew 23:5). Their long tassels, their priestly robes, their seats of honor in the synagogue didn't impress Jesus. All their showiness sickened Him. His warning to us is this: What may seem sacred might actually be sacrilege to God.

"How will you escape being condemned to hell?" (Matthew 23:33). Jesus decried the religious leaders, with a litany of rebukes in Matthew chapter 23, for their greed, self-indulgence, legalism, and murderous inclinations against those who are truly of God. Seven *"Woe to you"* pronouncements were made against the Pharisees, who "[did] not practice what they preach" (Matthew 23:3). Pulpits today are filled with "spiritual" leaders just like the Pharisees, who one day will face the same chilling condemnation—from Jesus Himself.

So what can you do if you continually find yourself in a spiritually abusive situation?

- **Submit yourself to God's authority.** You are accountable to

God first and to human authorities second. "Am I now trying to win the approval of men, or of God? Or am I trying to please men? If I were still trying to please men, I would not be a servant of Christ" (Galatians 1:10).

- **Talk about your concerns with spiritual leaders** who are not involved in your abusive situation. God desires peace, unity, and reconciliation among Christians. "Be completely humble and gentle; be patient, bearing with one another in love. Make every effort to keep the unity of the Spirit through the bond of peace" (Ephesians 4:2-3).

- **Consider how the spiritually abusive attitude of others** is affecting your spiritual life, your relationships with family members and friends, and your sense of personal value. "I urge you, brothers, to watch out for those who cause divisions and put obstacles in your way that are contrary to the teaching you have learned. Keep away from them" (Romans 16:17).

- **Separate yourself from abusive situations** and seek out people who have a positive influence and encourage you. "Encourage one another and build each other up, just as in fact you are doing" (1 Thessalonians 5:11).

Submission and Spiritual Leaders

QUESTION: "Do I always have to submit to spiritual leaders, even when I know they are abusive? After all, the Bible says, 'Submit yourselves for the Lord's sake to every authority instituted among men' (1 Peter 2:13)."

ANSWER: Spiritual abusers love to manipulate others by telling them that they must always submit to spiritual authority. This is wrong! When the apostle Paul was facing trial at the hands of the Jewish religious leaders, he knew he would be executed. Therefore, rather than submitting to religious leaders in Jerusalem who were not following God, Paul appealed to stand trial in Rome before the secular court of Caesar. However, before appealing to Caesar, Paul unknowingly insulted the Jewish high priest. When Paul was told whom he had insulted, he agreed that no one should speak evil about the ruler of the Jewish people. We should always *respect* spiritual authority, but we do not need to *obey* it if it doesn't line up with God's truth.

"At this the high priest Ananias ordered those standing near Paul
to strike him on the mouth. Then Paul said to him,
'God will strike you, you whitewashed wall!
You sit there to judge me according to the law,
yet you yourself violate the law by commanding that I be struck!'
Those who were standing near Paul said,
'You dare to insult God's high priest?'
Paul replied, 'Brothers, I did not realize that he was the high priest;
for it is written: "Do not speak evil about the ruler of your people"'"
(ACTS 23:2-5).

F. How to Move from Legalism to Grace

"Amazing grace, how sweet the sound…" Who hasn't heard these familiar words that begin what is probably one of the most favored hymns of all time? The author, John Newton (1725–1807), was captain of a ship engaged in slave trade. He transported his share of the six million African slaves brought to the Americas during the eighteenth century. While on a homeward voyage, his ship encountered a violent storm and, fearing all was lost, he exclaimed, "Lord, have mercy on us!"

After leaving the slave trade and for the rest of his life, Newton referred to that day as the day when he understood the limitless grace of God. Newton spent the last 43 years of his life as a minister who fully understood the dynamics of divine grace—God's gift to everyone irrespective of "good deeds or earned worth." God's amazing grace is the means by which we are saved from original sin, given the power to live a life pleasing to God, and granted eternal salvation.

"This righteousness from God comes through faith
in Jesus Christ to all who believe.
There is no difference,
for all have sinned and fall short of the glory of God,
and are justified freely by his grace
through the redemption that came by Christ Jesus"
(ROMANS 3:22-24).

"Amazing grace! How sweet the sound
That saved a wretch like me!

I once was lost, but now am found,
Was blind, but now I see.
Through many dangers, toils, and snares,
I have already come;
'Tis grace hath brought me safe thus far,
And grace will lead me home."[26]

If your heart's desire is to move from legalism to grace, you need to…

G—**GIVE UP** trying to please God through your own efforts.

- Understand that the law is not a spiritual code for you to follow in order to earn God's favor.

- Understand that you will fail if you think you can fulfill the law in your own strength.

- Understand that you need not fear when you fail to measure up (and you will). Just rely on Christ to be your Redeemer. Remember:

"There is now no condemnation for those who are in Christ Jesus,
because through Christ Jesus the law of the Spirit of life set me free
from the law of sin and death"
(ROMANS 8:1-2).

R—**REALIZE** that God's love is a free gift—complete and unconditional.

- You are under the "grace principle" of life if you are a Christian.

- You have not been delivered from bondage in order to focus on a code of rules and regulations.

- You need to know that because of the everlasting love of the Lord, you are free in Christ. Remember:

"We have been released from the law so that
we serve in the new way of the Spirit,
and not in the old way of the written code"
(ROMANS 7:6).

A—Accept that Christ, through His Holy Spirit, is living in you to empower you to please God.

- Remember, Satan and death and sin were defeated at the cross.

- Remember, you received the gifts of salvation, eternal life, justification, righteousness, and glorification not by any of your own efforts, but through faith in Jesus Christ.

- Remember, you died to your old life, and your new life is now lived by faith in Christ, who earned these things *for* you. Remember:

> *"I have been crucified with Christ and I no longer live,*
> *but Christ lives in me. The life I live in the body,*
> *I live by faith in the Son of God,*
> *who loved me and gave himself for me"*
> (Galatians 2:20).

C—Commit to reading God's Word.[27]

- Know that the ways of the world are not God's ways.

- Know that by reading the Word of God you will know the ways of God…especially in the areas of your weakness.

- Know that God will use His Word to conform you to His character. Remember:

> *"Do not conform any longer to the pattern of this world,*
> *but be transformed by the renewing of your mind.*
> *Then you will be able to test and approve what God's will is—*
> *his good, pleasing and perfect will"*
> (Romans 12:2).

E—Experience the freedom of trusting God to fulfill His plan and purpose for you.[28]

- It's up to you to focus on the truth that God promises to complete His purpose for you.

- It's up to you to drop the mentality that "God loves me only when I'm good and rejects me when I'm bad."
- It's up to you to appropriate God's free gift of grace. Remember:

> *"Being confident of this, that he who began a good work in you*
> *will carry it on to completion until the day of Christ Jesus"*
> (PHILIPPIANS 1:6).

G. How to Biblically Answer Legalistic or Abusive Arguments

Paul referred to them as "disputable matters" (Romans 14:1).

He was concerned about finger-pointing that was taking place within the church. Believers were judging each other over matters not of sin but of the conscience. One man ate meat, and another didn't. One man considered a certain day of the week more sacred than the others; another considered them all alike. "Each one should be fully convinced in his own mind…Let us stop passing judgment on one another" (Romans 14:5,13).

The apostle further recognized that what lurked under the surface of all this judgment was pride—a "looking down" on others that caused disunity and shifted people's focus off of spiritual matters of far greater importance. The Bible says,

> *"The kingdom of God is not a matter of eating and drinking,*
> *but of righteousness, peace and joy in the Holy Spirit,*
> *because anyone who serves Christ in this way*
> *is pleasing to God and approved by men"*
> (ROMANS 14:17-18).

══════ Only the New Testament, Not the Old, Is Valid ══════

ARGUMENT: Because the Bible says we are no longer under the law but under grace, Christians don't need to read the Old Testament—just the New. After all, Galatians 3:25 says, "Now that faith has come, we are no longer under the supervision of the law."

ANSWER: The Bible encompasses both the Old and New Testaments—both make up the *whole* written Word of God. While Jesus fulfilled in Himself the requirements of the law given through Moses (Matthew 5:17),

God's entire Word is vital for us today because *both* the Old and New Testaments...

— Reveal the character of God and are thus necessary to gain a complete picture of God
— Reveal how God has intervened in human life
— Reveal His purpose for us
— Reveal His plans for the future
— Reveal a validation of each other and comprise the authoritative Word of God

Even the apostle Paul, who wrote about the misuse of the Old Testament Law, stated this:

> *"We know that the law is good if one uses it properly"*
> (1 TIMOTHY 1:8).

Polygamy Is Valid Today

ARGUMENT: God blessed David and other Old Testament leaders who had multiple wives. That confirms God approved of polygamy. Those who believe in the whole Bible should be permitted to take multiple wives and enjoy polygamous relationships.

ANSWER: Just because certain situations are presented in the Bible does not mean that God approved of them. Just because several suicides are reported in Scripture does not imply, "Go and do likewise!" Don't make the mistake of assuming that God was silent about polygamous relations:

— In the first mention of marriage in the Bible, the Lord laid the foundation for the one man-one woman union. Genesis 2:24 states, "For this reason a man will leave his father and mother and be united to his wife, and they will become one flesh."
— The Bible *does not* say *wives*! Note that Genesis 2:24 is repeated in the New Testament by Jesus in Matthew 19:5 and Mark 10:7 and by Paul in Ephesians 5:31.
— The New Testament adds that to "be above reproach," a spiritual

leader must be "the husband of but one wife"—not *wives* (1 Timothy 3:2).

— Interestingly, all countries and cultures that have their laws rooted in biblical morality require that the marriage relationship be exclusively one husband and one wife.

Note Paul's words to the church in Corinth:

> *"Since there is so much immorality,*
> *each man should have his own wife,*
> *and each woman her own husband"*
> (1 CORINTHIANS 7:2).

Too Many, Too Young: The FLDS Polygamy Problem

Just who is in danger? Seeing children at play typically evokes warm feelings in me, but that warmth quickly turns cold if I learn that some of these children are actually *child brides*. In fact, my frequent plea is, "Can't these children be protected?"

Any woman in the Fundamentalist Church of Jesus Christ of Latter Day Saints (FLDS) could conceivably be wife number 12, 13, or 14—enmeshed in a religion that celebrates polygamy. And the chilling aspect of the multiple marriages is the painful portrait of the child bride. Many young women who are given away in marriage are underage and commonly have up to ten children by the time they're 30 years old.[29]

The girls are readily identifiable by their bouffant hair and baggy prairie dresses, and the boys by their dark overalls and long-sleeved shirts. This controversial cult broke away from the mainstream Mormon Church* and has repeatedly been the target of criminal investigations.

In April 2008, the predatory environment inside the FLDS community prompted a Child Protective Services raid and the subsequent removal of more than 400 children. The court ruled that most of the children had to be returned to their homes, but 12 sect members were

---

* Many people contact our ministry with questions about cults and specifically about polygamy.

ordered to stand trial on various charges, including sexual assault and failure to report child abuse.

Raymond Jessop, who allegedly had nine wives, was the first to be tried on the charge of sexual assault of a child. He was married to a 15-year-old girl who gave birth to Jessop's child at age 16. (Jessop was more than double her age.) In November of 2009, Jessop was convicted and sentenced to ten years in prison.[30]

According to the cult's doctrine, "polygamy is *necessary* for complete salvation."[31] The leader, known as the Prophet, controls every family by allocating wives. He commits further spiritual abuse by removing wives from their husbands if the Prophet feels those husbands have dishonored or disrespected him. So it is to every man's benefit to hold the Prophet in highest esteem, because the more wives and children he has, the greater his stature—now and in eternity. And the young girls, who are treated like chattel and have no choice regarding marriage, are often forced to cohabit with elderly men or close relatives.

Although the Bible—one of the FLDS group's four "holy books"— says, "Everyone must submit himself to the governing authorities" (Romans 13:1), obviously they disregard this instruction. When one of Jessop's young wives was in labor for several days and needed medical attention, their Prophet (once on the FBI's top-ten fugitives list) told Jessop not to take her to a hospital. According to his journal, seized by authorities, he wrote, "I knew that the girl being 16 years old, if she went to the hospital, they could put Raymond Jessop in jeopardy of prosecution as the government is looking for any reason to come against us there."[32]

What kind of spiritual leader would allow any young girl to suffer medically to protect an illegal polygamous person? Answer: *One who misuses his position of spiritual authority to achieve his agenda.* It's leaders like these who will ultimately be held accountable by the God of the Bible for their illegal and indecent acts.

Jesus issued a stern warning for people like these who lead children to rebel against governmental authorities and to commit immoral acts:

> *"Things that cause people to sin are bound to come,*
> *but woe to that person through whom they come.*

> *It would be better for him to be thrown into the sea*
> *with a millstone tied around his neck*
> *than for him to cause one of these little ones to sin"*
> (LUKE: 17:1-2).

Baptism for the Dead Is Biblical

ARGUMENT: Baptism for the dead will bring salvation to everyone for whom I am baptized and will enable me to advance in the heavenly realm.

ANSWER: Those who hold to this belief claim that the apostle Paul spoke of such a practice in 1 Corinthians 15:29: "Now if there is no resurrection, what will those do who are baptized for the dead? If the dead are not raised at all, why are people baptized for them?"

But look carefully at the Bible itself, at 1 Corinthians chapter 15:

— The mention of people being baptized to save the souls of the dead is found nowhere else in Scripture. In fact, this interpretation was condemned as heresy by many of the early church fathers.

— Paul wrote 1 Corinthians 15 in response to false teachers who had infiltrated the church and claimed that "there is no resurrection of the dead" (verse 12). He wrote the chapter to affirm the historical fact of the resurrection of the dead.

— In chapter 15 we find evidence that the practice of baptism for the dead is based on false teaching from false teachers:

- More than 500 eyewitnesses attested to Christ's resurrection from the dead, most of whom were still alive at the time Paul wrote the chapter (verses 5-7).

- Ultimately, a major *inconsistency* is evident: If the false teachers did not believe in life after death, then why were people being baptized for the dead? Paul was simply saying, "If you reject the resurrection of the dead, you shouldn't baptize for the dead. To do so is illogical!"

- Those practicing baptism of the dead were the false

teachers—not Paul or the other Christians. That is evident because Paul referred to the ones being baptized as "those" and "people"—not "I," "you," or "we."

- Even for those who believe in the resurrection, the practice of baptizing someone on behalf of the dead in order to earn another person's salvation cannot be reconciled with Scripture. The Bible says that salvation comes as a gift of God's grace, and only through each individual's *faith* in Christ. That is, salvation is by *faith alone*, not any work such as baptism. Ephesians 2:8-9 states, "It is by grace you have been saved, through faith—and this not from yourselves, it is the gift of God—not by works, so that no one can boast."

The Bible clearly teaches that there are no opportunities for salvation *after* a person has died:

> *"Man is destined to die once,*
> *and after that to face judgment"*
> (HEBREWS 9:27).

Wives Must Submit to Their Husbands, No Matter What

ARGUMENT: Because God says wives are to submit to their husbands, as a wife, I must submit to whatever my husband says even if it violates my conscience. Ephesians 5:22 says, "Wives, submit to your husbands as to the Lord."

ANSWER: In the Bible, a "hierarchy" of submission exists to guide our decision making:

— Based on Ephesians 5:21, we should "submit to one another out of reverence for Christ." This is *mutual submission* and includes both husbands and wives deferring to the appropriate desires of each other.

— The very next verse says, "Wives, submit to your husbands" (verse 22), which should be read with the corollary verse, "Husbands, love your wives as Christ loved the church" (verse 25).

However, if a husband asks a wife to rob a bank with him, she should not submit because...

— The Bible also says a Christian should "submit himself to the governing authorities" (Romans 13:1). However, if the government instructs you to gas hundreds of people (as done in Nazi Germany), you should not submit because...

— Ultimately, "We must obey God rather than men!" (Acts 5:29). One of God's Ten Commandments states, "You shall not murder" (Exodus 20:13). Clearly the highest authority is God, next is the governing authorities, and then the husband. With all that in mind, no one should ever submit to that which is not of God.

For example, if an angry husband is physically abusing his wife or engaging her in any illegal activity and then "hitting her over the head" with what Ephesians 5:22 says about submission, her response should be biblical—*by calling for help*, even from the police, if necessary (Romans 13:1). If he gets angry and shouts, "You aren't being a Christian," her response should be biblical—*by getting out of harm's way.* Proverbs 22:24 says, "Do not make friends with a hot-tempered man, do not associate with one easily angered." If he tries to manipulate her into not taking legal action against him, her response should be biblical—*by allowing him to suffer the consequences of his actions.* Proverbs 19:19 says, "A hot-tempered man must pay the penalty; if you rescue him, you will have to do it again."

Never submit to abuse. The situation will only get worse if you do. Violence is never right in God's sight.

> *"Give up your violence and oppression*
> *and do what is just and right"*
> (Ezekiel 45:9).

Wearing Jewelry Is Forbidden

ARGUMENT: Wearing jewelry is worldly and prohibited by God. First Peter 3:3-4 says, "Your beauty should not come from outward adornment, such as braided hair and the wearing of gold jewelry and fine clothes. Instead, it should be that of your inner self, the unfading beauty of a gentle and quiet spirit, which is of great worth in God's sight."

ANSWER: If you refuse to wear jewelry based on 1 Peter chapter 3, you have a major ethical dilemma because you must also refuse "the putting on of clothing," which is also stated in the literal translation of this verse. Likewise, 1 Timothy 2:9 states that women should "dress modestly, with decency and propriety, not with braided hair or gold or pearls or expensive clothes." However, many biblical passages speak *positively* about wearing jewelry and fine clothing—and even about God being the giver of both! Therefore, when looking at the whole counsel of God, the biblical position has to be that any item of *external beauty*—like attractive jewelry, clothing, and hairstyles—should never be regarded as more valuable than the *internal beauty* of a humble heart and a sensitive spirit. The stigma against jewelry is unbiblical when the numerous Scriptures that present jewelry in a positive light are considered:

— In Proverbs 25:12, Solomon, the wisest of all men said, "Like an earring of gold or an ornament of fine gold is a wise man's rebuke to a listening ear." Because the rebuke of a wise person is presented as good, obviously a gold earring or ornament is also presented as good.

— In Genesis chapter 24 we read that Abraham sent his chief servant on a journey to bring back a wife for his son. Abraham told the servant that an angel would lead him to her. The chosen bride-to-be was given a "gold nose ring...and two gold bracelets," which were provided by Abraham (verse 22). Later, "The servant brought out gold and silver jewelry and articles of clothing and gave them to Rebekah" (verse 53). Here, all items of jewelry are presented in the most positive light.

— According to Genesis 41:41-43, after Pharaoh put Joseph "in charge of the whole land of Egypt," Joseph wore a "signet ring... [and] a gold chain around his neck."

— In Numbers 31:48-50, we read that Moses' officers "brought as an offering to the LORD the gold articles...armlets, bracelets, signet rings, earrings and necklaces—to make atonement."

— Job 42:10-11 tells us that after the Lord made Job prosperous again, "all his brothers and sisters and everyone who had known him before came and...each one gave him a piece of silver and a gold ring."

— In Song of Songs 1:10-11, Solomon describes the beauty of his bride-to-be: "Your cheeks are beautiful with earrings, your neck with strings of jewels. We will make for you earrings of gold, studded with silver."

— According to Song of Songs 4:9, Solomon says to his bride, "You have stolen my heart...with one glance of your eyes, with one jewel of your necklace."

— In Ezekiel 16:11-13, God describes Himself as adorning Israel "with jewelry: I put bracelets on your arms and a necklace around your neck, and I put a ring on your nose, earrings on your ears and a beautiful crown on your head. So you were adorned with gold and silver."

— In Haggai 2:23, the Lord Almighty says He will take His servant and "make you like my signet ring, for I have chosen you." Notice that the Lord Himself promised to make His servant like a choice signet ring for Himself!

— In Luke chapter 15, Jesus shared a poignant story about a prodigal son who, upon returning home, experienced the full forgiveness of his father, who ran to his son and called out, "Quick!...Put a ring on his finger...For this son of mine was dead and is alive again; he was lost and is found" (verses 22-24). Realize that the purpose of this parable is to describe the compassionate, forgiving heart of the heavenly Father toward us. Therefore, God the Father figuratively bestows a ring upon us when we are truly repentant and willing to come home to Him.

In conclusion, refusing to wear "rings and things" does not make a person more spiritual. Likewise, the fact that some people choose to wear jewelry does not make them more worldly. When it comes to issues such as these, throughout the Bible the primary issue is the heart. Where is it focused? Your first priority should be to set your heart on the spiritual things of God. Then all other choices in life will fall right in line.

> *"Set your minds on things above, not on earthly things"*
> (COLOSSIANS 3:2).

Hair Length and Head Coverings

ARGUMENT: In church services, women should wear a head covering and wear their hair long. The Bible says, "Every woman who prays or prophesies with her head uncovered dishonors her head—it is just as though her head were shaved...Does not the very nature of things teach you...that if a woman has long hair, it is her glory? For long hair is given to her as a covering" (1 Corinthians 11:5,14-15).

ANSWER: To understand these cultural mandates, we must understand the *context* of why Paul wrote these words to the Corinthian church.

Paul's comments regarding women's hair length and head coverings were clearly in response to the thousand priestesses and prostitutes at the Temple of Aphrodite on Acrocorinth who did not cover their heads and who wore their hair short. The purpose of Paul's words was to protect Christian women from being thought of as sexually immoral or as prostitutes if they were to cut their hair and thus dishonor themselves, their husbands, or their church. According to Jewish law, an adulterous woman had her hair cut off (Numbers 5:11-31).

If any of the temple prostitutes became Christians, they were required to wear a head covering (Greek, *peribolaion*) until their hair had time to grow long. This custom was necessary in that era (but not today) because of what short hair symbolized to the people.

Wearing Red Is Forbidden

ARGUMENT: Wearing any shade of red is worldly and is prohibited because of its association with sin and harlotry. Isaiah 1:18 says, "'Come now, let us reason together,' says the LORD. 'Though your sins are like scarlet, they shall be as white as snow; though they are red as crimson, they shall be like wool.'"

ANSWER: Nowhere in the Bible do we find a prohibition against wearing red.

This passage from Isaiah is not attaching the color red to sin, but rather is using red to illustrate the cleansing effect of the red blood of Christ.

Jeremiah 4:30 is often misinterpreted in the same way: "What are you doing, O devastated one? Why dress yourself in scarlet and put on jewels of gold?...You adorn yourself in vain." Obviously, scarlet was considered beautiful, but because Israel was spiritually desolate, this passage presents a contrast: Israel had outer beauty, not inner beauty. This passage isn't saying that God's people should never wear anything beautiful. Rather, it's saying that our outer beauty should be a reflection of our inner beauty. (See Ezekiel 16:1-16.)

There are many Bible passages that present the color red in a positive light:

— Proverbs 31:21—The woman in Proverbs 31:10-31 is often called the Proverbs 31 woman. This virtuous, godly, ideal woman has no fear for her household—her entire family—for in the winter, "all of them are clothed in scarlet."

— Exodus 26:1—The curtains of the Tabernacle were made with *scarlet* thread.

— Exodus 28:33—The high priest in the Tabernacle wore *scarlet* on the hem of his robe when he entered the presence of the Lord within the Holy of Holies.

— Numbers 4:7-8—The table of showbread in the Holy Place was entirely covered with a *scarlet cloth*.

— Nahum 2:3—The army God chose to defeat enemy nations had *red* shields and wore *scarlet* garments.

— Isaiah 63:1-2—The One stained with *crimson red*, the One robed in splendor, is a prophetic picture of Christ after His second coming and His victorious judgment over the ungodly. He is the triumphant King of kings and Lord of lords (Revelation 19:13-16).

Women Are Forbidden to Wear Pants

ARGUMENT: It is sinful for women to wear pants because Deuteronomy 22:5 states, "A woman must not wear men's clothing, nor a man wear women's clothing, for the LORD your God detests anyone who does this."

Answer: This Scripture cannot apply to women wearing pants because...

— When God gave this command to the Israelites, men did not wear pants, but rather garments like robes that, in the original Hebrew text of the Old Testament, were called *kethoneth*. Ironically, men and women wore the same garments!

— Most biblical scholars report that this prohibition was a response to a cross-dressing ritual common in the Canaanite religion. To cross-dress is to wear clothing designed to give a person the *appearance* of being the opposite sex and to make that person feel like the opposite sex.

— Presently, cross-dressing is considered to be practiced by those who struggle with gender identity issues, most specifically, those called *transvestites*. Cross-dressing is incongruent with the Bible, which declares that each person's physical body is intricately formed by God. Subsequently, to reject one's own sexuality is to reject God's design. "You created my inmost being; you knit me together in my mother's womb" (Psalm 139:13).

— Originally, God Himself made clothing for Adam and Eve that was so similar that the Hebrew word *kethoneth* described the specific garment He made for each of them. "The LORD God made garments [*kethoneth*] of skin for Adam and his wife and clothed them" (Genesis 3:21).

— Most cultures do not consider pants to be exclusively men's clothing.

In the New Testament, the subject of how women are to dress is communicated by Paul: "Women [should] dress modestly, with decency and propriety" (1 Timothy 2:9). Consequently, the only restrictions on women's clothing are these: Whatever women wear, it should be modest, decent, and appropriate.

The Dietary Laws in the Old Testament Must Be Kept

Argument: Because God gave dietary laws for the benefit of His people, we should abide by them today in order to live a blessed life. Those who do not adhere to the dietary laws will be doomed. Leviticus 11:47 says, "Distinguish between the unclean and the clean, between living creatures that may be eaten and those that may not be eaten."

ANSWER: Jesus repealed the Old Testament dietary laws to demonstrate that righteousness could not be obtained by observing the law. Even if certain dietary principles are still considered beneficial, Jesus made it clear that personal holiness cannot be achieved through what is eaten and what is not:

— Mark 7:18-19—Jesus asked, "Are you so dull?…Don't you see that nothing that enters a man from the outside can make him 'unclean'? For it doesn't go into his heart but into his stomach, and then out of his body. (In saying this, Jesus declared all foods 'clean.')"

— Acts 10:15—The apostle Peter, when confronted about keeping the Old Testament dietary law, was reprimanded by the Lord, who said, "Do not call anything impure that God has made clean."

— Colossians 2:16-17—The apostle Paul explained that the Old Testament dietary laws were repealed because they were not the reality but merely a foreshadowing of Christ, who is the reality. The coming of Christ did away with the shadow. Paul said, "Do not let anyone judge you by what you eat or drink, or with regard to a religious festival, a New Moon celebration or a Sabbath day. These are a shadow of the things that were to come; the reality, however, is found in Christ."

— Romans 14:3,14—Paul himself declared all food clean by saying, "I am fully convinced that no food is unclean in itself. But if anyone regards something as unclean, then for him it is unclean" (verse 14). Earlier he made the point that no one should spiritually condemn another for eating or not eating certain foods. Such condemnation constitutes spiritual abuse: "The man who eats everything must not look down on him who does not, and the man who does not eat everything must not condemn the man who does, for God has accepted him" (verse 3).

Saturday Is the Only Valid Day of Worship

FIRST ARGUMENT: One of the Ten Commandments is, "Remember the Sabbath day by keeping it holy" (Exodus 20:8). To be obedient to God, all worship services must take place on Saturday or else they are not valid. Because God rested on the seventh day following His creation of the universe, we are supposed to rest on the Sabbath day. Genesis 2:2 says, "By the seventh day God had finished the work he had been doing; so on the seventh day he rested from all his work."

ANSWER: To understand and apply this fourth commandment correctly, we must first understand the background of the Sabbath:

— The word *Sabbath* does not mean "Saturday."

— The English word *Sabbath* comes from the Hebrew root *shabbat*, which means "to cease." When referring to the day of rest, the form of the word is intensive, signifying a *complete cessation of activity—a complete rest* from work.[33]

— In God's eyes, believers must cease from working to try to gain His acceptance. According to the New Testament, the Sabbath of the Old Testament was merely a foreshadowing of the fact that Christ is to be our "rest." Colossians 2:16-17 says, "Do not let anyone judge you by what you eat or drink, or with regard to a religious festival, a New Moon celebration or a Sabbath day. These are a shadow of the things that were to come; the reality, however, is found in Christ."

— Authentic Christians enter into a never-ending "Sabbath rest" in which they stop trying to attain righteousness and receive Christ's righteousness as their own. They enjoy a never-ending relationship with the Lord and receive His never-ending acceptance: "There remains, then, a Sabbath-rest for the people of God" (Hebrews 4:9).

— We are to stop seeking to please God in our own strength and rest in our secure relationship with Jesus—rest in our never-ending relationship with Christ our Lord: "Anyone who enters God's rest also rests from his own work, just as God did from his" (Hebrews 4:10).

When you choose to rely on Christ as your Lord and Savior, no amount of work makes you acceptable to God. Only Christ's finished work on the cross makes you acceptable.

SECOND ARGUMENT: Because Jesus kept the Saturday Sabbath, we too should keep the Saturday Sabbath.

ANSWER: The reason Jesus kept all the Jewish laws, including the Saturday Sabbath, was that He was born in a Jewish family "under law" (Galatians 4:4). But our relationship to the law changed after Christ's death on the cross. The Bible says, "Christ is the end of the law" (Romans 10:4), meaning He had fulfilled the law for us so we would no longer be under the law.

THIRD ARGUMENT: The Bible states that Christian leaders like Paul and Barnabas worshipped on Saturday.

ANSWER: Paul and Barnabas did go to the Saturday services in the local synagogues, but their sole purpose was to proclaim the good news of the gospel. They proclaimed that the promised Messiah had come. For example:

— In a synagogue in Antioch, Paul said, "I want you to know that through Jesus the forgiveness of sins is proclaimed to you. Through him everyone who believes is justified from everything you could not be justified from by the law of Moses" (Acts 13:38-39).

— At the next synagogue the response was huge: "At Iconium Paul and Barnabas went as usual into the Jewish synagogue. There they spoke so effectively that a great number of Jews and Gentiles believed" (Acts 14:1).

— When Paul and Silas "had passed through Amphipolis and Apollonia, they came to Thessalonica, where there was a Jewish synagogue. As his custom was, Paul went into the synagogue, and on three Sabbath days he reasoned with them from the Scriptures" (Acts 17:1-2).

Remember, in Romans 1:16 Paul clearly stated that the gospel was to be presented "first for the Jew." The most logical place to find the Jewish people was the Jewish synagogue on the Saturday Sabbath.

FOURTH ARGUMENT: For almost 300 years, the early Christian church worshipped on Saturday. Many historical writings have concluded that the Roman emperor Constantine, in the year AD 325, changed the Sabbath to Sunday.

ANSWER: Such "historical writings" are based on fiction rather than fact, as seen in the documented writings of the early church fathers. While Constantine did make a proclamation that Sunday was to be the legal day of rest, he didn't change the Sabbath from Saturday to Sunday. Christians had already worshipped on Sunday *centuries* before Constantine made his declaration. Constantine merely *legalized* what they were doing. Here is proof:

— Around AD 110, Ignatius wrote, "…no longer observing Sabbaths but fashioning their lives after the Lord's Day [Sunday] on which our life also rose through Him."[34]

— Around AD 95, the *Didache* (considered the earliest written teachings of the church apart from the Bible) stated, "And on the Lord's own day [Sunday] gather yourselves together and break bread and give thanks…"[35]

— Around AD 150, Justin Martyr said, "But Sunday is the day on which we all hold our common assembly…Jesus Christ our Savior on the same day rose from the dead."[36]

Yet even more important is the fact two different New Testament books written by two different authors referred to the Sunday worship services:

— Luke, the author of Acts and the Gospel of Luke, wrote, "On the first day of the week we came together to break bread. Paul spoke to the people and, because he intended to leave the next day, kept on talking until midnight" (Acts 20:7).

— Paul instructed believers to give their offerings at the Sunday church services: "Now about the collection for God's people: Do what I told the Galatian churches to do. On the first day of every week, each one of you should set aside a sum of money in keeping with his income, saving it up, so that when I come no collections will have to be made" (1 Corinthians 16:1-2).

FIFTH ARGUMENT: Those who do not practice a Saturday Sabbath will be cut off from all true believers and will be doomed. Exodus 31:14 says, "Observe the Sabbath, because it is holy to you. Anyone who desecrates it must be put to death; whoever does any work on that day must be cut off from his people."

ANSWER: This entire passage (Exodus 31:12-17) reveals that the Sabbath was given exclusively to the children of Israel to set them apart from all other people. It reveals the absolute reality that the "work of salvation" was done by Jesus *alone* and the fate of those who seek to gain salvation by their own works is eternal death and separation from God. If being doomed to hell is the horrific fate of those who do not observe a Saturday Sabbath, consider:

— Of the Ten Commandments, this fourth commandment was the only one *not repeated* in the New Testament.

— Neither Jesus nor any of the New Testament writers mentioned it.

— The apostle Paul left the sacred day of worship up to each person simply as a matter of preference or conscience. Then he admonished us to stop judging others over this issue: "One man considers one day more sacred than another; another man considers every day alike. Each one should be fully convinced in his own mind" (Romans 14:5).

H. How to Know Whether Divine Healing Is Guaranteed for Everyone Today

One major tenet of the "Prosperity Gospel" asserts that physical suffering will always be alleviated when you place the proper amount of faith in God's healing power. We are told that all we need to do is *name* the needed healing and, in faith, *claim* the healing in the name of Jesus, and we will be healed (hence the term name-it-and-claim-it theology).

This assumption is based on the fact that Jesus healed *all* the sick who came to Him when He was on earth. "When evening came, many who were demon-possessed were brought to him, and he drove out the spirits with a word and healed all the sick. This was to *fulfill* what was spoken through the prophet Isaiah: 'He took up our infirmities and carried our diseases'" (Matthew 8:16-17, emphasis added).

However, does the fact Jesus healed people during His time on earth mean that all people today are to seek healing from Him as well? Some religious leaders use Matthew 8:16-17 to teach that all of our illnesses can be healed by Jesus Christ—if only we would have enough faith. But Matthew 8:16-17 refers directly to a prophecy found in Isaiah 53:4-5:

> *"Surely he took up our infirmities and carried our sorrows,*
> *yet we considered him stricken by God,*
> *smitten by him, and afflicted.*
> *But he was pierced for our transgressions,*
> *he was crushed for our iniquities;*
> *the punishment that brought us peace was upon him,*
> *and by his wounds we are healed."*

Knowing the meaning of the word "fulfill" in Matthew 8:17 is key to resolving the misunderstandings about this passage.

Let's say, for example, that you've bought a house and signed a contract for a 20-year mortgage. Once you make your last payment, the contract is *fulfilled:*

— If the mortgage company calls and tells you to continue making the monthly mortgage payment, would you comply? Of course not! You have already fulfilled your obligation to the contract.

— In the same way, Isaiah's prophecy was "fulfilled" in Matthew 8:17. Just as it would be incorrect for a mortgage company to expect you to keep making house payments after you had fulfilled the contract—after the debt had been paid in full—it would be incorrect to assume that Jesus would always heal every infirmity after He confirmed His identity as the Messiah.

— The prophecy that the Messiah would heal all the sick had been fulfilled in the person of Jesus and proved to the people that He was indeed the promised Messiah. This truth is validated by the fact that after Jesus fulfilled the prophecy and was crucified, buried, resurrected, and had ascended to heaven, He did not heal the apostle Paul, even after the apostle had made multiple requests for healing. When Paul asked God three times to deliver him from a "thorn in the flesh," God refused and said,

"My grace is sufficient for you, for my power is made perfect in weakness" (2 Corinthians 12:7-9).

Remember that Paul was used mightily of God and is considered the world's greatest Christian missionary. When Paul wasn't healed, it wasn't because he lacked enough faith. Nor was it because God lacked the power to heal Paul. Rather, God had a purpose in allowing Paul to experience this malady, just as God had a purpose in allowing Jesus to heal all who came to Him when He was living on earth.

— Note that Timothy also did not receive a miraculous healing. In regard to Timothy's illnesses, Paul told Timothy to "stop drinking only water, and use a little wine because of your stomach and your frequent illnesses" (1 Timothy 5:23). If the cure for all physical problems is prayer for healing, why would Paul recommend a medicinal cure? (Wine has certain medicinal properties.) Was it because Timothy did not have enough faith? If so, why didn't Paul raise that issue? The reason Paul recommended that Timothy take wine was because he knew God doesn't heal every sickness and ailment that comes along. *Not all prayer will be answered in accordance with our requests,* even when we have the most sincere heart and the deepest faith.

— Jesus, God the Son, prayed in the Garden of Gethsemane, "Father, if you are willing, take this cup from me" (Luke 22:42). Yet He still experienced the torture and torment of the cross.

— Jesus' prayer reveals the correct attitude toward requests for healing. He said, "Yet not what I will, but what you will" (Mark 14:36). If God chooses not to heal us, we must trust that He has a reason for not doing so. We are to trust His plan for our life.

Ask and You Will Receive

QUESTION: "The Bible says, 'Ask and you will receive' (John 16:24). I was told all I had to do was *name* and *claim* what I wanted…in Jesus' name. If I would sincerely *believe,* I could expect to *receive*—which clearly hasn't happened! I'm angry with God. Why hasn't He answered my prayers?"

Answer: Your anger at God is based on an *unrealistic expectation*. While you were completely sincere in making your request, those who taught you the expectation that God will honor any request brought before Him are wrong. Their name-it-and-claim-it theology is not biblical:

- When you look at the whole counsel of God—when you read all the Scriptures on this subject in their accurate context—you will see that the believe-and-receive doctrine doesn't measure up as biblically accurate.

- Consider the apostle Paul, whose pedigree was impressive, yet he knew little health and wealth. Although 100 percent in the will of God, he was also weak and "in want." Rather than naming it and claiming it, he said, "I know what it is to be in need, and I know what it is to have plenty. I have learned the secret of being content in any and every situation, whether well fed or hungry, whether living in plenty or in want. I can do everything through him who gives me strength" (Philippians 4:12-13).

- Jesus tells us that whatever we ask in faith, we will receive: "I tell you, whatever you ask for in prayer, believe that you have received it, and it will be yours" (Mark 11:24). At face value, this verse appears to back up the belief that God will give us whatever we ask—as long as we believe, we will receive it. Yet the apostle John provides important clarification for us, saying that your desire *must* conform to God's will. Only then will God look upon your request with favor and bring it to pass:

  > *"If we ask anything according to his will, he hears us. And...we know that we have what we asked of him"*
  > (1 John 5:14-15).

I. Recovery from Legalism and Spiritual Abuse

Their priorities and practices couldn't have been more different, making one thing perfectly clear: Jesus was indeed the good shepherd, and the Pharisees were the false shepherds.

Jesus taught truth. .... The Pharisees spread lies.

Jesus embraced sinners. ...... The Pharisees shunned sinners.

Jesus healed the sick. .... The Pharisees hindered the sick.

In the end, the Pharisees *fleeced the sheep*, whereas *Jesus died for the sheep*. And Jesus lives today to be *your* shepherd—to shepherd you through all of life. When you come under His care and place your total trust in Him, He will remain faithful as the shepherd of your soul.

> *"I am the good shepherd.*
> *The good shepherd lays down his life for the sheep"*
> (JOHN 10:11).

Recovery

The following is an acrostic for the word *recovery*.

R—REALIZE that you have been in a legalistic/abusive situation.

- Acknowledge to yourself, to God, and to someone else that you have been spiritually deceived and deeply wounded.

- Acknowledge your willingness to have believed the lies you have embraced.

- Acknowledge your personal responsibility for propagating those lies to others without personally verifying their validity. Remember, the Bible says,

> *"If we confess our sins, he is faithful and just*
> *and will forgive us our sins and purify us from all unrighteousness.*
> *If we claim we have not sinned,*
> *we make him out to be a liar and his word has no place in our lives"*
> (1 JOHN 1:9-10).

E—EXERCISE your freedom in Christ.

- Renounce being in bondage to the lies of legalism and embrace the truth that you have been forgiven and set free.

- Renounce your excessive allegiance to any spiritual leader or church and embrace Jesus as your spiritual head and leader.

- Renounce the laws you have been living under and embrace the One who has set you free from the law. Remember, the Bible says,

> *"If the Son sets you free, you will be free indeed"*
> (JOHN 8:36).

C—CORRECT your concept of God.

- Study the Bible for yourself to learn the true character of God.
- Study the books of Galatians and Hebrews and Romans chapters 3–8, which proclaim your liberty in Christ.
- Study the Gospel of John and the epistle of 1 John to see the loving heart of the Father. Remember, the Bible says,

> *"How great is the love the Father has lavished on us,*
> *that we should be called children of God! And that is what we are!*
> *The reason the world does not know us is that it did not know him"*
> (1 JOHN 3:1).

O—OPEN yourself to healthy Christian relationships.

- Realize that your fear and distrust of authentic Christians is based on your abusive situation, then refuse to judge others for the sins of some.
- Realize that God created you to fellowship with others and that He will use other Christians to bring love, nurture, and healing into your heart.
- Realize that God wants to use you to bring comfort into the lives of others who have also experienced spiritual abuse. Remember, the Bible says,

> *"Praise be to the God and Father of our Lord Jesus Christ,*
> *the Father of compassion and the God of all comfort,*
> *who comforts us in all our troubles, so that we can comfort*
> *those in any trouble with the comfort we ourselves have received*
> *from God. For just as the sufferings of Christ flow over into our lives,*
> *so also through Christ our comfort overflows"*
> (2 CORINTHIANS 1:3-5).

V—Voice your cares and concerns to God.

- Tell God your deepest doubts, hurts, and fears as well as the deepest longings of your heart.

- Tell the Lord about the guilt and anger you feel over having been deceived.

- Tell the Lord how you feel about having been used to satisfy the unquenchable hunger of another person for power and position. Remember, the Bible says,

> *"Trust in him at all times, O people;*
> *pour out your hearts to him, for God is our refuge"*
> (Psalm 62:8).

E—Enlist the help of spiritually mature, grace-filled mentors.

- Seek relationships with those who have unquestioned wisdom and integrity.

- Seek those who love the Lord and who cling to the Word as their guide to knowing God.

- Seek a spiritual mentor who will encourage you to accurately interpret the Bible for yourself. Remember, the Bible says,

> *"He who walks with the wise grows wise,*
> *but a companion of fools suffers harm"*
> (Proverbs 13:20).

R—Rest in the finished work of Christ.

- Deny your fleshly compulsion to do good works in order to gain the approval of God. Claim the righteousness of Christ as your own.

- Deny condemning thoughts that assault your mind and your emotions. Claim the cleansing forgiveness of Christ, who has washed you whiter than snow.

- Deny the lie that you need to prove yourself worthy of salvation. Claim the fact that God loved you and Jesus died for you in spite of your sin. Remember, the Bible says,

"At just the right time, when we were still powerless,
Christ died for the ungodly...God demonstrates his own love
for us in this: While we were still sinners, Christ died for us"
(ROMANS 5:6,8).

Y—YIELD yourself to the Holy Spirit, who lives within you.

- Trust the Holy Spirit to guide you into truth and to protect you from error.

- Trust the Holy Spirit to empower you to love the Lord your God with all your heart, soul, mind, and strength and to live a life that is pleasing to Him and that glorifies Him.

- Trust the Holy Spirit to fulfill God's promise to conform you to the character of Christ. Remember, the Bible says,

"When he, the Spirit of truth, comes, he will guide you into all truth.
He will not speak on his own; he will speak only what he hears,
and he will tell you what is yet to come"
(JOHN 16:13).

"In the essentials, unity. In the nonessentials, liberty.
And in all things, charity." Precious child of God, you don't
need to work or to do one more act to gain God's approval.
You have His approval—you are accepted in the Beloved!

=== *Spiritual Abuse—Answers in God's Word* ===

QUESTION: "Why does God make salvation a gift through our faith and not through our works?"

ANSWER: "It is by grace you have been saved, through faith—and this not from yourselves, it is the gift of God—not by works, so that no one can boast" (Ephesians 2:8-9).

QUESTION: "Once we have been justified by faith, are we still under the law?"

ANSWER: "The law was put in charge to lead us to Christ that we might be justified by faith. Now that faith has come, we are no longer under the supervision of the law" (Galatians 3:24-25).

QUESTION: "Is my spirituality judged by what I eat or drink or whether I keep the Sabbath day?"

ANSWER: "Do not let anyone judge you by what you eat or drink, or with regard to a religious festival, a New Moon celebration or a Sabbath day. These are a shadow of the things that were to come; the reality, however, is found in Christ" (Colossians 2:16-17).

QUESTION: "If I can't become righteous by observing the law, what is the point of the law?"

ANSWER: "No one will be declared righteous in his sight by observing the law; rather, through the law we become conscious of sin" (Romans 3:20).

QUESTION: "Can I earn righteousness by keeping the law?"

ANSWER: "I do not set aside the grace of God, for if righteousness could be gained through the law, Christ died for nothing!" (Galatians 2:21).

QUESTION: "Is Saturday more sacred than the other days of the week?"

ANSWER: "One man considers one day more sacred than another; another man considers every day alike. Each one should be fully convinced in his own mind" (Romans 14:5).

QUESTION: "What does the Bible say about trying to win someone's approval and not being able to say no?"

ANSWER: "Am I now trying to win the approval of men, or of God? Or am I trying to please men? If I were still trying to please men, I would not be a servant of Christ" (Galatians 1:10).

QUESTION: "Why should sin no longer be my master?"

ANSWER: "Sin shall not be your master, because you are not under law, but under grace" (Romans 6:14).

QUESTION: "After the passing of the Old Testament law, is there no covenant to live by? Are there no laws?"

ANSWER: "This is the covenant I will make with them after that time, says the Lord. I will put my laws in their hearts, and I will write them on their minds" (Hebrews 10:16).

QUESTION: "From what has Christ set us free?"

ANSWER: "It is for freedom that Christ has set us free. Stand firm, then, and do not let yourselves be burdened again by a yoke of slavery" (Galatians 5:1).

VERBAL AND EMOTIONAL ABUSE

VERBAL AND EMOTIONAL ABUSE

Victory over Verbal and Emotional Abuse

"You're worthless!" "You'll never amount to anything!" "I wish you had never been born!" Words like these, spoken to a child, can wound the heart for a lifetime.

Another kind of abuse takes place in adulthood when control is the name of the game. Threats like, "If you leave me, I'll hurt the children!" or "I've taken the keys—you're not going anywhere!" are both emotionally and verbally abusive and are ways of maintaining control in relationships.

Abuse can also be perpetrated without a word—degrading looks, obscene gestures, and threatening behaviors can inflict immense pain and impede emotional growth.

If you can relate to any of these abusive scenarios, please know you don't have to let an abuser make you feel worthless. Jesus said that God not only knows each and every sparrow, but He also knows you intimately and considers you to be of far greater worth than them:

> *"Are not five sparrows sold for two pennies?*
> *Yet not one of them is forgotten by God.*
> *Indeed, the very the hairs of your head are all numbered.*
> *Don't be afraid; you are worth more than many sparrows"*
> (LUKE 12:6-7).

I. DEFINITIONS OF VERBAL AND EMOTIONAL ABUSE

A. What Is Emotional Abuse?

Emotional abuse is the unseen fallout from all other forms of abuse: physical, mental, verbal, sexual, and even spiritual. People often minimize the importance of emotions. Yet feelings can be the driving force behind choices made by deeply wounded people, and those choices can be detrimental if not rooted in a true understanding of who we are. Emotional abuse strikes at the very core of who we are—crushing our confidence, whittling away at our sense of worth, suffocating our spirit. The Bible says,

> *"A cheerful heart is good medicine,*
> *but a crushed spirit dries up the bones"*
> (Proverbs 17:22).

- **Emotional abuse is any ongoing negative behavior** used to control or hurt another person. Emotional abuse ranges from consistent indifference to continual belittling of character.

  — All forms of abuse—emotional, verbal, mental, physical, spiritual, and sexual—damage a person's sense of dignity and God-given worth.

  — All forms of abuse wound the spirit and therefore are emotionally abusive.

Proverbs, the book of wisdom, poses this probing question:

> *"A crushed spirit who can bear?"*
> (Proverbs 18:14).

- **Emotional abuse or "psychological mistreatment" scars the spirit** of the one abused.

  — The damage from emotional abuse can last far longer than damage from any other kind of abuse. A broken arm will soon heal; a broken heart may take a lifetime to heal.

  — After extended periods of emotional abuse, many victims lose hope, feeling that life is not worth living.

The book of Proverbs states it this way:

> *"Hope deferred makes the heart sick"*
> (Proverbs 13:12).

- **Emotional abuse can be passive-aggressive.** Passive-aggressive abuse is a means of exercising indirect, underhanded control over another person.

— *Passive-aggressive abusers* express their anger through non-assertive, covert behavior. To gain control in a relationship, these abusers often use manipulation as a means of placing themselves in a position of dependence. Then, with underlying anger, they become faultfinders of the people on whom they depend.[1]

— *Victims of passive-aggressive people feel perplexed* and dismayed at being the target of punitive and manipulative behaviors.

— *Friends of passive-aggressive abusers often become enmeshed* in trying to comfort or console them in response to their claims of unjust treatment and their inability to handle life on their own.

Passive-aggressive abusers need to recognize and resolve their very real anger and take to heart God's warning:

> *"Do not be quickly provoked in your spirit,*
> *for anger resides in the lap of fools"*
> (ECCLESIASTES 7:9).

- **Emotional abuse can be either *overt* or *covert*.**
  — *Overt abuse* clearly expresses that a person is useless or unloved (as when one is belittled as a child).[2]
  — *Covert abuse* occurs by sending the same message in subtle ways that may or may not be intended to cause harm by the perpetrator (as when one is ignored as a child).[3]

Biblical Example of
Both Overt and Covert Abuse: Tamar
(Read 2 Samuel chapter 13.)

OVERT ABUSE

Tamar, daughter of King David, was raped by her half-brother Amnon and then was openly and blatantly despised and shunned by him.

Covert Abuse

Their father, King David, indirectly rejected Tamar by failing to execute justice on her behalf when he refused to hold Amnon accountable for his sin. David, in essence, let his son off the hook by totally ignoring the sexual violation of his daughter.

Emotional Abuse in Scripture

Question: "What does the Bible say about emotional abuse?"

Answer: The Bible doesn't use the term *emotional abuse*, but it does instruct us as to how we are to treat one another. The Bible details the kinds of attitudes and actions we should show and carry out toward one another. If we follow these guidelines, we will never abuse anyone.

> *"Do nothing out of selfish ambition or vain conceit,*
> *but in humility consider others better than yourselves.*
> *Each of you should look not only to your own interests,*
> *but also to the interests of others"*
> (Philippians 2:3-4).

B. What Is Verbal Abuse?

Verbal abuse is a form of overt emotional abuse. A skilled woodsman wields his ax carefully, chopping repeatedly on a designated spot until the targeted tree falls. This lumberjack takes pride in controlling himself and his dangerous tool, never striking a careless blow. Likewise, a verbal abuser uses his tongue like a sharp weapon to hack away at another person. This abuser is skilled in his ability to strike a blow—he wields derogatory, deceitful words with a precision intended to caustically cut the heart and injure the soul.

> *"Your tongue plots destruction;*
> *it is like a sharpened razor,*
> *you who practice deceit"*
> (Psalm 52:2).

- **Verbal abuse is the systematic, ongoing use of harmful words** or sharp tones in an attempt to control or dominate another person.

— *Abuse* is mistreatment: the destructive misuse of something or someone.

— *Verbal abuse* is always destructive.

Those who practice verbal abuse may, sometimes unconsciously, delight in its power to destroy.

> *"You love every harmful word,*
> *O you deceitful tongue!"*
> (PSALM 52:4).

• **Verbal abuse injures the feelings of others** with reviling, insulting, or contemptuous words. The Hebrew word for "revile" is *gadaph*, from a root word that means "cut" or "wound."[4] The psalmist said,

> *"My disgrace is before me all day long,*
> *and my face is covered with shame*
> *at the taunts of those who reproach and revile me,*
> *because of the enemy, who is bent on revenge"*
> (PSALM 44:15-16).

• **Verbal abuse often seeks to injure the reputation of others.** It does this by…

— Using tactics such as backbiting, barbs, or belittling talk

— Using strategies such as slander, slurs, and lies

The Bible says this about verbal abusers:

> *"You love evil rather than good,*
> *falsehood rather than speaking the truth"*
> (PSALM 52:3).

C. What Is Brainwashing?

When soldiers are taken captive, enemy combatants will sometimes attempt to brainwash them—an effective tactic used in psychological warfare. This term refers to a systematic, forcible process of indoctrination that puts pressure on prisoners to relinquish their beliefs and accept opposing views.[5]

It's not only prisoners of war who are exposed to attempts at brainwashing. You may find that a member of your family or a supervisor at work is trying to brainwash you. In whatever circumstance brainwashing occurs, the damage can be devastating. That's because the goal of brainwashing is to systematically and persistently wear away at your sense of self-worth and confidence—to the point that you distrust yourself, doubt your decisions, and even lose touch with reality.

The Bible warns…

> *"Those people are zealous to win you over,*
> *but for no good. What they want is to alienate you from us,*
> *so that you may be zealous for them"*
> (GALATIANS 4:17).

Verbal and Emotional Tactics Employed in Brainwashing

VERBAL BRAINWASHING

— *Intimidation*: Implying that your failure to comply with all demands or to adopt all of the abuser's attitudes or beliefs will result in severe consequences

— *Indoctrination:* Implanting repeated messages contrary to your presently held values or beliefs

— *Discreditation:* Belittling your "outside" family and friends who disagree with the abuser

— *Degradation:* Engaging in name-calling, insults, ridicule, and humiliation

— *Accusation:* Claiming that your thoughts are childish, stupid, or crazy

> *"They do not speak peaceably, but devise false accusations*
> *against those who live quietly in the land"*
> (PSALM 35:20).

EMOTIONAL BRAINWASHING

— *Isolation:* Depriving you of all outside sources of emotional and social support

— *Interrogation:* Inducing exhaustion by keeping you up late, interrupting your sleep, causing sleep deprivation, or wearing you down physically or emotionally

— *Militization:* Enforcing excessive compliance with trivial demands

— *Falsification:* Withdrawing emotional support but later denying the withdrawal

— *Deception:* Intentionally failing to keep promises and agreements

— *Exploitation:* Using you or someone close to you for selfish interests or gain

The psalmist accurately presents what the victim of such treatment would experience:

> *"The enemy pursues me, he crushes me to the ground;*
> *he makes me dwell in darkness like those long dead.*
> *So my spirit grows faint within me;*
> *my heart within me is dismayed"*
> (PSALM 143:3-4).

Besieged, Broken, and Brainwashed:
The Patty Hearst Story

Three words will forever be associated with the life of Patty Hearst: "Kidnapped Newspaper Heiress."[6]

On February 5, 1974, I remember this banner headline flashing across multiple newspapers and news magazines. Worldwide, stories detailed how this 19-year-old college student was gagged and whisked away from her apartment by a small band of domestic terrorists—the Symbionese Liberation Army, or SLA.[7]

SLA militants perceived themselves as urban revolutionaries and wanted to be viewed as "defenders of the people"—raucous rebels remembered for taking down the ruling class. One motive for kidnapping Patty was to use her in a prisoner exchange for two arrested SLA militants charged with murder. The other was to coerce Patty's father, Randolph Hearst, to drain his "fattened bank accounts" to feed the state's hungry.

The first two months of Patty's kidnapping could only be described as *terrorizing:* days and nights filled with verbal, emotional, and physical abuse. She was confined to a closet, continually blindfolded, and repeatedly raped. To help keep the SLA in the media spotlight, she was forced to make scripted tape recordings to affirm she was still alive.

When several weeks passed without any communication from Patty, loved ones feared the worst. Then in April, the silence was broken—by a tape recording featuring a very different Patty. The heiress declared that she had turned rebel and she now wanted the world to identify her as "Tania."

Patty explained that the SLA had given her two options: (1) be released, or (2) join the SLA to fight for the freedom of the oppressed. Patty chose the latter, with her decision sounding definite: "I have chosen to stay and fight."[8]

Patty's aversion-turned-allegiance toward her SLA captors is symptomatic of those experiencing a phenomenon known as the Stockholm syndrome. The term was coined following a weeklong siege at a Swedish bank in 1973, during which two bank robbers took four hostages and the traumatized captives developed a close bond with their captors. Conditions were intolerable and inhumane, yet when police finally flushed out the robbery suspects, the four hostages encircled the robbers, trying to protect them from harm. One woman even claimed she was in love with one of the criminals and planned to marry him upon his release from prison.[9]

Just weeks after joining the SLA, Tania fought her first battle, but it wasn't for the purpose of stomping out social injustice. Donning a black beret and wielding a machine gun, Tania was caught on camera robbing a San Francisco bank, threatening to shoot anyone who got in the way. The photos taken by the bank's security cameras sent shockwaves around the world: Was Patty a victim or a victimizer? Was she a forced—or free—accomplice?

Aware of the "brainwashing" buzz in the media, Patty released another recording: "My gun was loaded. At no time did my comrades intentionally point their guns at me. As for being brainwashed, the idea is ridiculous to the point of being beyond belief."[10]

The SLA moved its militants to a "safe house" in Los Angeles, but they weren't safe for long. FBI and police discovered their hideout and, after a gun battle, the house burned to the ground, leaving behind six charred bodies. The world wondered: Did Patty die for a warped revolution? But an argument had prevented Patty and two of the SLA comrades from getting to the house, so the traumatized trio watched the entire shootout on television.

About ten months later, with new recruits, the SLA resumed "combat operations" and raided another bank to fund its "civil war" against the government. In this robbery, a shotgun blast killed a 42-year-old mother of four. Patty, waiting outside, drove the getaway car.[11]

Finally, on September 17, 1975, Patty was arrested—19 months after her kidnapping. The SLA disbanded, and Patty's role as a revolutionary came to an end.

Patty was charged with bank robbery, and the most brilliant legal mind of the time—in an effort to get her acquitted—built her defense around the argument that she had been brainwashed. The attorney had Patty recant, in court, every word and deed committed by Tania, and Patty testified that after being raped repeatedly for months, her mind was no longer her own. "I couldn't even think thoughts for myself anymore because I had been so programmed," Patty stated.[12] "I had been…held in a closet for two months and…abused in all manner of ways. I was very good at doing what I was told."[13]

Sadly, the jury rejected the brainwashing defense and sentenced Patty to seven years in prison, of which she served nearly two years. The president of the United States commuted her sentence, and later she received a presidential pardon.

Sociologists and criminologists today understand far more about the mechanics of mind control than when Patty Hearst was tried. Experts now acknowledge that Patty was undoubtedly a victim of brainwashing—of verbal and emotional abuse, of manipulative mind control—who had attempted to explain, "I had no free will until I was separated from them."[14]

Realize that you don't have to be a literal captive to succumb to the debilitating effects of brainwashing. Those subjected to incessant barrages of hostile attacks—about a person or an idea—become vulnerable to brainwashing, especially when the attackers are in positions of power. Within families, sometimes the victim is like a helpless bird who is mysteriously selected to be pecked to death by its nest-mates, leaving that member maimed and alienated.

Unlike Patty Hearst, most adults are not physically held captive, and therefore need to learn how to recognize and resist coercive persuasion. Likewise, we need to take steps to remove ourselves from the source of brainwashing attempts—and *stay away* until those efforts have ceased. Otherwise, when negativism is spewed, we can become poisoned by the toxic fumes.

Only after Patty Hearst became separated from her brainwashers could she see the truth so the truth could set her free. Similarly, if someone is trying to control your mind, you must separate yourself from that person and situation so you can *see the truth*. As Jesus said, when you know the truth, "the truth will set you free."[15]

II. Characteristics of Verbal and Emotional Abuse

Words possess immense power. Through words, God created the world (Genesis chapter 1). Through the Word made flesh (John 1:14), God saved the world. Words can be life-giving as well as life-threatening—life-giving by inspiring us to be all we were meant to be, and life-threatening by destroying our hopes and dashing our dreams. Ultimately, words move from being positive to being abusive when they hurt our hearts and harm our relationships. The Bible says,

"The tongue has the power of life and death"
(Proverbs 18:21).

A. What Differentiates Grievous Words from Gracious Words?

Words have the ability to build others up or to tear others down. Ephesians 4:29 says, "Do not let any unwholesome talk come out of your mouths, but only what is helpful for building others up according to their needs, that it may benefit those who listen."

GRIEVOUS WORDS THAT HURT	GRACIOUS WORDS THAT HEAL
• **Attacking a Person** — "You *are* inherently wrong." — "You *are* intrinsically bad."	• **Addressing an Action** — "You *did* something wrong." — "You did something bad."
• **Yelling** — "Shut up!" — "You look awful."	• **Discussing** — "Please listen, we need to talk about _____." — "Let's talk about what might be more appropriate for you to wear."
• **Name-calling** — "You stupid idiot!" — "You crazy fool!"	• **Instilling Hope** — "You are good at _____." — "You have positive qualities."
• **Insulting** — "You're worthless!" — "You're disgusting!"	• **Complimenting** — "You have tremendous value." — "You have many qualities I find appealing."
• **A Negative Picture of the Past** — "I wish you'd never been born." — "I should have had an abortion."	• **A Positive Picture of the Past** — "I was glad the day you were born." — "I knew God had a special purpose for you before you were ever born."
• **A Negative Picture of the Present** — "You can't do anything right." — "Get lost!"	• **A Positive Picture of the Present** — "You do a lot of things right." — "You'll always have a home in my heart."
• **A Negative Picture of the Future** — "You'll never amount to anything." — "You're hopeless."	• **A Positive Picture of the Future** — "God has a wonderful plan for your life." — "God has a future filled with hope for you."

"'I know the plans I have for you,' declares the LORD,
'plans to prosper you and not to harm you,
plans to give you hope and a future'"
(JEREMIAH 29:11).

B. What Are Some of the Many Faces of Abuse?

Abuse wears many faces—faces as varied as the people who give it or receive it. Abuse can be subtle or blatant, quiet or loud, smooth or abrasive. But with all its differences, abuse is always either verbal or nonverbal in delivery, and it always deeply impacts your personal and social life. As the psalmist said of an abuser:

"His speech is smooth as butter,
yet war is in his heart;
his words are more soothing than oil,
yet they are drawn swords"
(PSALM 55:21).

VERBAL ABUSE	NONVERBAL ABUSE
• Accusing	• Abandoning the family
• "Advising" excessively	• Abusing mentally, spiritually, emotionally, physically
• Backbiting	• Acting overly suspicious
• Badgering	• Arriving late as a form of control
• Bashing	• Being chronically irresponsible
• Belittling	• Brandishing weapons
• Betraying	• Changing rules continually
• Blame-shifting	• Committing adultery
• Brainwashing	• Damaging property
• Breaking promises	• Deceiving others
• Bullying	• Displaying excessive jealousy
• Complaining chronically	• Driving recklessly
• Controlling conversations	
• Criticizing unjustly or excessively	

VERBAL ABUSE	NONVERBAL ABUSE
• Cursing	• Embezzling funds
• Degrading	• Excluding others
• Demanding compliance	• Favoring others
• Demanding false confessions	• Forcing sex or encouraging sexual perversion
• Demanding that unrealistic expectations be met	• Giving unsolicited "help" to manipulate
• Demeaning	• Glaring condescendingly
• Denying that the abuse ever occurred	• Hanging up the phone on someone
• Denying that the abuse is wrong	• Hiding items (car/house keys, money, jewelry, important documents)
• Destroying credibility	• Ignoring
• Dictating orders	• Interfering with another's work
• Disgracing	• Interrupting sleep
• Gossiping	• Intimidating physically
• Humiliating	• Invading another's personal space
• Insulting	• Isolating from family
• Interrupting constantly	• Killing another's pet
• Laughing at abusive behavior	• Making insulting gestures
• Lying or twisting the truth	• Making unwanted visits
• Making fun of a person's fear	• Manipulating with excessive gifts
• Making negative comparisons to others	• Monitoring another's phone calls
• Making racial slurs	• Opening another's mail
• Manipulating children	• Ostracizing
• Minimizing what is wrong	• Overindulging to get control
• Mocking	
• Name-calling	
• Playing verbal mind games	

VERBAL ABUSE	NONVERBAL ABUSE
• Ridiculing	• Playing cruel tricks
• Scapegoating	• Pouting with pity parties
• Shaming	• Prohibiting another's decision making
• Slandering	• Prohibiting friendships with others
• Speaking profanity	• Prohibiting private conversations
• Switching reality	• Raping
• Teasing	• Refusing to leave when asked
• Terrorizing	• Refusing to listen or validate feelings
• Threatening	• Rejecting one's own child
• Threatening suicide in order to control	• Slamming doors and drawers
• Twisting Scripture	• Sneering
• Undermining other relationships	• Stalking
• Using coarse talk	• Stealing
• Using put-downs	• Threatening with gestures
• Violating the context of conversations	• Walking away as a power play
• Wounding with sarcasm	• Withdrawing emotionally
• Yelling/screaming	• Withholding love, compliments, credit, or finances

C. What Characterizes Classic Passive-Aggressive Behavior?

Passive-aggressive behavior is a form of *covert control. Overt abuse*—such as bashing someone physically, a verbal rage, or name-calling—is easy to identify. But *covert abuse*—such as shunning, slighting, or ignoring someone—can be much more subversive and difficult to detect, though it is just as emotionally abusive.

Passive-aggressive people express anger indirectly and seek to control others in evasive, underhanded, or deceitful ways. While some people seem unaware that they engage in such hurtful behavior patterns, others are quite intentional about it. The Bible makes it clear that…

> *"No one who practices deceit will dwell in my house;*
> *no one who speaks falsely will stand in my presence"*
> (PSALM 101:7).

The tactics used in this type of emotional abuse may include the following:

- Invalidating

  "I never said that." "Your recall is wrong." "I don't know what you are talking about."

- Minimizing

  "You're just too sensitive." "You're exaggerating." "You're making a big deal out of nothing."

- Countering

  "You couldn't possibly feel that way." "You've got it all wrong." "You don't know what you're talking about."

- Trivializing

  "If you had really studied for the test, you would have gotten 100 instead of 98." "Your efforts really fell short." "You're giving yourself too much credit."

Methods of Sabotage

To gain covert control and power, the passive-aggressive, emotionally abusive person will use some of the following methods:[16]

- Foster chaos

  Control others by intentionally leaving work and projects incomplete

- Tell lies or half-truths

  Control others with unjustified excuses for not fulfilling commitments

- Procrastinate

  Control others by intentionally missing deadlines, thus displaying no regard for the negative impact on others

- Be chronically late

  Control others by keeping people waiting

- Be ambiguous

  Control others by sending mixed messages, leaving others in a wake of confusion about what was said or what was meant

- Caustic counsel

  Control others by offering unsolicited advice on a continual basis

- Be passively indifferent

  Control others by giving the impression that their concerns are heard and important, but then disregarding them

- Manipulative protecting and helping

  Control others by extending help with the intention of causing a sense of indebtedness

- Be a quick-change artist

  Control others by changing the subject and diverting attention from conversations that feel personally threatening

- Withhold affirmation

  Control others by failing to give deserved compliments and deserved credit

- Cross boundaries

  Control others by taking advantage of those with few or no personal boundaries

When Saul's men were sent to watch David's house and to kill him, David prayed,

> *"For the sins of their mouths, for the words of their lips,*
> *let them be caught in their pride"*
> (PSALM 59:12).

D. What Are Examples of Emotionally Abusive Rejection?

Rejection is common to all of us. At one time or another we have been unjustly rejected by a prospective employer, not chosen by a team captain, jilted by a suitor, or ignored by an acquaintance. In those types of instances, the hurt doesn't usually last long or leave permanent scars. However, there are some types of rejection that can cut like a knife or pierce us like an arrow to the heart.

> *"Not a word from their mouth can be trusted;*
> *their heart is filled with destruction.*
> *Their throat is an open grave;*
> *with their tongue they speak deceit"*
> (PSALM 5:9).

- **Examples of overt, abusive rejection** include a parent who...
  — deserts the family.
  — tells a child, "I wish you had never been born."
  — tells a child, "You are a disgrace to this family."
  — tells a child, "You're just like your sorry father."
  — tells a child, "I wish you were more like your brother."
  — tells a child, "You will never amount to anything."
  — tells a child, "You were a mistake... You were an accident... You are the wrong gender."

> *"I cannot lift my head, for I am full of shame*
> *and drowned in my affliction"*
> (JOB 10:15).

- **Examples of covert, abusive rejection** include a parent who...
  — constantly raises the bar with unreasonable standards and demands more than the child is capable of giving.
  — withholds love.

— overindulges.

— overprotects.

— divorces and begins to withdraw.

— commits suicide.

> *"See, O LORD, how distressed I am! I am in torment within,*
> *and in my heart I am disturbed"*
> (LAMENTATIONS 1:20).

E. What Is the Cost of Constant Abuse?

There is always a price to be paid for pain, a loss to be incurred by the recipient of abusive words and hurtful gestures. The cost is often unseen—an extensive, inner deprivation that can continue to damage the soul for a lifetime. As the wisest among men wrote…

> *"The tongue that brings healing is a tree of life,*
> *but a deceitful tongue crushes the spirit"*
> (PROVERBS 15:4).

Victims of Abuse May Experience…

- Loss of self-worth . . . . increased self-doubt
- Loss of self-confidence . . . . increased self-consciousness
- Loss of self-perception . . . . increased self-criticism
- Loss of happiness . . . . increased emotional flatness
- Loss of freedom . . . . increased vigilance
- Loss of inner peace . . . . increased peace-at-all-costs behavior
- Loss of self-assurance . . . . . increased insecurity
- Loss of security . . . . increased desire to escape
- Loss of trust . . . . increased distrust
- Loss of sexual identity . . . . . increased sexual confusion

- Loss of a clear conscience . . increased guilt or shame
- Loss of friendship . . . . increased isolation
- Loss of faith . . . . increased fear
- Loss of safety . . . . increased anxiety
- Loss of self-respect . . . . increased self-destruction
- Loss of optimism . . . . increased pessimism
- Loss of pride . . . . increased self-hatred
- Loss of hope . . . . increased despair

The Bible says,

> "Those God foreknew he also predestined
> to be conformed to the likeness of his Son"
> (ROMANS 8:29).

F. What Characterizes Healthy vs. Unhealthy Relationships?

Are you in an abusive relationship? Have you experienced an unhealthy dynamic between you and someone close to you? Many people fail to recognize that they are in an abusive relationship because abuse has been "their normal" for so long. If you look closely, you can evaluate the health of any relationship by seeing the type of fruit it produces—whether the fruit is good or bad. Jesus said,

> "A good tree cannot bear bad fruit, and
> a bad tree cannot bear good fruit.
> Every tree that does not bear good fruit is cut down
> and thrown into the fire.
> Thus, by their fruit you will recognize them"
> (MATTHEW 7:18-20).

======= *The Fruit Test* =======

As a help for realistically evaluating a relationship close to you, take "The Fruit Test." On the left side of each fruit, mark *yes* or *no* for yourself, and on the right side, mark *yes* or *no* for the other person in the relationship.

CIRCLE "Y" FOR YES AND "N" FOR NO

FRUIT OF THE ABUSIVE SPIRIT (what sin produces)		FRUIT OF THE HOLY SPIRIT (what the Spirit produces)	
"If you keep on biting and devouring each other, watch out or you will be destroyed by each other... The acts of the sinful nature are obvious: sexual immorality, impurity and debauchery; idolatry and witchcraft; hatred, discord, jealousy, fits of rage, selfish ambition, dissensions, factions" (GALATIANS 5:15,19-20).		*"The fruit of the Spirit is love, joy, peace, patience, kindness, goodness, faithfulness, gentleness and self-control. Against such things there is no law"* (GALATIANS 5:22-23).	
Yourself	**Other Person**	**Yourself**	**Other Person**
Y/N **Biting** Y/N		Y/N **Love** Y/N	
Has a sharp, biting tongue that often hurts the heart		Seeks to do what is in the best interest of another	
Y/N **Devouring** Y/N		Y/N **Joy** Y/N	
Is so overpowering and dominant that the identity of another seems to be destroyed		Lives with an inner gladness of heart regardless of challenging circumstances	
Y/N **Hatred** Y/N		Y/N **Peace** Y/N	
Displays disdain or animosity toward another person		Displays tranquility in the midst of hardships and trials	
Y/N **Discord** Y/N		Y/N **Patience** Y/N	
Starts arguments that result in tension and strife		Endures difficulties calmly without complaint	

FRUIT OF THE ABUSIVE SPIRIT (what sin produces)		FRUIT OF THE HOLY SPIRIT (what the Spirit produces)	
Y/N **Jealousy** Y/N		Y/N **Kindness** Y/N	
Views others as rivals, and possessively wants to exclude them		Expresses genuine care and helps with a benevolent heart	
Y/N **Rage** Y/N		Y/N **Goodness** Y/N	
Displays out-of-control anger		Displays moral character and godly virtue with a pure heart	
Y/N **Selfishness** Y/N		Y/N **Faithfulness** Y/N	
Seeks to satisfy personal desires with little or no regard for the desires of another		Is loyal to appropriate significant relationships	
Y/N **Dissension** Y/N		Y/N **Gentleness** Y/N	
Frequently voices disagreements and disapproval		Treats others with sincere respect, displaying a soothing disposition	
Y/N **Factions** Y/N		Y/N **Self-control** Y/N	
Causes splits between others instead of seeking unity		Exercises restraint rather than choosing to be undisciplined	

(Ask someone close to you—someone you trust and who will tell you the truth—to help you evaluate your responses.)

The Bible says,

> *"Produce fruit in keeping with repentance"*
> (LUKE 3:8).

III. CAUSES OF VERBAL AND EMOTIONAL ABUSE

"How can he be so cruel?" "How can she be so insensitive?" "Why would he talk that way?" These are *real questions* that victims of abusers may ask. Understanding the *real answers* can give you wisdom and discernment regarding your relationships.

> *"Surely you desire truth in the inner parts;*
> *you teach me wisdom in the inmost place"*
> (PSALM 51:6).

A. What Breeding Ground Brings Forth Abusers?

Has someone implied that you are abusive? If this implication has a kernel of truth to it, do you want to change? In order to heal from the wounds of the past, you need to face the fact that your past was painful. After this acknowledgement, seek to understand the painful impact those wounds have had on your relationships, both past and present. At this point you can courageously choose to face the areas in your life that need healing, or you can refuse to do so and remain a victim of your past—and continue to make others a victim of your past as well.

If you choose the path of healing, cling to these words:

> *"Heal me, O Lord, and I will be healed;*
> *save me and I will be saved,*
> *for you are the one I praise"*
> (Jeremiah 17:14).

Background of Abusers

Evaluate your childhood. What were your relationships like during your preschool years? During your years in school? During your adolescence? What feelings do you remember? Were you usually sad, glad, mad, scared? The list below may help you to remember.

- I experienced some type of abuse from one or both of my parents.
- I felt "different" as a child.
- I felt belittled or bullied by my schoolmates.
- I stuffed my emotions.
- I learned my parents' ways of maintaining control.
- I didn't have a safe place to express my feelings.
- I thought that "my normal" was normal—but it wasn't.
- I never dealt with my underlying feelings of anger.
- I never developed sensitivity to the feelings of others.

Can you relate to this statement by the psalmist?

> *"I was overcome by trouble and sorrow"*
> (Psalm 116:3).

Childhood Feelings of Abusers

As children, those who become abusers usually felt singled out. They felt that they were different in at least several of these areas:

- Too short or too tall
- Too fat or too thin
- Too dark or too light (skin color)
- Physical features too large (nose, ears, feet)
- Physical features undesirable (freckles, acne, teeth, hair color)
- Athletically challenged (awkward or uncoordinated)
- Academically challenged (mentally slow, LD, ADD, or ADHD)
- Physically challenged (disability, poor eyesight, hearing problem, or speech difficulties)

Do you recognize the truth in these words of Jesus?

> *"Which of you by worrying can add one cubit to his stature?"*
> (MATTHEW 6:27 NKJV).

Predisposing Influences in the Childhood of Abusers

Not all children who experience abuse become abusers; however, *most abusers have been abused* in one way or another. This raises the question: Why do some children become abusers while others do not? Certain factors predispose future abusers to make particular choices about how they respond to their experiences. One thing they all have in common: Each young spirit was crushed by heartache. The Bible says,

> *"Heartache crushes the spirit"*
> (PROVERBS 15:13).

TEMPERAMENT

— The child is willful and assertive.

— The child is confident and forceful.

— The child lacks compassion and empathy for others.

— The child exerts power and control over peers.

PERSONALITY

— The child is aggressive and impulsive.

— The child is competent and secure.

— The child has an inflated ego and a sense of entitlement.

— The child is competitive and dominates relationships.

ENVIRONMENT

— The child experiences some form of abuse within the home.

— The child spends excessive, unsupervised hours watching violent TV programs and sitcoms laced with sarcasm.

— The child forms the belief that being mean to others is the best form of self-protection.

— The child is unable to express anger and frustration safely at home.

B. Why Do Some Inflict Abuse, and Others Receive or Reject Abuse?

Different Responses to Abuse

All children are affected by abusive treatment. Some take the path of succumbing to abuse and defining themselves by the negativity of that abuse. Others take the path of rising above the abuse and defining themselves by positive, character-building values.

> *"As for the deeds of men—by the word of your lips*
> *I have kept myself from the ways of the violent.*
> *My steps have held to your paths; my feet have not slipped"*
> (PSALM 17:4-5).

Different Paths to Travel

Many people wonder, *Why did I have to travel down this path of abuse?* You might not know the exact answer for some time. Or, you might never know the full answer, but you *can* know that as long as you continue to entrust your life to the Lord, He will direct your path each step of the way. Through Him, you can be an *overcomer.* You can be more than a conqueror over the abuse that now defeats you.

"In all these things we are more than conquerors
through him who loved us"
(ROMANS 8:37).

1. THE PATH OF VICTIMS

— Children *internalize* abusive experiences.

— Children *blame* themselves for the abuse.

— Children *feel* deserving of abuse.

— Children *seek out* abusers who look strong.

— Children *remain* victims of abusers.

2. THE PATH OF ABUSERS

— Children *internalize* abusive experiences.

— Children *blame* others for the abuse.

— Children *feel* that others are deserving of abuse.

— Children *seek out* the weak in order to look strong.

— Children *become* abusers.

3. THE PATH OF OVERCOMERS/CONQUERORS

— Children initially internalize their abusive experiences, but later *externalize* them.

— Children initially blame themselves or others for the abuse, but later *forgive* all involved in the abuse—including themselves.

— Children initially feel deserving of abuse, but later *feel* deserving of loving, trusting relationships.

— Children initially seek out abusers or victims, but later *seek out* well-adjusted people.

— Children initially remain victims or become abusers, but later reject both roles and *become* emotionally healthy.

Truly, the path to overcoming is through Christ:

"Thanks be to God!
He gives us the victory through our Lord Jesus Christ"
(1 CORINTHIANS 15:57).

===== **Staying in Abusive Relationships** =====

QUESTION: "Why do people who are being abused continue to stay in abusive relationships?"

ANSWER: One major reason is fear. Isaiah 21:4 says, "My heart falters, fear makes me tremble." Abusers can use fear as a powerful weapon to control another person. One effective strategy they use to instill fear is to communicate demeaning messages, such as verbal threats that warn of physical harm. Another tactic for creating fear is to leave or to withdraw emotional support.

Ultimately, the resulting fear is that of not having the three basic needs met—the needs for love, significance, and security.[17] Yet the Lord wants us to turn from fear to faith and to trust Him to meet our deepest needs.

> *"Fear of man will prove to be a snare,*
> *but whoever trusts in the LORD is kept safe"*
> (PROVERBS 29:25).

C. What Is the Root Cause of Abusive Relationships?

Clarifying the Impact of Relationships

Healthy relationships are those in which the people involved have a clearly defined sense of their own identities. Without a clear understanding of who we are and of the worth God has given us, it is hard to maintain functional, ongoing relationships that enrich everyone involved. A relationship will not always be smooth, but it can provide a safe, trusting environment in which there is no fear of intimacy and where each person knows how to communicate personal needs and desires to the other.

Unhealthy relationships generally reflect an inability to understand and work within appropriate boundaries. Because unhealthy boundaries are almost always the result of being raised in some variation of a dysfunctional family, the likelihood that children raised in such families will develop healthy boundaries without some form of direct intervention is minimal.

The pain that children experience from not having their God-given needs for love, significance, and security[18] met in childhood carries over into each subsequent relationship—in which they are likely to expect or insist that these needs be met, often in illegitimate or abusive ways.

Sadly, abusive fathers fail to take to heart this admonition of Scripture:

"Fathers, do not exasperate your children;
instead, bring them up in the training and instruction of the Lord"
(Ephesians 6:4).

Correcting the Beliefs of Victims

Wrong Belief of Victims

"I am responsible for the way others treat me. I deserve to be mistreated because, at my very core, I am a bad person. Therefore, bad things should happen to me. If I would just be a better person, people would treat me better. I don't have a choice about being mistreated. I must be doing something wrong or I wouldn't be treated this way. If I just try harder to do what is expected, I can make things better. If I can't, maybe I deserve to be unhappy."

Right Belief of Victims

"I realize that I have been living a lie, believing that I am to blame for being mistreated and believing that my happiness will come from a human relationship. I have a choice about how I respond to anyone who mistreats me. I don't want to have a false loyalty to anyone who abuses me. Nor do I want to have the false expectation that if I can just change, the abuse will stop. I will no longer live for the approval of others; instead, I will rely on the Lord to meet my inner needs. My value and worth come from Him alone, and He loves me unconditionally. Only the Lord can meet all my needs."

"Am I now trying to win the approval of men, or of God?
Or am I trying to please men? If I were still trying to please men,
I would not be a servant of Christ"
(Galatians 1:10).

Correcting the Beliefs of Abusers

Wrong Belief of Abusers

"I am not responsible for the way I treat others; they are to blame. If people wouldn't make me mad, I wouldn't treat them badly. They are the ones who should change, not me. There's nothing wrong with me. People just need to accept me the way I am."

Right Belief of Abusers

"I realize that I am responsible for the way I respond to others. No one deserves to be mistreated. No matter how people act toward me, how I act toward them is my choice. If I have given my heart to Jesus, then God has given me the power, through His Holy Spirit within me, to treat everyone with love and respect. I don't need to try to control people because God is in control, and He is the only one who can meet my deepest needs." This right belief is based on the exhortation to

> *"be compassionate and humble. Do not repay evil with evil*
> *or insult with insult, but with blessing, because to this you*
> *were called so that you may inherit a blessing"*
> (1 PETER 3:8-9).

═══════════ Overcoming Damage from the Past ═══════════

QUESTION: "How can I overcome the damage that I suffered in my past? Why do I keep repeating the same unhealthy relational patterns, and how can I change these harmful behaviors?"

ANSWER: God often allows difficulties in life to wake us up to our need to understand our personal attitudes and actions, and then with that understanding we can take responsibility for them. You will find yourself drawn to the same relational dynamics over and over until you overcome the past by allowing God to train you through discipline, and thus to produce a harvest of peace and righteousness in you. Truly...

> *"God disciplines us for our good, that we may share in his holiness.*
> *No discipline seems pleasant at the time, but painful.*
> *Later on, however, it produces a harvest of righteousness*
> *and peace for those who have been trained by it"*
> (HEBREWS 12:10-11).

IV. STEPS TO SOLUTION

A. A Key Verse to Memorize

> *"Love does no harm to its neighbor.*
> *Therefore love is the fulfillment of the law"*
> (ROMANS 13:10).

B. A Key Passage to Read and Reread

Have you ever spilled a glass of milk and watched helplessly as it poured across the tabletop and over the edges onto the floor below? You wish you could somehow catch it and pour it back into the glass, but the liquid flows all too quickly between your fingers and cannot be contained. You are left with a mess to clean up.

It normally takes just a few minutes to wash a table and clean up spilled milk splashed across the floor. But it takes much longer when it comes to cleaning up after our hurtful words. Once they have been spilled onto a person, damaging the soul and inflicting great emotional pain, it takes time and the healing counsel of God's Word to restore wholeness and repair the abusive relationship. And if there is no repentance from the abuser and no help sought by the abused, the effects of verbal and emotional abuse can last a lifetime, causing permanent scars of sorrow on the heart of the abused. God hears and judges your every word as it spills out from the overflow of your heart!

"How can you who are evil say anything good?
For out of the overflow of the heart the mouth speaks.
The good man brings good things out of the good stored up in him,
and the evil man brings evil things out of the evil stored up in him.
But I tell you that men will have to give account
on the day of judgment for every careless word they have spoken.
For by your words you will be acquitted,
and by your words you will be condemned"
(MATTHEW 12:34-37).

═══════════════ *Words* ═══════════════

W—Words that are good do not come from the mouths
of those who are evil. . . . . verse 34

O—Out of the overflow of your heart come the words
you say. . . . . verse 34

R—Righteousness flows from good that is stored in
your heart. . . . . verse 35

D—Deeds of evil are stored in the heart of one who is evil. . . verse 35

S—Spoken words said in carelessness will bring
condemnation to the speaker on the day
of judgment. . . . . verses 36-37

C. How to Identify the Language of Love

Abuse occurs when one person repeatedly interacts with another person in an unloving manner. Abuse violates the way God tells us to love one another. The best description of love is found in 1 Corinthians chapter 13, often called the Love Chapter. If you wonder whether you are being verbally abused, write out the exact words spoken to you and ask yourself…

- "How does this make me feel?"
- "Does this sound like a conversation between those who respect each other?"
- "Does this sound like a conversation between those who care for each other?"
- "Would Jesus speak to me in this way?"
- "If I said these words, how would the other person react?"

Compare the words spoken to you with God's description of love in 1 Corinthians 13:4-8 and the standard He has set for us:

> *"Love is patient, love is kind.*
> *It does not envy, it does not boast, it is not proud.*
> *It is not rude, it is not self-seeking,*
> *it is not easily angered, it keeps no record of wrongs.*
> *Love does not delight in evil but rejoices with the truth.*
> *It always protects, always trusts, always hopes, always perseveres.*
> *Love never fails"*
> (1 CORINTHIANS 13:4-8).

The Language of Love Inventory

LOVE IS…	YES OR NO?
Patient—Are these words spoken in haste?	_____
Kind—Are these words unkind?	_____

LOVE IS NOT…
Proud—Are these words prideful? _____
Rude—Are these words disrespectful? _____
Self-seeking—Are these words self-serving? _____
Easily angered—Are these words hostile? _____

LOVE DOES NOT…
Envy—Are these words selfishly possessive? _____
Boast—Are these words bragging? _____
Delight in evil—Are these words malicious? _____

LOVE ALWAYS…
Protects—Do these words attack? _____
Trusts—Do these words create doubt? _____
Hopes—Do these words create despair? _____
Perseveres—Do these words lessen motivation? _____

LOVE…
Keeps no record of wrongs—Are these words based
    on past wrongs? _____
Rejoices with the truth—Do these words reflect
    untruthfulness? _____
Never fails—Do these words reflect loss of love? _____

The Bible says,

> *"Love must be sincere.*
> *Hate what is evil; cling to what is good"*
> (ROMANS 12:9).

D. How to Have Victory over Verbal Abuse

Is there any hope for those who have been verbally abused? Granted, change doesn't come overnight, but with hard, consistent work progress can be made…authentic change can occur…and victory can be achieved.

Those who seek to control or to overpower you with verbal bombardments may not be as strong and self-assured as they appear. If they express inappropriate anger toward you, realize that their assaults are not about you, but about them! The source of their insensitive attacks is a heart that suffers from emotional pains or dysfunctions from the past and from their choice to respond to those pains by abusing others. In addition, keep in mind that you may have unresolved anger from abuse in your own past that magnifies the abuse you are experiencing now. If that is the case, the Bible has this helpful word of instruction:

> *"Get rid of all bitterness, rage and anger, brawling and slander,*
> *along with every form of malice.*
> *Be kind and compassionate to one another, forgiving each other,*
> *just as in Christ God forgave you"*
> (Ephesians 4:31-32).

Steps to Victory

1. Face the Problem

- Decide to identify any verbal abuse. Does the other person...
  - — say things that seem designed to make you feel guilty?
  - — claim always to be right?
  - — put you down in humorous or sarcastic ways?
  - — become your "judge and jury"?
  - — bring up the past over and over?
- Decide that you will no longer tolerate the abusive behavior.
- Decide to communicate your position to the abuser.
- Decide that you will look at and resolve your anger from past or present verbal abuse.

The Bible says,

> *"Search me, O God, and know my heart;*
> *test me and know my anxious thoughts.*
> *See if there is any offensive way in me,*
> *and lead me in the way everlasting"*
> (Psalm 139:23-24).

2. UNDERSTAND THE SOURCE OF THE PROBLEM

- Know that many verbal abusers were themselves abused or neglected in one way or another as children. (Some, however, were not abused as children and simply learned abusive behavior later in life.)

- Know that verbal abusers lack sympathy and feel justified in their abuse.

- Know that uncontrolled outbursts of anger can be triggered by depression, fear, hurt, stress, anxiety, worry, frustration, or insecurity.

- Know that you are *not* the cause of the abuse (although you will be blamed).

The Bible says...

> *"The heart of the discerning acquires knowledge;*
> *the ears of the wise seek it out"*
> (PROVERBS 18:15).

3. CONFRONT THE PROBLEM PERSON

- Communicate an attitude of caring.
    "I want you to know that I care about you."

- Communicate that you have been deeply hurt by the abusive behavior.
    "I feel deeply hurt by your tone of voice when you talk to me."

- Communicate your desire for a positive relationship, but make it clear that you will no longer tolerate verbal attacks.
    "I want to support you and I want us to have a good relationship, but I will no longer tolerate abusive behavior from you."

- Communicate truth without condemnation or judging.
    "I want our relationship to continue, but if you choose to continue belittling me, I will know that you don't value me. We therefore have no basis for a relationship, and I will leave."

The Bible says,

> *"The wise in heart are called discerning,*
> *and pleasant words promote instruction"*
> (Proverbs 16:21).

4. Take Responsibility for Yourself

- Resist becoming defensive.
- Resist retreating into a shell.
- Resist playing the familiar victim-martyr role.
- Resist seeking retaliation.

The Bible says,

> *"Do not repay anyone evil for evil.*
> *Be careful to do what is right in the eyes of everybody.*
> *If it is possible, as far as it depends on you,*
> *live at peace with everyone"*
> (Romans 12:17-18).

5. View the Abusive Person from God's Perspective

- See the person as someone for whom Christ died.
- See the person as having God-given worth.
- See the person as capable of being changed by Christ.
- See the person as having legitimate God-given needs that God alone can meet and that God is willing to meet.

The Bible says,

> *"Be completely humble and gentle;*
> *be patient, bearing with one another in love."*
> (Ephesians 4:2).

6. Love Unconditionally

- Love is not a feeling, but a commitment to do what is right.
- Love looks for legitimate ways to meet the needs of another.

- Love seeks to do what is in the best interests of another.
- Love says, "I care about our relationship, and I will work to make it a positive, healthy one."

The Bible says,

> *"Hatred stirs up dissension,*
> *but love covers over all wrongs"*
> (Proverbs 10:12).

7. Practice a Powerful Prayer Life

- Remember that God cares about both of you more than you care about each other.
- Remember that prayer is the surest path to healing and wholeness.
- Remember that you need to pray for healing for both you and your abuser.
- Remember to thank God for all that He is teaching you in the midst of this trying time.

The Bible says,

> *"Pray continually; give thanks in all circumstances,*
> *for this is God's will for you in Christ Jesus"*
> (1 Thessalonians 5:17-18).

E. How to Change the Course of an Abusive Relationship

You can curtail verbal and emotional abuse by developing a plan to prevent yourself from being controlled. You cannot change another person, but you can change yourself so that the abusive tactics used on you in the past are no longer effective and cease to ensnare you. As you determine the appropriate boundaries, realize that these boundaries are designed to guard your soul—your mind, will, and emotions. The Bible says,

> *"In the paths of the wicked lie thorns and snares,*
> *but he who guards his soul stays far from them"*
> (Proverbs 22:5).

Determining Your Plan of Action

1. **State clearly, in a conversation or a letter, what you are willing to accept and not accept from the abuser.**[19]

   — Communicate your position in a positive way.

   — Do not justify yourself. Do not be apologetic, just state the boundary:

   — "I want our relationship to continue, but...

   > ...I am not willing to listen to your name-calling."

   > ...I am not willing to hear your accusations concerning (*name*) any longer."

   — Talking negatively is counterproductive.

   > ..."I am not willing to be controlled by your silent treatment any longer."

   — Keep your statements short and succinct.

Remember:

> *"A man of knowledge uses words with restraint,*
> *and a man of understanding is even-tempered"*
> (PROVERBS 17:27).

2. **Announce the consequence you will enforce if the abuser violates your requests.**

   — Your response should be a matter of separating yourself from the abuser.

   — You cannot change the abuser's behavior, but you can remove yourself from frequent exposure to unacceptable behavior.

   — "I want to visit with you, but...

   > ...if you call me a name again, I will leave for a period of time."

   > ...if you persist in making that accusation, I will end our conversation."

...if you give me the silent treatment, I will go and find someone else to talk with."

— Consequences are part of God's divine plan.

Remember:

> *"A man reaps what he sows"*
> (GALATIANS 6:7).

3. Enforce the consequence every single time abuse occurs.

— Do not bluff! The abuser needs to know that you are going to act consistently on your words.

— Plan on the abuser testing you multiple times.

— In your mind and heart...

  • Say *no* to manipulation.

  • Say *no* to pressure.

  • Say *no* to control.

– Eventually your abuser will stop using an abusive tactic—but only after that tactic proves ineffective.

Remember:

> *"Let your 'Yes' be yes, and your 'No,' no"*
> (JAMES 5:12).

4. Hold your ground and absolutely do not negotiate.

— Because verbal abusers do not use words fairly, negotiation will not work.

— Instead of being willing to talk out the problem, your abuser will seek to wear you out.

— Simply state that when the behavior stops, you look forward to a renewed relationship.

  • "I am not willing to discuss this topic any longer."

  • "I have stated clearly what I will not accept."

  • "When you are ready to respect my requests, let me

know. I look forward to enjoying being together at that time."

— Keep your words brief and to the point.

Remember:

> *"When words are many, sin is not absent,*
> *but he who holds his tongue is wise"*
> (PROVERBS 10:19).

5. **Respond when your boundary is violated—never react on gut emotion or out of anger.**

— Expect the abuser to violate your boundary, but don't react.

— Expect the abuser to violate your boundary again…and again! But don't react.

— If you react, you will find yourself back under the control of the abuser.

— Respond by detaching yourself from the abuser and enforcing your repercussions.

  • Do not *cry* because you feel hurt.

  • Do not *beg* because you feel fearful.

  • Do not *explode* because you feel frustrated.

Remember:

> *"The end of a matter is better than its beginning,*
> *and patience is better than pride.*
> *Do not be quickly provoked in your spirit,*
> *for anger resides in the lap of fools"*
> (ECCLESIASTES 7:8-9).

6. **Solicit the support of one or two wise, objective people to help you through this process.**

— Include supporters as you analyze and identify the problem.

— Include supporters as you determine how to articulate your plan.

— Include supporters as you enforce the repercussions.

— Include supporters—friend, mentor, counselor—to help you through this critical period.

- Discuss the situation with your supporters.
- Discuss the tactics used on you.
- Discuss the plan of action.

Remember:

"Listen to advice and accept instruction,
and in the end you will be wise"
(Proverbs 19:20).

The time it takes to defuse a volatile, abusive relationship is limited. But during that limited time...

- Expect manipulative maneuvers and emotional ups and downs.
- Assume your actions will make the abuser angry.
- Allow your abuser to react without reacting yourself.
- Do not seek to placate this person—it won't work.

Think of this time period as comparable to having surgery. It is a painful experience, but it provides the only hope for healing and having a new, healthy relationship.

Remember:

"The tongue of the wise brings healing"
(Proverbs 12:18).

F. How to Confront and Cope with Emotionally Abusive People

Although victims of verbal and emotional abuse generally feel inadequate and powerless to stop an abusive relationship, appropriate confrontation is often necessary to defuse such abuse. Ignoring it won't make it go away. Wishful thinking won't make it better. And believing that loyalty means remaining quiet is dangerously erroneous.

When hurtful words and actions are exposed as unacceptable and viewed as intolerable, the foundation is laid for change to occur. That change will come slowly and will likely be met with much resistance by the abuser. When power is the goal and control is at stake, an unrepentant abuser will repeatedly change tactics in an attempt to maneuver around each boundary you set, always looking for some way to put you in a position to be manipulated. To remain silent in such a relationship is not love but fear, and is harmful rather than helpful. [20]

According to God's Word…

"Better is open rebuke than hidden love"
(PROVERBS 27:5).

Start Educating Yourself

- *Emotional abuse can go on for years* before victims realize the dynamic in the relationship isn't normal.
- *Abusers are calculating, and their behavior is deliberate.* It is designed to keep them in control.
- *Much of your discouragement will begin to dissipate* once your eyes are opened to the tactical behavior of the abuser. Only then will you be able to establish a more level playing field.

Heed the words of the wisest man who ever lived on earth:

"Let the wise listen and add to their learning,
and let the discerning get guidance"
(PROVERBS 1:5).

Set Boundaries [21]

- *Communicate that you will no longer be treated with disrespect.*
  "I feel greatly disrespected because of the way you are treating me. I will not stay here if you continue to disrespect me."
- *Specify what behavior is unacceptable.*
  "I won't continue to talk with you if you continually interrupt me."
- *Refuse to accept excuses and reasons for repeated inconsiderate behavior.*
  Suppose the other person says, "I didn't mean to be late; some people I needed to see came by." You can respond in a firm but

pleasant tone, "That does not make what you did acceptable because you could have phoned me. From now on—unless you call—I will go on with my plans without you."

The Bible says,

"Pleasant words are a honeycomb,
sweet to the soul and healing to the bones"
(PROVERBS 16:24).

Seize the Moment

- *Speak up as soon as the abuser begins to change the subject* or to twist your words around to mean something other than what you intended.

    "You just changed the meaning of my words. I didn't say that. What I said was (_____). Now, what are you hearing me say?"

- *Repeat back to the abuser* the incorrect or unreasonable words said to you.

    "What you are saying is (_____). Is that accurate?"

- *Remain calm.* Your abuser wants a strong reaction from you.

    "Do we need to discuss this at a later time? If you want to continue now, I need you to speak with more restraint, or this conversation will have to wait."

Remember this truth:

"The quiet words of the wise are more to be heeded
than the shouts of a ruler of fools"
(ECCLESIASTES 9:17).

Seek to Surface the Abuser's Hostility

- *Acknowledge that you sense anger* in your abuser.

    "I sense that you are feeling angry."

- *Confirm that being angry is permissible.* Never attempt to humor an abuser out of anger.

    "At times anger is justified."

- *Help your abuser recognize the cause of the anger,* but don't try to psychoanalyze the individual.

  Ask, "What triggered your anger?"

Realize...

> *"The purposes of a man's heart are deep waters,*
> *but a man of understanding draws them out"*
> (PROVERBS 20:5).

Soften the Confrontation Process

- *Confront the behavior,* not the person.

  "I care about you, but I dislike what you are doing. What can I do to help you stop (_____)?"

- *Avoid threats, sarcasm, hostility, put-downs, or judgment* of the other person's intentions.

  "If you are angry with me, talk with me and help me to understand why. But please stop your present behavior."

- *Ask again if necessary* (respectfully), when you don't get a clear, direct answer.

  "Let me ask again. Why did you tell me you were coming to the ceremony, but then never showed up?"

Take to heart this admonition from God's Word:

> *"Live a life worthy of the calling you have received.*
> *Be completely humble and gentle;*
> *be patient, bearing with one another in love.*
> *Make every effort to keep the unity of the Spirit*
> *through the bond of peace"*
> (EPHESIANS 4:1-3).

Stay in the Present

- *Focus on the issue at hand.*

  "I need for us to focus on this issue and to resolve it."

- *Don't bring up past issues.*

    "We cannot change the past, but we can do things differently now."

- *Don't let the other person get you off track.*

    "I realize this topic may bring up other issues, but we need to stay on this subject for now and find a solution for it."

Apply this counsel from God's Word:

> *"Let your eyes look straight ahead, fix your gaze directly before you.*
> *Make level paths for your feet and take only ways that are firm.*
> *Do not swerve to the right or the left; keep your foot from evil"*
> (Proverbs 4:25-27).

Squelch Unrealistic Expectations

- *Don't put all of your hope in the expectation that an abuser will change,* but put your confidence in God and His sufficiency.

- *Be aware that you cannot make the abuser change* no matter what you do, how much you try, or how good you are as a person.

- *Know that change will occur only after the abuser admits to having a problem* and begins to receive the help and support needed to turn from that problem.

Keep the following in mind:

> *"If we claim to be without sin,*
> *we deceive ourselves and the truth is not in us.*
> *If we confess our sins,*
> *he is faithful and just and will forgive us our sins*
> *and purify us from all unrighteousness"*
> (1 John 1:8-9).

Strengthen Your Relationship with the Lord

- *Look first to the Lord for discernment* about your relationship.

- *Ask the Lord to give you wisdom, insight, and direction* as you seek to honor Him in all your relationships.

- *Read Scripture and take God at His word* in order to renew your mind so that you will not continue to live as a victim, but as a victor.

- *Get involved in a Bible study.* Memorize and daily rehearse Scripture passages that emphasize your worth and the authority you have as a child of God.

- *Live dependently on Christ,* who lives within you.

- *Don't try to live out of your own resources.* Multiple times throughout the day, present yourself to the Lord and acknowledge your total dependence upon His resources.

Remember these words from the Lord to the apostle Paul, and Paul's response:

> "'My grace is sufficient for you,
> for my power is made perfect in weakness.'
> Therefore I will boast all the more gladly about my weaknesses,
> so that Christ's power may rest on me"
> (2 CORINTHIANS 12:9).

G. How to Build Personal Boundaries

All countries have clear geographical boundaries, and many protect these boundaries by exercising strict control over who enters or leaves. In addition, all countries have laws that apply to everyone living or traveling within those boundaries. People must do the same when it comes to protecting themselves.[22] Certainly we don't need to use roadblocks, soldiers, and guns, but God does want us to establish personal boundaries in our relationships so we can preserve our emotional health and protect the treasure God has in us. We need to carefully guard who has access to our hearts and minds.

Do you feel that someone often takes advantage of you? Are you expected to meet all the needs of someone else? Do certain people expect you to help them but then fail to help you when needs arise? Does someone take advantage of you at work by relentlessly piling on one task after another? Do you feel manipulated by someone's lies, half-truths, procrastination, and lateness? Those are the results when you lack emotional boundaries. When those kinds of breaches occur often, they become significant threats to your freedom to serve God and become all He wants you to be. Learn to *draw the line* with people who cross your boundaries and put you in bondage. You can do this by remembering this truth:

> *"It is for freedom that Christ has set us free.*
> *Stand firm, then, and do not let yourselves*
> *be burdened again by a yoke of slavery"*
> (Galatians 5:1).

Step #1: Place Boundaries Around Your Heart

Be careful where and upon whom you spend your emotions. Put firm boundaries around the things in which you are emotionally invested. Completely giving your heart away will cause you to stumble and will cause your devotion to turn from God to someone else.

> *"Above all else, guard your heart,*
> *for it is the wellspring of life"*
> (Proverbs 4:23).

Step #2: Learn that It's Okay to Say No

Many people who lack boundaries are not in touch with their true feelings. Or if they are, they don't think they have the right to say no. Do not listen to lies about being selfish or uncaring when you refuse to comply with someone's wishes. Jesus set boundaries while He was here on earth, and at times He found it necessary to say no to people, including His disciples. He knew there are times when it's best to say no. Jesus said,

> *"Let your 'Yes' be 'Yes,' and your 'No,' 'No'"*
> (Matthew 5:37).

Step #3: Start Being Assertive

People who are nonassertive would benefit from assertiveness training classes. Nonassertive behavior allows others to violate your personal rights; by your behavior, you actually permit the infringement. The reason people typically give for being nonassertive is to avoid any kind of conflict, but the consequences are horrendously hurt feelings and deeply devalued self-worth. Assertively standing up for yourself in a respectful, appropriate manner is in accord with these instructions from Jesus:

"If your brother sins against you,
go and show him his fault, just between the two of you.
If he listens to you, you have won your brother over"
(MATTHEW 18:15).

======= *Assertiveness Training 101* =======

WAYS TO DELIVER YOUR MESSAGE WITHOUT INCITING ANGER

"WHEN I..."

Describe a specific behavior of the other person that violates one of your boundaries.

- "When I hear your anger escalate, I get concerned."
- "When I hear that several people have been invited for dinner and I have not been given sufficient advance notice, I am caught off guard."

"THE RESULT IS..."

Describe specifically how the other person's behavior affects your life and, as a result, how you feel. (Avoid saying, "You make me...")

- "The result is I feel hurt and frustrated because I think that instead of *yelling*, we should be *talking* about the problem."
- "The result is I feel embarrassed, ill-prepared, and inadequate because I might not have enough food on hand to prepare, and I also feel taken advantage of."

"I WOULD..."

Describe what you would like to hear or to have happen.

- "I would appreciate you being aware when you start getting angry so you can consciously choose to speak in a more normal tone of voice."
- "I would appreciate your checking with me before asking anyone to join us for dinner."

Step #4: Draw the Line

Each of us have personal, emotional, and physical boundaries that should not be crossed and certainly not invaded. Do you know your specific boundaries? Do you know how to respond when your boundaries have been trampled? Do you know where to draw the line? To help identify your boundaries, pay attention when your emotions are intense, dark, or guilt-ridden in response to something someone has said or done to you. That's a sign your boundaries are being crossed. The following responses will help you educate those in your life who are verbally and emotionally crossing the line! Remember:

> *"Wounds from a friend can be trusted,*
> *but an enemy multiplies kisses"*
> (Proverbs 27:6).

Ways to Draw the Line

INFORM: "Do you realize you are speaking loudly?"
"Do you know how your words sound?"
"Do you know that you are saying things that make me feel uncomfortable?"

IDENTIFY: "Please lower your voice."
"Please stop using that kind of language."
"Please explain your anger."

IMPLORE: "Stop insulting me with your words."
"Stop these painful outbursts."
"Stop hurting me in this way."

INSIST: "You must stop speaking to me in that tone of voice."
"You will have to change this way of communicating with me."
"You may not continue to degrade me in this way."

INSTRUCT: "I will no longer allow you to hurt me like this."
"I will no longer allow you to talk to me this way."
"I will no longer allow that tone of voice in my presence."

INVITE: "I am open to working this out when you choose to be reasonable."

> "I care about you and our relationship, but you must change
> your ways of communicating with me."
>
> "I am willing to go to counseling with you if you will agree to
> do so."

IMPACT: "I am now leaving in order to protect myself."

"Because this behavior is unacceptable to me, I am going to
distance myself from you for awhile."

"If you continue with this behavior, I will consider all my
options regarding our relationship."

Step #5: Appropriate God's Will for Your Life

Are your emotions and will dominated by a strong, controlling personality? Close the door on your fear of displeasing others, particularly your abuser, by establishing boundaries. Begin to redefine your own, separate identity by daily choosing to live according to God's will.

> *"You did not receive a spirit that makes you a slave again to fear,*
> *but you received the Spirit of sonship.*
> *And by him we cry, 'Abba, Father'"*
> (ROMANS 8:15).

God's Will for You

- God's will is that you be treated with respect.

  > *"Show proper respect to everyone"*
  > (1 PETER 2:17).

- God's will is that you be heard and taken seriously.

  > *"Everyone should be quick to listen, slow to speak"*
  > (JAMES 1:19).

- God's will is that you express appropriate anger toward others
  and that anger toward you be expressed appropriately.

  > *"In your anger do not sin"*
  > (EPHESIANS 4:26).

- God's will is that you participate in and benefit from mutual submission.

  > *"Submit to one another out of reverence for Christ"*
  > (EPHESIANS 5:21).

- God's will is that you speak truthfully from your heart and that others speak truthfully to you.

  > *"Each of you must put off falsehood and*
  > *speak truthfully to his neighbor"*
  > (EPHESIANS 4:25).

- God's will is that you be allowed to make mistakes and to take responsibility for them, and that others take responsibility for their mistakes as well. The apostle Paul wrote,

  > *"Not that I have already obtained all this,*
  > *or have already been made perfect,*
  > *but I press on to take hold of that for*
  > *which Christ Jesus took hold of me"*
  > (PHILIPPIANS 3:12).

- God's will is that you be able to say no without feeling guilty.

  > *"Say 'No' to ungodliness and worldly passions"*
  > (TITUS 2:12).

- God's will is that you refuse that which violates your conscience.

  > *"I strive always to keep my conscience clear before God and man"*
  > (ACTS 24:16).

- God's will is that you give and receive only justifiable rebukes.

  > *"He who rebukes a man will in the end gain more favor*
  > *than he who has a flattering tongue"*
  > (PROVERBS 28:23).

- God's will is that you appeal to a higher authority if need be. The apostle Paul, when slandered by Jewish leaders, said,

"If the charges brought against me by these Jews are not true,
no one has the right to hand me over to them. I appeal to Caesar!"
(ACTS 25:11).

- God's will is that you remove yourself from an abusive situation.

"Do not make friends with a hot-tempered man,
do not associate with one easily angered"
(PROVERBS 22:24).

- God's will is that you seek emotional and spiritual support from others.

"Let us not give up meeting together…
but let us encourage one another"
(HEBREWS 10:25).

Dealing with Hurtful Words

QUESTION: "How can I deal with the hurtful things my husband says to me?"

ANSWER: When things are peaceful between the two of you, ask, "If we could have a better relationship with each other, would you want it?" When your spouse responds affirmatively, say, "I want that too. But sometimes we get into verbal battles that are not best for us or for the kids. So I've decided just to step out of the room when that happens in the future and then come back later. I'm going to do this because spoken words cannot be taken back any more than toothpaste squeezed out can be put back into the tube."

"Wisdom will save you from the ways of wicked men,
from men whose words are perverse"
(PROVERBS 2:12).

H. How to Let God Heal Your Broken Heart

No one escapes the pain of a broken heart. In the Hebrew text of the Old Testament, the word translated "brokenhearted" can also mean "shattered."[23] And no one lives very long in this fallen world without experiencing that shattering and the all-encompassing pain that accompanies it.

Many never heal from heartbreak because they avoid dealing with their pain by blocking out, denying, or burying the memories. But the path the Lord has prepared will heal your deepest hurts if you allow Him into the innermost part of your heart so He can spread His soothing balm throughout your entire being—spirit, soul, and body.

> *"May God himself, the God of peace, sanctify you through and through.*
> *May your whole spirit, soul and body be kept blameless*
> *at the coming of our Lord Jesus Christ.*
> *The one who calls you is faithful and he will do it"*
> (1 THESSALONIANS 5:23-24).

I. The First Action You Can Take Toward Healing

The first step for you to take on the Lord's path toward healing is to enter into a loving relationship with Him. To help you understand the relationship that God wants to have with you, there are four points from His Word that you need to know. You'll find them in the appendix on pages 411–13.

J. Additional Actions You Can Take Toward Healing

Whether you are a new believer or you've been one for years, the path to healing is a process that takes time. As you walk with the Lord, ask Him to help you take these steps toward healing.

- **Give your heart to the Lord, allowing Him to be your Deliverer.**
    - Acknowledge your inability to heal yourself and accept the fact that God is the source of all growth and healing.
    - Realize that the abuse you have suffered may have altered your brain chemistry and created some physical problems.
    - Ask the Lord to heal your past pain and soothe your soul as you take refuge in Him and draw on His strength.

    > *"The LORD is my rock, my fortress and my deliverer;*
    > *my God is my rock, in whom I take refuge"*
    > (PSALM 18:2).

- **Know that you are never alone.**
    - Realize that everyone experiences loneliness and pain—it's part of the path of life.

— Continually thank the Lord that He is always with you.

— Build a network of friends who care about you and who will support you both spiritually and emotionally.

> *"The LORD himself goes before you and will be with you;*
> *he will never leave you nor forsake you.*
> *Do not be afraid; do not be discouraged"*
> (DEUTERONOMY 31:8).

- **Search for the truth.**
  — Discern the truth about what has caused your past wounds and your present struggles.

  — Search out the truths of God's Word that will help strengthen and encourage you.

  — Seek truths from biblical principles and the wise counsel of trustworthy people to aid you in understanding and addressing your situation.

  > *"Guide me in your truth and teach me,*
  > *for you are God my Savior,*
  > *and my hope is in you all day long"*
  > (PSALM 25:5).

- **Address your legitimate emotional needs.**[24]
  — Understand that you have three God-given needs—for love, for significance, and for security.

  — Understand that proper self-esteem comes from viewing yourself through God's eyes.

  — Understand that God never withholds His love from you, though you may not have felt that you were loved by your parents or your spouse.

  > *"You are a forgiving God, gracious and compassionate,*
  > *slow to anger and abounding in love"*
  > (NEHEMIAH 9:17).

- **Pay attention to your feelings and perceptions.**
  — See the abuse for what it is—actual abuse!

— Know that you are not going crazy; you are not going nuts.

— If you felt abused, acknowledge that what happened is unacceptable.

> *"You will know the truth,*
> *and the truth will set you free"*
> (JOHN 8:32).

- **Clear your mind of confusion.**

  — Realize that you have been a victim of confusing, mixed messages.

  — Seek help from a safe, trustworthy person to sort through the confusing words and to distinguish the truths from the lies.

  — Refuse to be confused if the abuser attempts to reverse the blame onto you or counters what you are saying.

  > *"God is not a God of confusion but of peace"*
  > (1 CORINTHIANS 14:33 ESV).

- **Acknowledge your destructive feelings.**

  — Make a list of any destructive thoughts and emotions, such as bitterness, hatred, a desire for revenge, or an unwillingness to forgive.

  — Be honest with God about these. He knows you have them, and He understands why.

  — Ask God to cleanse you from all destructive feelings and attitudes.

  > *"Cleanse me with hyssop,*
  > *and I will be clean;*
  > *wash me, and I will be whiter than snow"*
  > (PSALM 51:7).

- **Forgive your abuser.**

  — List each offense committed against you by each abuser.

  — Release each offense and the pain it caused into the hands of God.

— Choose, as an act of your will, to release each abuser to God for His judgment.

> *"Bear with each other and forgive*
> *whatever grievances you may have against one another.*
> *Forgive as the Lord forgave you"*
> (COLOSSIANS 3:13).

- **Allow yourself to grieve.**

  — Write down all the losses that have occurred in your life.

  — Allow yourself time to grieve. Weep by yourself or with a friend.

  — Write the word *finished* beside each painful memory.

  > *"There is a time for everything,*
  > *and a season for every activity under heaven...*
  > *a time to weep...a time to mourn and a time to dance"*
  > (ECCLESIASTES 3:1,4).

- **Realize that healing is a process, not an event.**

  — Refuse to seek quick fixes and painless solutions.

  — Develop an understanding of the activities that promote healing.

  — Grow in patience as you embrace the journey of the healing process.

  > *"As an example of patience in the face of suffering,*
  > *take the prophets who spoke in the name of the Lord.*
  > *As you know, we consider blessed those who have persevered"*
  > (JAMES 5:10-11).

- **Reach out and minister to others.**

  — Ask God for a compassionate heart that is sensitive toward those who have experienced abuse.

  — Be prepared to share your experience when God brings other victims across your path.

— Ask God to fill you with a passionate desire to comfort others by sharing your healing with them.

"The Father of compassion and the God of all comfort…
comforts us in all our troubles,
so that we can comfort those in any trouble with the comfort
we ourselves have received from God"
(2 Corinthians 1:3-4).

Releasing Bitterness When the Abuser Has Died

Question: "How can I release the bitterness toward my abuser, who is now dead?"

Answer: Although you cannot confront your abuser in person, you can indirectly confront by saying *what you would want to say* (or need to say) as though your abuser is in front of you.

• Consider the "chair technique." Imagine the person seated in a chair placed in front of you. Say the things you would say to the person if you were actually seated across a table from him. Express your feelings about what was done to you and the ramifications it had on your life. Then forgive the person and explain that you have taken the person off of your emotional hook and placed the person onto God's hook.

• Write a letter to your abuser stating every painful memory and read it over the person's grave or at a place where you can openly "speak" to the person as though you were in his presence. Then at the close, choose to forgive by releasing your abuser into the hands of God.

• Make a list of all painful as well as positive memories. After completing the list, go back to the beginning and write the word *past* next to each memory. Acknowledge and accept that the past is in the past. Release all the pain as well as the person into the hands of God.

The fact that your abuser has died does not mean that you cannot forgive and therefore bitterness will remain lodged in your heart and mind. You *can* forgive. The Bible says,

> *"See to it that no one misses the grace of God*
> *and that no bitter root grows up to cause trouble and defile many"*
> (Hebrews 12:15).

K. How to Recover from Abuse

Recovery—healing—is a process that occurs over time and is a result of hard, productive work. Rarely is it accomplished in a moment or in a single experience. But regardless of the time frame, victory is assured for those who have entrusted their lives to Jesus.

> *"The Lord...*
> *holds victory in store for the upright,*
> *he is a shield to those whose walk is blameless,*
> *for he guards the course of the just*
> *and protects the way of his faithful ones"*
> (Proverbs 2:6-8).

We can sum up all the practical insights and suggested solutions for recovery in nine steps that are illustrated in the following confessions:

Step 1

"I recognize that I am powerless to heal my damaged emotions resulting from abuse, and I look to God for the power to make me whole."

Step 2

"I acknowledge that God's plan for my life includes victory over my experiences of abuse."

Step 3

"The person who abused me is responsible for the acts committed against me and for the words spoken to me. I will not accept the guilt and the shame resulting from those acts or words."

Step 4

"I am looking to God and His Word to find my identity as a worthwhile and loved human being."

Step 5

"I am honestly sharing my feelings with God and with at least one other person as I try to identify those areas in need of cleansing and healing."

Step 6

"I am accepting responsibility for the ways I have responded to abuse."

Step 7

"I am willing to accept God's help in moving forward to forgive myself and those who have offended me, and to trust Him in the process of doing so."

Step 8

"I am willing to mature in my relationship with God and with others."

Step 9

"I am willing to let God use me as an instrument of His healing and restoration in the lives of others."

By faith, I claim the words of the psalmist:

> *"You turned my wailing into dancing;*
> *you removed my sackcloth and clothed me with joy,*
> *that my heart may sing to you and not be silent.*
> *O LORD my God, I will give you thanks forever"*
> (PSALM 30:11-12).

Sticks and stones can break your bones but words can break your heart. Therefore, guard your heart against the hurting words of others and open your heart to the healing words of God.

Verbal and Emotional Abuse—Answers in God's Word

QUESTION: "Does God expect me to live at peace with everyone—even abusive people?"

ANSWER: "Do not repay anyone evil for evil. Be careful to do what is right in the eyes of everybody. If it is possible, as far as it depends on you, live at peace with everyone" (Romans 12:17-18).

QUESTION: "How can I avoid conceit so that I won't look only to my own interests?"

ANSWER: "Do nothing out of selfish ambition or vain conceit, but in humility consider others better than yourselves. Each of you should look not only to your own interests, but also to the interests of others" (Philippians 2:3-4).

QUESTION: "Why should I give thanks in the midst of all circumstances?"

ANSWER: "Pray continually; give thanks in all circumstances, for this is God's will for you in Christ Jesus" (1 Thessalonians 5:17-18).

QUESTION: "How much power does the tongue have?"

ANSWER: "The tongue has the power of life and death" (Proverbs 18:21).

QUESTION: "What do reckless words do? What can bring healing?"

ANSWER: "Reckless words pierce like a sword, but the tongue of the wise brings healing" (Proverbs 12:18).

QUESTION: "Is there any hope or a future for me?"

ANSWER: "'I know the plans I have for you,' declares the LORD, 'plans to prosper you and not to harm you, plans to give you hope and a future'" (Jeremiah 29:11).

QUESTION: "Should I ever rebuke an abuser?"

ANSWER: "He who rebukes a man will in the end gain more favor than he who has a flattering tongue" (Proverbs 28:23).

QUESTION: "How should I pray for the Lord to heal me?"

ANSWER: "Heal me, O LORD, and I will be healed; save me and I will be saved" (Jeremiah 17:14).

QUESTION: "Why do I need to forgive others?"

ANSWER: "If you forgive men when they sin against you, your heavenly Father will also forgive you. But if you do not forgive men their sins, your Father will not forgive your sins" (Matthew 6:14-15).

QUESTION: "What will happen if I have more fear of people than trust in the Lord?"

ANSWER: "Fear of man will prove to be a snare, but whoever trusts in the LORD is kept safe" (Proverbs 29:25).

VICTIMIZATION
Victory over the Victim Mentality 213

VICTIMIZATION

Victory over the Victim Mentality

Here they come again...those painful memories that permeate your heart and pummel your thoughts and emotions. You feel caught like a frightened bird in a cage with no way to freedom. It happened so long ago. You had hoped to move on, yet once again your heart feels like it is under attack, as though arrows were whizzing through the iron bars on your cage and piercing your heart with deep, debilitating pain.

Do you live your life trying to cope with a crippling crisis from your past, hoping to somehow get beyond it, to forget it? Well, the good news is that God wants so much more for you than just to *cope*. He wants to help you *overcome* your painful past and *conquer* the destructive patterns that have developed in your life as a result of your past victimization. He wants you to grow in maturity through His grace and to reach out and help others in similar pain.

You don't have to remain captive to your feelings of powerlessness. God wants to set you free from the cage that has far too long held you captive and robbed you of peace. He offers you His power for healing and changing. And when you experience true healing and personal transformation, you also gain true freedom. Like a bird out of a cage, you can experience freedom today and have bright hope for tomorrow! All because of the fact that...

"it is for freedom that Christ has set us free.
Stand firm, then,
and do not let yourselves be burdened
again by a yoke of slavery"
(GALATIANS 5:1).

I. DEFINITIONS OF VICTIMIZATION

She was the daughter of a king, but she became a desolate woman. Her position guaranteed a lifetime of honor and recognition, but instead she spent most of her life in seclusion and disgrace.

Tamar's earlier years were characterized by beauty and innocence. These qualities about her captivated and tortured a certain young man, her half brother, Amnon. "Amnon became frustrated to the point of illness on account of his sister Tamar, for she was a virgin, and it seemed impossible for him to do anything to her" (2 Samuel 13:2).

But Amnon's shrewd cousin came up with a plan that made the impossible possible.

A. What Is a Victim?

Jonadab counseled Amnon, "Go to bed and pretend to be ill…When your father comes to see you, say to him, 'I would like my sister Tamar to come and give me something to eat. Let her prepare the food in my sight so I may watch her and then eat it from her hand'" (2 Samuel 13:5). Amnon had no trouble figuring out the rest of the plan.

When King David attended to his "sickly" son Amnon, he dutifully honored his son's request to beckon Tamar to his bedside. Tamar prepared cakes and brought them to Amnon, but instead of grabbing hold of the cakes, he grabbed hold of Tamar. "'Don't, my brother!' she said to him. 'Don't force me. Such a thing should not be done in Israel! Don't do this wicked thing. What about me? Where could I get rid of my disgrace? And what about you? You would be like one of the wicked fools in Israel. Please speak to the king; he will not keep me from being married to you'" (2 Samuel 13:12-13).

Tamar's voice of reason went unheeded, and Amnon, determined to satisfy his fleshly appetite, proceeded to forcibly rape his half sister. "He refused to listen to her, and since he was stronger than she, he raped her" (2 Samuel 13:14). In so doing, Amnon proved himself to be "one of the wicked fools in Israel."

> *"In his arrogance the wicked man hunts down the weak,*
> *who are caught in the schemes he devises"*
> (PSALM 10:2).

A *victim*[1] is a person who experiences adversity, who is powerless to change the situation. For example, a person can be a victim of an unwanted divorce, infidelity, spiritual abuse, suicide, elder abuse, stalking, sexual harassment, or of alcoholic parents.

Tamar was clearly the victim of Amnon. And as his victim, she experienced all three of the following definitions of a victim:

1. *A victim is a person who* is tricked or duped.

   Examples include someone who is a victim of robbery, identity theft, fraud, kidnapping, cult entrapment, and other dishonest schemes.

2. *A victim is a person who* is injured, destroyed, or sacrificed.

   Examples include someone who is a victim of incest, domestic violence, rape, satanic ritual abuse, a drunk driver, homicide, a natural disaster.

3. *A victim is a person who* is subjected to oppression, hardship, or mistreatment.

   Examples include someone who is a victim of any verbal, emotional, sexual, physical, racial, or economic abuse.

> *"Men cry out under a load of oppression;*
> *they plead for relief from the arm of the powerful"*
> (JOB 35:9).

===== **God Sees Your Grief** =====

QUESTION: "Does God even see the grief I carry in my heart as a result of being victimized?"

ANSWER: Yes, He sees your grief, He takes it seriously, and He acts on it.

> *"You, O God, do see trouble and grief;*
> *you consider it to take it in hand.*
> *The victim commits himself to you;*
> *you are the helper of the fatherless"*
> (PSALM 10:14).

B. What Victims Are Mentioned in the Bible?

Tamar's tragic loss of innocence was but the first in a string of abuses committed by Amnon, who, after maliciously victimizing Tamar, "hated her with intense hatred. In fact, he hated her more than he had loved her" (2 Samuel 13:15).

Amnon commanded Tamar to get out of his presence and had a servant put her out when she refused to leave. He repudiated the notion of taking her as his bride, which the law required, and told the servant to bolt the door behind her. Lust had been camouflaged as love, and Amnon would one day discover that Tamar was not the only victim of his sexual sin. The Bible asks the following rhetorical questions:

> *"Can a man scoop fire into his lap without his clothes being burned?*
> *Can a man walk on hot coals without his feet being scorched?"*
> (Proverbs 6:27-28).

One Hebrew word in the Old Testament that is used to speak of a victim is *chelekah*, which means "hapless, unfortunate, the unlucky."[2] We find it used in Psalm 10:8, which says, "He [the wicked man] lies in wait near the villages; from ambush he murders the innocent, watching in secret for his victims." Other Old Testament translations of the word *victim* are…

- the slain
- the killed
- the casualties
- the slaughtered
- the dead
- the defiled
- the wounded

According to these translations, Jesus was a willing victim of our sins—He, the innocent One, laid down His life for the guilty.

> *"He was pierced for our transgressions,*
> *he was crushed for our iniquities;*
> *the punishment that brought us peace was upon him,*
> *and by his wounds we are healed"*
> (Isaiah 53:5).

The Gift that Keeps on Giving:
The Nicholas Green Story

They could have been *bitter,* but instead they became *bolder.*
Reginald and Maggie Green decided to vacation in the beautiful
Italy countryside in early fall of 1994. They brought along their two

small children so they could enjoy family time together. Home for the Greens was Bodega Bay, California, a coastal town 70 miles north of San Francisco.

A tragic encounter on an Italian highway forever changed the course of the Greens' lives. Two men, Francesco Mesiano and Michele Iannello, both in their twenties, pulled alongside the Greens' rented vehicle and attempted to rob them. Shots were fired, and one bullet lodged in the head of seven-year-old Nicholas, who was sitting in the back seat beside his four-year-old sister. [3]

Shortly afterward, Nicholas died. The Greens' tragedy could have been like so many other stories that make headlines for a day and then fade into the background. Public interest usually wanes while private grief wells within the hearts of hurting families trying to pick up the pieces of their lives.

But instead, Reginald and Maggie's young boy found a special place in the hearts of millions all around the world. Nicholas Green is a household name in Italy, where parks, hospitals, and schools are named after him. That's because his parents, while immersed in heart-rending grief, chose to move *beyond their pain*. After Nicholas' death, Reginald and Maggie donated their son's organs and corneas to seven Italians, saving lives and restoring eyesight to those desperate to receive true help in their lives, *desperate to see God's hope for their lives*. [4]

This selfless, lifesaving act stunned the Italian nation. Up to that time, organ donations had been rare. This incident unleashed an outpouring of compassion and admiration for the Green family, as well as a national soul-searching about how the Italian populace ought to respond when facing a similar situation. The response proved to be more than thought-provoking—*it produced powerful results*.

Organ donations in Italy soon quadrupled, placing that nation near the top for organ donations in Europe. And the tragic yet tenderhearted story of Nicholas' death inspired a movement called the Nicholas Effect, prompting people around the globe to become organ donors and, in turn, garner the great joys of giving to others. [5]

In addition, Reginald began the Nicholas Green Foundation, a nonprofit organization dedicated to furthering the cause of organ and tissue donation worldwide and raising public awareness about the shortage of donors. As a noted journalist himself, Reginald inspired others through his two books, *The Nicholas Effect: A Boy's Gift to the World* and *The Gift that Heals: 42 Transplant Stories.*

This young boy's story even made its way onto film with the 1998 made-for-TV movie *Nicholas' Gift.* It had such a great impact that it received an Emmy nomination.

Despite all the positive efforts and noble work that have resulted from his son's death, Reginald is first to admit that it doesn't take away the pain of his loss. "The sense that life is missing a vital ingredient is there all the time"—but giving to others and donating "does put something on the other side of the balance."[6]

The citizens of Bodega Bay were also inspired to do something special to observe the loss of one of their own. An 18-foot bell tower was constructed in their coastal community, from which 140 bells have been hung—almost all sent by Italians. The centerpiece bell, which stands 30 inches high, has Nicholas' name on it, along with the names of the seven recipients of Nicholas' organs. It came from a foundry that has been making bells for the papacy in Rome for 1000 years.[7] Coastal winds almost continually move the bells to chime, reminiscent of children at play.

The Green family found victory over the victim mentality by giving tangibly to others—by giving inspiration, by giving hope, and by discovering that when you give, you truly receive much more. Jesus said it best: "It is more blessed to give than to receive" (Acts 20:35).

C. What Is the Victim Mentality?[8]

Tamar was devastated by Amnon's heartless disregard for her feelings and wishes, her plans and dreams. And the deep disdain he felt toward her after forcing himself on her was more than she could bear.

How could he disgrace her as though she had no worth and then discard her as though she had no value? How could she ever hold her head high again and take pride in her position in life?

Amnon had not only taken Tamar's purity, he had taken her future as well.

To express her deep sorrow and shame, Tamar tore her richly ornamented robe, which symbolized her status as a virgin daughter of the king, and placed ashes on her head. And "she put her hand on her head and went away, weeping aloud as she went" (2 Samuel 13:19).

- *The victim mentality* is a mind-set in which a person who was once a victim continues to hold on to old thought patterns and feelings of powerlessness even when the victimization has ended.

- *The victim mentality* causes individuals to see others as powerful and themselves as weak and powerless.

- *The victim mentality* leads those who were genuinely powerless to stop abuse in the past to assume the same powerless state in the present. Before they can fully embrace the future that the Lord has planned for them, they must replace this faulty assumption with God's truth.

- *The victim mentality* can cause a person to consciously or subconsciously deny responsibility for his or her actions. The individual continues to manifest self-destructive attitudes and actions while blaming others for the undesirable results. Victory requires a new mind-set:

> *"We demolish arguments and every pretension that sets itself up against the knowledge of God, and we take captive every thought to make it obedient to Christ"*
> (2 CORINTHIANS 10:5).

======= **Victim Mentality** =======

QUESTION: "What will help me overcome a victim mentality?"

ANSWER: You can overcome a victim mentality by changing the way you see God and the way you see yourself in relationship to Him, thus changing the way you see yourself in relationship to others and to events in your life. As a past victim, you may have been defenseless, but now you are no longer without power:

> *"In all these things we are more than conquerors through him who loved us"*
> (ROMANS 8:37).

D. What Questions Do Victims Ask God?

Once revered as royalty and now ravaged by rape, Tamar moved into the house of her compassionate brother, Absalom. Abandoned by Amnon, the one who should have taken her into his home, she held no hope that marriage and family could ever be a part of her future. She was further wounded when her father, though furious with Amnon, did not hold him accountable for his sin against her. Thus, no one executed justice on her behalf. "Tamar lived in her brother Absalom's house, a desolate woman" (2 Samuel 13:20).

However, there was one who did not turn a deaf ear or blind eye to Tamar's suffering. And Absalom found the opportune moment to avenge his sister's rape two years later. At a festive time of shearing sheep, Absalom instructed his servants to wait until Amnon was "in high spirits from drinking wine" (2 Samuel 13:28) and then, at his command, kill him. The servants obeyed Absalom's instructions, and Amnon was violently murdered for his violation of Tamar. Scripture warns us...

> *"When the sentence for a crime is not quickly carried out,*
> *the hearts of the people are filled with schemes to do wrong"*
> (ECCLESIASTES 8:11).

Probably the most frequently and fervently asked question by victims of abuse is this:

Where Are You, God?

Why do You hide in times of trouble?
Why do You let the godless rule?
Victims are ambushed, crushed, and downtrodden.
Wicked men care not. They're prideful and cruel
and say to themselves,
"God has forgotten! He won't see."
I feel You are absent...that You never see.
Yet You encourage and lift the afflicted,
breaking the strong arm of evil siege.
Since You do hear the cry of the wounded,
cradling my heart in angel's wings,
You help me gaze upon heaven's glory.
You, O God, are my Father, my King!

—BASED ON PSALM 10

E. What Is God's Heart for the Victim?

God is a God of love, and He created us for love relationships. He hates violence, and He takes up the cause of victims who fall prey to violent words and deeds. He will execute justice one day on behalf of all victims. And woe to those who will face the judgment of God, who sees all and knows all! Nothing is hidden from Him.

> *"Nothing in all creation is hidden from God's sight.*
> *Everything is uncovered and laid bare*
> *before the eyes of him to whom we must give account"*
> (Hebrews 4:13).

Be assured…

- God hears the cry of the battered and abused. "You hear, O Lord, the desire of the afflicted; you encourage them, and you listen to their cry" (Psalm 10:17).

- God holds the victim of abuse in the palm of His hand. "Do not fear, for I am with you; do not be dismayed, for I am your God. I will strengthen you and help you; I will uphold you with my righteous right hand" (Isaiah 41:10).

- God will rescue the victim of abuse and violence. "He will rescue them from oppression and violence, for precious is their blood in His sight" (Psalm 72:14).

- God confirms the victim's value and worth. "Are not five sparrows sold for two pennies? Yet not one of them is forgotten by God. Indeed, the very hairs of your head are all numbered. Don't be afraid; you are worth more than many sparrows" (Luke 12:6-7).

- God brings good out of the evil deeds of others. "The Lord works out everything for his own ends—even the wicked for a day of disaster" (Proverbs 16:4).

From Victim to Victor: The Stormie Omartian Story

In the second year of our young ministry, I had the privilege of interviewing a lovely guest—one who had experienced the extraordinary freedom of moving from hopelessness to genuine hope for her heart.

Her story begins as a little girl who spent much of her early life locked in a little closet under a stairway—a closet where the family laundry was stored. In that small space Stormie had to sit cramped and cross-legged on a large pile of soiled clothes overflowing from a laundry basket. Musty smells, darkness, and the sounds of mice scampering around were all a regular part of Stormie's daytime world, which was spent largely in that closet.

Stormie never knew what trigger would prompt her mother to banish her to the bleak prison of fearful isolation. On this particular day she had simply asked for a glass of water. "Get in the closet until I can stand to see your face!" her mother yelled with disdain.[9] At least Stormie knew she would be released in the evening when her father returned from work, for her mother kept Stormie's closet captivity a complete secret from him.

Stormie always envisioned her father one day "coming to her rescue"—sweeping her up and forever freeing her from her mother's verbal, emotional, and physical abuse. But he never came. Always "dead tired"—as he described it—from another hard day's work, he was blind to the disturbing behavior in his own home that resulted in horrific abuse of his little girl.[10]

Compounding Stormie's desperate situation was the family's secluded living environment—a Wyoming farm 20 miles from the closest town. There were no neighbors nearby and no playmates available to help Stormie build her social skills. Long-term isolation and limited social interaction led to speech impediments and relationship difficulties that, later in life, required major help for Stormie to overcome.[11]

The need to attend school eventually freed Stormie from her small, dark prison, but it didn't stop her mother's verbal, emotional, and physical abuse. One day after returning home from school, Stormie's mother grabbed her by the hair, slammed her against a door, and slapped her wildly as she screamed: "You murderer! You murderer!

You've killed an innocent child! I hope you're happy with yourself, you [expletive]!"

What could possibly have triggered such an outburst? A friend's mother had miscarried a baby, and for some reason Stormie's mother blamed it on her. A week earlier, Stormie had stayed overnight at her friend's house and the next day, the friend's mom drove Stormie home. Realize that the drive home happened a week before the miscarriage. What bizarre reasoning for such horrid brutality![12]

That terrifying incident occurred during Stormie's last year of junior high. She was preparing to accept full responsibility for what had happened when her friend assured her that the miscarriage was in no way her fault. From that day forward, Stormie was engulfed with hatred toward her mother.

Stormie's mother continually told Stormie she was crazy. The painful environment at home prompted so much anxiety, fear, and self-loathing that one day, at age 14, Stormie decided to swallow pills from a bathroom medicine cabinet in an attempt to permanently end her agony. To this day, Stormie remembers what was going through her mind. "My intention was to die...not to attract attention."[13]

Ironically, Stormie's mother rescued her from the overdose—forcing her to throw up—but never sought help for her emotionally distraught daughter. Stormie's suicide attempt was never again discussed.

In the years that followed, alcohol, drugs, the occult, and promiscuous relationships provided temporary diversions from her emotional pain, but despair and depression were ever-present. Two unplanned pregnancies ending with abortions only compounded Stormie's guilt and heartache.[14] Desperation for affection and a deathly fear of being alone set Stormie up for an inability to say no to wrong relationships.

Although Stormie achieved considerable success as an actress, model, and singer, the emotional fallout from the abuse she suffered as a child still hung like a dark storm cloud over her life.

When Stormie was 28 years old, she accepted Christ as her Savior. Two years later, she married Christian singer and songwriter Michael Omartian at their Los Angeles-area church. Though sincere and steadily growing in her faith, Stormie knew something was still terribly wrong. Depression, panic attacks, and even thoughts of suicide continued to torment her.

Counselors at Stormie's church suggested they attack the problem through prayer and fasting. She made a list of her every known sin. Then on an appointed day, Stormie specifically renounced each one from her long list. Her prayer partners then addressed spirits of futility, despair, fear, rejection, suicide, and torment. "I was not demon-possessed," she said, "but these spirits had oppressed me at points where I had given them place through my sins of unforgiveness and disobedience to God."[15]

"The next morning I awoke without any feelings of depression whatever—no thoughts of suicide, no heaviness in my chest, no fearful anticipation of the future...Day after day it was the same. I never again experienced those feelings, nor the paralysis that accompanied them. I had gone into that counseling office knowing Jesus as Savior, but I came out knowing Him also as my Deliverer."[16]

In 1976, Stormie and Michael joyfully welcomed their first child into the world—Christopher Scott. "I will never be like my mother," she assured herself confidently upon his arrival. "My child will have the best care I can give him."[17]

Christopher's relentless crying, however, soon triggered powerful emotions Stormie could hardly comprehend. "The frustration built until I finally snapped," she recalls. "I slapped my baby on the back, the shoulder and the head...I was out of control."[18]

To her horror, God begin to reveal her own latent abusive tendencies. "It was shocking to discover that I had all the potential in me to be an abuser. It was built in me from childhood. I had seen that violent, out-of-control behavior before—in my mother. I knew it wasn't my child I hated. It was *me*. And now I also saw that it wasn't *me* that my mother hated; it was herself."[19]

Unlike her earlier deliverance, which was immediate, Stormie's deliverance from child-abusing tendencies was "long and slow"—a gradual process of recovery as God gently and lovingly peeled back layer after layer of pain and wrong thinking.

Through the years since her conversion, God continued to faithfully heal the many wounds in Stormie's life. But one wound remained painfully raw—her strained relationship with her mother. Stormie begged God for a redeemed mother-daughter bond, and He assured her that He would provide—through the birth of a daughter! Contemplating a second pregnancy at nearly 40 years of age frightened Stormie, but she did, indeed, conceive.

"From the moment of Amanda's birth, the healing began. Just like an open wound heals slowly day by day, I felt a wound in my emotions, in my heart somewhere, begin to heal. Every day with Amanda brought more wholeness and more fulfillment." [20]

Through it all, Stormie says, "I learned about the power of prayer... and the transformation that takes place when it becomes our priority. I learned that the more I obeyed God, the more I changed.

"In fact, God changed me and my life so much over the years that today I hardly recognize myself from the person I used to be. And the best part is...I know that what He did in me, He can do in anyone." [21]

Stormie Omartian, one of America's most beloved authors with well over 13 million books sold, [22] was transformed from a cowering *victim* to a confident *voice* now heard around the world—a compassionate, compelling voice that communicates the help and healing of Jesus to all who need hope. And who doesn't need hope!

II. Characteristics of the Victim Mentality

They were a nation of victims brutalized by the insecurities of a powerful leader and empire. The Israelite population exploded in the land of Egypt, and a new Egyptian king feared the people would make a formidable alliance with his country's enemies. Proposing to "deal shrewdly with them" (Exodus 1:10), he subjected the entire nation to slavery, establishing taskmasters "over them to oppress them with forced labor...and worked them ruthlessly. They made their lives bitter with hard labor in brick and mortar and with all kinds of work in the fields; in all their hard labor the Egyptians used them ruthlessly" (verses 11-14).

At the heart of a victim's wounded emotions is the feeling of powerlessness, a feeling that one is unable to make healthy choices in circumstances and relationships. Left with a damaged sense of self-worth, unhealed victims of abuse develop unhealthy beliefs and behaviors. And because of a past lack of control, some victims have a hidden fear of being controlled in the present. Therefore, they themselves may become overcontrolling.

Other victims resign themselves to not being in control and have a hidden fear of not being controlled. Therefore, they may become codependent. Both types of unhealthy fear and responses can produce negative spiritual and physical side effects because of the victims' unresolved emotional difficulties. The cry of a victim's heart is often...

> *"be merciful to me, LORD, for I am faint;*
> *O LORD, heal me, for my bones are in agony"*
> (PSALM 6:2).

A. What Is the Profile of a Victimized Person?

False guilt brings death of the soul. Victimizers leave their innocent victims with abiding feelings of rejection and personal defectiveness. The constant fear that their "stains" will be exposed causes victims to develop destructive ways of relating to others. These self-protective patterns of behavior are pitfalls to healthy adult relationships and decrease the ability to know God intimately, as explained by righteous Job in the Bible:

> *"If I am guilty—woe to me!*
> *Even if I am innocent, I cannot lift my head,*
> *for I am full of shame and drowned in my affliction"*
> (JOB 10:15).

A victimized person typically exhibits several of these characteristics:

A—Ambivalent	Experiences conflicted emotions about pain and pleasure and gives mixed emotional signals to others
B—Betrayed	Expects rejection and is unable to trust or have faith in God or others
U—Unexcitable	Lacks passion for both good and bad, and merely seeks to be free of conflict with others and has a flat response to circumstances without emotional highs or lows

S—Self-absorbed	Consumed with self-protection and unable to show sensitivity to others
E—Emotionally Controlled	Disengages from true feelings and becomes blind to the feelings of others
D—Dependent on Self	Seeks to be in control because of a reluctance to depend on God or others

The constant cry of many victims is…

> *"My soul is in anguish"*
> (Psalm 6:3).

B. What Are the Standard Statements of Victims?

The words we say to others don't necessarily reflect the words we say to ourselves. Both "other-talk" and "self-talk" reveal what is in our hearts, but what we say to ourselves has the greater power over our lives. If we rehearse negative statements in our minds, we will build prison walls in our minds that will keep us in bondage to a low sense of self-worth.

Some of the most frequent and fervent statements made by victims of abuse are listed below. Place a check mark (✓) beside the ones that apply to you.

- ☐ I am a worthless and unlovable person.
- ☐ I am bad if I feel angry.
- ☐ I am better off with bad love than no love at all.
- ☐ I am defective.
- ☐ I am obligated to bring about change when I see that it is needed.
- ☐ I am responsible for the behavior and feelings of those around me.
- ☐ I am terrible because I hate my victimizer.
- ☐ I am wrong for having needs.
- ☐ I must be dependent on others because they are wiser and stronger than I am.
- ☐ I must be unlovable if the people I care for reject me.
- ☐ I must keep peace at any price.

- ☐ I must take care of myself because no one else is trustworthy.
- ☐ I need the approval of other people in order to be happy.
- ☐ I will be loved if I am good.
- ☐ I will never let anyone get close enough to me to hurt me again.
- ☐ I will never measure up.
- ☐ My feelings are less important than the feelings of others.
- ☐ My feelings are not important at all.
- ☐ My mistakes only confirm my worthlessness.

Whatever the contributing factors to your low estimation of your worth, they are held in place by negative thinking that you have embraced over the years. But the low opinion of yourself can be overcome by replacing those negative words with God's Word:

> *"Do not conform any longer to the pattern of this world,*
> *but be transformed by the renewing of your mind.*
> *Then you will be able to test and approve what God's will is—*
> *his good, pleasing and perfect will"*
> (ROMANS 12:2).

C. What Are Some Emotional Side Effects of Victimization?

The people of Israel "groaned in their slavery and cried out, and their cry for help because of their slavery went up to God" (Exodus 2:23).

God heard their cry and raised up a resilient though somewhat reluctant deliverer. Moses, along with his brother, Aaron, approached the Egyptian Pharaoh about allowing the Israelites to go and conduct a feast to the Lord in the wilderness. In utter disregard to the God of the Israelites, Pharaoh not only refused the request but multiplied the Israelites' misery by no longer providing straw to help make bricks, yet required that they maintain the same level of production.

When the production levels fell, the Egyptian taskmasters beat the Israelite foremen. In consternation the foremen confront Moses and Aaron, saying,

> *"May the LORD look upon you and judge you!*
> *You have made us a stench to Pharaoh and his officials*
> *and have put a sword in their hand to kill us"*
> (EXODUS 5:21).

As happened in the case of the Israelites, those who have been extensively victimized generally struggle with severe emotional side effects such as...

Low Self-worth[23]

Those who have a low sense of self-worth usually find themselves...

—accepting abuse

—accepting blame

—accepting condemnation

—accepting injustice

—being critical of self and others

—being desperate for approval

—being unable to set boundaries

—being unable to accept compliments

—being a people-pleaser

—being defensive

Those who have a warped view of themselves and others often have a warped view of God. When people feel unworthy of love, respect, and approval from others, often they feel even more unworthy of God's love, respect, and approval.

Their faulty beliefs lead them to draw faulty conclusions about God, and their wrong beliefs about God serve only to sabotage their relationship with God and kill any hope of being valued and used by God.

If you struggle with feeling devalued and insignificant, remember Jesus' words:

> *"Consider the ravens:*
> *They do not sow or reap,*
> *they have no storeroom or barn;*
> *yet God feeds them.*
> *And how much more valuable you are than birds!"*
> (LUKE 12:24).

═══ Worth Your Weight in Gold ═══

QUESTION: "What does the Bible say about my worth?"

ANSWER: Perhaps you've heard the expression that someone is "worth his weight in gold." This saying actually comes from the Bible—you'll find it in Lamentations 4:2. Just think about how much worth that would literally be!

If gold were selling at $250 per ounce, one pound (16 ounces) of gold would be worth $4,000. And a person who weighs 150 pounds would be worth $600,000—well over half a million dollars.[24]

Interestingly, the Bible presents a person's worth as too great to be measured in mere monetary terms. Peter says that your faith alone is "more precious than gold" (1 Peter 1:7 NKJV). Are you beginning to see how much you, combined with your faith, are worth in the eyes of God? You are indeed precious to God. You have God-given worth—in fact, this is how much He loves you:

> *"This is how God showed his love among us:*
> *He sent his one and only Son into the world*
> *that we might live through him"*
> (1 JOHN 4:9).

Dependency[25]

The victims of abuse often form various addictions or dependencies, such as dependency...

—on food	—on social status
—on drugs/alcohol	—on financial security
—on people	—on personal abilities
—on religion	—on material possessions
—on physical appearance	—on professional success

======= Addiction =======

QUESTION: "Why is addiction so common among people who have been victimized?"

ANSWER: Typically, victimization robs its recipients of feeling content and whole—they feel needy and look for something or someone to complete them and fulfill their deepest needs.

God created us with three inner needs—for unconditional love, significance, and security.[26] When these needs are not met in healthy ways, people generally try to get them met in illegitimate ways—sometimes through various addictions.

Addictions are mood-altering—whether through a chemical (alcohol), a behavior (gambling), or a person (codependency). If you have been victimized, you need to let the Lord be your Need-meeter, your Deliverer.

When you humble your heart before Christ and invite Him into your life, He will help deliver you from any addictions in your life:

> *"For he will deliver the needy who cry out,*
> *the afflicted who have no one to help"*
> (Psalm 72:12).

Fear[27]

Fear is a common side effect experienced by victims of abuse. They may exhibit fear...

—of abandonment	—of authority figures
—of rejection	—of God
—of failure	—of unexpected changes
—of affection	—of unfamiliar places
—of intimacy	—of unpredictable situations

- *Fear* can be real or imagined, rational or irrational, normal or abnormal.
- *Fear* acts as a protective device placed in us by our Creator to activate all of our physical systems when we are faced with real danger.
- *Fear* triggers the release of adrenaline in the body that propels us to action—action often called "fight, flight, or freeze."
- *Fear* is a natural emotion designed by God. However, prolonged fear or fearfulness is not designed by God, for fearfulness means living in a *state of fear* or having a *spirit of fear.*

> *"God has not given us a spirit of fear,*
> *but of power and of love and of a sound mind"*
> (2 Timothy 1:7 nkjv).

Excessiveness

Yet another emotional side effect of victimization is excessiveness...

—in control
—in seriousness
—in work
—in organization
—in relationships

—in appearance
—in safety
—in rules
—in details
—in thoughts

The human mind is in many ways like a machine with built-in safety features. When a victim feels overloaded and stressed, the mind can consciously or unconsciously be trained to focus excessively on some object or action as a means of providing a measure of temporary emotional or mental relief.

The danger is that the excessive attention or action often becomes so strong the person feels powerless to control it. But the One who created the mind can certainly reprogram it through the power of His Spirit and His Word. That is why God instructs us to...

> *"offer your bodies as living sacrifices,*
> *holy and pleasing to God—this is your spiritual act of worship.*
> *Do not conform any longer to the pattern of this world,*
> *but be transformed by the renewing of your mind.*
> *Then you will be able to test and approve what God's will is—*
> *his good, pleasing and perfect will"*
> (ROMANS 12:1-2).

Compulsiveness

Those who are victimized will often display a compulsiveness...

—about perfectionism
—about irresponsibility
—about daily routines
—about cleanliness
—about orderliness

—about personal rituals
—about repeated victimization
—about dieting
—about exercise
—about locking doors

Those who feel controlled by compulsive behaviors need to know that...

> *"God will meet all your needs*
> *according to his glorious riches in Christ Jesus"*
> (PHILIPPIANS 4:19).

- *Perfectionists* seem highly motivated to produce, yet their behavior is actually a compulsive drive to protect themselves from feelings of worthlessness.[28] They live under the law of God (seeking to earn approval and worth) instead of living under the grace of God (accepting unearned approval and worth). In striving to perform perfectly, they often…

  C—Control environment, situations, and others[29]

  O—Object to criticism and correction

  M—Major on the minors

  P—Procrastinate until the last minute

  U—Underestimate time needed to complete tasks

  L—Lack joy and creativity

  S—Sacrifice relationships for projects

  I—Imagine rejection from others

  V—Vacillate in making decisions

  E—Express intolerance toward others

- *Perfectionists* may appear confident, conscientious, and highly productive, but they are full of self-doubts and fears that the slightest mistake will cause other people to withdraw, be disappointed, or to reject them.

- *Perfectionists* become overly sensitive to the opinions and feedback of others, often disregarding their own healthy instincts.

- *Perfectionists* often live in an overly cautious way, reluctant to try new things, take a risk, or tackle big projects for fear of failing or appearing inadequate in the eyes of others.

- *Perfectionists* would be wise to recall the words of the apostle Paul: "Are you so foolish? After beginning with the Spirit, are you now trying to attain your goal by human effort?" (Galatians 3:3). Likewise, all who engage in compulsive behaviors need to heed the warning of the prophet Isaiah:

> *"The word of the LORD to them will become: Do and do, do and do,*
> *rule on rule, rule on rule; a little here, a little there—*
> *so that they will go and fall backward, be injured and snared and captured"*
> (ISAIAH 28:13).

===== Perfection =====

QUESTION: "Since we are called to be 'perfect' (2 Corinthians 13:11), is it really possible to never sin?"

ANSWER: Christians are called to "be perfect" in the sense of spiritual maturity and becoming spiritually whole. The meaning of the word "perfect" in the original Greek text is not "sinless, faultless, flawless," but rather, "mature, whole, complete." Other translations say, "Become complete" (NKJV), "aim for perfection" (NIV), and

> *"grow to maturity"*
> (2 CORINTHIANS 13:11 NLT).

D. What Are Some Physical and Mental Side Effects of Victimization?[29]

The continual victimization of the Israelites by the Egyptian rulers obviously affected them physically and mentally, which led to the emotional distress expressed in their anger toward Moses.

Physical abuse impacts the whole person—body, soul, and spirit. As the Israelites struggled to keep up with the backbreaking work assigned by their Egyptian taskmasters, their spirits became broken as well. In their exhausted state of body and mind, they became greatly discouraged and grew angry at Moses, blaming him for their hardship.

Moses, in turn, was dismayed by the sudden turn of events and fervently poured out his feelings to God:

> *"Moses returned to the LORD and said,*
> *'O Lord, why have you brought trouble upon this people?*
> *Is this why you sent me?*
> *Ever since I went to Pharaoh to speak in your name,*
> *he has brought trouble upon this people,*
> *and you have not rescued your people at all'"*
> (EXODUS 5:22-23).

Like the Israelites, those who are subjected to repeated victimization often suffer from some of the following physical and mental problems:

- **Disorders**
  - substance abuse/addictions
  - anorexia/bulimia/overeating
  - self-injury or self-endangerment
  - dissociation/splitting

- **Memory disturbances**
  - memory blocks
  - flashbacks
  - memory loss
  - body memories

- **Sexual difficulties**
  - frigidity/impotence
  - promiscuity/prostitution
  - sexual identity confusion
  - defensive reactions to touch

- **Sleeping disruptions**
  - nightmares
  - insomnia/restlessness
  - fear of going to bed or to sleep
  - awakening frequently to avoid sleeping too soundly

The pressing prayer of many who have experienced victimization is...

> *"Listen to my cry, for I am in desperate need;*
> *rescue me from those who pursue me,*
> *for they are too strong for me.*
> *Set me free from my prison,*
> *that I may praise your name"*
> (PSALM 142:6-7).

========= Dissociative Identity Disorder =========

QUESTION: "At times I appear to have completely different personalities. Although my normal tone of voice, movements, and expressions are different, I'm not aware of it because the changes occur when I seem to lose track of time. Could this be related to the sexual abuse I experienced as a child?"

ANSWER: Yes. If you experienced severe traumatic abuse at least once before the age of seven, you may be experiencing symptoms associated with dissociative identity disorder (DID).

- DID is the term used in the psychological community since 1994 to describe what had previously been called multiple personality disorder.

- The defining feature of this disorder is that a part of a person's identity becomes detached or "dissociated."

- Dissociation is characterized by the presence of two or more "parts or identities," with vast differences between each part.

- Each identity has distinct behaviors, mannerisms, and possibly even physical attributes, such as right- or left-handedness, allergies, and eyesight.

- When the walls separating traumatic events from the conscious mind begin to crumble, flashbacks of the once-cloistered events begin "seeping through" to the conscious mind. Generally this begins to occur when people are in their mid to late twenties or thirties.

- The process of "integration" consists of bringing into the mainstream of consciousness the trauma and pain carried by each part of the person's identity so it can be processed, so healing can occur, and so each part can then become integrated back into the whole.

DID is neither a mental illness nor can it be attributed to substance abuse or a general medical condition. By God's design, the mind is created with the capability to *dissociate* so one part of a child can privately carry severe pain and trauma without the child's having a mental or emotional breakdown. In that respect, DID is a gift from God. As the Bible says,

"I praise you because I am fearfully and wonderfully made;
your works are wonderful, I know that full well"
(PSALM 139:14).

E. What Are Some Spiritual Side Effects of Victimization?

Not only did the Israelites suffer crippling emotional, physical, and mental side effects from generations of slavery in Egypt, they also suffered spiritual side effects.

After years of suffering and crying out to God for a deliverer, when the time was right for God to answer their cries and send Moses to them, they had great difficulty trusting him. Their hearts were full of doubts not only about him but also about God.

Moses tried to reassure the people with words of God's plan to free them from the yoke of the Egyptians by performing mighty acts of judgment. God had promised to take them as His own people and give them the land He swore to give to their forefathers. However, despite Moses' efforts, their bitter bondage was a barrier to their willingness to believe what he said to them.

"Say to the Israelites:
'I am the LORD, and I will bring you out from under the yoke of the Egyptians.
I will free you from being slaves to them,
and I will redeem you with an outstretched arm and
with mighty acts of judgment.
I will take you as my own people, and I will be your God…
And I will bring you to the land I swore with uplifted hand
to give to Abraham, to Isaac and to Jacob…'
Moses reported this to the Israelites,
but they did not listen to him
because of their discouragement and cruel bondage"
(EXODUS 6:6-9).

As was the case with the Israelites, those who are repeatedly victimized often struggle with obstacles to their spiritual growth. They have…

- **A knowledge of God but little personal experience of God**
  — Knowing God is all-powerful, all-knowing, and everywhere-present

- Knowing God is a force to be reckoned with
- Knowing God is eternal and sovereign

- **Anger at God for not stopping the abuse**
  - Thinking God is responsible for the bad things that have happened to them
  - Thinking God is cruel and unloving
  - Thinking God is unfair and unjust

- **Difficulty forming an intimate relationship with God**
  - Struggling with being honest and open with God
  - Struggling with believing the promises of God
  - Struggling with giving their hearts and lives to God

- **Distrust of God for allowing the abuse**
  - Considering God to be unrestricted and undiscerning in the use of His power
  - Considering God to be a liar
  - Considering God to be undependable

- **Fear of God's anger and displeasure**
  - Seeing God as impossible to please
  - Seeing God as punitive and vindictive
  - Seeing God as condemning

- **Feelings of rejection and unworthiness**
  - Feeling that God has abandoned them
  - Feeling that God has ascribed no value to them
  - Feeling that God has thrown them on the garbage heap

- **Projected the attributes of their abuser onto God**
  - Believing that God is hurtful and insensitive
  - Believing that God is selfish and controlling
  - Believing that God is inconsistent and unpredictable

- **Sought to gain God's approval**
  - Hoping God will bless them for their sacrificial giving
  - Hoping God will bless them for their church-related activities
  - Hoping God will bless them for their service to others

- **Warped negative perceptions of God**
  - Perceiving God as distant and disinterested
  - Perceiving God as indifferent to their pain
  - Perceiving God as unavailable

Some spiritual strugglers become so embittered:

> *"they say to God, 'Leave us alone!*
> *We have no desire to know your ways'"*
> (Job 21:14).

Others, however, choose to reach out in faith to lay hold of the promises of God:

> *"The gospel...is the power of God for the salvation of everyone who believes...*
> *'Come!' Whoever is thirsty, let him come;*
> *and whoever wishes, let him take the free gift of the water of life...*
> *'Come to me, all you who are weary and burdened,*
> *and I will give you rest.*
> *Take my yoke upon you and learn from me,*
> *for I am gentle and humble in heart,*
> *and you will find rest for your souls'"*
> (Romans 1:16; Revelation 22:17; Matthew 11:28-29).

F. What Are Some Self-defeating Survival Skills?

God's actions got the attention of the Israelites, and after 430 years of living in Egypt, the people of Israel finally escaped their oppressor—but not until after God poured forth horrific plagues upon Egypt. Hail mixed with fire, an invasion of locusts, the death of all of Egypt's firstborn...those were among ten plagues that culminated with the Egyptians virtually pushing the

Israelites out the door. They couldn't get them to leave their country soon enough, and were even plundered by the Israelites before they departed!

God saw the pain of His people and was moved to provide help and restoration:

> *"I will take you as my own people,*
> *and I will be your God.*
> *Then you will know that I am the LORD your God,*
> *who brought you out from under the yoke of the Egyptians"*
> (EXODUS 6:7).

All of us have developed ways of avoiding unpleasant situations and responsibilities, but those operating out of a victim mentality have become experts at self-protection. Developed early in life through modeling or sheer creativity, these skills were learned responses and ways of relating that were necessary for surviving abusive situations.

These behaviors often operate subconsciously and can undermine nonabusive relationships and sabotage the healing process.

Only by walking in the truth of God's Word through the power of His Spirit within us can we overcome.

> *"Teach me your way, O LORD, and I will walk in your truth;*
> *give me an undivided heart, that I may fear your name"*
> (PSALM 86:11).

Survival Personalities

The Dependent gives up personal responsibility in many areas of life and uses helplessness to get support from others. This disguise, adopted for protection, sends the message "I need you," but in adulthood it becomes a powerful means of controlling and manipulating others.

The Pleaser abides by the motto "peace at any price." By constant compliance with the wishes or desires of others, this individual pays a high price for approval and acceptance. As an adult, the Pleaser has lost a great deal of personal identity.

The Fixer has low sense of self-worth and attempts to fix it by becoming responsible for and fixing others. Fixers are often seen as very loving, self-sacrificing, and spiritual—though often these traits are merely for show, used to avoid addressing their own needs seriously.

The Performer appears highly competent and seems to have it all together. A perfect performance for every act is the Performer's unattainable goal. Although there is a certain amount of personal satisfaction in doing so much so well, this person is inwardly paralyzed by the fear of being found to have inadequacies.

The Controller feels secure only when in control. As an adult, the Controller comes across as self-assured, always right, and, for the most part, looking good. A fear of vulnerability is what makes this wounded lamb act like a lion.

The Martyr is a great and constant sufferer. Anyone who has been abused needs and deserves the compassion of others. The Martyr, however, controls others by continuing to elicit compassion for having experienced devastating abuse.

Rather than affirm these self-designed and self-defeating survival skills, the Bible presents another option:

> *"Since we are surrounded by such a great cloud of witnesses,*
> *let us throw off everything that hinders*
> *and the sin that so easily entangles,*
> *and let us run with perseverance the race marked out for us.*
> *Let us fix our eyes on Jesus,*
> *the author and perfecter of our faith,*
> *who for the joy set before him endured the cross,*
> *scorning its shame,*
> *and sat down at the right hand of the throne of God"*
> (HEBREWS 12:1-2).

G. What Are the Victim's Broken Boundaries?[31]

Because of past physical and emotional abuse, victims may continue to have difficulty establishing and maintaining personal boundaries. And adults who relate to others out of a victim mentality often have difficulty being appropriately honest and assertive. They validate the words spoken by Isaiah the prophet:

"Justice is driven back,
and righteousness stands at a distance;
truth has stumbled in the streets,
honesty cannot enter"
(Isaiah 59:14).

If you think you have difficulty establishing and maintaining appropriate boundaries, take the following…

Test for Broken Boundaries[32]

- ☐ Do you find it difficult to make decisions and stick with them when opposed?
- ☐ Do you feel you must seek opinions from others before making a decision?
- ☐ Do you feel hesitant to give your opinion when asked?
- ☐ Do you fear expressing what you really feel?
- ☐ Do you lack confidence in your convictions?
- ☐ Do you avoid certain people because you fear embarrassment?
- ☐ Do you find it difficult to maintain eye contact with another person?
- ☐ Do you find it difficult to ask others for help?
- ☐ Do you do favors for others even when you know you shouldn't?
- ☐ Do you avoid asking people to return overdue items they have borrowed?
- ☐ Do you have difficulty receiving sincere compliments?
- ☐ Do you need a great deal of assurance from others?
- ☐ Do you do more than your share of work on a project?
- ☐ Do you have difficulty pointing out situations that are unfair?
- ☐ Do you ever say yes when you want to say no?

If you checked any of those boxes, you may be operating with a victim mentality. Be aware that

> *"fear of man will prove to be a snare,*
> *but whoever trusts in the LORD is kept safe"*
> (PROVERBS 29:25).

H. What Are the Victim's Codependent Tendencies?

Someone who is *codependent* is dependent on another person to the point of being controlled or manipulated by that person. We should have a healthy interdependence on others in the sense that we should value and enjoy each other, and love and learn from each other, but we should not allow ourselves to become totally dependent on each other.

An interdependent relationship involves a healthy, mutual give-and-take where neither person looks to the other to meet each and every need. But many people who have experienced victimization form *misplaced dependencies* on others. Those kinds of relationships are not healthy. God intends for us to live in total dependence on Him alone, and to realize He will work through others to meet some of our needs. We should not expect or look to others to do so.

Again and again, the Bible portrays how godly people learn to have a *strong dependence* on the Lord rather than a *weak dependence* on each other. The apostle Paul said we should...

> *"not rely on ourselves but on God"*
> (2 CORINTHIANS 1:9).

- **Codependent people may appear capable and self-sufficient,** yet in reality they are insecure, self-doubting, and in need of approval.

  — This need for approval can result in an *excessive sense of responsibility.*

  — It can also result in a dependence on *people-pleasing performance.*

However, the Bible says our primary focus should not be on pleasing people, but rather on pleasing God.[33]

> *"We instructed you how to live in order to please God,*
> *as in fact you are living.*
> *Now we ask you and urge you*
> *in the Lord Jesus to do this more and more"*
> (1 THESSALONIANS 4:1).

- **Classic codependent relationships** are typically characterized by an emotionally *weak person* who feels the need to be connected to an emotionally *strong person.*
  - The so-called *strong one* is actually weak because of the need to be needed.
  - Both are insecure and become entangled in a web of emotional bondage.
  - The two combine to produce a destructive cycle of manipulation and control, draining joy and happiness out of life.
  - Because this destructive dynamic is often subconscious, both parties can feel innocent of any wrongdoing.

Yet God knows that the self-absorbed motives of codependent persons are consumed with trying to fill an empty emotional bucket that has no bottom.[34]

> *"All a man's ways seem innocent to him,*
> *but motives are weighed by the LORD"*
> (PROVERBS 16:2).

III. CAUSES OF A VICTIM MENTALITY

Bitter circumstances surrounded Naomi, *and she blamed no one but God.*
Widowed and left childless upon the death of her two adult sons, bitterness, fear, and insecurity were all Naomi felt as she contemplated leaving Moab to return to her homeland, Israel. She urged her two daughters-in-law, Orpah and Ruth, to find refuge among their relatives, but they insisted on returning to Israel alongside her. "No, my daughters. It is more bitter for me than for you, because the LORD's hand has gone out against me!" (Ruth 1:13).

Naomi further compelled the two women to leave. Orpah eventually decided to return to her own family, but Ruth remained loyal to her mother-in-law. Naomi gave up her pleading when she realized the degree of Ruth's determination.

> *"Don't urge me to leave you or*
> *to turn back from you.*
> *Where you go I will go,*
> *and where you stay I will stay.*

> *Your people will be my people*
> *and your God my God"*
> (RUTH 1:16).

Everyone who has been victimized has felt overwhelmed by trauma. Many often end up arriving at distorted conclusions about themselves and their world. These incorrect beliefs lead wounded hearts to adopt faulty reactions and behaviors that hide their intense hurt and build walls that act as barriers to intimacy with God.

Yet the Lord lovingly uses failures and problem relationships to reveal unresolved emotional problems. As God calls each one of us to account, His desire is to break down the dividing walls and heal hurting hearts in order to set prisoners free.

> *"The Spirit of the Lord is on me,*
> *because he has anointed me to preach good news to the poor.*
> *He has sent me to proclaim freedom for the prisoners*
> *and recovery of sight for the blind,*
> *to release the oppressed"*
> (LUKE 4:18).

A. Why Does Setting Up Spiritual Walls Lead to a Victim Mentality?

The town of Bethlehem stirred upon the arrival of Naomi and her daughter-in-law. "The women exclaimed, 'Can this be Naomi?'" (Ruth 1:19). Naomi couldn't bear to recall the meaning of her name, a name that signified pleasantness or sweetness. The name Mara, identified with bitterness, seemed far more appropriate for her circumstances.

> *"'Don't call me Naomi,' she told them.*
> *'Call me Mara,*
> *because the Almighty has made my life very bitter.*
> *I went away full, but the LORD has brought me back empty.*
> *Why call me Naomi?*
> *The LORD has afflicted me;*
> *the Almighty has brought misfortune upon me'"*
> (RUTH 1:20-21).

Often those who develop a victim mentality view themselves as spiritual...

Prisoners of the Past

FAULTY REACTIONS	DISTORTED CONCLUSIONS	BIBLICAL TRUTH
Blaming God	"This is God's fault." "God is not fair!"	"He is the Rock, his works are perfect, and all his ways are just. A faithful God who does no wrong, upright and just is he" (Deuteronomy 32:4).
Harboring anger toward God	"How could God let this happen to me?" "God doesn't care about me."	"The LORD is righteous in all his ways and loving toward all he has made" (Psalm 145:17).
Refusing to trust God	"I can't depend on God." "I don't believe in God."	"Trust in the LORD with all your heart and lean not on your own understanding" (Proverbs 3:5).
Fearing God	"I'm afraid of God." "I want to hide from God."	"The LORD is my light and my salvation—whom shall I fear? The LORD is the stronghold of my life—of whom shall I be afraid?" (Psalm 27:1).
Doubting God's love	"God certainly doesn't love me." "I don't deserve God's love."	"Great is his love toward us, and the faithfulness of the LORD endures forever" (Psalm 117:2).

Left unchecked, such anger, disbelief, fear, and doubt can build up spiritual walls that separate victims from the truths of Scripture and lead to the onset of a victim mentality.

B. Why Does Erecting Emotional Walls Lead to a Victim Mentality?

The two widows, Naomi and Ruth, were alone and virtually destitute. They were without any means of supporting themselves and had to rely completely on God's provision.

Rather than sink into depression and self-pity, Ruth had an idea and asked Naomi if she could carry it out. Ruth would follow the custom of the poor and follow behind the harvesters in the fields of fellow Hebrews and pick up the remnants of grain that they dropped. Ruth's suggestion brought hope to Naomi—hope that Ruth would be able to gather enough grain to put food on the table so they wouldn't starve. The outcome, of course, would be in the hands of the Lord.

> *"Ruth the Moabitess said to Naomi,*
> *'Let me go to the fields and pick up the leftover grain*
> *behind anyone in whose eyes I find favor.'*
> *Naomi said to her, 'Go ahead, my daughter'"*
> (RUTH 2:2).

Often those who develop a victim mentality view themselves as *emotional...*

======= *Prisoners of the Past* =======

FAULTY REACTIONS	DISTORTED CONCLUSIONS	BIBLICAL TRUTH
Bitterness	"I hate living in this family." "I wish I were someone else."	"See to it that no one misses the grace of God and that no bitter root grows up to cause trouble and defile many" (Hebrews 12:15).
False Guilt	"This is my fault." "I must not tell; I'll get in trouble."	"Surely you desire truth in the inner parts; you teach me wisdom in the inmost place" (Psalm 51:6).

Faulty Reactions	Distorted Conclusions	Biblical Truth
Shame	"Something must be wrong with me." "I am a bad person."	"I praise you because I am fearfully and wonderfully made; your works are wonderful, I know that full well" (Psalm 139:14).
Unforgiveness	"I'll never forgive them." "I wish they were dead."	"If you hold anything against anyone, forgive him, so that your Father in heaven may forgive you your sins" (Mark 11:25).
Fear	"What will happen to me if someone finds out?" "What if someone hurts me again?"	"I sought the Lord, and he answered me; he delivered me from all my fears" (Psalm 34:4).
Hopelessness	"Things have never been good." "Life will never get better."	"I am still confident of this: I will see the goodness of the Lord in the land of the living" (Psalm 27:13).
Self-centeredness	"I never have fun or enjoy life like others do." "It's hard to think of anything but my unhappiness."	"The Lord will fulfill his purpose for me; your love, O Lord, endures forever" (Psalm 138:8).

Left in place, these emotional walls prevent the truth of God's Word from penetrating the soul, and a victim mentality takes hold.

C. Why Does Raising Relational Walls Lead to a Victim Mentality?

In the midst of grief and uncertainty, Naomi couldn't conceive that God was orchestrating circumstances for her blessing—and the link through which He would make this happen was loyal Ruth.

To provide food for herself and her mother-in-law, Ruth chose to glean grain in a field that happened to belong to Boaz, a relative of Naomi's deceased husband, Elimelech. He was a godly and gracious man, amply providing for and protecting Ruth while she worked.

A glimmer of hope shone in Naomi's sad eyes when Ruth told her where she was gleaning:

> "'The LORD bless him!' Naomi said to her daughter-in-law.
> 'He has not stopped showing his kindness to the living and the dead.'
> She added, 'That man is our close relative;
> he is one of our kinsman-redeemers'"
> (RUTH 2:20).

Often those who develop a victim mentality view themselves as *relational...*

=== *Prisoners of the Past* ===

FAULTY REACTIONS	DISTORTED CONCLUSIONS	BIBLICAL TRUTH
Fear	"People are unsafe." "I must protect myself."	"Do not be afraid of any man, for judgment belongs to God" (Deuteronomy 1:17).
Distrust	"People are unreliable." "I must guard myself."	"There is a friend who sticks closer than a brother" (Proverbs 18:24).

Faulty Reactions	Distorted Conclusions	Biblical Truth
Anger	"People are perpetrators." "I must avenge myself."	"Do not take revenge, my friends, but leave room for God's wrath, for it is written: 'It is mine to avenge; I will repay,' says the Lord" (Romans 12:19).
Insecurity	"People are selfish." "I must fend for myself."	"All the believers were together and had everything in common. Selling their possessions and goods, they gave to anyone as he had need" (Acts 2:44-45).

As victims of abuse move on with their lives, many outgrow their faulty and immature ways of thinking about life. They put away the past and begin to seek fulfillment through achieving personal goals such as service to the Lord, marriage, children, career, financial success, and other personal accomplishments.

Unfortunately, the patterns these victims developed as children in order to survive remain part of their personalities. These patterns may become iron-clad, protective walls around emotional pain or hurt, and they may keep self-awareness, vulnerability, and true intimacy in relationships at bay.

Although those who have been victimized as children yearn for mature love, often a journey back into their silenced hearts seems too threatening[35] and the hidden deceptions too deep to understand.

> *"The heart is deceitful above all things and beyond cure.*
> *Who can understand it?"*
> (Jeremiah 17:9).

D. Why Does Fostering Fear Lead to a Victim Mentality?[36]

Fear does not appear in a vacuum. There is always something that sets up a person to be controlled by fear, and there is always something that serves to trigger that fear. The setup occurred in the past, while the trigger occurs in the present. Finding the truth about your fear will provide wisdom as to why you are being controlled by present fear and being held captive to a victim mentality.

> *"Surely you desire truth in the inner parts;*
> *you teach me wisdom in the inmost place"*
> (PSALM 51:6).

Past Setups for Fear

- **Monumental Experiences**
    — Traumatic events
    — Scary situations
    — Abusive relationships
    — Fearful role models

    Realize the reason for your fear and tell yourself the truth about the past and the present. "When I was a child, I talked like a child, I thought like a child, I reasoned like a child. When I became [an adult], I put childish ways behind me" (1 Corinthians 13:11).

- **Emotional Overload**
    — Pent-up unacknowledged feelings
    — Unrealistic expectations
    — Harsh, stressful environment
    — Demanding, rejecting authority figures

    Realize the reason for your fear and allow the Lord to help you heal from your hurts. "Humble yourselves, therefore, under God's mighty hand, that he may lift you up in due time. Cast all your anxiety on him because he cares for you" (1 Peter 5:6-7).

- **Situational Avoidance**
    — Refusal to face fears
    — Rejection of chances for change

— Reinforcement of fears

— Repetition of negative thought patterns

Realize the reason for your fears and allow the Lord to help you face your fears. "I am the LORD, your God, who takes hold of your right hand and says to you, Do not fear; I will help you" (Isaiah 41:13).

- **Dismal Outlook**

  — Anticipation of danger and disaster

  — Expectation of frustration and failure

  — Belief of lies

  — Rejection of truth

Realize the reason for your fears and tell yourself the truth. "Whatever is true, whatever is noble, whatever is right, whatever is pure, whatever is lovely, whatever is admirable—if anything is excellent or praiseworthy—think about such things" (Philippians 4:8).

E. Why Does Victimization Lead to Codependency?

Just as day follows night, codependency predictably follows victimization. They tend to go hand in hand, and for good reason. Each fosters the other and imprisons victims in a repetitive, painful cycle—a cycle God wants to break so He can bring freedom.

> *"It is for freedom that Christ has set us free.*
> *Stand firm, then,*
> *and do not let yourselves be burdened again*
> *by a yoke of slavery"*
> (GALATIANS 5:1).

===== Codependency =====

QUESTION: "How are victimized children set up to become codependent adults?"

ANSWER: No one sets out to be emotionally addicted. Love-cravings often are created in childhood because there is "no water in the well"—their "love buckets" are empty. These children may become adult love-addicts because they…

- did not receive enough positive affirmation as children
- grew up feeling unloved, insignificant, and insecure
- experienced a traumatic separation or a lack of bonding
- felt and continue to feel intense sadness and a profound loss at being abandoned
- experienced repeated rejection from their parents
- felt and continue to feel extreme fear, helplessness, and emptiness

Children with empty love-buckets create a fantasy about some "savior" who will remove their fear and finally make them feel whole. As adults, they still behave like emotionally needy children who…

- believe that being loved by someone—anyone—is the solution to their emptiness
- enter relationships believing they cannot take care of themselves
- assign too much value and power to the other person in a relationship
- have tremendously unrealistic expectations of the other person
- try to "stick like glue" to the other person in order to feel connected
- live in fear that those who truly love them will ultimately leave them

The plight of a love addict would seem without solution were it not for the Lord, who is the only true Savior, the One who loves them unconditionally and eternally. He gives this assurance in the Bible:

> *"I have loved you with an everlasting love;*
> *I have drawn you with loving-kindness"*
> (JEREMIAH 31:3).

F. What Is the Root Cause of a Victim Mentality?

Having lost her love for life, Naomi now saw hope on the horizon.

In ancient Israel, it was customary for the nearest relative to have the first opportunity to buy or redeem a deceased person's property, and Naomi wanted to sell a field that belonged to Elimelech. Boaz was interested in buying the field, but there was a nearer kinsman the property had to be offered to first.

Initially the man was interested. But then he heard the legal transaction would involve acquiring the widow, Ruth. Apparently the property had passed into the hands of Ruth's late husband, Mahlon, upon his father's death. It was necessary "to maintain the name of the dead with his property" (Ruth 4:5).

The kinsman declined the entire offer, and Boaz purchased the field and took Ruth as his wife. A son, Obed, was born, and pleasantness was restored to the once-embittered Naomi.

> *"The women said to Naomi:*
> *'Praise be to the LORD,*
> *who this day has not left you without a kinsman-redeemer.*
> *May he become famous throughout Israel!*
> *He will renew your life and sustain you in your old age.*
> *For your daughter-in-law, who loves you*
> *and who is better to you than seven sons,*
> *has given him birth'"*
> (RUTH 4:14-15).

Victims who remain imprisoned by a victim mentality do so because of a belief system that keeps them locked into feeling they are powerless to change. Thus they tend to resist accepting responsibility for their personal healing and growth.

WRONG BELIEF OF THE VICTIM

"I was powerless to change my life growing up, and I am powerless to change it now. What has happened to me has defined me, and I do not deserve anything better. Besides, I am not as adequate or as good as others, and the fear of being discovered as the failure I am overwhelms me."

RIGHT BELIEF FOR THE VICTIM

As a child of God, you have Christ living in you. He gives you the power to change. You can give Him your fear of failure and accept the responsibility to overcome your past because God is faithful—He will do it! You can take your every thought captive and begin a process of reprogramming your mind so you can become emotionally, relationally, and spiritually healthy. Determine that you will "demolish arguments and every pretension that sets itself up against the knowledge of God, and…take captive every thought to make it obedient to Christ" (2 Corinthians 10:5).

You are able to do this because…

> *"his divine power has given [you] everything [you] need*
> *for life and godliness through [your] knowledge of him*
> *who called [you] by his own glory and goodness"*
> (2 PETER 1:3).

IV. STEPS TO SOLUTION

Apart from the supernatural work of the Spirit of God within the lives of victims, there is no solid solution to the serious side effects of being victimized.

Such a work is based on having a personal relationship with God, on seeing Him as He really is—a gracious and compassionate heavenly Father who is full of tender mercies. This requires replacing distorted images of God with the truth about His character. It requires maturing in the Lord, walking with Him on a daily basis, confiding in Him, and learning to trust Him for life itself.

Understanding the life-changing effects of being victimized by others is not for the purpose of placing blame, becoming bitter, or for excusing our failures. It is accepting the fact that facing ourselves is necessary for identifying and replacing past problematic programming with the transforming Word of God.

> *"For the word of God is living and active.*
> *Sharper than any double-edged sword,*
> *it penetrates even to dividing soul and spirit,*
> *joints and marrow;*
> *it judges the thoughts and attitudes of the heart"*
> (HEBREWS 4:12).

A. A Key Verse to Memorize

"You, O God, do see trouble and grief;
you consider it to take it in hand.
The victim commits himself to you;
you are the helper of the fatherless"
(Psalm 10:14).

B. A Key Passage to Read and Reread

Read all of Psalm 91, and focus particularly on verse 11:

"He will command his angels concerning you
to guard you in all your ways"
(Psalm 91:11).

His Guardian Angels Have Watch-care over You

- Rest in the presence of almighty God — verse 1
- Trust in the defense of your loving God — verse 2
- Believe in the faithfulness of your God — verses 3-7
- See your vindication as coming from God — verse 8
- Live in the safety of your sheltering God — verses 9-10
- Know you are guarded by angels sent from God — verses 11-13
- Rely on the protection of your loving God — verse 14
- Call on your Savior and God for deliverance — verses 15-16

C. How to Analyze Your Anger

Those who have been caught in a cage of victimization—those who feel powerless because of someone else's entrapment—can understandably feel anger stemming from one or more of these four sources: hurt, injustice, fear, and frustration.

Anger is like the red light on our car dashboard that blares *Something's wrong! Something's wrong!* Anger can serve as a gift that motivates us to look at why we were victimized in the first place and how we can break free.

Probing into buried feelings from your past can be painful. That's why it may seem easier to stay angry than to uncover the cause, turn loose of your "rights," and grow in maturity.[37] The Bible gives specific, practical solutions in the form of three "do not's":

> *"'In your anger do not sin':*
> *Do not let the sun go down while you are still angry,*
> *and do not give the devil a foothold"*
> (EPHESIANS 4:26-27).

One of the first steps toward overcoming a victim mentality is to look at your present anger patterns and the picture they paint of your past victimizations. Learning the cause of your anger will aid you in learning how to resolve your anger.

The Four Causes of Anger

1. Hurt[38]—Your Heart Is Wounded

Everyone has a God-given inner need for *unconditional love*.[39] When you experience rejection or emotional pain of any kind, anger can become a protective wall that keeps people and pain away.

2. Injustice[40]—Your Right Is Violated

Everyone has an inner moral code that produces a sense of what is right and wrong, fair and unfair, just and unjust. When you perceive that an injustice has occurred against you or others (especially those whom you love), you may feel angry. If you hold on to the offense, the unresolved anger can begin to make a home in your heart.

3. Fear[41]—Your Future Is Threatened

Everyone is created with a God-given inner need for *security*.[42] When you begin to worry, feel threatened, or get angry because of a change in circumstances, you may be responding to fear. A fearful heart reveals a lack of trust in God's perfect plan for your life.

4. Frustration[43]—Your Performance Is Not Accepted

Everyone has a God-given inner need for *significance*.[44] When your efforts are thwarted or do not meet your personal expectations, your sense of significance may feel threatened. Frustration over unmet expectations of yourself or of others is a major source of anger.

"Man's anger does not bring about the righteous life that God desires"
(James 1:20).

Search your heart and determine that you will not allow anger to dictate your decisions or control your emotions. Instead, turn your hurts, rights, fears, and frustrations over to God and enter into a total dependence upon Him to meet your needs. Remember:

> *"The Lord will guide you always;*
> *he will satisfy your needs in a sun-scorched land*
> *and will strengthen your frame.*
> *You will be like a well-watered garden,*
> *like a spring whose waters never fail"*
> (Isaiah 58:11).

D. How to Free Yourself from Unresolved Anger

She fled to an isolated place, but was found by almighty God.

Hagar was the maidservant of Sarai, the woman through whom God had promised both a blessed heir for her husband, Abram, and descendants as numerous as the stars. But when day after day after day passed with no son yet conceived, Sarai proposed her own plan for fulfilling God's promise—a plan that directly involved Hagar.

Sarai proposed that Abram have sexual relations with Hagar. And if she conceived, the child born from their union would be considered Sarai's own. Because Sarai's suggestion was customary for the time, Abram followed her advice and, along with a child being conceived, a struggle was birthed between the two women:

> *"After Abram had been living in Canaan ten years,*
> *Sarai his wife took her Egyptian maidservant Hagar*
> *and gave her to her husband to be his wife.*
> *He slept with Hagar, and she conceived.*
> *When she knew she was pregnant,*
> *she began to despise her mistress"*
> (Genesis 16:3-4).

Many of us assume that once we reach adulthood, our pain from childhood will just disappear and no longer affect us. But this "disappearing act" does not happen unless we identify our past pains from childhood and resolve them. While we are not the sum of our experiences, we are shaped by our *responses* to our experiences.

God does not want us to store up the bad things that happened to us by stockpiling our anger. Rather, He wants us to be like a storehouse from which the bad fruit of anger and resentment, distrust and fear is discarded and the good fruit of joy and peace, patience and kindness, and forgiveness are retained.

> *"The good man brings good things out of the good stored up in him,*
> *and the evil man brings evil things out of the evil stored up in him"*
> (MATTHEW 12:35).

Resolving Anger Rooted in Childhood Victimizations

The next time anger wells up in your heart or uncontrollable tears stream down your face, ask yourself:

- What am I feeling: hurt, injustice, fear, or frustration?
- Did I have any of these same feelings when I was a child?

Here is how you can face your anger from the past and begin to see how your present anger is connected to your unresolved childhood anger:

- *Ask God to reveal* buried hurts, injustices, fears, and frustrations from your childhood.
- *Take four pieces of paper* and label one "Hurt," one "Injustice," one "Fear," and one "Frustration." Then write down every instance of each you can remember from your life.
- *Release your anger* over each instance to God and replace the anger with God's peace.
- *Forgive and pray* for those toward whom you have harbored anger.
- *Burn the pages* as a sacrificial offering to God.
- *Ask God to reveal* the relationship between your past and present anger.
- *Ask close family members and friends* what they think makes you angry and how they know when you are angry.

- *Ask forgiveness* from anyone you have offended by your anger.
- *Assume personal responsibility* for your present feelings of anger.
- *Meditate on how God has demonstrated His great love for you.*

If your heart yearns for love and acceptance, remember:

> *"This is how God showed his love among us:*
> *He sent his one and only Son into the world that we might live through him.*
> *This is love: not that we loved God,*
> *but that he loved us and sent his Son as an atoning sacrifice for our sins"*
> (1 John 4:9-10).

E. How to Find the Key to Your Locked Prison Cage

Sarai complained to Abram about Hagar's mistreatment of her, and Abram gave her the authority to do as she pleased regarding Hagar. Sarai immediately began to treat her harshly.

Hagar then fled to a lonely place by a spring in the wilderness, but soon found she was not alone. God compassionately spoke to her, instructing her to return and submit to Sarai. He assured Hagar that her offspring would be greatly multiplied. However, this offspring was not the promised seed yet to be fulfilled through Abram and Sarai.

> *"You are now with child and you will have a son.*
> *You shall name him Ishmael, for the Lord has heard of your misery.*
> *He will be a wild donkey of a man;*
> *his hand will be against everyone and everyone's hand against him,*
> *and he will live in hostility toward all his brothers"*
> (Genesis 16:11-12).

Finding freedom is a process that takes time and has periods of regression. You may have seasons when it seems like no progress is being made at all. The first step in the process is deciding that you want to heal and believing that healing *is possible* with God. As you place your hope in Him and seek His plan for you, wait patiently for the Lord to lovingly show you the way.

> *"No one whose hope is in you will ever be put to shame,*
> *but they will be put to shame who are treacherous without excuse.*
> *Show me your ways, O Lord, teach me your paths"*
> (Psalm 25:3-4).

Healing Is Possible

QUESTION: "After someone has been victimized, is healing really possible?"

ANSWER: Yes, through the power of the Lord. It will take time, but healing is a positive process through which you will experience spiritual growth.

> *"Heal me, O LORD, and I will be healed;*
> *save me and I will be saved"*
> (JEREMIAH 17:14).

As you begin the process of healing—of finding freedom from your bondage to victimization—there are several painful realities you will need to face and work through.

Face Your Prison

Recognizing your prison walls is necessary in order to tear those walls down and experience the freedom—the total freedom—God has planned for you. Ask yourself:

— Do I feel there is no way out of my situation?

— Do I think love is based on my performance?

— Do I feel powerless in my relationships?

— Do I lie to avoid conflict?

— Do I think other people are better than me?

— Do I have a lack of trust in people?

— Do I have difficulty saying *no*?

— Do I fear rejection?

Acknowledging your bondage and your need to break through the walls that are keeping you from having healthy relationships is critical to the healing process.

— Acknowledge your bondage by confessing it to God.

— Acknowledge your realization that your bondage has hindered both your relationship with God and your relationships with others.

— Acknowledge your need for God's divine intervention in your life.

— Acknowledge your dependence on Him to empower you to walk in freedom.

— Acknowledge your need for a new way of thinking about Him, yourself, and others.

— Acknowledge your need to see yourself from God's viewpoint.

— Acknowledge your need to understand what constitutes a healthy relationship from God's perspective.

— Acknowledge your bondage by sharing it with one or two trusted confidants who will agree to hold you accountable and help you work toward becoming mature in Christ.

Remember the admonition in God's Word that we are to...

> *"carry each other's burdens,*
> *and in this way you will fulfill the law of Christ"*
> (GALATIANS 6:2).

═══════════ **God Is Trustworthy** ═══════════

QUESTION: "Who can I trust to help me?"

ANSWER: God knows how to make sense out of your confusion, and He is completely trustworthy. He will also bring trustworthy persons into your life to aid you in your healing process and to provide healthy, long-term relationships that help keep you on the path toward healing.

> *"Trust in the LORD with all your heart*
> *and lean not on your own understanding;*
> *in all your ways acknowledge him,*
> *and he will make your paths straight"*
> (PROVERBS 3:5-6).

Face Your Past[45]

- **Remembering past victimization** is sometimes the first step toward healing.

To induce memory, God often uses...

—flashbacks   —dreams and nightmares

—parenthood   —a significant death

—media coverage   —touch

—victory over an addiction   —the testimony of others

- **Journaling can help you** to move through the stages of remembering.

  Writing down your thoughts and feelings helps you...

—face the fact of the abuse

—recall the feelings associated with the abuse

—uncover hidden fury associated with the abuse

—process your feelings about the abuse

—objectify the abuse

—organize the events surrounding the abuse

—discover the ramifications of the abuse

—gain insights into any present abuse

You'll want to memorize this Scripture passage:

*"I have been deprived of peace; I have forgotten what prosperity is.
So I say, 'My splendor is gone and all that I had hoped from the LORD.'
I remember my affliction and my wandering, the bitterness and the gall.
I well remember them, and my soul is downcast within me.
Yet this I call to mind and therefore I have hope:
Because of the LORD's great love we are not consumed,
for his compassions never fail"*
(LAMENTATIONS 3:17-22).

Trouble Remembering

QUESTION: "What if I'm having trouble remembering?"

ANSWER: Ask the Lord to bring to your mind anything He wants you to remember. Pray, "Lord, I'm willing to face whatever painful situations that occurred years ago. I know that I don't have to remember everything in order to be emotionally whole. Enable me to remember what You want me to remember."

Realize:

> *"The advantage of knowledge is this:*
> *that wisdom preserves the life of its possessor"*
> (ECCLESIASTES 7:12).

Face Your Patterns of Behavior[46]

- **Realizing what you are doing** to get your inner needs met can provide meaningful insight. Ask yourself:
  — Am I compromising my values in order to feel loved?
  — Am I violating my conscience in order to feel secure?
  — Am I being a perfectionist, a workaholic, a fixer in order to feel significant?
  — Am I cycling through one idolatrous codependent relationship after another in a vain attempt to fill my love bucket?

Remember:

> *"No temptation has seized you except what is common to man.*
> *And God is faithful;*
> *he will not let you be tempted beyond what you can bear.*
> *But when you are tempted,*
> *he will also provide a way out so that you can stand up under it"*
> (1 CORINTHIANS 10:13).

Codependent Relationships

QUESTION: "How do I stop falling into codependent relationships? And how can I have my craving for love met in a way that honors God?"

ANSWER: Any of us can move from codependency to a healthy, mutual give-and-take in our relationships. When the pain in your relationship is greater than your fear of abandonment, the motivation for change is powerful. To break out of your codependency, you must...

- *Confront the fact that you are codependent.* Before you can break free of codependency's grasp, you must admit your love addiction.

- *Confront the consequences of your codependency.* Accept responsibility for how your past experiences and reactions have hurt your adult relationships.

- *Confront your painful emotions.* Understand that you will have pain no matter what you choose. If you leave your codependent relationships, you will hurt, but if you stay, you will also hurt. The only hope for healing is leaving the codependent lifestyle altogether and resolving the emotional wounds that are drawing you into codependent relationships.

- *Confront your secondary addictions.* Recognize that, in an effort to numb the emotional pain of the relationship, codependency often leads to other addictions, such as chemical dependency, sexual addiction, compulsive eating, or excessive spending.

- *Confront your current codependent relationship(s).* Acknowledge your role and stop relating through old, familiar, codependent patterns.

- *Confront your codependent focus.* Stop focusing on what the other person is doing and start focusing on what you need to do to become emotionally healthy.

- *Confront your codependent conflicts.* Do not allow yourself to become trapped in heated arguments or to become emotionally hooked by the bad behavior of another person.

- *Confront what you must leave in order to receive what you truly need.* Leave your childish, dependent thinking (*I can't live without you.*) and enter into healthy adult thinking (*I want you in my life, but if something were to happen, I could still live without you*).

- *Confront your need to build mature, non-codependent relationships.* Establish several interdependent relationships—not just one exclusive relationship.

Take to heart the admonition of Scripture:

> *"Let us…go on to maturity"*
> (Hebrews 6:1).

People-pleaser

QUESTION: "How can I stop being a people-pleaser?"

ANSWER: The best way to eliminate an undesirable belief or behavior is by replacing it with a desirable one.

- Begin by knowing the truth about yourself and the reality of God's love for you through studying God's Word.
- Ask God to open your eyes and mind to His truth.
- Why seek the temporary approval of a person when you can have the permanent approval of God?
    — Start living for God's approval by living according to His Word.
    — Stop looking to people for acceptance.

The problem with many relationships today is that each person sees the other as the source of supply for the meeting of personal needs. Unfortunately, no one is perfect enough or consistent enough always to meet the expectations of another. In truth, there is only one dependable Source: His name is Jesus Christ.

> *"Am I now trying to win the approval of men, or of God?*
> *Or am I trying to please men?*
> *If I were still trying to please men,*
> *I would not be a servant of Christ"*
> (GALATIANS 1:10).

Biblical Dependency

QUESTION: "Is any form of dependency biblical?"

ANSWER: God wants us to depend on *Him* to meet our needs, and not other people. To develop a biblical dependency on God, you must...

- **Rely** on Him, not on people or things or self-effort. "My salvation and my honor depend on God; he is my mighty rock, my refuge" (Psalm 62:7).

- **Believe** that He will meet all of your needs. You can safely reveal your hurts, your fears, and your needs to God. He will be your Need-meeter. "God is able to make all grace abound to you, so that in all things at all times, having all that you need, you will abound in every good work" (2 Corinthians 9:8).

- **Trust** in Him to take care of your loved ones. "Trust in him at all times, O people; pour out your hearts to him, for God is our refuge" (Psalm 62:8).

- **Rely** on Christ, whose life within you will enable you to overcome any destructive dependency. "The one [Christ] who is in you is greater than the one [Satan] who is in the world" (1 John 4:4).

=========== **Negative Patterns** ===========

QUESTION: "How do I overcome negative behavior patterns?"

ANSWER: Know that in Christ you are set free from old patterns of sin. Make choices that are in accord with His Word, allowing Him to reshape your thoughts and your responses.

> *"We know that our old self was crucified with him*
> *so that the body of sin might be done away with,*
> *that we should no longer be slaves to sin"*
> (ROMANS 6:6).

Face Your Private Secret[47]
Understanding the bondage that secrets create is essential to breaking down prison walls.

— Talking about the past brings it into reality.

— Telling someone else gives your past credibility.

— Telling the secret breaks its power over you.

— Telling brings what was done in the dark out into the light for healing.

Scripture reminds us...

"'Can anyone hide in secret places so that I cannot see him?' declares the LORD.
'Do not I fill heaven and earth?' declares the LORD...
Therefore confess your sins to each other
and pray for each other so that you may be healed.
The prayer of a righteous man is powerful and effective"
(JEREMIAH 23:24; JAMES 5:16).

Too Embarrassed to Tell

QUESTION: "Why tell anyone? It's too embarrassing."

ANSWER: Many victims feel responsible for their abuse. This can lead to feelings of shame and a strong desire to keep the events secret. The power of "the secret" keeps you in bondage and must be broken. You are not responsible for the abuse that you experienced. You can declare with Job,

"Let God weigh me in honest scales
and he will know that I am blameless"
(JOB 31:6).

Face Your Pain[48]

Walking through the emotional pain of victimization is one of the most difficult but most necessary steps in breaking down the walls that keep you in bondage.

— Pain confirms your abuse.

— Pain unrevealed is pain unhealed.

— Pain expressed is often pain released.

— Pain is unpleasant but not unbearable.

Be assured:

"If we confess our sins,
he is faithful and just and will forgive us our sins
and purify us from all unrighteousness"
(1 JOHN 1:9).

Painful Memories

QUESTION: "How can I bear to recall such painful memories?"

ANSWER: The Lord will help you, and He will bear your burdens. Take one day at a time, depending on the Lord.

> *"Praise be to the Lord,*
> *to God our Savior,*
> *who daily bears our burdens"*
> (PSALM 68:19).

Face Your Victimizer—only if it is safe to do so[49]

Standing up for yourself and taking back control over your life and body is liberating in itself.

— Pray for God's timing and the preparation of your heart and the heart of the victimizer.

— Identify realistic goals that you hope to accomplish through the confrontation.

— Write down what you plan to say and rehearse it with someone beforehand.

— Be prepared for the offender to deny having abused you.

— When the time is appropriate, talk with your perpetrator one on one, or take someone you trust with you if you think it is necessary.

— Let go of secret hopes and expectations. Know that your confrontation is biblical:

> *"If your brother sins against you,*
> *go and show him his fault"*
> (MATTHEW 18:15).

Confronting the Abuse

QUESTION: "When do I confront?"

ANSWER: When it is safe and when you can confront positively and in strength. Remember:

> *"Reckless words pierce like a sword,*
> *but the tongue of the wise brings healing"*
> (Proverbs 12:18).

Words you could say:

- "I want you to know that I remember the abusive things you did to me when I was a child, and I want you to know it profoundly impacted my life."
- "How did you justify those harmful acts toward me?"
- "Have you gone to counseling to fully understand the reasons you committed such abusive acts?"
- "What preventative actions are you now taking to not harm another person?"
- "I also want you to know that I have a new life in Christ, and He has enabled me to forgive you. He is healing my wounds and giving me joy and peace."
- "My prayer for you is that you will accept Jesus into your heart as your Lord and Savior so He can heal you too."

Realize:

> *"The wise in heart are called discerning,*
> *and pleasant words promote instruction"*
> (Proverbs 16:21).

Releasing Bitterness When the Offender Is Dead

Question: "How can I release the bitterness I feel toward my victimizer, who is now dead?"

Answer: Although you cannot confront your victimizer in person, you can confront indirectly by saying what you would want or need to say as though your offender is in front of you.

- Consider the "chair technique." Imagine the person seated in a chair placed in front of you. Say the things you would say to the person as if you were actually seated across a table from him or her. Express your feelings about what was done to you and the ramifications those events have had on your life. Then forgive the person and explain that you have taken him or her off of your emotional hook and placed the person onto God's hook.

- Write a letter to your victimizer, stating every painful memory. Read it over the person's grave or at a place where you can openly speak to the person as though you were in each other's presence. Then at the close, choose to forgive by releasing your victimizer into God's hands.

- Make a list of all painful as well as positive memories. After completing the list, go back to the beginning and write the word *past* next to each memory. Acknowledge and accept that the past is in the past. As an act of your will, release all the pain as well as the person into God's hands. Take the person and the pain off of your emotional hook and put him or her onto God's hook.

The fact that your victimizer has died does not mean you cannot forgive and thereby prevent bitterness from establishing a foothold in your heart and mind. The Bible says,

> *"See to it that no one misses the grace of God*
> *and that no bitter root grows up to cause trouble and defile many"*
> (Hebrews 12:15).

Face Your Pardon[50]

Learning the truth about guilt and forgiveness is a major key to living in freedom.

— Forgive yourself.

— Forgive the offender.

— Forgive anyone who has overtly or covertly victimized you.

— Forgiveness gives you freedom by taking vengeance out of your hands and putting the matter in God's hands to avenge.[51]

> *"We know him who said,*
> *'It is mine to avenge; I will repay,' and again,*
> *'The Lord will judge his people'"*
> (Hebrews 10:30).

========== **Reason for Forgiving** ==========

QUESTION: "Why should I forgive?"

ANSWER: The obvious answer to the question, "Why forgive?" is this: Because God says so! But *why does God say so*? First, because *others* need it. And second, because *you* need it![52] Long ago, George Herbert said that the person who cannot forgive "breaks the bridge over which all must pass if they would ever reach heaven; for everyone has need to be forgiven."[53]

The Bible is clear regarding forgiveness:

> *"Bear with each other*
> *and forgive whatever grievances you may have against one another.*
> *Forgive as the Lord forgave you"*
> (COLOSSIANS 3:13).

========== **Forgiveness** ==========

QUESTION: "How can I forgive?"

ANSWER: "To err is human, to forgive, divine."[54] This famous quote from Alexander Pope is a heavenly reminder to all of us. However, the earthly reality is more like this: "To err is human, to blame it on someone else is more human!" Oh, how much easier it is to blame than to forgive. But we are called by God to forgive. And when you do forgive, genuine forgiveness draws you into the heart of God, and your life takes on the divine character of Christ.

> *"You show that you are a letter from Christ,*
> *the result of our ministry,*
> *written not with ink but with the Spirit of the living God,*
> *not on tablets of stone but on tablets of human hearts"*
> (2 CORINTHIANS 3:3).

— Make a list of all the offenses caused by your offender and the pain each one caused you.

— Imagine right now that a hook is attached to your collarbone. And imagine attached to the hook all the pain resulting from the wrong that was done to you.

— Ask yourself, *Do I really want to carry all that pain with me for the rest of my life?* The Lord wants you to take all the pain from the past and release it into His hands.

— Then take the one who offended you off of your emotional hook and place that person onto God's hook. The Lord knows how to deal with your offender—in His time and in His way. God says,

> *"It is mine to avenge; I will repay"*
> (DEUTERONOMY 32:35).

ARGUMENT: "I cannot forgive and forget. I keep thinking about being hurt."

ANSWER: When you choose to forgive, you don't get a case of "holy amnesia." However, after facing the hurt and confronting the offender, close off your mind to rehearsing the pain of the past. Do not focus on your hurt, but on your healing.

> *"Forget the former things; do not dwell on the past"*
> (ISAIAH 43:18).

Face Your Predicament[55]

Knowing God permitted your victimization—but in no way caused it or condoned it—is paramount! God hates evil and violence and will one day totally obliterate all evil and evil practices. He will pronounce eternal judgment on all who persist in their evil ways.

> *"I will punish the world for its evil, the wicked for their sins.*
> *I will put an end to the arrogance of the haughty*
> *and will humble the pride of the ruthless"*
> (ISAIAH 13:11).

Columbine

It was April 20, 1999, and the two teenagers had planned for months to celebrate the birthday of their hero. It would be a birthday tribute that no high school student would forget—complete with fireworks. So...happy birthday, Adolf Hitler!

Dylan Klebold and Eric Harris walked into Columbine High School in Littleton, Colorado, armed with a pair of sawed-off shotguns, a semiautomatic handgun, and about a dozen homemade bombs. The scene was reminiscent of a video the two hate-filled students had made for a school project, in which they had depicted themselves carrying fake firearms and killing students. The teacher never showed the video to the class, deeming it far too graphic.[56]

Equally graphic and disturbing was what Klebold and Harris posted on a Web site. Racist rhetoric riddled its pages. But even more chilling was the outline of a plan to commit mass murder in Littleton and destroy the lives of the teachers and students they hated. A deputy at the Jefferson County sheriff's office had been directed to the Web site and an affidavit was written for a search warrant, but it was never filed.[57]

Klebold and Harris, who always wore black attire, had a reputation for being bullies. Their disdain primarily targeted Christians, minorities, and athletes. They filled their minds with nihilistic music, which denies the existence of morality and traditional values and instead advocates revolution, assassination, and terrorism. And on this fateful day, the two who loved to play violent video games were dressed in black trench coats and acted out their violence as mass murderers. Before turning their guns on themselves, Klebold and Harris shot and killed 12 students and 1 teacher, and left others seriously injured.

Rachel Scott was their first victim. They shot her twice in the legs and once in her mid-section while she was eating lunch just outside of the library. But the bloodthirsty pair wasn't satisfied...

Rachel tried to crawl away to find cover as the two gunmen walked off, but suddenly Harris turned back, grabbed Rachel by the hair, pulled her head up, and asked, "Do you believe in God?"

Rachel responded, "You know I do."

Harris pointed his gun to her head and, before pulling the trigger, coldly blurted out, "Then go be with him."[58] *And so she did.*

Another young woman would share an experience almost identical to Rachel's. Cassie Bernall had been studying in the library when Klebold and Harris stood over her and asked her the same question—whether she believed in God. Her simple response, "Yes," prompted a shot almost at point-blank range. She died immediately. The irony is that, not long before, Cassie's response might have been no. Before giving her life to Christ, she had dabbled in the occult and had even entertained thoughts about murdering her own parents.[59]

The widely reported news of the shootings shocked and saddened millions worldwide. Meanwhile, the brave stances for Christ evidenced that day reverberated through the Christian community as word solemnly spread of its newest young martyrs. On the day of Rachel Scott's funeral, during which tribute was paid to her faith in Christ, the CNN network reached its largest audience ever.[60]

Cassie Bernall's story was recounted at a teen mission in Michigan and deeply inspired the 73,000 who were in attendance. Christian organizations on college campuses across the United States reported a resurgence in participation as young people were moved to reexamine their faith. One young man said Cassie's affirmative response about believing in God had opened the doors for him to share his faith because his unsaved friends were so perplexed as to why, with a gun pointed at her head, she didn't say *no*.[61] Cassie's testimony also moved contemporary Christian artist Michael W. Smith to write the touching song *This Is Your Time,* which was released in 1999.

Consider the irony: While the two gunmen perceived themselves as snuffing out the lives of these two Christians, the result was that untold thousands of people heard their stories and either received Christ or were inspired to live more boldly. In Rachel Scott's journal, in an entry dated April 20, 1998—exactly one year prior to her death—we find these words: "I am not going to apologize for speaking the Name of Jesus. I am not going to justify my faith to them, and I am not going to hide the light that God has put into me. If I have to sacrifice everything...I will."[62]

Hundreds of thousands of bloggers have read and been influenced by Rachel's words. Mark blogged back, "I believe that, like Rachel, each of us should make a decision for Christ now, because, like Rachel, we never know how much time we have left on Earth."[63] Even many people who do not share Rachel's faith have been deeply touched. Luis wrote [sic], "im not a Christian or neither do i have any interest in the christian beliefs but...i cant stop thinkin about her... shows me how much she is influencing me, Rachel is God's gift to humanity."[64] Jeff shared the impact of Rachel's testimony: "I was one of the millions [sic] hearts you have touched…i am 44 years old and I will never forget u."[65]

In light of the overwhelming response to her journal entry and martyrdom, Rachel could have easily said to the two terrorists, "You intended to harm me, but God intended it for good to accomplish what is now being done, the saving of many lives" (Genesis 50:20).

Because we know God is sovereign, we know he permitted the tragedy at Columbine to take place. But that does not mean He caused or condoned it. In the end, He took that which was meant for evil and turned it to good.

And God can do the same in your life. Though He may have permitted your victimization, you need to…

— *Reason* in your mind that God did not create us as puppets, but He gives each person a free will with the ability to choose right or wrong.

— *Realize* that human will must always be separated from God's will.[66]

— *Remember* that allowing sin is not the same as causing or agreeing with sinful actions.

— *Recognize* that God will judge sin and sinful people in His time and in His way.

— *Recall* that God did not rescue His own Son from evil people and their evil deeds but allowed Him to suffer an excruciatingly painful victimization and death.

— *Rejoice* that, while God permits evil, He has the desire and power to redeem both those injured by victimization and those who victimize others. He wants to restore them to wholeness and use them to accomplish His divine purposes.

— *Reckon* that your life is but a vapor. Yet God loves you as His own child and plans to conform you into the very image of His beloved Son, Jesus Christ.

"We are more than conquerors through him who loved us.
For I am convinced
that neither death nor life, neither angels nor demons,
neither the present nor the future, nor any powers,
neither height nor depth, nor anything else in all creation,
will be able to separate us from the love of God
that is in Christ Jesus our Lord....
For those God foreknew he also predestined
to be conformed to the likeness of his Son"
(ROMANS 8:37-39,29).

Questioning or distrusting that which does not line up with our perceptions or that which we do not understand is quite natural. It is also natural to
be confused when the inexplicable occurs. So when we're victimized, it's second nature to ask God, "Why?" Even righteous Job questioned God.

So, during times of uncertainty...

— *Remind yourself that God has a perfect plan* for your life that cannot be thwarted by anything or anyone. "I know that you can
do all things; no plan of yours can be thwarted...For the LORD
Almighty has purposed, and who can thwart him? His hand
is stretched out, and who can turn it back?" (Job 42:2; Isaiah
14:27).

— *Remind yourself that nothing takes God by surprise* and that He
always goes before you to direct your path. He always holds
you with His hand. "You hem me in—behind and before; you
have laid your hand upon me...Where can I go from your
Spirit? Where can I flee from your presence?...If I rise on the
wings of the dawn, if I settle on the far side of the sea, even
there your hand will guide me, your right hand will hold me
fast" (Psalm 139:5,7,9-10).

— *Remind yourself that God's ways are not your ways* and His
thoughts are high above yours. You cannot foresee His plans or
comprehend His strategy. "How great are your works, O LORD,
how profound your thoughts! ...'For my thoughts are not your
thoughts, neither are your ways my ways,' declares the LORD.
'As the heavens are higher than the earth, so are my ways higher

than your ways and my thoughts than your thoughts.'…Therefore, holy brothers, who share in the heavenly calling, fix your thoughts on Jesus, the apostle and high priest whom we confess" (Psalm 92:5; Isaiah 55:8-9; Hebrews 3:1).

— *Remind yourself that God loves you desperately* and that He will bring good from everything that happens to you, even evil things done by evil people. "We know that in all things God works for the good of those who love him, who have been called according to his purpose" (Romans 8:28).

— *Remind yourself that God has a spiritually prosperous future* planned for you, one that is full of hope. "'I know the plans I have for you,' declares the LORD, 'plans to prosper you and not to harm you, plans to give you hope and a future'" (Jeremiah 29:11).

— *Remind yourself that God is all-powerful, all-knowing,* always present, thoroughly righteous, and that He has a good reason for everything He allows in your life. "He who forms the mountains, creates the wind, and reveals his thoughts to man, he who turns dawn to darkness, and treads the high places of the earth—the LORD God Almighty is his name…The LORD has established his throne in heaven, and his kingdom rules over all…Consider it pure joy, my brothers, whenever you face trials of many kinds, because you know that the testing of your faith develops perseverance. Perseverance must finish its work so that you may be mature and complete, not lacking anything" (Amos 4:13; Psalm 103:19; James 1:2-4).

— *Remind yourself that you are but clay in God's hands,* dust formed into a human being by your heavenly Father, who knit you together in your mother's womb and recorded your every day in His book before ever there was one. "Remember that you molded me like clay. Will you now turn me to dust again?…For you created my inmost being; you knit me together in my mother's womb…All the days ordained for me were written in your book before one of them came to be" (Job 10:9; Psalm 139:13,16).

God Is with Us When We Suffer

QUESTION: "Where was God when I was being abused?"

ANSWER: Among God's many attributes are His omniscience (He is all-knowing) and His omnipresence (He is present everywhere). Though God never wills evil, He is with us when we suffer.[67] And though He does not promise to remove suffering in this present sinful life, He does promise to remove it from the life to come. "The eyes of the LORD are everywhere, keeping watch on the wicked and the good...He will wipe every tear from their eyes. There will be no more death or mourning or crying or pain, for the old order of things has passed away" (Proverbs 15:3; Revelation 21:4).

God Will Punish the Offender

QUESTION: "Why doesn't God punish the offender?"

ANSWER: He will punish the wicked and lift up the innocent in His chosen time and in His chosen way. "The power of the wicked will be broken, but the LORD upholds the righteous" (Psalm 37:17).

F. How to Break the Cycle of Rejection

Victimization and rejection are constant companions and construct strong prison walls around the hearts of many victims. The messages they relay to their captives are bitterly painful and terribly destructive. The lies they convey must be countered with the truth of Scripture.

> *"Surely you desire truth in the inner parts;*
> *you teach me wisdom in the inmost place"*
> (PSALM 51:6).

When you experience...

A Sense of Rejection

Tell yourself the truth: "Just because someone withholds love from me doesn't mean everyone will withhold love from me. God will always listen to me and will never withhold His love from me." Psalm 66:20 says, "Praise be to God, who has not rejected my prayer or withheld his love from me!"

A Sense of Worthlessness

Tell yourself the truth: *Just because someone doesn't value me doesn't mean no one values me. God valued me enough to send Jesus to die for me so that I can spend eternity with Him.* "This is how God showed his love among us: He sent his one and only Son into the world that we might live through him" (1 John 4:9).

A Sense of Self-hate

Tell yourself the truth: *Just because someone has judged and condemned me doesn't mean I should condemn myself. God will never condemn me because I am in Christ's family.* "Who will bring any charge against those whom God has chosen? It is God who justifies. Who is he that condemns? Christ Jesus, who died—more than that, who was raised to life—is at the right hand of God and is also interceding for us" (Romans 8:33-34).

Remember...

- Jesus knew to expect unjustified hatred, and He tells you to expect unjustified hatred. "I have chosen you out of the world. That is why the world hates you" (John 15:19).

- Jesus knew to expect persecution, and He tells you to expect persecution. "If they persecuted me, they will persecute you also" (John 15:20).

- Jesus had enemies yet He loved them, and He tells you to love your enemies and do good to them. "Love your enemies, do good to them" (Luke 6:35).

- Jesus prayed for those who persecuted Him, and He tells you to pray for your persecutors. "Pray for those who persecute you" (Matthew 5:44).

- Jesus modeled forgiveness toward those who sinned against Him, and He tells you to forgive those who sin against you. "If you forgive men when they sin against you, your heavenly Father will also forgive you" (Matthew 6:14).

- Jesus understood that those who rejected Him were really rejecting His Father, and He tells you that those rejecting you are really rejecting Him. "He who rejects you rejects me" (Luke 10:16).

- Jesus said He would be rejected, but in the end there would be blessing. And He tells you that you will be rejected, but in the end there will be blessing. "Blessed are you when men hate you, when they exclude you and insult you and reject your name as evil, because of the Son of Man" (Luke 6:22).

- Jesus expected trouble as He submitted to the Father's purpose, yet He was an overcomer. And He tells you to expect trouble, but when trouble comes, if you will submit to the Father's purpose, you'll be an overcomer! "Everyone born of God overcomes the world. This is the victory that has overcome the world, even our faith" (1 John 5:4).

In order to break the cycle of rejection in your life...

Focus on Facts, Not on Feelings

A—Admit the rejection of the past and acknowledge its pain.

C—Claim God's acceptance and unconditional love.

C—Choose to forgive those who rejected you.

E—Expect future rejection because you live in a fallen world.

P—Plant Scripture in your mind to produce new and truthful thought patterns.

T—Thank God for what you've learned through your rejection.

E—Encourage others as an expression of Christ's love.

D—Draw on the power of Christ's life within you.

"You, dear children, are from God and have overcome them, because the one who is in you is greater than the one who is in the world"
(1 JOHN 4:4).

G. How to Conquer Irrational Fear

The love of God is the antidote for fear. The presence of overwhelming fear is the absence of confidence in the character of the God of the Bible and the assurance of His love for you. If your perception is that God is not "for you," then you have only your personal resources on which to rely and your personal philosophy about life to comfort and sustain you. How you respond to fear is often directly related to what you believe about God and what you believe about His promises regarding you and your life. The truth is…

> *"The LORD is faithful to all his promises*
> *and loving toward all he has made"*
> (PSALM 145:13).

When you feel afraid of a person or a situation…

- **Ask** yourself whether what you are afraid of is actually going to happen.
- **Assess** whether what you fear is something that is even likely to happen.
- **Realize** that fixating on your fear guarantees its repetition.
- **Understand** that most fears have nothing to do with what's actually happening.
- **Identify** the past trauma(s) that first instilled your fear.
- **Determine** whether the fear you are presently feeling is current. Ask yourself:
  — What past fear am I bringing into the present?
  — When did this fear first begin?
  — How old do I feel emotionally when I feel this fear?
  — Where am I when I feel this fear?
  — What is going on when I feel this fear?
  — How is this fear affecting my life now? What is it costing me?
- **Tell yourself**, "I will not let this fear run my life. I will not let past or present fears control me."
- **Repeat** this phrase over and over: "That was then, and this is now. That was then, and this is now."
- **Determine** to get out of the grip of fear.
- **Do** what it takes to control your fear and to change from being fearful to being confident and peaceful.
- **Decide** to live in the here and now and act in a way that is not based on fear.

- **Share** your fear and your plan for change with a trustworthy person who will keep you accountable.

> *"The LORD himself goes before you and will be with you;*
> *he will never leave you nor forsake you.*
> *Do not be afraid; do not be discouraged"*
> (DEUTERONOMY 31:8).

H. How to Purge Yourself of Perfectionism

Those who are victimized as children often become perfectionists as adults in the hope of gaining acceptance and approval from those significant to them. If you are caught in the trap of perfectionism, remember that self-talk is powerful. What you rehearse in your mind greatly impacts your feelings and behavior. Practice telling yourself what God has declared to be true about you:

- *I don't always have to measure up—no one is perfect.* "All have sinned and fall short of the glory of God" (Romans 3:23).

- *I never have to fear losing God's love because of anything I might or might not do.* "I am convinced that neither death nor life, neither angels nor demons, neither the present nor the future, nor any powers, neither height nor depth, nor anything else in all creation, will be able to separate us from the love of God that is in Christ Jesus our Lord" (Romans 8:38-39).

- *I can live without fear of being condemned, even when I fail to meet the expectations of those who genuinely love me.* "There is no fear in love. But perfect love drives out fear, because fear has to do with punishment. The one who fears is not made perfect in love" (1 John 4:18).

- *I can confidently take on new challenges. I'm not limited to doing only those things at which I excel.* "The LORD will be your confidence and will keep your foot from being snared" (Proverbs 3:26).

- *I don't have to worry about finding the perfect job or selecting the ideal situation because I can trust God to prepare the way for my future.* "We are God's workmanship, created in Christ Jesus to do good works, which God prepared in advance for us to do" (Ephesians 2:10).

- *I am free to enjoy life. God doesn't want me to be in bondage to a set of rules and regulations.* "If the Son sets you free, you will be free indeed" (John 8:36).

- *My salvation is a free gift! It's not based on what I deserve or earn through work and other achievements.* "It is by grace you have been saved, through faith—and this not from yourselves, it is the gift of God—not by works, so that no one can boast" (Ephesians 2:8-9).

- *God does not expect me to become Christlike in my own power. God assumes responsibility for bringing me to maturity.* "Being confident of this, that he who began a good work in you will carry it on to completion until the day of Christ Jesus" (Philippians 1:6).

I. How to Define and Deal with Guilt and Shame

Everyone who has been victimized as a child struggles with overwhelming feelings of guilt and shame. Left unresolved, these "terrible twins" reap havoc and destruction in the lives of those trying to heal from past victimization. Unless they are correctly defined and dealt with God's way, healing cannot happen and the blessings of life cannot be fully enjoyed.

"I have set before you life and death, blessings and curses.
Now choose life...love the LORD your God, listen
to his voice, and hold fast to him"
(DEUTERONOMY 30:19-20).

============ Overcoming Guilt and Shame ============

QUESTION: "How can I overcome the guilt and shame I feel as a result of being blamed for the abusive things done to me? Did I really deserve this abuse? Was it really my fault?"

ANSWER: Abusive people are notorious for blaming their actions on their victims. *Blame shifting* is a means of controlling others and breaking down any possibility of resistance. No one deserves abuse. And no one makes another person abusive. Abusers alone are responsible for their actions. You are not to blame for what your abusers chose to do. The shame belongs to them alone, not to you. Remember:

*"No one whose hope is in you [Jesus] will ever be put to shame,
but they will be put to shame who are treacherous without excuse"*
(PSALM 25:3).

Shame Is Not the Same as Guilt

QUESTION: "Are guilt and shame the same?"

ANSWER: No. Shame focuses on you, whereas guilt focuses on your behavior.

- **Shame** is a painful emotion of disgrace caused by a strong sense of real or imagined guilt.

- **Shame** is experienced when your guilt moves from knowing you have *done* something bad to feeling that *you are* bad.

- **Shame** focuses on who you are, whereas guilt focuses on what you've done.[68]

- **Shame** creates an inner desire to maintain rigid control over emotions and behavior, whereas guilt creates a desire to change or justify emotions and behavior.

- **Shame** produces inner loneliness that fosters unhealthy dependencies, whereas guilt produces inner longings that foster healthy repentance in relationships.

- **Shame** steals the joy of your salvation, whereas guilt confessed restores joy in salvation.

If you struggle with shame, remember the blessed words of the apostle Paul...

*"Blessed are they whose transgressions are forgiven,
whose sins are covered.
Blessed is the man
whose sin the Lord will never count against him"*
(ROMANS 4:7-8).

True Guilt and False Guilt

QUESTION: "What is the difference between true guilt and false guilt?"

ANSWER: Meet two kinds of guilt:

- **True guilt** refers to the fact of being at fault, deserving punishment, and requiring a sacrificial offering.[69]

- **True guilt** results from any wrong attitude or action that is contrary to the perfect will of God.

- **True guilt** speaks truth, gently leading you to repentance and forgiveness.

- **False guilt** arises when you blame yourself even though you've committed no wrong or you've already confessed and turned from your sin.

- **False guilt** keeps you in bondage to three destructive weapons: shame, fear, and anger.[70]

- **False guilt** taunts and condemns, bringing dishonor and inner shame.

Those plagued by feelings of false guilt would benefit from following the apostle Peter's advice:

> *"Be self-controlled and alert.*
> *Your enemy the devil prowls around like a roaring lion*
> *looking for someone to devour"*
> (1 PETER 5:8).

Responding to False Guilt

QUESTION: "How should I respond to false guilt?"

ANSWER: The next time the viewing screen of your mind begins to replay sins you have repented of or sins committed against you for which you feel responsible, realize that this taunting comes from Satan, the accuser, to discourage you. Ask yourself:

- "What am I hearing?" (I'm hearing an accusation.)

- "What am I feeling?" (I'm feeling false guilt.)

- "What are the facts?" (I am not guilty. I am fully forgiven.)

- Use Scripture as your standard when it comes to feelings of false guilt. Because you have received Jesus Christ as your personal Savior and He died to take away your sins, you are not guilty.

- Turn Romans 8:33-34 into a prayer: "Thank You, Father, that You have justified me and don't condemn me and don't want me to condemn myself. These feelings of false guilt are not valid because I have accepted Christ's sacrifice and turned from my sin."

> *"Who will bring any charge*
> *against those whom God has chosen?*
> *It is God who justifies.*
> *Who is he that condemns?*
> *Christ Jesus, who died—more than that,*
> *who was raised to life—*
> *is at the right hand of God and is also interceding for us"*
> (ROMANS 8:33-34).

J. How to Claim Your Identity in Christ

For us who are Christians to walk in victory, we need to identify the lies we believe about ourselves and exchange them for the truth about who we really are in Christ. For lasting change to occur, we must cast aside the lies and constantly rely on the truths of Scripture.

> *"[You] were taught in him in accordance with the truth that is in Jesus.*
> *You were taught, with regard to your former way of life,*
> *to put off your old self…to be made new in the attitude of your minds;*
> *and to put on the new self,*
> *created to be like God in true righteousness and holiness"*
> (EPHESIANS 4:21-24).

- *You are chosen by God.*
  "*He chose* us in him before the creation of the world to be holy and blameless in his sight" (Ephesians 1:4).

- *You are adopted by God.*
  "In love he predestined us to be *adopted* as his sons through Jesus Christ, in accordance with his pleasure and will" (Ephesians 1:4-5).

- *You are a child of God.*

  "To all who received him, to those who believed in his name, he gave the right to become *children of God*" (John 1:12).

- *You are born again.*

  "You have been *born again*, not of perishable seed, but of imperishable, through the living and enduring word of God" (1 Peter 1:23).

- *You are a new creation.*

  "If anyone is in Christ, he is a *new creation*; the old has gone, the new has come!" (2 Corinthians 5:17).

- *You have a new nature.*

  "In him you were also circumcised, in the *putting off of the sinful nature*, not with a circumcision done by the hands of men but with the circumcision done by Christ" (Colossians 2:11).

- *You have a new heart.*

  "I will give you a *new heart* and put a new spirit in you; I will remove from you your heart of stone and give you a heart of flesh" (Ezekiel 36:26).

- *You have a new spirit.*

  "I will put *my Spirit* in you and move you to follow my decrees and be careful to keep my laws" (Ezekiel 36:27).

- *You have a new mind.*

  " 'Who has known the mind of the Lord that he may instruct him?' But we have the *mind of Christ*" (1 Corinthians 2:16).

- *You are clothed with Christ.*

  "All of you who were baptized into Christ have *clothed* yourselves with Christ" (Galatians 3:27).

- *You are baptized into Christ.*

  "We were therefore buried with him through *baptism* into death in order that, just as Christ was raised from the dead through the glory of the Father, we too may live a new life" (Romans 6:4).

- *You are hidden in Christ.*

  "You died, and your life is now *hidden* with Christ in God" (Colossians 3:3).

- *You are sealed with the Spirit of Christ.*

  "You also were included in Christ when you heard the word of truth, the gospel of your salvation. Having believed, you were marked in him with *a seal*, the promised Holy Spirit, who is a deposit guaranteeing our inheritance until the redemption of those who are God's possession—to the praise of his glory" (Ephesians 1:13-14).

- *You are redeemed.*

  "In him we have *redemption* through his blood, the forgiveness of sins, in accordance with the riches of God's grace" (Ephesians 1:7).

- *You are washed.*

  "That is what some of you were [wicked]. But you were *washed*, you were sanctified, you were justified in the name of the Lord Jesus Christ and by the Spirit of our God" (1 Corinthians 6:11).

- *You are purified.*

  "If we walk in the light, as he is in the light, we have fellowship with one another, and the blood of Jesus, his Son, *purifies* us from all sin" (1 John 1:7).

- *You are justified.*

  "Since we have been *justified* through faith, we have peace with God through our Lord Jesus Christ" (Romans 5:1).

- *You are totally accepted by Christ.*

  "Accept one another, then, just as Christ *accepted* you, in order to bring praise to God" (Romans 15:7).

- *You are totally blameless before Christ.*

  "He has reconciled you by Christ's physical body through death to present you holy in his sight, *without blemish* and free from accusation" (Colossians 1:22).

- *You are totally righteous in Christ.*

  "God made him who had no sin to be sin for us, so that in him we might become the *righteousness of* God" (2 Corinthians 5:21).

- *You are totally complete in Christ.*

  "In Christ all the fullness of the Deity lives in bodily form, and you have been given *fullness* [made complete] in Christ, who is the head over every power and authority" (Colossians 2:9-10).

- *You are totally perfect in Christ.*

  "By one sacrifice he has made *perfect* forever those who are being made holy" (Hebrews 10:14).

- *You are free from accusation.*

  "He has reconciled you by Christ's physical body through death to present you holy in his sight, without blemish and *free from accusation*" (Colossians 1:22).

- *You are free from condemnation.*

  "There is now *no condemnation* for those who are in Christ Jesus" (Romans 8:1).

- *You are free from the law.*

  "My brothers, you also *died to the law* through the body of Christ, that you might belong to another, to him who was raised from the dead, in order that we might bear fruit to God" (Romans 7:4).

- *You are saved from God's wrath.*

  "Since we have now been justified by his blood, how much more shall we be *saved from God's wrath* through him!" (Romans 5:9).

- *You have been made an heir of God.*

  "You are no longer a slave, but a son; and since you are a son, God has made you also an *heir*" (Galatians 4:7).

- *You have inherited everything you need to be godly.*

  "His divine power has given us *everything we need* for life and *godliness* through our knowledge of him who called us by his own glory and goodness" (2 Peter 1:3).

- *You have inherited a new nature in Christ.*

  "Through these he has given us his very great and precious promises, so that through them you may participate in the *divine nature* and escape the corruption in the world caused by evil desires" (2 Peter 1:4).

- *You have inherited every spiritual blessing.*

  "Praise be to the God and Father of our Lord Jesus Christ, who has blessed us in the heavenly realms with *every spiritual blessing* in Christ" (Ephesians 1:3).

- *You have inherited eternal life.*

  "This is the testimony: God has given us *eternal life*, and this life is in his Son" (1 John 5:11).

K. How to Know Your Real Self-worth

Victimization sabotages the self-worth of its victims. To be devalued by another person can leave lasting scars and sends a strong message that the victim has little or no worth. Such lies are clearly countered by the words of Jesus:

> *"Look at the birds of the air;*
> *they do not sow or reap or store away in barns,*
> *and yet your heavenly Father feeds them.*
> *Are you not much more valuable than they?"*
> (Matthew 6:26).

If you are struggling over your worth and value to God, memorize...

Psalm 139

Realize that God knows all about you. . . . . .verses 1-6

Remember that God is always with you. . . . . . .verses 7-12

Respect the fact that God created you. . . . . . .verses 13-14

Recognize that God uniquely designed you. . .verses 15-16

Receive God's loving thoughts toward you.   . .verses 17-18

Renounce God's enemies as enemies to you. . .verses 19-22

Respond to God's changing you.   . . . . .verses 23-24

As you meditate on Psalm 139, accept the truth that you are W-O-R-T-H-Y:

W—Work on eliminating negative attitudes and beliefs.

O—Obtain a scriptural understanding of having love for yourself.

R—Refuse to compare yourself to others.

T—Thank God for His unconditional love for you.

H—Hope in God's promise to make you more and more like Christ.

Y—Yield your talents and abilities to helping others.

When you were a child, you did not have control over those in authority over you, but that is no longer the case. You are now able to choose those with whom you associate, and you can certainly control your self-talk. Therefore, you can take an active part in replacing the distorted view you have of yourself with God's view of you. And you can begin by starting to…

- **Accept yourself.**
    - — Stop striving for perfection or to be like someone else.
    - — Realize the Lord made you for a purpose, and He designed your personality and gave you the gifts and abilities He wanted you to have in order to accomplish His purpose for you.

    > *"Many are the plans in a man's heart,*
    > *but it is the LORD's purpose that prevails"*
    > (PROVERBS 19:21).

- **Thank God for encouraging you.**
    - — Acknowledge and praise God for the abilities He has given you and the things He has accomplished through you.

— Engage in biblically based, encouraging self-talk and mute the condemning critic inside your head.

> *"May our Lord Jesus Christ himself and God our Father,*
> *who loved us and by his grace gave us eternal encouragement*
> *and good hope, encourage your hearts and strengthen you*
> *in every good deed and word"*
> (2 THESSALONIANS 2:16-17).

- **Accept the compliments of others.**
  — To discount the positive comments of those who have heartfelt appreciation for you is to discount their opinions and their desire to express their gratitude to you.
  — Practice graciously accepting compliments and turning them into praise to God for the affirmation that He is at work in you and producing good fruit through you.

  > *"This is to my Father's glory, that you bear much fruit,*
  > *showing yourselves to be my disciples"*
  > (JOHN 15:8).

- **Release past negative experiences and focus on a positive future.**
  — Refuse to dwell on negative things said or done to you in the past and release them to God.
  — Embrace the work God is doing in your life now and cooperate with Him by dwelling on Him, His character, and His promises to you to fulfill His purposes in you.

  > *"It is God who works in you to will and to act*
  > *according to his good purpose"*
  > (PHILIPPIANS 2:13).

- **Live in God's forgiveness.**
  — God has extended forgiveness to you for all of your sins (past, present, and future), so confess and repent of

anything offensive to God. Do not set yourself up as a higher judge than God by refusing to forgive yourself.

— Lay harsh judgment of yourself aside and accept that you will not be made fully perfect and totally without sin until you stand in the presence of Christ and are fully conformed to His image.

> *"Dear friends, now we are children of God, and what we will be has not yet been made known. But we know that when he appears, we shall be like him, for we shall see him as he is. Everyone who has this hope in him purifies himself, just as he is pure"*
> (1 John 3:2-3).

- **Benefit from mistakes.**
    — Realize that you can learn from your mistakes as well as from the mistakes of others, and decide to view your mistakes as opportunities to learn needed lessons.
    — Ask God what He wants to teach you from your mistakes; listen to Him and learn. Then move forward with a positive attitude and put into practice the insights you have gained.

> *"'My [Jesus'] grace is sufficient for you, for my power is made perfect in weakness.' Therefore I [Paul] will boast all the more gladly about my weaknesses, so that Christ's power may rest on me"*
> (2 Corinthians 12:9).

- **Form supportive, positive relationships.**
    — Realize that critical people are hurt people who project their feelings of inadequacy onto others in an attempt to ease their own emotional pain.
    — Minimize the time you spend with negative, critical people—whether family, friends, or co-workers—and seek out those who encourage and support you both emotionally and spiritually.

> *"He who walks with the wise grows wise, but a companion of fools suffers harm"*
> (Proverbs 13:20).

- **Formulate realistic goals and plans.**
  — Elicit the help of others to identify your strengths and weaknesses as well as the gifts God has given you, plus the things you are persuaded God has called you to do.
  — Prayerfully set some reasonable, achievable goals that capitalize on your strengths, and make a plan for how you will set about to accomplish those goals.

  > *"Do you not know that in a race all the runners run,*
  > *but only one gets the prize?*
  > *Run in such a way as to get the prize"*
  > (1 CORINTHIANS 9:24).

- **Identify your heart's desires.**
  — Make a list of the things you have dreamed of doing but have never attempted because of a fear of failure or a lack of self-assurance.
  — Share each desire with the Lord, asking Him to confirm to you which ones are from Him. Then lay out the steps you need to take in order to accomplish them.

  > *"Delight yourself in the LORD*
  > *and he will give you the desires of your heart"*
  > (PSALM 37:4).

- **Plan for success.**
  — Anticipate any obstacles to accomplishing your goals and desires and plan strategies for overcoming them.
  — Think of yourself achieving each of your goals and doing the things God has put on your heart to do.

  > *"May he give you the desire of your heart*
  > *and make all your plans succeed"*
  > (PSALM 20:4).

- **Celebrate each accomplishment.**
  — Your feelings of self-worth and self-confidence will grow with the acknowledgment of each accomplishment.

— Rejoice with the Lord and the significant people in your life over the things God has done through you and for you. Affirm and celebrate your success.

"There, in the presence of the LORD your God, you and your families
shall eat and shall rejoice in everything you have put your hand to,
because the LORD your God has blessed you"
(DEUTERONOMY 12:7).

- **Envision a ministry.**
  — Look ahead to the future instead of being a prisoner to the past.

  "Forget the former things; do not dwell on the past.
  See, I am doing a new thing! Now it springs up; do you not perceive it?
  I am making a way in the desert and streams in the wasteland"
  (ISAIAH 43:18-19).

  — Allow your mistreatment to be the making of your ministry to bring comfort to others.

  "Praise be to the God and Father of our Lord Jesus Christ,
  the Father of compassion and the God of all comfort,
  who comforts us in all our troubles, so that we can comfort those
  in any trouble with the comfort we ourselves have received from God"
  (2 CORINTHIANS 1:3-4).

Mistreatment is no stranger to any of us. Why then, in the face of misfortune, do some victims see themselves as having little value, while others live victoriously in light of their true value? What makes the difference?

The victorious Christian learns priceless lessons through victimization, such as sensitivity, empathy, compassion for other vicitms. Reaching out to others with a compassionate heart will give hope to *their* hearts. You can pass this hope of victory on to others and be powerfully used by God.

The blessing comes when you focus not on what you are getting, but on what you are giving. Jesus suffered immense mistreatment, yet He was not burdened with any sense of low self-worth. His ministry of compassion models for us the truth that truly…

"it is more blessed to give than to receive"
(ACTS 20:35).

L. How to Construct a New Chain of Events

As God begins to free us from the old chains of bondage, we begin to see His grace operating in our lives through new channels of personal support and exciting opportunities for service.

The final step toward healing is choosing not to continue to look inward, reliving past pain and sorrow, but choosing to look outward for occasions to help others. Survivors of abuse are especially sensitive and empathetic toward other wounded hearts who need someone to show them the way.

And while you're reaching out, God is reaching in, touching your heart with the miracle of healing!

> *"Is not this the kind of fasting I have chosen:*
> *to loose the chains of injustice and untie the cords of the yoke,*
> *to set the oppressed free and break every yoke?*
> *Is it not to share your food with the hungry*
> *and to provide the poor wanderer with shelter—*
> *when you see the naked, to clothe him,*
> *and not to turn away from your own flesh and blood?*
> *Then your light will break forth like the dawn,*
> *and your healing will quickly appear;*
> *then your righteousness will go before you,*
> *and the glory of the LORD will be your rear guard"*
> (ISAIAH 58:6-8).

Links of the Chain

Link 1:   Place all of your trust and confidence in God to complete the good work He has begun in you.

Link 2:   Make your relationship with God your first priority.

Link 3:   Respond to the opportunities for personal support and continued spiritual growth that God will place in your path.

       —Attend a church that preaches and honors the Word of God.

       —Get involved in Bible study and growth seminars.

       —Develop a few healthy relationships and establish accountability.

Link 4:   Be prepared for God to open the door of opportunity for you to share small portions of your experience with someone—even before you think you are ready.

—Trust Christ to give you wisdom and appropriate words to say.

—Focus on the hope you have found in Jesus Christ for true healing.

Link 5:   Consider your personal prayer life to be foundational.

Link 6:   Realize your family is the first field of ministry opportunity.

Link 7:   Seek God's leading when new avenues of ministry open up.

Link 8:   See new people who come into your life as divine appointments from your Lord.

Link 9:   Begin to see your life as a whole new way that God can bring beauty out of ashes.

Link 10:   Recognize the tremendous value of service to others.

> *"Come and listen, all you who fear God;*
> *let me tell you what he has done for me"*
> (Psalm 66:16).

"God wanted to prove that He can take care of a dirty, unwanted child. He could help me endure the beatings, the sexual abuse, and the rejection from my father as well as from my mother. God wanted to prove a point, and He did. Now I have the privilege of telling thousands of people that God can take 'nobodys' and make them into 'somebodys' for His name's sake."[71]

—DORIE VAN STONE

M. How to Support Survivors on the Road to Becoming Overcomers

Everyone has been touched either directly or indirectly by some form of victimization. That means all of us are in a position now or will be in a position in the future to further a survivor's journey on the way to becoming an overcomer…to travel from merely coping to thriving…from struggling to winning…from pain to peace…from victim to victor.

As you travel that road with someone dear to you, make it your goal to…

- *Listen* with your heart, without judging, without questioning.
- *Believe* what you hear, without doubting, without qualifying.
- *Validate* the injury, the feelings, the pain, and the loss with words, with emotional responses, with actions.
- *Comfort* with compassion, with words, with Scripture, without pity.
- *Encourage* counseling, group support, sharing the secrets.
- *Learn* about victimization, about the healing process.
- *Strengthen* in the Lord, with prayer, with Scripture.
- *Express* your thoughts, your feelings, your goals, your boundaries.
- *Support* the healing process, with time, with words, with actions.
- *Respect* the commitment to healing, the time healing takes, the space healing requires, the process of healing.
- *Accommodate* progressive changes, flashbacks, anger.

God heals the broken heart when you give Him all the pieces. He washes the wounds…mends the mind… tallies the tears. He empowers you to rise above abuse and become all He created you to be.

Victimization—Answers in God's Word

QUESTION: "How am I to bear up under the pain of unjust suffering? Is there an example for me to follow?"

ANSWER: "It is commendable if a man bears up under the pain of unjust suffering because he is conscious of God…To this you were called, because

Christ suffered for you, leaving you an example, that you should follow in his steps" (1 Peter 2:19,21).

QUESTION: "Where was the Lord when I was so brokenhearted and crushed?"

ANSWER: "The LORD is close to the brokenhearted and saves those who are crushed in spirit" (Psalm 34:18).

QUESTION: "How can I look forward to the future and know that God will make my path straight when the path of my past was so devastatingly crooked?"

ANSWER: "Trust in the LORD with all your heart and lean not on your own understanding; in all your ways acknowledge him, and he will make your paths straight" (Proverbs 3:5-6).

QUESTION: "Where can I find the rest and the hope that God promises to those who trust in Him for salvation?"

ANSWER: "Find rest, O my soul, in God alone; my hope comes from him. He alone is my rock and my salvation; he is my fortress, I will not be shaken" (Psalm 62:5-6).

QUESTION: "After having been terribly hurt by people who should have cared for and protected me, how will I ever be able to trust that God's will for me is good?"

ANSWER: "Do not conform any longer to the pattern of this world, but be transformed by the renewing of your mind. Then you will be able to test and approve what God's will is—his good, pleasing and perfect will" (Romans 12:2).

QUESTION: "Is there any good news of freedom the Lord has for me, an oppressed prisoner of a painful past?"

ANSWER: "The Spirit of the Lord is on me, because he has anointed me to preach good news to the poor. He has sent me to proclaim freedom for the prisoners and recovery of sight for the blind, to release the oppressed" (Luke 4:18).

QUESTION: "Am I to confront the people in my life who have sinned against me?"

ANSWER: "If your brother sins against you, go and show him his fault, just between the two of you. If he listens to you, you have won your brother over" (Matthew 18:15).

QUESTION: "Can God's Word actually heal my damaged emotions and rescue my life from what seems like a grave of hopelessness and insecurity?"

ANSWER: "He sent forth his word and healed them; he rescued them from the grave" (Psalm 107:20).

QUESTION: "How will I ever be free from the pain and damage of my past?"

ANSWER: "If the Son sets you free, you will be free indeed" (John 8:36).

QUESTION: "Am I to forgive the grievances I have against others who have mistreated me?"

ANSWER: "Bear with each other and forgive whatever grievances you may have against one another. Forgive as the Lord forgave you" (Colossians 3:13).

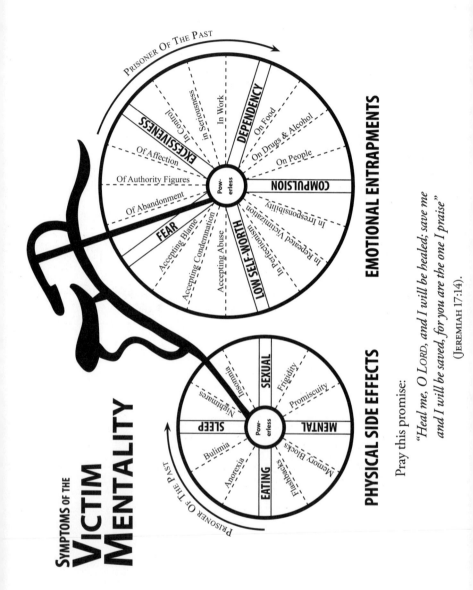

Symptoms of the VICTIM MENTALITY

EMOTIONAL ENTRAPMENTS

PRISONER OF THE PAST

EXCESSIVENESS
- In Control
- In Seriousness
- Of Affection
- Of Authority Figures
- Of Abandonment

DEPENDENCY
- In Work
- On Food
- On Drugs & Alcohol
- On People

FEAR
- Accepting Blame
- Accepting Condemnation
- Accepting Abuse

LOW SELF-WORTH
- In Perfectionism
- In Repeated Victimization
- In Irresponsibility

COMPULSION

Pow-erless

PHYSICAL SIDE EFFECTS

PRISONER OF THE PAST

SLEEP
- Insomnia
- Nightmares

SEXUAL
- Frigidity
- Promiscuity

EATING
- Bulimia
- Anorexia

MENTAL
- Flashbacks
- Memory Blocks

Pow-erless

Pray this promise:

"Heal me, O Lord, and I will be healed; save me and I will be saved, for you are the one I praise" (Jeremiah 17:14).

WIFE ABUSE
Assault on a Woman's Worth 305

WIFE ABUSE

Assault on a Woman's Worth

He is prominent and highly esteemed, praised for his significant contributions to the community. What woman wouldn't feel fortunate to be his wife? She certainly has all the finer things in life. And the children have the best that money can buy. How could she think of destroying such a picture-perfect family? How could she risk losing her security or stepping into an unknown future?

Where would she go? What could she do? How would she support herself? Even worse, if she began to expose the terrible truth, would she lose the children?

She felt so hopeless. Who would believe her? No one could conceive that such a pillar of the community could pummel his wife night after night with painful punches.

She was skilled at hiding her feelings as well as her bruises. With swollen, tear-stained eyes, she wrongfully reasoned, *It's mostly my fault anyway!*

But her Creator God knew the undeniable truth.

> *"You hear, O LORD, the desire of the afflicted;*
> *you encourage them, and you listen to their cry,*
> *defending the fatherless and the oppressed,*
> *in order that man, who is of the earth,*
> *may terrify no more"*
> (PSALM 10:17-18).

I. DEFINITIONS OF WIFE ABUSE

God designed the marriage relationship to balance, to benefit, to better both the husband and the wife. With the first marriage on earth, He created

Eve to be the perfect companion for Adam. He intended the pair to love, honor, and cherish each other all the days of their lives, and His intention is still the same for every married couple today.

But in too many homes around the world, the marriage *bond* has become *bondage*—shared lives have become shattered by abuse. Husbands are berating, belittling, and betraying their wives. Yet these assaults are kept hidden from the outside world. The sacred relationship created by God has been undermined by one mate hurting or even harming the other.

Any form of abuse is a flagrant violation of the marriage vow, "To have and to hold from this day forward…to love and to cherish, 'til death do us part." And although such abuse usually takes place behind closed doors, it is blatantly evident before the eyes of the Lord.

> *"Nothing in all creation is hidden from God's sight.*
> *Everything is uncovered and laid bare*
> *before the eyes of him to whom we must give account"*
> (Hebrews 4:13).

A. What Is Abuse?

While abusive acts are committed by both husbands and wives, in cases of domestic violence approximately 95 percent of the victims are women.[1] Although abusive treatment has a long history of being tolerated—socially and even legally—abuse has always grieved the heart of God.

In certain countries, wife beating is considered a cultural norm. The majority of health-care workers in such countries, both male and female, condone husbands using physical force against their wives under certain circumstances, which results in abused women receiving little or no emotional support from the national health-care system. For example, if a Turkish wife criticizes her husband, the public supports his inflicting her with painful blows as her rightful punishment.[2]

Often, women in other countries who suffer abuse get little help from those around them, but help is available from Someone above them. God promises to stay close to the brokenhearted, to show compassion to the abused and to comfort them.

> *"He heals the brokenhearted and binds up their wounds"*
> (Psalm 147:3).

- **Abuse** means "to mistreat, hurt, or injure."[3]
- **Abuse** and **violence** are often used interchangeably, although the word violence implies an escalation of abuse and introduces the element of fear of harm as a means of control.[4]
- **Violence,** in Hebrew, is most often a translation of the word *chamas,* which means "to wrong" or "treat violently."[5] *Chamas* is also translated as "malicious, destroy, wrong, crime, ruthless, plunder," and "terror."[6]

God feels strong opposition against anyone who is
abusive or violent toward another. "'I hate a man's covering
himself with violence...' says the LORD Almighty"

(MALACHI 2:16).

- **Domestic violence** and **family violence** are the legal terms for physical spousal abuse, child abuse, elder abuse, or any other type of physical abuse that takes place within the home or family.[7]
- **Domestic violence** refers to a pattern of coercive and violent behavior exercised by one adult in an intimate relationship with another.[8]
- **Domestic violence** is *not* an issue of "marriage problems" or "irreconcilable differences" solved by "conflict resolution." This kind of abuse...

    A—**Affects** everyone in the family

    B—**Bridges** all levels in society: racial, religious, geographic, and economic

    U—**Undermines** the value of others

    S—**Seeks** to dominate others

    E—**Escalates** in intensity and frequency

Spiritual leaders, community officials, family, and friends need to be responsive when informed of spousal abuse. Abuse of any kind should never be tolerated nor hidden under the cover of male supremacy or "godly submission." To the contrary, the God of the Bible is a God of refuge, a stronghold of support and defense against violence:

> *"My rock, in whom I take refuge,*
> *my shield and the horn of my salvation.*
> *He is my stronghold, my refuge and my savior—*
> *from violent men you save me"*
> (2 Samuel 22:3).

Abuse and Punishment for Sins

Question: "Would God condone my husband's abusing me in order to punish me for my sins?"

Answer: No. While Scripture repeatedly shows God using one nation to bring judgment on another nation, there is not a single instance in which God used the violence of one mate to punish the other mate. God hates sin, and abuse is sin. The truth is:

- An abusive mate is abusive simply as a result of choosing wrong over right.
- While you may be the *recipient* of your husband's abuse, you are not the *reason* for that abuse. The violence of your husband exposes his sinfulness, not your sinfulness.

God's instruction for all of us is to...

> *"Do what is just and right...Do no wrong or violence"*
> (Jeremiah 22:3).

The All-American Abuser: The O.J. Simpson Story

He could be charming...and *chilling*.

He could bedazzle the crowd on the football field, yet belittle, berate, and beat his wife behind closed doors. Local police reports documented numerous trips to their home for incidents such as hitting her, kicking her, smashing family photos, throwing her to the ground, pushing her out of a moving car, throwing her clothes out of the house, bashing her car with a baseball bat, and repeatedly stalking her.[9]

In 1994, Orenthal James Simpson—the all-star running back and pro football Hall of Famer more commonly known as O.J. or "The Juice"—stunned the world when he was arrested on the charge of murdering his ex-wife Nicole and her friend Ron Goldman.[10]

A pretrial hearing disclosed that Nicole had been victimized by O.J. for 17 years, with more than 50 allegations of spouse abuse. In 1989, for example, O.J. pleaded no contest to beating his wife and threatening to kill her. He was sentenced only to probation, fined $700, and ordered to perform community service.

Two years before her murder, Nicole filed for divorce from O.J., citing an abusive relationship. She was hoping that by no longer living under the same roof with O.J. the brutal cycle of abuse would stop. While divorce papers and restraining orders were legally designed to "shut the door" to Nicole, the legendary running back believed he had the right to bust through the door anytime he wanted.

On one such occasion, police officers were summoned to Nicole's home. They found her cowering in the bushes in her front yard—bloodied and terrorized—wearing nothing but a bra and sweatpants. Nicole wanted the police to charge O.J. with breaking and entering. Instead, they assured *him* they would keep the incident as quiet "as legally possible"—after all, he was their hero.

Nicole's words to the officers that day revealed her all-too-frequent and frustrating plight: "You never do anything. You always come here and you never arrest him."[11] Nicole actually found herself caught in *two* cycles of abuse: She was suffering first at the hands of an unpredictably violent ex-husband, and second at the hands of an apathetic, neglectful police force.

On October 3, 1995, following what was described as the most publicized criminal trial in history, the stunning verdict reverberated around the world: O.J.—acquitted! A virtually airtight case, plus a sordid police record of wife battering, convinced countless millions of people who watched on television that a guilty verdict was assured. Instead, Simpson walked out of the Los Angeles County courtroom a free man.

Free? Just 20 days later the civil trial began. It concluded on February 4, 1996, with the jury finding that O.J. willfully and wrongfully caused the death of Ron Goldman and that he had committed battery with malice and oppression against the two victims. The jury found O.J. liable and awarded the plaintiffs $8.5 million in damages.

At the root of O.J.'s abusive nature was jealous possessiveness. The beatings were intended to rein in Nicole—to control her, to show her who was really in charge of her life. Experts in domestic violence believe this possessiveness manifested itself in the methodology employed in the murders: Ron's body was marked with torturous taser wounds, and ultimately both he and Nicole were viciously slashed across their throats.[12]

The Bible says husbands are to love their wives sincerely and sacrificially. But O.J.'s interpretation of love justified his violence as revealed by his own words. In an inconceivably bizarre quote in a Florida newspaper, O.J. said, "Let's say I committed this crime...Even if I did do this, it would have been because I loved her very much, right?"[13]

While this infamous criminal case did little to stir O.J.'s conscience, other men were deeply impacted—*and perhaps just in time*. One fax received by Simpson's prosecutors simply read, "You may have just saved my wife's life, for as I listened to you describing Simpson's abuse, I recognized myself."[14]

Our ministry at Hope for the Heart offers written and recorded resources on over 100 topics. During 1995, the number one resource requested by people was our material on wife abuse. And the most common response to our *Biblical Counseling Keys* on wife abuse has been, "I haven't known what to say or do. Now I've found real help!"

B. What Are the Different Types of Abuse?[15]

Do you think you can always identify abuse when it is happening? Chances are, probably not. Abusive behavior can be aggressive or passive, physical or psychological, direct or indirect. Regardless of the method, all abusive behavior comes from those with hardened hearts who want to punish, coerce, and control.

Although abusers treat their mates unjustly, they blame their mates for making them abusive. They say things like, "You made me do it!" and "If it weren't for you, I would never have done it!" The actions of the abusive husband are "never" his fault—or so he hurtfully says.

After the pileup of put-downs, harsh beatings, and even sadistic sexual acts, wives can tragically start to think, *He's probably right. It really is all my fault.* But God knows the abusive husband is *entirely wrong.* And He knows precisely what is in the abuser's heart: Along with deception resides another evil—injustice.

> *"In your heart you devise injustice,*
> *and your hands mete out violence on the earth"*
> (PSALM 58:2).

Verbal Abuse

Verbal abuse is the use of words or tone of voice in an attempt to control or hurt another person or to destroy that person's self-worth. Like physical abuse, verbal abuse is devastating within a marriage—it is a destroyer of respect, trust, and intimacy. Place a check mark (✓) beside any of the following behaviors that are applicable to you.

Verbally abusive language is characterized by:

____ *Badgering* with excessive questioning or accusations

____ *Belittling* by mocking or name-calling

____ *Blaming* you for the abuse

____ *Confusing* with mind games or twisting what is said

____ *Controlling* with criticism or sarcasm

____ *Degrading* with public or private put-downs

____ *Demoralizing* by making light of the abusive behavior

____ *Devaluing* by demeaning family or friends

____ *Disempowering* by continually dictating orders

____ *Disrespecting* by denying that the abuse ever happened

____ *Insulting* with coarse language or profanity

____ *Intimidating* with yelling or threats

____ *Manipulating* with threats of self-injury or suicide

_____ *Overpowering* by always claiming to be right

_____ *Paralyzing* by threatening to report you as an unfit parent

_____ *Shaming* with humiliation or guilt trips

_____ *Silencing* with constant interruptions or changing topics

_____ *Telling* half-truths or lies

The internal negative impact of verbal abuse can last much longer than the external negative impact of physical violence. Name-calling, derogatory comments, persistent shaming, ridicule, and threats are devastating and highly destructive, making the victim (whether husband or wife) even more vulnerable to being controlled by the abuser. The psalmist says of the verbal abuser…

> *"His mouth is full of curses and lies and threats;*
> *trouble and evil are under his tongue"*
> (Psalm 10:7).

Emotional Abuse

While all forms of mistreatment are emotionally abusive, certain overt behaviors can be labeled as *emotional abuse*. All acts of emotional abuse will fit into one of two categories: passive or aggressive. Place a check mark (✓) beside any of the following behaviors that are applicable to you.

Passive emotional abuse is characterized by:

_____ *Avoiding* giving deserved compliments to you

_____ *Brooding* and sulking when around you

_____ *Changing* your passwords linked to financial accounts

_____ *Denying* your request to leave when you ask

_____ *Displaying* continual irritability around you

_____ *Disrespecting* your rights, opinions, or feelings

_____ *Failing* to return to your home at a reasonable time

_____ *Forbidding* access to your money, checkbook, and credit cards

_____ *Holding back* appropriate attention from you

_____ *Keeping* you from getting help to overcome an addiction

____ *Manipulating* your children

____ *Monitoring* all of your computer usage

____ *Neglecting* your important family gatherings

____ *Refusing* to express true feelings with you

____ *Rejecting* your need for emotional support

____ *Resisting* helping you with the children

____ *Stopping* you from receiving important information

____ *Unwillingness* to take a fair share of responsibility with you

____ *Using* the "silent treatment" against you

____ *Withholding* a listening ear from you or a response
    requested by you

The psalmist describes the feelings of the person who is emotionally
abused:

> *"My soul is in anguish...I am...utterly crushed;*
> *I groan in anguish of heart"*
> (Psalm 6:3; 38:8).

Aggressive emotional abuse is characterized by:

____ *Blocking* the doorway when you are arguing

____ *Breaking* promises to you or not keeping agreements

____ *Checking* up on you continually

____ *Damaging* your treasured items   fam photos

____ *Demanding* that you behave adoringly in public—after
    abusing you

____ *Driving* recklessly to instill fear in you   ?

____ *Expressing* excessive anger toward you

____ *Forbidding* your necessary medical treatment

____ *Harassing* you with unwanted phone calls

____ *Hiding* your car keys as a means of control

____ *Interfering* with your work

____ *Interrupting* your sleep

____ *Intimidating* you with threatening gestures or body language

____ *Isolating* you from family and friends

____ *Making* unwanted visits to you

____ *Manipulating* your decision making

____ *Monitoring* all of your phone calls

____ *Prohibiting* your participation in major decisions

____ *Stalking* you

____ *Suspecting* your activities with excessive jealousy

____ *Threatening* you with weapons

The psalmist describes the aggressive emotional abuser:

> *"In his arrogance the wicked man hunts down the weak,*
> *who are caught in the schemes he devises"*
> (PSALM 10:2).

Physical Abuse/Violence

Physical abuse involves a person's use of physical size, strength, presence, or position to control or hurt someone else. It often begins with verbal threats of physical harm, such as "You'll wish you had never been born!" and escalates to actual physical abuse, in which the threats become reality.

The first act of violence—with no immediate repercussion—makes it easier for the abuser to be violent again. Once the taboo is broken—"never hit a woman"—minor attacks can escalate into major assaults. Place a check mark (✓) beside any of the following behaviors that you have committed or that you have received.

Acts of violence include:

__ Pushing/shoving	__ Pinning down
__ Breaking bones	__ Slapping/striking
__ Punching	__ Destroying property
__ Kicking/stomping	__ Pulling hair
__ Threatening death	__ Grabbing/choking
__ Twisting arms	__ Using weapons (stabbing/shooting)

__ Confining/locking up   __ Hitting walls

__ Harming pets   __ Binding/chaining

__ Shaking severely   __ Killing pets

__ Scratching/pinching   __ Slamming doors

__ Kidnapping children   __ Poking/piercing

__ Throwing objects   __ Harming children

__ Burning/scalding   __ Breaking teeth

__ Killing children   __ Biting/spitting

__ Breaking items

The Bible warns us to stay away from those who are violent:

> *"Do not envy wicked men, do not desire their company;*
> *for their hearts plot violence, and their lips talk about making trouble"*
> (PROVERBS 24:1-2).

Sexual Abuse and Violence

Because many men believe that their wives are to be submissive to all their desires, many women experience sexual abuse—some even without realizing it. Place a check mark (✓) beside any of the following that you have experienced.

Sexual abuse includes:

____ *Sexually* degrading attitudes and treatment

____ *Discrimination* based on gender

____ *Withholding* sexual intimacy and romance

____ *Unjust* accusations of extramarital affairs

____ *Brazen* flirtation with members of the opposite sex

____ *Misuse* of Scripture to justify sex "on demand"

____ *Threats* of forced sex

____ *Threats* of going elsewhere for sexual gratification

____ *Adultery*

____ *Obscene* gestures

____ *Forced* sex (mate rape)

_____ *Sodomy* (forced oral or anal sex)

_____ *Homosexual* acts (rejecting sexual fidelity with wife)

_____ *Forced* involvement in perverse sexual acts

_____ *Using* objects on sexual parts

_____ *Forced* exposure to pornography

_____ *Coerced* sexual acts with others

The writer of Hebrews firmly states God's position on the sexual relationship in marriage:

> *"Marriage should be honored by all,*
> *and the marriage bed kept pure,*
> *for God will judge the adulterer and all the sexually immoral"*
> (Hebrews 13:4).

Forced Marital Sex

Question: "Is it ever right for a husband to demand sex from or force sex on his wife?"

Answer: No. God's purpose for sex in marriage is for procreation and for pleasure.

Sex within marriage is designed to establish a bond, not a barrier.

- Forced sex is rape.
- Forced sex produces fear that also prevents intimacy.
- Forced sex is lust, not love.

> *"Love cares more for others than for self.*
> *Love doesn't want what it doesn't have.*
> *Love doesn't...force itself on others, isn't always 'me first'"*
> (1 Corinthians 13:4-5 msg).

Husband/Male Abuse

Husbands/men who are abused by women...

— Are most often passive, sick, or elderly

— Are usually too embarrassed to reach out for help because they fear ridicule

— Are often regarded as objects of revenge by the wives they've abused

— Are entitled to the same legal protection from civil authorities as wives who are abused

— Are provided the same rights as women to take the same course of action

— Are often victimized by women previously abused by males in childhood

Wives who abuse men…

— Are often still angry at males who abused them in childhood

— Are often still angry at their husbands for previously abusing them

Women who overgeneralize and say, "*All* men are alike" or who have only negative things to say about men will one day have to face their failure to live up to the following scripture:

> *"Do not accuse a man for no reason—*
> *when he has done you no harm"*
> (Proverbs 3:30).

Characteristics of Abusive Women

Question: "What are some characteristics of women who are abusive toward men?"

Answer: The characteristics often fall into three categories:[16]

- *Alcohol abuse*—Women who abuse men are frequently alcoholics.

- *Psychological disorders*—At least 50 percent of women who abuse or are violent toward men are afflicted with Borderline Personality Disorder (BDP), which also contributes to suicide, chronic lying, erratic moods, sexual difficulties, and addiction to alcohol.

- *Unrealistic expectations*—Women who have unrealistic expectations of their relationship with men may, as a result, blame the shortcomings of men for their depression, anxiety, or caustic behavior.

> *"The wise woman builds her house,*
> *but with her own hands the foolish one tears hers down"*
> (PROVERBS 14:1).

C. What Is Misogyny?

His words are repugnant and his philosophy is reprehensible—especially to God, the Creator of women as well as of men.

The young Austrian philosopher Otto Weininger intended to create a wave of public debate with his 1903 work *Sex and Character*, but instead had to settle for a ripple of controversy as his treatise on the sexes was largely discredited by academia. Among other things, Weininger stated, "The complete female knows neither a logical nor a moral imperative, and the words law, duty, duty to oneself are the words that sound most alien to her," and "Genius is identical to depth. Just try to connect the words deep and woman... and everybody will hear the contradiction."[17]

Otto Weininger was a misogynist, a hater of women—a miserable, misguided man who ended his life by suicide. The last Scripture verse a misogynist would want to read is 1 Corinthians 11:7, which proclaims, "The woman is the glory of man."

- **Misogyny** is "hatred and distrust of women."[18] The word *misogyny* comes from the Greek word *misogynia* (*misein*, which means "to hate," and *gune*, which means "woman").[19]
- **Misogynists** have often experienced mental, emotional, or physical harm from women during childhood, or they have been "brainwashed" to believe that women are bad, cruel, or completely inept and irresponsible. Therefore, they overgeneralize and assume all women are the same. Their behavior toward women, especially their own wives, reflects the bitterness and hatred stored within their hearts.

"The good man brings good things out of the good stored up in him,
and the evil man brings evil things out of the evil stored up in him"
(Matthew 12:35).

- **Misogynists...**
  — Have a gender prejudice against all women
  — Think women are weak and thus despise them
  — Feel both threatened and enraged by a woman's tears
  — Act both lovingly and hatefully toward women
  — Primarily use mental and emotional abuse to control women

The words of the wise King Solomon can be applied to the misogynist:

"There is a time when a man lords it over others to his own hurt"
(Ecclesiastes 8:9).

D. What Is Misandry?

Her words are equally repugnant, and her philosophy is equally reprehensible—especially to God, who is the Creator of men as well as women.

Valerie Solanas, who died in 1988, was a radical American feminist and misandrist who derived a measure of infamy not only for attempting to murder acclaimed pop art painter Andy Warhol, but also for founding SCUM, the Society for Cutting Up Men. Her accompanying manifesto was filled with revolting hate for men.

While many of her words about men are clearly cutting and cruel, others can only be deemed as deeply deranged: "To call a man an animal is to flatter him..." And, "Life in this society being, at best, an utter bore and no aspect of society being at all relevant to women, there remains to civic-minded, responsible, thrill-seeking females only to overthrow the government, eliminate the money system, institute complete automation, and destroy the male sex." [20]

As we can expect, the Bible presents a view opposite of that held by misandrists:

"A man...is the image and glory of God"
(1 Corinthians 11:7).

As with misogyny, God is both angered by and anguishes over the attitudes and actions of those who belittle and berate anyone created in His image. "In the image of God he created him; male and female he created them" (Genesis 1:27).

- **Misandry** is the hatred and/or oppression of males.
- **Misandrists** have typically experienced some form of abuse at the hands of significant males during their childhood or adult years. As a result, they *overgeneralize* and reason that all men are going to act in a similar fashion toward them. Their behavior toward men, especially their husbands, reflects the bitterness, fear, and hatred stored within their hearts.

- **Misandrists…**
  — Harbor prejudice against all men
  — Think all men are evil, sexually abusive, oppressive, or violent
  — Fear the strength of a male, assuming his strength will be used to subjugate or abuse
  — Alternate between loving and hateful actions toward men
  — Manipulate men with sex and punish them with mental and emotional abuse

Many prostitutes are misandrists, and the writer of Proverbs warns against such women:

> *"Do not let your heart turn to her ways or stray into her paths.*
> *Many are the victims she has brought down; her slain are a mighty throng.*
> *Her house is a highway to the grave, leading down to the chambers of death"*
> (Proverbs 7:25-27).

E. Where Is God in All of This?

Neither victimizer nor victim can escape the penetrating gaze of God. *The victimizer* who has become desensitized to the violence he inflicts needs to remember that God is noting every slap, punch, and word that harms the victim. Unless there is confession and repentance, a day of accounting and judgment is coming.

The victim who is continually abused by a mate and has become desensitized to the pervasive presence of God needs to remember not to mistake the silence of God for the absence of God. God has taken note of *every* abusive incident, and as you pour out your heart to Him, He will always be with you, even during times of suffering.

Never think of God as just a bystander in life who passively watches as the innocent suffer and the wicked prosper. Never! In fact, He became a part of our tragically broken world as the son of the Virgin Mary. Jesus persistently endured unjust suffering, and it all climaxed at the most pivotal point in history, the crucifixion. God the Father watched God the Son's suffering with a broken heart even though He knew that only His Son's death could pay the penalty for the sins of the world.

When the deepest part of your heart cries His name, He responds with deep love and compassion. And even though God's purpose for allowing you to suffer may seem shrouded in a cloud of mystery and you cannot see His hand at work in your life, you can always trust His heart because…

> *"God is our refuge and strength,*
> *an ever-present help in trouble"*
> (Psalm 46:1).

God's Heart on Violence

- God hates violence. "The Lord examines the righteous, but the wicked and those who love violence his soul hates" (Psalm 11:5).

- God judges those who are violent. "God said to Noah, 'I am going to put an end to all people, for the earth is filled with violence'" (Genesis 6:13).

- God is angry with violent behavior. "Must they also fill the land with violence and continually provoke me to anger?" (Ezekiel 8:17).

- God prohibits violent people from positions of church leadership. "Since an overseer is entrusted with God's work, he must be blameless—not overbearing, not quick-tempered, not given to drunkenness, not violent, not pursuing dishonest gain" (Titus 1:7).

- God commands those who are violent to change. "Give up

your violence and oppression and do what is just and right"
(Ezekiel 45:9).

Taking Action Against Abuse

QUESTION: "How do I know if I should take action when I or someone I know is a victim of abuse?"

ANSWER: Whenever anyone, yourself included, is being abused, you need always to take some sort of action, even if it does not involve confronting the abuser. A safe rule of thumb is to never confront an abuser in a way or at a place that would put you in harm's way.

- If you know you are not being led by the Lord to confront, then do not confront.

- If you think you are to confront but it is not safe to do so alone, take someone with you who can keep the situation physically and emotionally safe for you. Generally speaking, there is safety in numbers.

- If someone is being abused and the person is powerless to stop the abuse, intervene on the person's behalf. Either confront the abuser yourself, report the abuse to someone who can confront, or direct the victim to someone for counseling and protection.

- If the victim is a minor, the abuse must always be reported to legal authorities where required by law. Even if it is not required by law, it should still be reported.

- If the abused person has not directly asked for your help, a good first step is to state simply and kindly that you are available should that person ever need to talk or need anything else. This will help the person to realize that someone cares and that help is available.

Righteous Job related the role and reputation he had as a rescuer:

> *"Whoever heard me spoke well of me,*
> *and those who saw me commended me,*
> *because I rescued the poor who cried for help,*
> *and the fatherless who had none to assist him"*
> (JOB 29:11-12).

II. Characteristics of Wife Abuse

They're all around us, but seldom do you know it, for they are masterful at masking their pain.

Sadly, one out of every three women worldwide is a victim of abuse. And these women come from all walks of life—yes, *all*! We find them among the rich and poor, the young and old, the educated and not, the employed and not, the religious or not. Abuse abides by no boundaries.

It can be your favorite aunt or your friend who sits with you at a little café for lunch. You may very well know someone who perhaps just last night was dragged to the floor and beaten. Those long sleeves she's wearing—year round—could be a hint of horrific abuse at home.

Abused women shroud themselves in secrecy to cover up their painful emotions, bruises, and gashes. However, God not only sees the abuse, but will also hold the abuser accountable for his degrading, violent behavior. The Bible says,

> *"Because of your stubbornness and your unrepentant heart,*
> *you are storing up wrath against yourself for the day of God's wrath"*
> (Romans 2:5).

A. What Is the Cycle of Abuse?

Like a volcano, abuse doesn't start with a sudden outburst of physical force, but rather with intense, internal pressure that builds to the point of eruption. Abusive patterns develop in three stages that are cyclical, becoming increasingly violent with each progressive stage.

Family members who fall victim to the repercussions of these stages feel traumatized by the mere anticipation of a violent outburst. Unfortunately, the escalating nature of abuse is not curbed without intense intervention and appropriate accountability. From the psalmist comes a clear call to action:

> *"Call him [the wicked and evil man] to account for his wickedness*
> *that would not be found out"*
> (Psalm 10:15).

The Cycle of Abuse[22]

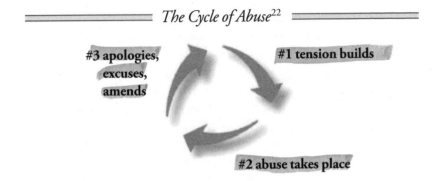

#3 apologies, excuses, amends

#1 tension builds

#2 abuse takes place

Agitated Stage

— Anxiety and tension mark the beginning phase of abuse. The abusive husband communicates dissatisfaction over something small and blames his wife. Then by inflicting verbal and emotional abuse, he maintains *passive psychological* control over his wife, thus creating a fear of some type of pain.

— During this stage, many victims buy into the lies spoken to them and accept responsibility for an abusive mate's unhappiness. Therefore, they try to adjust their own behavior in an effort to appease the abuser and thereby relieve the tension in their homes. However, these efforts only provoke more anger because the abuser does not want to be appeased, but to explode.

> *"From the fruit of his lips a man enjoys good things,*
> *but the unfaithful have a craving for violence"*
> (Proverbs 13:2).

Acute Stage

— In this phase, the pressure becomes so intense that the abuser erupts and gives full vent to rage. When violent behavior is unleashed, family members, outsiders, or police are often called on to defuse the rage.

— This acute stage of *aggressive* behavior doesn't last long, but over time these overpowering outbursts become more frequent and more dangerous.

"An angry man stirs up dissension,
and a hot-tempered one commits many sins"
(PROVERBS 29:22).

Apologetic Stage
— During this "honeymoon phase," the abuser becomes contrite, even sweet, and the abused feels soothed by these outwardly loving actions. With renewed hope for change and the deep desire to have a successful marriage, the abused views these overtures as genuine, heartfelt apologies and extends forgiveness.
— But, as with all honeymoons, they don't last, and the cycle of anger occurs again…and again…and again.
— This temporary honeymoon phase is characterized by the victimizer's dramatic transformation from being villainous to virtuous.
— This transformation is generally demonstrated by some or all of the following behaviors:

• acceptance of responsibility	• helpfulness	• promises
• apologies	• peacemaking	• remorse
• bargaining	• penitence	• romance
• gifts	• pleading	• tears

However, God says there is a vast difference between remorse and repentance, between regretting past behavior and changing future behavior:

"Godly sorrow brings repentance that leads to salvation
and leaves no regret, but worldly sorrow brings death"
(2 CORINTHIANS 7:10).

B. What Is the Situational Setup for Abuse?
In an abusive marriage, both spouses bring emotional deficits into the relationship, creating an unhealthy dynamic. For the cycle of abuse to be broken, one person in the relationship must change. Either the abuser must stop abusing or the abused must stop accepting abuse.

The abusive husband needs to stop perceiving his wife as a piece of property and instead recognize that he is inflicting pain on a precious *person* created in the image of God—a person highly valued by God. This change of mind-set will make a real difference in the relationship.

The abused wife needs to place her dependence on God rather than falsely believing she cannot function without her abusive husband. A change of mind-set will help bring change in an abusive relationship.

It takes only one person to break free from the painful cycle that keeps them both in a downward spiral. Though difficult, release is possible, especially through the power of the Lord.

> *"My eyes are ever on the LORD,*
> *for only he will release my feet from the snare"*
> (PSALM 25:15).

The Setup for Abuse

Notice the characteristics and attitudes exhibited by the husband and wife within an abusive relationship:

THE ABUSIVE HUSBAND	THE ABUSED WIFE
• Low self-worth	• Low self-worth
• Emotionally dependent	• Emotionally dependent
• Emotionally depressed	• Emotionally depressed
• Feels powerless or impotent	• Feels powerless or impotent
• Believes in gender supremacy	• Believes in family unity
• Views her as an unworthy object	• Views him as a powerful person
• Exaggerated jealousy/ possessiveness	• Exaggerated guilt/shame
• Insatiable ego	• Insecure ego
• Short fuse	• Long fuse
• Explosive emotions	• Stifled emotions

- Lives with suspicion
- Fears being betrayed
- Afraid of losing her

- Uses sex to establish dominance
- Often abuses alcohol

- Displays anger
- Blames her for abuse
- Believes she is the problem
- Stressful work environment
- Possesses weapons

- Lives with fear
- Fears being abandoned
- Afraid of losing financial/ emotional security

- Uses sex to establish intimacy
- May or may not abuse alcohol

- Denies anger
- Accepts blame for abuse
- Believes she is the problem
- Stressful home environment
- Avoids weapons

The psalmist accurately describes the anguish of the abused:

"If an enemy were insulting me,
I could endure it; if a foe were raising himself against me,
I could hide from him. But it is you...my companion, my close friend,
with whom I once enjoyed sweet fellowship"
(PSALM 55:12-14).

C. What Is the Cost of Being Constantly Abused?

There is always a price to be paid for pain—a loss to be incurred by the recipient of abusive words and hurtful acts. The cost is often unseen, an extensive, inner deprivation that can continue to damage the soul for a lifetime. How ironic that the tongue can serve as both an instrument of healing and an inflictor of heartache!

"The tongue that brings healing is a tree of life,
but a deceitful tongue crushes the spirit"
(PROVERBS 15:4).

The Cost of Being Abused

• Loss of self-worth	Increased self-doubt
• Loss of self-confidence	Increased self-consciousness
• Loss of self-perception	Increased self-criticism
• Loss of happiness	Increased emotional flatness
• Loss of freedom	Increased vigilance
• Loss of inner peace	Increased peace-at-all-costs mentality
• Loss of self-assurance	Increased anxiety
• Loss of security	Increased insecurity
• Loss of trust	Increased distrust
• Loss of sexual identity	Increased sexual confusion
• Loss of a clear conscience	Increased guilt or shame
• Loss of friendship	Increased isolation
• Loss of faith	Increased fear
• Loss of safety	Increased desire to escape
• Loss of self-respect	Increased self-abasement
• Loss of optimism	Increased pessimism
• Loss of personal pride	Increased self-hatred
• Loss of hope	Increased despair

Those who suffer the damaging effects of abuse can find hope and healing as they cling to the promise of God stated by the apostle Paul:

> *"Those God foreknew he also predestined*
> *to be conformed to the likeness of his Son"*
> (ROMANS 8:29).

D. What Is the Cost of Being Constantly Abusive?

Just as there is a price for incurring pain, there is a price to be paid for inflicting pain. As with the abused, the abuser pays in ways that often escape the physical eye because the payment is extracted from the unseen soul of the abuser—from the mind, will, and emotions—as a result of a hardened heart. Proverbs 28:14 says,

"He who hardens his heart falls into trouble."

The Cost of Being Abusive

- Loss of self-control . . Increased abusive behaviors toward wife
- Loss of clear conscience . . . . Increased guilt, shame, and blaming others
- Loss of empathy . . Increased selfishness and self-centeredness
- Loss of compassion . . Increased hardness of heart toward others
- Loss of sound judgment . . . Increased denial and rationalization
- Loss of inner restraint . . Increased anger and rage toward others
- Loss of faith . . . . Increased fear and rebellion toward God
- Loss of self-esteem . . . . Increased self-aggrandizement and belittling of others
- Loss of self-worth . . Increased self-doubt and criticism of others
- Loss of self-respect . . . . Increased self-loathing and disregard for others
- Loss of perception . . . . . . Increased self-focus and dominance over others
- Loss of self-confidence . . . . Increased self-consciousness and control of others
- Loss of personal pride . . . . Increased self-abasement and abasement of others
- Loss of joy and happiness . . . . Increased sullenness and depression
- Loss of freedom . . . . Increased bondage to being abusive toward others
- Loss of inner peace . . . . Increased restlessness and agitation toward others
- Loss of security . . . . Increased insecurity and power plays
- Loss of friendship . . . . Increased isolation and emotional withdrawal

A classic example of the cost of being an unrepentant abuser is seen in the life of the Egyptian Pharaoh, the overbearing master of the ancient Israelites. Every plague God sent to Egypt was followed by an appeal to Pharaoh to let the Israelites go. And after every appeal, Pharaoh hardened his heart and treated the Israelites even more harshly than before. Finally, Pharaoh's hardened heart resulted in not only the death of his own son, but also the deaths of the firstborn in every house throughout his kingdom, along with the destruction of his awesome army.

The cost of being constantly abusive proved to be catastrophic for Pharaoh, and it can be equally catastrophic for abusive husbands who fall under the disciplining hand of God. The Bible says,

> *"Pharaoh's heart was hard and he would not let the Israelites go,*
> *just as the LORD had said through Moses...*
> *When Pharaoh stubbornly refused to let us [Israel] go,*
> *the LORD killed every firstborn in Egypt, both man and animal...*
> *When Pharaoh's horses, chariots and horsemen went into the sea,*
> *the LORD brought the waters of the sea back over them,*
> *but the Israelites walked through the sea on dry ground"*
> (Exodus 9:35; 13:15; 15:19).

E. What Choices Do the Abused Have?

Making Help Available

Women in third-world countries formerly had few or no options for fleeing an abusive spouse. That scenario is changing considerably with the availability of more residential shelters for battered women and children—as well as nonresidential, temporary shelters. There are also telephone hotlines devoted to helping women in crisis.

Where these options are not available, women should compile a list of "safe homes," a network of people in the community who will provide a haven when a woman is in harm's way. Some countries also have designated local places of worship as temporary shelters. The Bible encourages us all to...

> *"Seek justice, encourage the oppressed"*
> (Isaiah 1:17).

Determining Your Response

Staying with an abuser only to wait for the next violent episode is not your only option. You have more than one viable choice. Safety should be paramount, for until a safe haven is found, you will not have the emotional stability or state of mind to make sound decisions concerning how to get help for your abusive situation and healing for your marriage.

People in abusive relationships adopt various ways of responding to their mates, but you need to know that you have a God who not only watches over you, but who also—if you take refuge in Him—will guide you in the way you should go.

> *"You are my hiding place;*
> *you will protect me from trouble and surround me with songs of deliverance.*
> *I will instruct you and teach you in the way you should go;*
> *I will counsel you and watch over you"*
> (Psalm 32:7-8).

Victims of domestic violence typically choose to respond to their victimizers in one of the following ways:

The Ostrich Outlook
The ostrich chooses to deny the situation, minimize its seriousness, or rationalize the abuser's behavior—even to the point of self-blame. "If I just did everything right, my mate wouldn't be this way. It's all my fault!" This choice leads to an even greater loss of self-respect.

The Martyr Mate
The martyr decides to be a "silent sufferer" in a destructive relationship. This is a dangerous choice. To survive, this person must sacrifice the voice of truth in order to avoid contradicting the marriage partner and risking a violent reaction.

The Puppet Partner
The puppet opts out by disowning personal feelings, denying personal anger, and living emotionally divorced. This choice also leaves the person vulnerable to potential danger. Abusive marriages do not remain static; abuse that goes unchallenged becomes increasingly violent.

The Merry-Go-Round Mate
The merry-go-rounder has already divorced several abusive marriage partners and is still looking for another partner to provide love and support. With

these choices, this person keeps going in circles. Until insight is gained into the reasons for abusive behavior and there is a willingness to take steps to protect self and children, the pattern of abuse will continue. More than likely, this person will marry yet another abuser.

THE BOUNDARY BUILDER

The boundary builder chooses to set healthy boundaries. Only behavior that is acceptable and nonviolent is tolerated. This positive choice offers the possibility of permanent change. This person prays for God to give the wisdom and courage necessary both to stand up to the opposition that will invariably come and also for the ability to follow through with consequences as new standards are established for the way the couple will relate to one another.

THE DEPARTING DOVE

The departing dove leaves—at least for a while—to demonstrate the seriousness of the abuse. This choice is an attempt to force the abusive marriage partner to either deal with the abusive behavior or to suffer the consequence of losing a mate. While the abused mate seeks personal counseling, the abusive mate also needs to get professional help. If that help is refused, the couple will remain separated from one another. The departing dove's inner cry is...

"My heart is in anguish within me; the terrors of death assail me.
Fear and trembling have beset me; horror has overwhelmed me.
I said, 'Oh, that I had the wings of a dove!
I would fly away and be at rest—I would flee far away and stay in the desert;
I would hurry to my place of shelter, far from the tempest and storm'"
(PSALM 55:4-8).

===== **Allowing an Abuser to Return Prematurely** =====

QUESTION: "I've helped a physically abused woman obtain a restraining order, but she allowed her husband to return home prematurely. Why did she—like so many others—allow him to come back when the violence would be repeated?"

ANSWER: She will probably continue to go back to the abuser until she is convinced that...

- She can keep the family truly safe and secure apart from the abuser.

- She is worthy and deserving of a better life and better treatment.

Therefore, there must be a double safety net of both community services and individual support that is perceived as reliable. This means we all need to...

> *"speak up for those who cannot speak for themselves,*
> *for the rights of all who are destitute.*
> *Speak up and judge fairly;*
> *defend the rights of the poor and needy"*
> (PROVERBS 31:8-9).

III. CAUSES OF WIFE ABUSE

The way couples relate to each other often mirrors the way their parents related to each other. Most behavioral patterns—both positive and negative—are learned.

In abusive marriages, typically the husband, the wife, or both grew up in an abusive home where conflict resolution skills were not practiced. Therefore, a hostile, abusive environment was "normal" to them.

They didn't realize back then that *their normal* wasn't normal, and they don't realize now that their normal isn't normal. Sin patterns can be generational, but every succeeding generation has the ability to stop the cycle of abuse that has come down from one generation to the next—with God's help. The God of the Bible says,

> *"My people are destroyed from lack of knowledge"*
> (HOSEA 4:6).

A. Why Do Abusers Do It?

Behavior does not come out of a vacuum, but out of a person's heart, environment, and personal experience. Each person is born with a propensity toward self-will and is raised in an environment that either promotes violence and abuse or promotes love and respect. Beliefs about God, self, and others are formed, and behavior naturally follows.

Research has indicated that young boys who witness violence between their parents triple their chances of becoming abusive husbands. The home where a woman is devalued and traumatized becomes a more impactful model for inciting violence in boys than does being assaulted as a teenager. It is estimated that more than three million children are witnesses to spouse abuse in the United States each year as their parents fail to heed the wise words of the writer of Proverbs:[23]

> *"Train a child in the way he should go,*
> *and when he is old [mature] he will not turn from it"*
> (Proverbs 22:6).

The abuser does what he does because:

— He grew up watching abuse between his parents.

— He experienced abuse as a child.

— He views people as possessions rather than persons.

— He "loves things and uses people" instead of loving people and using things.

— He has not been taught how to love.

— He understands love to be conditional—if she pleases him, she will avoid his wrath and vindictiveness.

— He thinks he has the right to control her.

— He thinks he has the right to use force on her.

— He fears she could be unfaithful.

— He fears losing her.

— He becomes angry when she shows weakness.

— He sees himself as a victim.

— He thinks she has taken power from him.

— He blames her for his low self-esteem.

— He believes his power demonstrates his superiority.

— He wants to feel significant and in control.

— He possesses an unbiblical view of submission and authority.

— He handles stress immaturely.

— He has few or no coping skills.

— He thinks violence is the way to get even or to retaliate.

— He has learned that violence and other forms of abuse work.

— He hasn't suffered strong enough repercussions to deter him.

The writer of Ecclesiastes explains the impact on an abuser's heart when consequences are delayed:

> *"When the sentence for a crime is not quickly carried out,*
> *the hearts of the people are filled with schemes to do wrong"*
> (ECCLESIASTES 8:11).

B. What Do Abusers Believe?

The beliefs that people carry are what give birth to their behaviors. The problem, then, is obvious: Abusers and those they abuse have *faulty beliefs* about their relationships. Therefore, they both engage in *faulty behaviors* toward one another.

Of all the distorted beliefs swirling in the heads of abusive husbands, two primary factors agitate those distortions and spawn violent behavior. *Anger*: His wife fails to "measure up" on any number of fronts, thus fanning the flames of fury. *Blame*: His wife is allegedly the cause of his unhappiness, his losses, his failed friendships, etc., and the list could go on and on.

Distorted beliefs, a dangerous mind-set, and a difficult situation are all it takes to light the fuse for abuse and cause an explosion. False accusations and out-of-control anger are not the ways of God; however, they do reflect the ways of abusers:

> *"They do not speak peaceably, but devise false accusations"*
> (PSALM 35:20).

Some distorted beliefs include:

— Abuse is normal in relationships.

— Jealousy and possessiveness are characteristics of love.

— Beatings demonstrate caring concern.

— Sex is better after a fight.

— Men need to prove their masculinity, to always be in charge.

— Women need to be controlled, to be kept in line.

— Husbands have the right to control their wives.

— Women deserve to be mistreated.

These erroneous beliefs can be countered with God's truth and by praying,

> *"Teach me knowledge and good judgment,*
> *for I believe in your commands"*
> (Psalm 119:66).

C. Why Doesn't She Leave?

Those who grew up in healthy, nonabusive homes have no frame of reference for those who bow to abuse. But those who grew up in abusive homes know all too well the reasons the abused not only allow abuse, but also stay with their abusers. They understand the mentality because it is *their mentality.* They lived it as children, and now they are living it as adults. They are caught in the snare of abuse.

However, the Bible makes it clear:

> *"Fear of man will prove to be a snare,*
> *but whoever trusts in the* Lord *is kept safe"*
> (Proverbs 29:25).

An abused wife chooses *not* to leave her husband for a variety of reasons—reasons that are understood by all who have stood in her shoes, walked down her street, shared in her sorrows. She doesn't leave because of what she firmly believes and falsely feels.

She doesn't leave because of…[24]

- **What she fully believes:**
    - She believes she doesn't have a biblical right to separate in order to achieve a healthy relationship.
    - She believes abuse is normal and she must accept it.
    - She believes she must protect the family image at all costs.
    - She believes family "problems" are private and can't be shared.
    - She believes she has to stay because of what spiritual leaders say.
    - She believes the promises of her husband to never do it again.

She believes being a peace-at-any-price person is being loyal and godly.

She believes her husband and children are all she has.

She believes biblical submission in marriage permits abuse.

She believes there are no organizations or services to help her.

- **What she falsely feels:**

  She feels helpless, as if she has no power to leave or make it on her own.

  She feels she has no real worth or value.

  — She feels manipulated by threats of suicide.

  She feels she deserves to be abused and blames herself.

  She feels isolated from supportive people.

  She feels too much shame to tell about the abuse.

  She feels she is not heard or understood when she does share.

  She feels others don't want to hear about the abuse.

  She feels that explaining the details of the abuse again costs too much.

  She feels that having two parents in an unhealthy relationship is better for the children than having only one healthy parent.

- **What she firmly fears:**

  She fears if she tells and then he changes, people won't forgive him.

  She fears what her husband will do if she leaves.

  She fears he will take their children.

  She fears he will divorce her and she will become a single parent.

  She fears the financial consequences of separation or divorce.

  She fears living all alone.

  She fears being dependent on others for help.

  She fears the stigma of people learning about her abuse.

  She fears she is "crazy" because she is continually told she is.

The abused need to cry out to God,

"Ensure your servant's well-being;
let not the arrogant oppress me"
(Psalm 119:122).

Separation Without Divorce

Question: "If a wife separates from her husband, is she not ultimately divorcing her husband or at least opening the door to divorce?"

Answer: No, the husband is the one who has opened the door to separation by his violence—not the wife. He is accountable to God for his sin as well as the consequences of his sin.

- Separation is not divorce and does not open the door to divorce, but instead opens the door to safety and obedience to God.
- Separation is siding with God regarding His hatred of violence: "The Lord examines the righteous, but the wicked and those who love violence his soul hates" (Psalm 11:5).
- Separation from an abusive husband is trusting God to do what is best for her marriage rather than trusting in anything she might do. She takes literally the Bible's promise to her: "Trust in the Lord with all your heart and lean not on your own understanding; in all your ways acknowledge him, and he will make your paths straight" (Proverbs 3:5-6).

D. Why Does She Leave?

It is one of the most difficult things she will ever do, and it is one of the best things she could ever do.

Leaving—taking that crucial step to curtail the cycle of abuse—benefits everyone involved and ushers in the opportunity for a fresh, new beginning. The wife no longer lives in fear or faces abuse in her own home. The husband can better grasp the gravity of the abusive situation and seek biblical counseling. The children are protected and spared further trauma from witnessing their father abuse their mother.

But it is by no means easy for a wife to walk away from the abuser. It is critical to enlist a supportive circle of friends who can help her maintain her resolve and help meet her needs during such a vulnerable time. And above all, she needs to seek the guiding, protective hand of God to give her the grace and strength to take that first step out the door.

> *"I am he, I am he who will sustain you.*
> *I have made you and I will carry you;*
> *I will sustain you and I will rescue you"*
> (Isaiah 46:4).

She leaves because:

- She finally realizes her husband won't change if circumstances remain the same.
- She understands that leaving may be the only way to motivate him to change.
- She can now see him acting on his threats of severe physical, mental, or emotional abuse.
- She sees his abuse is occurring more frequently.
- She sees he has begun to abuse the children.
- She wants to prevent their children from adopting abusive mind-sets and behaviors.
- She has found help through friends, family, a church, or professional organizations.
- She realizes it is not God's will for anyone to be abused.
- She is afraid for her life or the lives of her children if they stay.
- She realizes there is a thin line between threats and homicide.

She needs to continuously pray,

> *"O righteous God,*
> *who searches minds and hearts,*
> *bring to an end the violence of the wicked*
> *and make the righteous secure"*
> (Psalm 7:9).

Scripture reveals that many times godly people did separate physically from their ungodly authorities because submission would have caused those godly people to violate God's standard or revealed will. Biblically, Christians are called to submit to governing authorities, unless doing so would lead to sin or harm. Notice that…

- Jesus escaped the murderous plots of the religious leaders.
- The disciples of Jesus defied the mandate from the religious leaders that they stop preaching about Jesus.
- David fled King Saul with God's blessing. Although David was one of the king's subjects, when Saul's actions became violent, David escaped.

> *"The LORD was with David but had left Saul…*
> *Saul tried to pin him to the wall with his spear,*
> *but David eluded him as Saul drove the spear into the wall.*
> *That night David made good his escape"*
> (1 SAMUEL 18:12; 19:10).

Submission

QUESTION: "Because Ephesians 5:21 teaches we are to submit to one another, isn't leaving an abusive spouse against the teaching of the Bible?"

ANSWER: The Bible teaches mutual submission in a loving relationship, not one-way submission in an abusive relationship. The specific biblical instruction to anyone around a hot-tempered, easily angered person is separation:

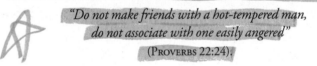

> *"Do not make friends with a hot-tempered man,*
> *do not associate with one easily angered"*
> (PROVERBS 22:24).

E. Why Does She Feel Guilty?

The Reasons for Her Guilt

There is an emotion associated with wife abuse that transcends all geographical boundaries and blinds women from seeing the truth about the abuse they suffer. That emotion is *false guilt*. It beguiles a woman into believing that the bruises, the slashes, the sexual violations really are all her fault, and not his.

> *"My guilt has overwhelmed me*
> *like a burden too heavy to bear"*
> (Psalm 38:4).

Blame-shifting by the berating husband who claims his abusive actions are the result of his wife's missteps can lead to her forming a "false guilt mindset" if she believes his lies and accepts responsibility for his abusive actions. False guilt adds another unhealthy dynamic to the already-wounded emotions of an abused wife.

She feels guilty because of his accusations that…

- She disobeyed him.
- She was arguing with him.
- She questioned him about how he was spending money.
- She questioned him about having girlfriends.
- She didn't prepare his meal on time.
- She wasn't sufficiently caring for the home or the children.
- She didn't have his clothes ready for him.
- She refused to have sex with him.

Thus, the guilt-ridden, falsely accused wife mentally and emotionally beats herself up, suffering needlessly as she says to herself, "My life is consumed by anguish" (Psalm 31:10).

How do the innocent come to bear the guilt of the guilty? Although this seems illogical, it is common among those who are continuously abused. In seeking to understand this painful phenomenon, it is helpful to define some relevant terms. As the Bible says,

> *"Blessed is the man [or woman] who finds wisdom,*
> *the man who gains understanding"*
> (Proverbs 3:13).

The Reasons She Shouldn't Feel Guilty

An abused woman should not feel guilt over moving out of harm's way. Note the differences between true guilt and false:

- *True guilt* is an emotional response as a result of any wrong attitude or action contrary to the perfect will of God—and it refers to the *fact* of being at fault.

— *True guilt* is a *fact*, not a *feeling*. *False guilt* is a self-condemning *feeling* not based on *fact*.

— *False guilt* is an emotional response of (1) self-blame even though no wrong has been committed or (2) self-blame that continues after having committed a sin even though the sin is confessed, repented of, and no longer a part of a person's life.

The prophet Isaiah explains true guilt by saying…

> *"We all, like sheep, have gone astray,*
> *each of us has turned to his own way"*
> (ISAIAH 53:6).

False guilt keeps you in bondage to three massive weapons of destruction: shame, fear, and anger.[25]

1. *False guilt is based on self-condemning feelings* that you have not lived up to your expectations or the expectations of someone else.

2. *False guilt is not resolved by confession* because there is nothing to confess.

3. *False guilt is resolved by rejecting lies and believing truth.* Revelation 12:10 says that Satan is the "accuser of our brothers." He loves to burden believers with false guilt and condemnation. Some of his favorite strategies are bringing up the past, reminding you of your failures, and making you feel unforgiven and unaccepted by God.

The apostle John describes the aim and destiny of Satan:

> *"The accuser of our brothers,*
> *who accuses them before our God day and night,*
> *has been hurled down"*
> (REVELATION 12:10).

Guilt and Shame

QUESTION: "How can I overcome the guilt and shame I feel as a result of being blamed for the abusive things done to me? Did I really deserve this abuse? Was it really my fault?"

ANSWER: Abusers are notorious for blaming their actions on those whom they abuse. *Blame-shifting* is a means of controlling others and breaking down any possibility of resistance.

Blame-shifting is effective with those...

— Who have a history of being abused and have been repeatedly told it is their fault

— Who believe bad things happen to only bad people, so they must be responsible for the abuse

— Who are children, for they are especially vulnerable to false guilt and shame heaped on them by those in authority over them

But the truth is...

— No one deserves abuse.

— No one makes another person sin.

— Abusers alone are responsible for their abusive acts. You are not to blame for what any abuser chooses to do.

Blame-shifters not only blame their victims but also shame them:

— Shame attacks your identity. (Guilt says, "I've *done* something bad," whereas shame says, "I *am* bad.")

— Shame does not focus on *what* you've done but on *who* you are.

— Shame will cause you to feel defective, which, in turn, causes a deep feeling of unworthiness and a continual fear of rejection.

— Shame belongs to the abuser alone, not to you.

Because shame attacks self-worth and produces self-loathing, it must be rooted out and replaced with a biblical view of how God sees you. It must be replaced with the truth. The psalmist says it this way:

> *"No one whose hope is in you [God] will ever be put to shame,*
> *but they will be put to shame who are treacherous without excuse"*
> (PSALM 25:3).

F. The Root Causes of Abuse

The Desire to Meet Inner Needs

Some people can't comprehend the *whys* of abuse. "Why do husbands do it? Why do wives accept it?" Within the heart of every person are three God-given inner needs—the needs for love, significance, and security.[26] At times we attempt to meet these needs illegitimately.

Abusers abuse their victims in order to *feel significant*. Those who are abused stay in abusive relationships in order to *feel secure*. To them, separation feels unbearable, or they feel terrified that the violence will escalate if they leave. God's solution is that both the abused and the abuser look to the Lord to meet their deepest inner needs:

> *"The LORD will guide you always;*
> *he will satisfy your needs in a sun-scorched land*
> *and will strengthen your frame.*
> *You will be like a well-watered garden,*
> *like a spring whose waters never fail"*
> (ISAIAH 58:11).

The Wrong Beliefs that Lead to Abuse

WRONG BELIEF OF THE ABUSER

The abuser abuses to feel significant.

> "My wife is to blame for what's happening. I have the right to expect certain things from my marriage partner who, after all, belongs to me. If I do not control my wife, I could lose her, so I'll do whatever it takes to remain in control."

RIGHT BELIEF FOR THE ABUSER

Here is what the abuser needs to say:

> "I alone am responsible for my abusive behavior and the way I respond to people and circumstances. My wife is not to blame because no matter what someone else does, I have a choice in how I treat others. Even if I lose my wife, I'll never lose God. He is my true source of significance and promises to meet my needs."

"My God will meet all your needs
according to his glorious riches in Christ Jesus"
(PHILIPPIANS 4:19).

WRONG BELIEF OF THE ABUSED
The abused accepts abuse to feel secure.

> "I'm to blame for what my husband does to me. I must be doing something wrong. If I just try harder to do what he expects of me, things will get better. If I don't do better, I could lose my husband along with my security. Or even worse, I could be killed. Pleasing my husband is my only hope for survival and security."

RIGHT BELIEF FOR THE ABUSED
Here is what the abused needs to say:

> "I'm not to blame for my husband's abuse, and I have been wrong in thinking my happiness will come from a human relationship. I can choose whether or not I am willing to be around anyone who mistreats me, including my husband. Even if I lose him, as a Christian, I will never lose Jesus, who lives in me. Because the Lord promises to be my provider, I will depend on Him to meet all of my needs. The Lord is my source of security."

"Your Maker is your husband—
the LORD Almighty is his name"
(ISAIAH 54:5).

G. How to Seek Significance and Find Security in God

Domestic violence does more than damage your body and disturb your thoughts. The pain goes much deeper, breaking your heart. You may feel hopeless and think, *I'll never be able to trust anyone again.* Unfortunately, this kind of heartache cannot simply heal itself over time, and no amount of positive actions can restore your sense of significance or security after being abused by the man you loved and trusted the most. There is only One who can provide eternal security and permanent change of heart.

The Lord offers hope and healing to all who are weary and broken. His path to healing will take time—you will not feel immediate physical safety, but God promises to give His presence, power, and protection to you. If you entrust your heart to Him, He will always walk beside you. You will never again face another day of fear, pain, or torment alone because the Lord says,

> *"Be strong and courageous.*
> *Do not be afraid or terrified because of them,*
> *for the LORD your God goes with you;*
> *he will never leave you nor forsake you"*
> (DEUTERONOMY 31:6).

If you desire to have your three God-given needs met and know the security that lasts forever, see the appendix on pages 411-413.

IV. STEPS TO SOLUTION

His arms once sweetly embraced you, but now they swing wildly toward you. His arms once tenderly held you, but now they severely harm you. You feel devastated, distraught, devalued.

As a victim of wife abuse, you feel submerged in both physical and emotional pain. You are traumatized and terrorized by a man who fails to heed this command of God: "Husbands, love your wives, just as Christ loved the church and gave himself up for her" (Ephesians 5:25). The arms where you once sought protection now petrify you.

But there are other arms—strong arms opening wide to you, longing to hold you and wanting to convey your worth. To God, you are a precious lamb. He wants to lead you like a shepherd to a place of peace. Turn to Him, ask for His help, seek His wisdom about finding protection from a scheming wolf. Find refuge and rest in His loving arms.

> *"He tends his flock like a shepherd:*
> *He gathers the lambs in his arms and carries them close to his heart"*
> (ISAIAH 40:11).

A. A Key Verse to Memorize

Oh that the abusive husband would heed the model set forth by the Lord Jesus, and treasure and tenderly care for what has been entrusted to him!

In the spiritual realm there exists a bridegroom and a bride, a beautiful portrayal of sacred and sacrificial love. Jesus is the bridegroom, and the church—all those who have trusted in Him as Savior and Lord—is the bride. Scripture testifies to the deep, abiding love Jesus has for His church—His bride, His people—ultimately evidenced by His sacrificial death on their behalf.

Jesus would never assault His bride's worth. He would never hurt or harm her in any way. As the bridegroom, He laid down His life for His bride.

> *"This is how we know what love is:*
> *Jesus Christ laid down his life for us"*
> (1 JOHN 3:16).

B. A Key Passage to Read and Reread

God Almighty sees and knows. Everything that is done behind closed doors—even in the darkest night—glares exceedingly bright before the eyes of God. He sees the secret assaults, the blackened eyes, the covered bruises.

For the abused: *Find peace in God.* Rest in His protective arms. He will help you and rescue you. Never is it His will for a wife to be harmed by her husband.

For the abuser: *Have a holy fear of God.* You will be held accountable for every vile word and violent act you've committed unless you confess your sin and change your ways. God is just—He must punish sin. His compassion overflows toward the one you are harming. The Bible makes it plain:

> *"Does he who formed the eye not see?*
> *Does he who disciplines nations not punish?"*
> (PSALM 94:9-10).

For the Abused: Psalm 91

> *"He who dwells in the shelter of the Most High*
> *will rest in the shadow of the Almighty.*
> *I will say of the LORD,*
> *'He is my refuge and my fortress, my God, in whom I trust.'*
> *Surely he will save you from the fowler's snare*
> *and from the deadly pestilence.*

He will cover you with his feathers,
and under his wings you will find refuge;
his faithfulness will be your shield and rampart...
If you make the Most High your dwelling—even the LORD,
who is my refuge...he will command his angels concerning you
to guard you in all your ways... 'Because he loves me,' says the LORD,
'I will rescue him; I will protect him, for he acknowledges my name.
He will call upon me, and I will answer him;
I will be with him in trouble, I will deliver him and honor him'"
(PSALM 91:1-4,9,11,14-15).

For the Abuser: Psalm 94

"O LORD, *the God who avenges,*
O God who avenges, shine forth.
Rise up, O Judge of the earth; pay back to the proud what they deserve...
They pour out arrogant words; all the evildoers are full of boasting...
Take heed, you senseless ones among the people;
you fools, when will you become wise?
Does he who implanted the ear not hear?
Does he who formed the eye not see?
Does he who disciplines nations not punish?
Does he who teaches man lack knowledge?...
You grant him relief from days of trouble, till a pit is dug for the wicked...
Who will rise up for me against the wicked?
Who will take a stand for me against evildoers?...
He will repay them for their sins and destroy them for their wickedness;
the LORD *our God will destroy them"*
(PSALM 94:1-2,4,8-10,13,16,23).

FOR THE ABUSED: PSALM 91

God Is...

- Your shelter . . . . verse 1
- Your resting place . . . . verse 1
- Your refuge . . . . verse 2
- Your fortress . . . . verse 2
- Your God . . . . verse 2
- Your Savior . . . . verse 3
- Your cover . . . . verse 4
- Your shield . . . . verse 4
- Your rampart . . . . verse 4
- Your dwelling . . . . verse 9
- Your guardian . . . . . verse 11
- Your rescuer . . . . . . verse 14
- Your protector . . . . verse 14
- Your answer . . . . . . verse 15
- Your deliverer . . . . . verse 15
- Your salvation . . . . . verse 16

FOR THE ABUSER: PSALM 94

You Are...

- Arrogant . . . . verse 4
- Boastful . . . . verse 4
- Senseless . . . . verse 8
- A fool . . . . verse 8

God Will...

- Avenge your victim(s) verse 1
- Judge you . . . . verse 2
- Pay you back what
  you deserve . . . . verse 2

God...

- Hears the abuse . . . . . verse 9
- Sees the abuse . . . . . . verse 9
- Punishes your sin . . . verse 10
- Knows your
  thoughts . . . . verse 10

God Will...

- Dig a pit for you . . . . verse 13
- Rise up against you . . verse 16
- Stand up against
  you . . . . verse 16
- Repay you for your
  sins . . . . verse 23
- Destroy you for your
  wickedness . . . . verse 23

C. How to Correct the Confusion

The woman who sincerely wants to please God but is not grounded in the Word of God can become captive to an incorrect understanding of biblical submission. She associates submission with accepting abuse, believing it's her call as a wife to suffer through kicks and punches. But nothing could be further from the heart of God, who never approves a husband's abuse.

One key to correcting the confusion is seeing Scripture in light of its context. Yes, the Bible says, "Wives, submit to your husbands" (Ephesians 5:22), but it also says, "Husbands, love your wives, just as Christ loved the church" (Ephesians 5:25), which is a clear mandate for husbands to treat their wives with compassion and tender care. Here are three helpful steps for examining Scripture accurately and contextually:

- Look at the surrounding verses.
- Look at the purpose of the passage or book in which the verse is found.
- Look at the whole counsel of God's Word on submission and love.
- Look at how we are to relate to one another:

> *"Do your best to present yourself to God as one approved,*
> *a workman who does not need to be ashamed*
> *and who correctly handles the word of truth"*
> (2 Timothy 2:15).

=== *Arguments and Answers* ===

Argument: "When Jesus said to turn the other cheek, He meant that you should submit to abuse."[27]

Answer: When you look at these words of Jesus, the context is the issue of rejecting retaliation: Refuse to retaliate evil for evil. Jesus was not advocating submitting to abuse: "You have heard that it was said, 'Eye for eye, and tooth for tooth.' But I tell you, Do not resist an evil person. If someone strikes you on the right cheek, turn to him the other also" (Matthew 5:38-39). The backdrop of Jesus' words about "turning the other cheek" was refusing to take personal revenge, not promoting or accepting abuse.

ARGUMENT: "Because Jesus submitted Himself to abuse, if you want to be Christlike, you must also submit to abuse."

ANSWER: It is important to notice that on numerous occasions when the enemies of Jesus sought to harm Him, He eluded them and escaped. However, when the time came for Him to take away the sins of the world, Jesus allowed His blood to be the payment price to purchase our forgiveness. Clearly, Jesus did not submit to abuse without purpose. "Jesus went around in Galilee, purposely staying away from Judea because the Jews there were waiting to take his life... Again they tried to seize him, but he escaped their grasp" (John 7:1; 10:39).

ARGUMENT: "First Peter 2:19 says we are called to endure unjust suffering. We are to take such suffering as being commendable before God. Peter wrote, 'It is commendable if a man bears up under the pain of unjust suffering because he is conscious of God.'"

ANSWER: This passage is not dealing with husbands and wives; rather, it speaks to first-century slaves who suffered under the hand of cruel masters. Twisting this passage to condone or justify marital or family abuse is a deceptive mishandling of the Word of God. We can learn from this passage that God gives grace to those who endure unjust suffering. However, this is not a call from God for wives to endure abuse by their husbands. To the contrary, men who abuse their wives do so because of their own ungodliness. And in Scripture, God specifically calls husbands and wives to sacrificially love each other and treat each other with respect: "Husbands, in the same way be considerate as you live with your wives, and treat them with respect as the weaker partner and as heirs with you of the gracious gift of life, so that nothing will hinder your prayers" (1 Peter 3:7).

The context of 1 Peter 3:7 refers to suffering because you are "conscious of God," which means you are suffering ridicule, criticism, and rejection because of your faith, not because you are a woman or you haven't met a husband's particular or unreasonable expectations.

ARGUMENT: "An abused woman should view suffering as her legitimate 'cross to bear.' As Matthew 16:24 says, 'If anyone would come after me [Jesus], he must deny himself and take up his cross and follow me.'"

ANSWER: Nowhere does the Bible indicate that the cross is an instrument of physical and emotional pain to be inflicted upon a woman by an abusive husband. It is not self-centered for a woman to escape or stop abuse. In context, Jesus was saying the cross is a symbol of death—death to self-centered living, death to self-rule so that the Lord can rule our hearts and lives. The very next verse confirms that the cross stands for yielding our lives to the Lord, and not abuse: "Whoever wants to save his life will lose it, but whoever loses his life for me will find it" (verse 25).

ARGUMENT: "God made men superior to women."

ANSWER: God made women and men different from one another, with different roles and functions. The Bible does not say that God regards one gender as superior and the other as inferior. Rather, He regards them as equal: "There is neither Jew nor Greek, slave nor free, male nor female, for you are all one in Christ Jesus" (Galatians 3:28).

ARGUMENT: "Because Ephesians 5:24 says wives should submit to their husbands in everything, a wife must submit unconditionally—even to abuse."[28]

ANSWER: This conclusion contradicts other Scripture passages. A "hierarchy of submission" was demonstrated when the apostles refused to obey the high priest and instead obeyed Jesus, who gave them the Great Commission to continue to teach about Him (Matthew 28:19-20). The disciples could have been severely punished for disobeying the high priest and instead submitting to God.

- Similarly, if a husband tells a wife to do something that God says is wrong, she must not submit to her erring husband, but instead submit to God.

- God clearly states His position that husbands are to treat their wives with respect, as well as His opposition to violence. In all things "we must obey God rather than men!" (Acts 5:29).

ARGUMENT: "Because the Bible says the husband is the head of the wife, a wife must not resist being abused by her husband."

ANSWER: A wife is to submit to the *headship* (or leadership) of her husband, but nowhere does the Bible imply she is to submit to the *abuse* of her husband. She is to respect his position, not be victimized by his power.

In Ephesians 5:23, the husband and wife relationship is compared to the relationship of Christ and the church. Christ is the head of His church, which is His body. Although the husband is the head of his wife, no head abuses its own body. A husband never chooses to beat his body with a hammer—unless, of course, he is out of his mind (mentally ill). Instead, he does whatever he can to protect and provide for his body. A godly husband will treat his wife in the same way that Christ cares for the church: "The husband is the head of the wife as Christ is the head of the church, his body, of which he is the Savior…Husbands ought to love their wives as their own bodies. He who loves his wife loves himself. After all, no one ever hated his own body, but he feeds and cares for it, just as Christ does the church" (Ephesians 5:23,28-29).

=========== **Submission vs. Your Conscience** ===========

QUESTION: "My husband says that because I am a Christian, I must submit to whatever is asked of me. Must I submit when pressured to do things that violate my conscience?"[29]

ANSWER: No, never violate your conscience. Keeping a clear conscience is an issue of your integrity. In the Bible, a "hierarchy" of submission exists to guide our decision making:

- First, we are to "submit to one another out of reverence for Christ" (Ephesians 5:21). This *mutual submission* includes both husbands and wives deferring to the appropriate desires of each other.

- Second, the verse that immediately follows says, "Wives, submit to your husbands" (verse 22), which should be read with the corollary verse, "Husbands, love your wives as Christ loved the church" (verse 25). *However,* if a husband asks his wife to rob a bank with him, she should not submit to him because…

- Third, the Bible also says we are to submit to governing authorities (Romans 13:1). *However,* if the government instructs you to gas hundreds of people (as happened in Nazi Germany), you should not submit because…

- One of God's Ten Commandments states, "You shall not murder" (Exodus 20:13). Ultimately, "We must obey God rather than men!" (Acts 5:29).

Clearly the highest authority is God, next is the governing authorities, and then the family. Thus, if your mate's request is illegal or against God's will, you must not submit.

"This is love for God: to obey his commands"
(1 JOHN 5:3).

D. How to Know Whether Your Husband Has Really Changed

Habitual patterns of abusive behavior rarely change unless there is significant intervention, professional guidance, or both. Sometimes, however, an abuser becomes so convicted of his harmful ways that the Lord is moved to give the person a new heart, new desires, and the power to change.

If your mate promises that change has occurred, you need to ask the Lord for the wisdom to carefully discern whether the change is only temporary and manipulative or your husband has truly taken personal responsibility for his abusive behavior. As Proverbs 2:12 says, "Wisdom will save you from the ways of wicked men, from men whose words are perverse."

As you seek to determine whether your mate's professed changes are real, ask yourself these questions:

— Do I no longer have a sense of fear when I am with my husband?
— Has my husband learned to control his anger without being verbally or emotionally abusive?
— Does my husband respect my right to disagree?
— Is my husband able to express his feelings of anger in a calm, nonthreatening way?
— Does my husband communicate feelings other than anger?
— Does my husband take personal responsibility for inappropriate behavior and no longer blame me or others?
— Do I feel I am being treated with respect?
— Does my husband show consistent love and refuse to harbor bitterness toward me?
— Does my husband include me in his decision making?
— Does my husband ask for my opinions and listen attentively to them?

— Does my husband share his heart with me?

— Does my husband express interest in my thoughts, feelings, and desires?

— Does my husband have an accountability group I can contact?

— Does my husband respect my need for other relationships?

Scripture is clear about the husband's role:

> *"Husbands, love your wives and do not be harsh with them"*
> (Colossians 3:19).

When Anger Hits Home:
The Raul and Sharon Ries Story

In the early years of our radio ministry, we often heard people say, "Thank you for tackling topics that other programs don't even touch." Because wife abuse was one of those taboo topics, I was so grateful to Sharon Ries for sharing her candid, compelling story with our Hope for the Heart family for an entire week. Now I want to share her story with you.

It all started with a "Hi ya,"[30] and before long the "bad boy" had swept the "good girl" off her feet.

As Raul strolled across the high school campus, Sharon was enraptured, imagining she was gazing at a dashing Spanish conqueror. Raul's brown skin and black wavy hair made the wannabe missionary girl temporarily lose sight of her spiritual focus.

After high school, she knew they couldn't marry. She had taken to heart what her Chilean missionary parents had told her: "Do not be unequally yoked."[31]

Yet their relationship deepened while Raul served in the Marines. Love letters, strewn with words of affection, linked their hearts from afar. And when Raul returned home, Sharon's once-firm boundaries crumbled—and she became pregnant.

Doubt consumed Sharon. Aware of Raul's reputation as a ladies' man, how could she marry a man she increasingly didn't *trust*?

Raul had grown up in a violent home where terror reigned. His compulsion to vent his rage led him to become a master of kung fu.

During the Vietnam War, hunting Viet Cong provided a new kind of exhilaration, where killing became the ultimate thrill. When Raul returned home, he brought an all-consuming rage with him.[32]

At age 20, Sharon stood before Raul uttering wedding vows. Because of the mess she had made of her life, she also silently recommitted herself to the Savior. "Lord, You're the answer to my situation—You're the *only* answer. I give my life to You, my child to You, and this man to You."[33]

Following the birth of their son and with another child on the way, restlessness dogged Raul. Sharon questioned him about his frequent late nights out. His abusive words: "Stupid…dummy…filthy witch… big nag"[34]…and a barrage of vile expletives shredded Sharon's sense of self-worth and security. His extramarital affairs prompted more questions from Sharon and more abuse from Raul. He threw their wedding album in her face, squeezed and bruised her limbs, and did kung fu kicks to her legs. Pain and humiliation became commonplace.

Sharon prayed and persevered…until Raul's abuse was unleashed toward their five-year-old son. Determined to shield him from danger, Sharon devised an escape plan. On Easter, she would leave.

Raul returned home Easter evening to an empty house and full suitcases. His wife's plans now obvious to him, he decided to counterattack. Pulling out his rifle, he reasoned, "If I can't have my family, nobody else is gonna have them!"[35] After killing them, he'd kill himself.

Raul figured Sharon and the kids were at church—"Little Miss Christian," he mused venomously. Awaiting the arrival of his prey, Raul turned on the television, idly flipping through the channels until a voice of reason penetrated the silence, with certain phrases catching his attention: "This is the real sign of love…fellowship with God… *you* can come to know that love…"[35] Raul's eyes locked on the screen. The man was talking about having a *relationship* with God, not just a *religion*. "Jesus died on the cross for *your* sins…When they drove the nails into His hands and feet, He took *your* punishment."

Tears began streaming down Raul's face, then waves of sobs. "Jesus offers you forgiveness…you are not beyond God's love." Raul dropped to his knees and gave his life to Jesus. He received God's free gift of salvation.[37]

With exuberant joy, Raul raced to Sharon's church, slipping in the back door just in time to hear, "Would anyone like to make a public profession of faith?"[38] Raul practically ran down the aisle. Sharon, however, was nowhere in sight. After being warmly received, Raul bounded home, eager to share the exciting news with Sharon, who had since returned. His enthusiasm was met by a door slammed in his face.

Sharon had reached a well-reasoned decision to remove her children and herself from harm's way. Sadly, harm was personified in her husband. She was serious about establishing a boundary—and Raul knew she was serious. Raul had crossed a godly boundary. This time, it would take more than words to regain her trust.

"Raul," she told him, after finally allowing him inside the living room, "it took me all of these years to make up my mind to leave you. And now, just when I've finally decided to go, you show up saying you're born again. Don't expect me to jump up and down with excitement, okay? To tell you the truth, I'm disappointed. I was looking forward to starting my life all over again."[39]

His declarations of "I'm changed!" weren't believed. He'd made those promises before. Raul then responded with uncharacteristic understanding. "I don't blame you. I really don't," he said. "But just watch—I'm going to show you that I'm changed."[40]

Wisely, Sharon required evidence of a changed life. She needed to see *new* attitudes and actions, not just a *temporary* change.

Indeed, there was change—Raul vacuumed the house (he had never done that before), cleaned the yard, didn't get drunk, didn't force Sharon to have sex, took time to read the Word, and attended church. But would this last?

About six months later, Raul got angry and grabbed Sharon's neck. She shrieked, "See, you haven't changed!" Immediately he dropped his hands and ran outside. Confused and alarmed by his abusive behavior, he turned to God for help. He knew this area of his life *had* to change—and soon.[41]

Raul found himself reading about Paul's persecution of the Jews before he became a believer. In Acts 9:4, Jesus appeared to Paul asking, "Why are you persecuting me?" Immediately, Raul realized that when he abused his wife, he was actually abusing Christ.

"That dramatic moment…was a major turning point," Raul said. "Realizing that when I hurt Sharon I was actually hurting Christ was the motivation I needed to change. I wanted to please God more than anything else. Never again did I physically abuse my wife."[42]

Were there new attitudes and actions? Oh, yes! And that is consistent with being a true Christian. Second Corinthians 5:17 explains, "If anyone is in Christ, he is a new creation; the old has gone, the new has come!" But what about Raul's lifelong violent habits? Raul learned to rely on the strength of Christ and His indwelling presence. He learned to claim Philippians 4:13: "I can do everything through Him who gives me strength."

Today Sharon—and tens of thousands of others—are sure God truly changed Raul. He has been the pastor of a church in California with more than 12,000 members and had a vibrant church-planting ministry in South America. He also hosts an international radio broadcast and has spoken at crusades at which thousands of people have come to Christ.

Ultimately, Raul found victory over violence. And it all began when Sharon learned the blessing of boundaries. The two are now one, their home is now whole, and *both* are growing more in conformity to the character of Christ.

E. How to Pay the Price of Reconciliation

Realizing the Cost of Change

Many men who have been startled by the seemingly abrupt departure or absence of their abused wives have asked, "How do I apologize to my wife and convince her that I won't hurt her anymore? And how do I ask her to take me back and give our marriage another chance?"

These are daunting questions that demand an answer if marriages damaged by abuse are to heal and become healthy.

If you are an abusive husband asking these questions, before approaching your wife with apologies, promises, and requests, consider what your wife needs from you and the changes you need to make to meet those needs. Once you know the *cost of reconciliation*, you need to determine if you are willing to pay the price. In this way, building a marriage is like building a tower:

"Suppose one of you wants to build a tower.
Will he not first sit down and estimate the cost to see
if he has enough money to complete it?
For if he lays the foundation and is not able to finish it,
everyone who sees it will ridicule him, saying,
'This fellow began to build and was not able to finish'"
(LUKE 14:28-30).

Recognizing the Steps Toward Change

If your answer is yes, and you are willing to pay the cost of reconciliation, then pray for God's wisdom regarding what you should say, and ask Him for the strength to…

CONFESS YOUR SIN

Be open and communicate honesty. "I know I have deeply wounded you and grievously sinned against both you and God by abusing you."

ASK FOR FORGIVENESS

Apologizing to your wife is a start, but you must also humbly ask for forgiveness. "I know I do not deserve your forgiveness and I do not expect you to forgive me immediately, but as time passes, I hope you will extend mercy and grace to me by forgiving me. Will you please forgive me or try to forgive me?"

ESTABLISH ACCOUNTABILITY

Be honest and vulnerable with people who can hold you accountable for your attitudes and actions.

— "I've joined a recovery group in which I'm fully disclosing my abusive acts toward you. At least one member talks to me daily and all are keeping my feet to the fire regarding the way I think about you and treat you. Most have been abusive toward their wives and their lives are changing. They're helping me see myself accurately and see the real reasons for my anger, which have nothing to do with you."

— "I know I've taken my anger out on you and blamed you, but I was wrong."

— "I'm the one to blame. You aren't the cause of my angry outbursts.

You aren't responsible for my anger. I'm the one responsible; I'm the one who chose to strike out at you rather than deal with the true root causes of my anger. For that I am deeply sorry and I truly apologize to you."

AIM FOR CHRISTLIKENESS

Determine to become conformed to the character of Christ regardless of your wife's response to you.

— "No matter what happens in our relationship, I'm completely committed to becoming a man of integrity and growing in Christlikeness."

— "With the Lord's help, I intend to become the man He created me to be. I am doing that by engaging in a men's Bible study group and by studying on my own and learning to talk to God on a regular basis throughout the day."

PROVE YOURSELF TRUSTWORTHY

Become a man your wife can trust.

— "You've been right not to trust me because I've not been trustworthy. I've hurt you when I should have protected you. I've robbed you of your self-respect when I should have given you respect. I've thought only of myself and what I've wanted from you when I should have first thought of you and what you've wanted from me."

— "I'm working hard to become someone you can trust to love and protect you, respect and care for you."

— "I'm committed to keeping my word to you and doing everything I tell you I'll do. I'll be truthful to you and no longer lie to you or even do something that would give me a reason to want to lie to you."

SACRIFICE YOUR SELF-RULE

Choose to be one with your wife and partner with her as an equal.

— "I realize that I've tried to control you, exerting power over you in every way I possibly could. I've berated you, intimidated you, physically overpowered you, and withheld good from you. I was wrong to have done those things to you."

— "I now know that God intended for us to share our resources equally and to make decisions jointly, to submit mutually and to love voluntarily, to talk openly and listen intently, to keep no secrets and to harbor no grudges.

"My goal is to have the kind of relationship with you that God designed for us from the beginning. I know it'll take time and hard work, but I am committed for the long haul and hope you'll wait while God works in me to change me."

— "I desire to be reconciled with you, but I want to do so on your terms. Please consider what you need to see from me in order to begin trusting me again and I will truly take to heart your request."

If your reason for reconciling with your wife is a selfish one, your attempts at restoration won't work! Marriages don't change until the people in the marriages change. A relationship improves only when the people in the relationship improve. Your wife obviously doesn't want more of the same unhealthy relationship, and she won't have a relationship with you until you change. Therefore, because you now know what change will cost, make a decision as to whether you are truly willing to do what is necessary to reconcile the relationship and rebuild the trust you shattered in the past.

F. How to Build Healthy Boundaries

If you are experiencing abuse from your husband, you need to draw a line in the sand. Your husband needs to know you will not tolerate his abuse. And if he crosses the line, a repercussion must follow. Perhaps you will leave home with the children, or you will notify the police, or you will call the pastor, or you will have certain individuals come who will take your husband out of the house.

Just as important as drawing a line in the sand is this: Ensure that the boundary doesn't get blurred by compromises or by a lack of resolve to enforce it. The only way to prevent abuse in the future is to stop it in the present. What you say you will do *you must do*—every time—or the cycle of abuse will rage on. The following Scripture passage reflects God's perfect will regarding violence:

"No longer will violence be heard in your land"
(Isaiah 60:18).

As you begin laying a firm foundation for building healthy boundaries with your husband (the following is an acrostic of the word B-O-U-N-D-A-R-I-E-S)...

B—Begin a new way of thinking about yourself, about God, and about abuse.

- God loves you and created you in His image.
- Abuse is a sin against God's creation; God did not create you to be abused.
- Don't think that abuse is normal—line up your thinking with God's thinking.

> *"Do not conform any longer to the pattern of this world,*
> *but be transformed by the renewing of your mind.*
> *Then you will be able to test and approve what God's will is—*
> *his good, pleasing and perfect will"*
> (Romans 12:2).

O—Overcome fear of the unknown by trusting God with the future. Personalize and memorize the following passages:

> *"The Lord himself goes before [me] and will be with [me];*
> *he will never leave [me] nor forsake [me]. [I will] not be afraid;*
> *[I will] not be discouraged"*
> (Deuteronomy 31:8).

> *"When I am afraid, I will trust in you...*
> *I sought the Lord, and he answered me;*
> *he delivered me from all my fears"*
> (Psalm 56:3; 34:4).

U—Understand the biblical mandate to hold abusers accountable.

- Confrontation is biblical.

- Confrontation can be used by God's Spirit to convict the abuser.
- Lack of confrontation enables abusers to continue abusing others.

"Call him to account for his wickedness
that would not be found out"
(Psalm 10:15).

N—Notify people of your needs (supportive friends, relatives, or others).
- They must believe you.
- They must be trustworthy.
- They must not divulge your new location to your husband if you leave.

"Carry each other's burdens, and in this way
you will fulfill the law of Christ"
(Galatians 6:2).

D—Develop God's perspective on biblical love, submission, and authority.
- Neither love, submission, nor authority ever give license for abuse.
- Neither love, submission, nor authority is to be imposed or demanded, but is to be voluntary.
- Neither love, submission, nor authority is designed by God to be a way of life for only some people, but for everyone.

"Submit to one another out of reverence for Christ"
(Ephesians 5:21).

A—Admit your anger and practice forgiveness.
- Confirm your hurt.
- Confess your anger.
- Choose to forgive your husband but not necessarily to reconcile with him.

"See to it that no one misses the grace of God and that
no bitter root grows up to cause trouble and defile many"
(HEBREWS 12:15).

R—RECOGNIZE your codependent patterns of relating and change the way
you respond.

- Don't respond fearfully, hiding the truth from your husband.
- Don't believe you can change your husband.
- Don't take responsibility for your husband's behavior.

"Am I now trying to win the approval of men, or of God?
Or am I trying to please men? If I were still trying to please men,
I would not be a servant of Christ"
(GALATIANS 1:10).

I—IDENTIFY healthy boundaries for yourself and commit to maintaining
them.

- Communicate your boundaries.
- State what you will do if your husband crosses your boundaries.
- Follow through when your boundaries are crossed.

  For example, state firmly, "The next time you use any force
  against me [or block me from leaving, etc.], I will call the police."
  Or, "You can no longer live at home." Or, "I will leave with the
  children." Then follow through with the promised action.

"A hot-tempered man must pay the penalty;
if you rescue him, you will have to do it again"
(PROVERBS 19:19).

E—ENSURE your personal safety (and that of your children) immediately.

- Have a plan of action.
- Involve your church. Find out ahead of time who you can contact for help.
- Plan ahead whom you will call and where you can go. Have the
  necessary numbers easily accessible.

"I will lie down and sleep in peace, for you alone,
O LORD, make me dwell in safety"
(PSALM 4:8).

S—**SEE** your identity as a precious child of God, an identity that cannot change even though your role as a wife may change.

- God chose you.
- God redeemed you.
- God adopted you.

"How great is the love the Father has lavished on us,
that we should be called children of God! And that is what we are!"
(1 JOHN 3:1).

Setting Boundaries Without Risk

QUESTION: "I know that I need to leave my abusive husband and establish boundaries with him. But how do I present the boundaries to him without putting myself at risk?"

ANSWER: What's vitally important is *what* you say and *how* you say it (with compassionate strength). At a time when your relationship is stable and peaceful, approach your mate. If you do not feel safe approaching him alone, ask someone you both respect to be present.

Tell your mate...

- "I love you and want our marriage to work."
- "If we could have the best relationship possible, would you want it?"
- "Just as there are penalties for crossing boundary lines in sports, there are penalties for crossing boundary lines in marriage. And you've crossed a boundary line in our marriage."
- "I absolutely will not live with an abusive person. Therefore, I have decided to leave and take the children with me."
- "Ultimately, *you* will decide whether we reconcile our marriage."
- "I will know what your decision is by your actions toward me."

- "If you really want us to live together again as husband and wife, I will know by the respect you show me and by the way you treat me."

- "You have the power to make or break our marriage through your actions. *The choice is yours.*"

You must carefully think about what you say, and then you must follow through with the consequences you establish. In this manner you will avoid the way of wives who are not wise:

> *"The wisdom of the prudent is to give thought to their ways"*
> (Proverbs 14:8).

G. How to Prepare a Safety Plan for Leaving

Battles on the home turf can turn into a full-scale war when an abused spouse chooses to leave. It is vital that you surround yourself with an army of people who will support and help protect you, as well as devote the necessary time to make critical preparations (legally, financially, etc.) for independent living.

Recognize and understand that threats of harm can escalate when an abusive husband realizes his wife is finally going to take decisive action. That is why comprehensive preparation as well as support and help from friends, family, counselors, pastors, and even legal authorities are desperately needed. *Never attempt to leave an abusive husband by yourself.*

Above all, seek refuge in the arms of your Deliverer, asking Him to guide and protect you as you attempt to march away from the war zone.

> *"Praise be to the Lord my Rock,*
> *who trains my hands for war, my fingers for battle.*
> *He is my loving God and my fortress,*
> *my stronghold and my deliverer, my shield,*
> *in whom I take refuge, who subdues peoples under me"*
> (Psalm 144:1-2).

Violent outbursts can occur at any time. A violent spouse may enter a blind rage when he discovers a different dynamic in the relationship. He begins to fear losing control of you and losing the family. The greatest danger comes when a husband learns his wife has intentions of leaving. A person who is wise will have prepared for the worst by having a safety plan for leaving.

> *"A prudent [person] sees danger and takes refuge,*
> *but the simple keep going and suffer for it"*
> (PROVERBS 22:3).

As you prepare your strategies for safety...[43]

Create a list of phone numbers you may need for emergencies.

— Local emergency number (for example, 9-1-1)

— Local police

— Women's shelter

— County Registry of Protective Orders

— Salvation Army

— Work number

— Employer's/supervisor's home number

— Church number

— Minister's home number

— Hotline for domestic violence

— Friends

Pray to God...

> *"Keep me, O LORD, from the hands of the wicked."*
> (PSALM 140:4).

Share the seriousness of your situation with trustworthy people.

— Ask whether you could stay with them at a moment's notice if the need were to arise.

— Ask trusted neighbors to call the police if they hear screams or hitting.

— Select a code word or phrase (such as *blue eggs*) or a signal (turning on a certain light) to use as a signal for your neighborhood friends and family to call the police.

— Store a bag of extra clothing and money at a confidant's house.

— Talk with a doctor or nurse about the violence. (Ask the doctor or nurse to take photographs of your injuries and to document the abuse in your medical records.)

— Contact a local shelter to discuss your options and ask them to help you devise a safety plan.

Pray to God...

> *"Blessed is he who has regard for the weak;*
> *the LORD delivers him in times of trouble"*
> (PSALM 41:1).

Plan an escape route.

— Identify which emergency exits you can use (doors, windows, elevator, stairwell) and practice getting out safely.

— If an argument begins, move away from any room containing potential weapons (such as the kitchen).

— Move to a room that has an exit (not a bathroom, a closet, or a small space where the abuser could trap you).

— Rehearse your escape plan with your children.

> *"Make level paths for your feet and take only ways that are firm"*
> (PROVERBS 4:26).

Teach your children safety secrets.

— Teach your children not to get into the middle of a fight, even if they want to help you.

— Teach them to stay out of the kitchen (away from knives).

— Teach them how to give your address and phone number.

— Teach them how to call the police.

— Teach them who to call for help.

— Teach them how to quickly and quietly escape (through a back door or a window).

— Teach them when to escape (such as when violence erupts or when they feel threatened).
— Teach them where to go for safety.

> *"Through knowledge the righteous escape"*
> (PROVERBS 11:9).

Place physical evidence of violence with a trusted confidant or in a safety deposit box.

— Documentation of physical injuries to you and your children
— Pictures of damaged property (such as broken furniture, doors, and walls)
— A log of the abuse by date and event
— Physical evidence of your mate's threats from letters and e-mails, voice mail, text messages, and answering machine messages

> *"They do not realize that I remember all their evil deeds.*
> *Their sins engulf them; they are always before me"*
> (HOSEA 7:2).

Identify essential or meaningful items you can gather quickly (but remember safety must be your first concern).

— Address book
— Children's favorite toys and blankets
— Medicines
— Pictures
— Sentimental items
— Your personal pets

> *"Gather up your belongings to leave the land,*
> *you who live under siege"*
> (JEREMIAH 10:17).

Keep important papers and documents easily accessible and together in one place (and remember that everything on this list can be replaced).

— Bank books, money, credit cards
— Birth certificates
— Current unpaid bills
— Deeds and other legal records (lease/rental agreement, house deed, mortgage payment book)
— Divorce papers
— Driver's license and registration
— Family medical records
— Insurance papers (health, car, house)
— Passport, green card, visa, work permit
— Protective order/restraining order (keep with you at all times)
— School records (K-12)
— College diploma
— Social Security cards
— Welfare identification
— Résumé
— Transcripts of children in college
— SAT/ACT scores

"Wisdom reposes in the heart of the discerning"
(Proverbs 14:33).

Cover your bases before leaving.
— Accumulate some emergency cash and keep it hidden or give it to a confidant for safekeeping.
— Transfer important digital files to external media and then delete them from the computer.
— Hide an extra set of car keys (also house and office keys).

— Open a checking and/or savings account in your name.

— Cancel any shared bank accounts or credit cards.

— Change passwords to online accounts that you'll need to access.

— Open a post office box in your name.

— Put aside jewelry, silver, or other valuables that your husband would not miss and that could be quickly sold for cash.

> *"If you are wise, your wisdom will reward you"*
> (PROVERBS 9:12).

Restraining Order and God's Will

QUESTION: "If I get a restraining order, am I going against the will of God as stated in 1 Corinthians 6:1,7?" ("If any of you has a dispute with another, dare he take it before the ungodly for judgment instead of before the saints?… Why not rather be cheated?")

ANSWER: No, the context of 1 Corinthians 6:1-8 is this: Avoid looking to nonbelievers to settle a dispute that is taking place between believers.

- The purpose of a restraining order is not to settle a dispute regarding unjust harm or loss, but rather to obtain protection *from* unjust harm or loss—possibly even loss of life.
- The intent of a restraining order is to protect people from physical harm, not to settle a dispute between Christians.
- God established through Moses the civil court system to handle problems between the people of God.
- We are called by God to submit to the civil authorities, and domestic violence is against both the civil law and the law of God.

> *"Everyone must submit himself to the governing authorities,*
> *for there is no authority except that which God has established.*
> *The authorities that exist have been established by God.*

> *Consequently, he who rebels against the authority*
> *is rebelling against what God has instituted,*
> *and those who do so will bring judgment on themselves"*
> (Romans 13:1-2).

H. How to Protect Yourself Outside the Home

Even if you, as an abused wife, no longer live under the same roof with your husband, you may still find yourself vulnerable to harm. While an abuser may find it more challenging to inflict harm after you leave the home, there are some abusers who are relentless in their pursuit for revenge.

Safety can be a constant challenge for you whether alone or in a crowd, at home or at work, in a subway or in a car. There is comfort to be found behind locked doors and bolted windows, but those aren't available in public places. So how do you live without fear and a sense of constant vulnerability?

Thankfully, you can take steps toward safety that can help reduce the risk of further abuse. But never fail to remember that the Lord God Almighty, not your abusive husband, is sovereign over your life. Seek refuge in Him.

> *"The name of the Lord is a strong tower;*
> *the righteous run to it and are safe"*
> (Proverbs 18:10).

Safety steps for being out and about

— Change your regular travel habits.

— Try to get rides with different people.

— Shop and bank in different places.

— Keep your court order and emergency numbers with you at all times.

— Obtain a cell phone and program it to call an emergency number or the police. (Keep it with you at all times.)

> *"The Lord will keep you from all harm—*
> *he will watch over your life"*
> (Psalm 121:7).

Safety steps for being at work

— Confide in a coworker about your unsafe situation.

— Explain your situation to the head of security at the office building.

— Give a picture of your husband to security, to your supervisor, and to friends at work.

— Ask your supervisors if they can make it harder for your abuser to find you at work.

— If you have a court order, keep a copy of it at work.

— Ask someone to screen your calls, if possible.

— Save abusive voice mails and e-mails you receive from your husband.

— Don't go to lunch alone.

— Ask a security guard, friend, or coworker to walk you to and from your car, bus, or other mode of transportation.

— Ask if your employer can help you find community resources.

"Rescue the weak and needy;
deliver them from the hand of the wicked"
(Psalm 82:4).

I. How to Use the Law in the United States

Sadly, many abused wives are so beaten down that they feel powerless to do anything to free themselves from the bondage they mistakenly believe is unbreakable. In truth, it is not only their husbands who keep them in bondage, but also their own passivity, rooted in fear and insecurities. They *choose* to stay in abusive relationships rather than to definitively act to bring about an end to their violent home life.

But today, unlike them, you can choose differently. With the help of the legal system and strong community support networks, you can begin developing a plan to break the cycle of abuse, once and for all. Do not believe the lies that you have to stay and endure abuse or that no one can or wants to help you. Help is available—from those around you and from the One above you.

"Rulers hold no terror for those who do right,
but for those who do wrong…Do what is right and he will commend you.

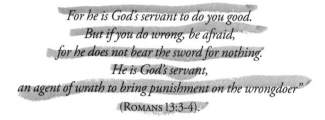

> *For he is God's servant to do you good.*
> *But if you do wrong, be afraid,*
> *for he does not bear the sword for nothing.*
> *He is God's servant,*
> *an agent of wrath to bring punishment on the wrongdoer"*
> (Romans 13:3-4).

If you stay in your home, take action and obtain a restraining order/protective order.

— Inform family members, friends, neighbors, and coworkers of the court order.

— Ask them to be ready to call the police if your husband appears and refuses to leave.

— Get an unlisted phone number for yourself.

— Take a good self-defense course.

— Keep a phone in a room you can lock from the inside.

— When you need to call the police, do so quickly.

— If police officers come, tell them what happened and get their names and badge numbers.

To those in law enforcement the Bible says,

> *"Let the fear of the Lord be upon you. Judge carefully,*
> *for with the Lord our God there is no injustice or partiality or bribery"*
> (2 Chronicles 19:7).

Take action if your home is not safe and secured.

— Install new locks on outside doors.

— Install deadbolt locks.

— Install locks on the windows and on the inside of your bedroom door.

— Install a security system.

— Install smoke detectors.

— Install an outside lighting system.

"You will know that your home is safe"
(Job 5:24 nlt).

Take action to protect your children and yourself by allowing a judge to issue protective orders.

— Have a judge order your husband to stay away from you or your children.

— Have a judge order your husband to leave your home.

— Have a judge order that you take temporary custody of your children and that your husband pay you temporary child support.

— Have a judge order the police to come to your home while your husband picks up his personal belongings.

— Have a judge order you to take possession of the car, furniture, and other belongings.

— Have a judge order your husband to go to a batterers' intervention program.

— Have a judge order your husband to not call you at work.

— Have a judge order your husband to turn over his guns to the police.

"We know that the law is good if one uses it properly"
(1 Timothy 1:8).

Take action if you are being harassed by phone.

— Consider getting caller ID tracking.

— Consider rejecting anonymous calls.

— Consider call-screening.

— Consider call-blocking.

— Consider call-tracing.

— Consider call-waiting caller ID.

— Consider a do-not-disturb function on your phones.

— Consider obtaining priority ringing.

"This is what the LORD Almighty says:
'Give careful thought to your ways'"
(HAGGAI 1:5).

Take action if you are worried about your safety or the safety of your children during scheduled visits.

— Show the judge pictures of your injuries.

— Tell the judge you do not feel safe when your husband comes to your home to pick up the children to visit with them.

— Ask the judge to order your husband to pick up and return the children at the police station or some other safe place.

— Ask that your husband's visits be only at very specific times so the police will know by reading the court order whether your husband is there at the wrong time.

— Tell the judge if your husband has harmed or threatened the children; ask that visits be supervised; think about who could do that for you.

— Get a certified copy of the court order.

"Protect me from men of violence who plan to trip my feet"
(PSALM 140:4).

Take action if you are concerned about your safety during any criminal proceedings.

— Show the prosecutor your court orders.

— Show the prosecutor medical records containing your injuries or pictures, if you have them.

— Tell the prosecutor the name of anyone who is helping you (a victim advocate or a lawyer).

— Tell the prosecutor about any witnesses to your injuries or abuse.

— Ask the prosecutor to notify you ahead of time if your husband is getting out of jail.

*"This is what the LORD says: 'Stand at the crossroads and look; ask for
the ancient paths, ask where the good way is, and walk in it, and you
will find rest for your souls. But you said, "We will not walk in it"'"*
(JEREMIAH 6:16).

Take action if you fear for your safety at the courthouse.

— Sit as far away from your husband as you can; you don't
have to look at or talk to him; you don't have to talk to his
family or friends if they are there.

— Bring a friend or relative with you to wait until your case is
heard.

— Tell a bailiff or sheriff that you are afraid of your husband,
and ask the person to look out for you.

— Make sure you have your court order before you leave.

— Ask the judge or the sheriff to retain your husband for a
while when court is over so you can leave quickly without
having any unwanted interaction.

— Call the police immediately if you think your husband is
following you when you leave.

— Take your protection order with you if you have to travel
to another state, either for work or for safety. It is valid
everywhere.

*"You will go on your way in safety,
and your foot will not stumble"*
(PROVERBS 3:23).

What Recourses Do Women Have?

QUESTION: "My friend's husband continues to be physically violent toward
her. Other than leaving with their children, what recourse does she have?"

ANSWER: A wife who has been victimized by her husband *should not be doubly victimized* by having to leave her own home. Though he is the violator,
don't assume that she should be the one to leave.

- She could first call a legal official (such as a district attorney) to inquire about the local laws governing protective orders and court orders that can force her husband to leave the premises.
- If she has difficulty getting information, she can call a shelter for battered women, a hotline for domestic violence, the Salvation Army, or an attorney who specializes in family law who can explain to her the ways she can legally protect her family.

Great comfort and assurance will come from those who are wise:

> *"The wise heart will know the proper time and procedure"*
> (ECCLESIASTES 8:5).

Protection Through the Legal System

QUESTION: "What protection is available through the legal system in the United States?"[44]

ANSWER: In the absence of a divorce action, a *peace bond* is issued before a justice of the peace in a civil court. This legal instrument is mainly used in cases involving domestic violence. In a divorce action, the attorney requests a *restraining order* to protect the abused from further harassment and violence. Such an order is usually issued by a family court judge. Keep the following in mind:

- The mere suspicion of violence or threats of violence are not enough to warrant the issuing of any order by a judge.
- Before a judge will consider issuing any order, police reports must contain documented reports of physical contact.

God promises to bless those who confront the guilty. Proverbs 24:25 says, "It will go well with those who convict the guilty, and rich blessing will come upon them."

If you live in a place where the legal system does not offer protection against domestic abuse, find help from a church or seek refuge with empathetic friends or neighbors. God is aware of your situation, and He will guide you to a place of safety.

"The LORD is my rock, my fortress and my deliverer;
my God is my rock, in whom I take refuge.
He is my shield and horn of my salvation, my stronghold"
(PSALM 18:2).

J. How to Realize Your Biblical Bill of Rights

The U.S. Bill of Rights, which comprises the first ten amendments to the U.S. Constitution, stands as a fundamental symbol for individual freedoms. Among other constraints, Congress can pass no law that prohibits the free exercise of religion, nor can it deprive any person of life, liberty, or property without due process of law.

And so it goes within the marriage relationship. Know the rights you have that are firmly embedded in an even more trustworthy document—*the Bible, the Word of God*. It includes the right to operate by faith and not by fear, and the right to seek to live a holy life, not a hellish one marked by abuse.

"God did not call us to be impure, but to live a holy life"
(1 THESSALONIANS 4:7).

Some people claim that when you come into a relationship with Christ, you give up all of your rights. This simply is not true. You always have the God-given right to live your life according to God's Word in order to accomplish God's will. For example, if your marriage partner tries to pressure you to commit a sinful act by using Scripture out of context (perverting the purpose of the command "wives, submit to your husbands"), God's will is that you *not* do it. Instead, you "must obey God rather than men" (Acts 5:29).

Here is the biblical bill of rights as viewed within the context of a marriage relationship:

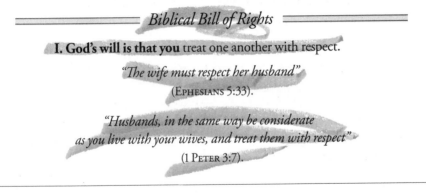

Biblical Bill of Rights

I. God's will is that you treat one another with respect.

"The wife must respect her husband"
(EPHESIANS 5:33).

"Husbands, in the same way be considerate
as you live with your wives, and treat them with respect"
(1 PETER 3:7).

II. God's will is that you experience mutual submission.

"Submit to one another out of reverence for Christ"
(Ephesians 5:21).

III. God's will is that you speak truth and have truth spoken to you in a loving manner.

*"Speaking the truth in love, we will in all things grow up
into him who is the Head, that is, Christ"*
(Ephesians 4:15).

IV. God's will is that you express anger and have anger expressed toward you in appropriate ways.

*"In your anger do not sin:
Do not let the sun go down while you are still angry"*
(Ephesians 4:26).

V. God's will is that you both spend personal time alone.

*"Very early in the morning, while it was still dark, Jesus got up,
left the house and went off to a solitary place, where he prayed"*
(Mark 1:35).

VI. God's will is that you use your unique talents and gifts to serve others.

*"Each one should use whatever gift he has received to serve others,
faithfully administering God's grace in its various forms"*
(1 Peter 4:10).

VII. God's will is that you enjoy freedom from fear.

*"You did not receive a spirit that makes you a slave again to fear,
but you received the Spirit of sonship. And by him we cry, 'Abba, Father'"*
(Romans 8:15).

VIII. God's will is that you both seek emotional and spiritual support from others.

*"Let us not give up meeting together...
but let us encourage one another"*
(Hebrews 10:25).

IX. God's will is that you report abuse to governmental authorities.

"Submit yourselves for the Lord's sake to every authority instituted among men…who are sent by him to punish those who do wrong and to commend those who do right… The authorities that exist have been established by God. Consequently, he who rebels against the authority is rebelling against what God has instituted, and those who do so will bring judgment on themselves"
(1 Peter 2:13-14; Romans 13:1-2).

X. God's will is that you leave an abusive relationship when it becomes necessary to do so.

"The prudent see danger and take refuge, but the simple keep going and suffer for it"
(Proverbs 27:12).

THE UNITED NATIONS UNIVERSAL DECLARATION OF HUMAN RIGHTS ARTICLES I, III, AND V, 1948

"All human beings are born free and equal in dignity and rights…
Everyone has the right to life, liberty and security of person…
No one shall be subject to torture or to cruel, inhuman
or degrading treatment or punishment."

K. How to Clarify the Church's Role and Reinforce Christlike Responses

Religion can be a *resource* or a *roadblock*, greatly depending on the *response* of the church leaders. As a *resource* it can provide the necessary safety and support for the abused to seek help and healing. As a *roadblock* it can turn a blind eye to abuse or rationalize it, thereby contributing to the victim's sense of self-blame.

Jesus had this to say about unresponsive spiritual leaders:

"You experts in the law, woe to you, because you load people down with burdens they can hardly carry, and you yourselves will not lift one finger to help them"
(Luke 11:46).

Motivating local churches to move from apathy to action—from ignorance to enlightenment—regarding domestic violence is a most worthy cause, but not necessarily an easy one to carry out. In accepting this critical challenge, consider the following straightforward suggestions:

- *Recruit* the support of church leaders to back your position and provide you with the necessary resources so that you can provide meaningful help. Educate yourself and your leaders to understand the complexity of the problem and how abusers typically disguise themselves within the religious community.

- *Realize* the great degree of difficulty for the abused to come forward and reveal the truth about their abusers. Explain that the abused often remain shrouded in silence for fear of retaliation or not being believed.

- *Remember* the primary importance of fully listening to the abused. Listen with your heart as well as with your ears so the abused feels sincerely heard.

- *Reassure* the abused that your church is a safe place. Keep shared information completely confidential, doing everything in your power to protect the abused's privacy and safety in this way.

- *Recognize* that women of color and different cultures are often most at risk. Factors such as fear of deportation, lack of familiarity with the language and legal system, cultural expectations for women to keep problems private, and lack of resources or education may contribute to their silence.

- *Rebuke* the abuser so that strong, godly leaders confront and counsel the abuser through the lengthy path of *repentance, restoration*, and *reconciliation*. Hold the abuser accountable to participate in a specialized recovery program, even if the pastoral team is unable to handle the counseling in-house at the church.

- *Refuse* to allow the abuser to use Scriptures such as Ephesians 5:22 out of context to justify abusive actions. Redirect abusers to Bible passages that show the importance of loving and respecting their wives and family members.

- *Refer* the abused person to trained counselors and specialized services to receive the safety and support needed for everyone in the family. Provide a list of phone numbers, services, support people, as well as an action plan that will arm the abused with necessary resources.

- *Resolve* to help break generational cycles of abuse. Abusers and those whom they abuse usually come from homes where they witnessed abuse or they experienced abuse themselves. Engage the children in counseling, for children from a violent home are more likely to become abusive or be abused and more likely to use alcohol or drugs.

- *Recommend* Bible study, prayer, and fasting to both the abuser and the abused. Encourage both the abused and abuser to establish the daily habit of having a time to study God's Word, pray, and cast every care on the Lord.

> *"My comfort in my suffering is this:*
> *Your promise preserves my life"*
> (Psalm 119:50).

L. How to Respond to Wife Abuse as a Pastor or Parishioner

If you are a church leader or a member of a church, you need a heightened awareness of the prevalence and dangers of domestic violence. *Make no mistake—abuse is occurring within your congregation.* Therefore, you need to know how to respond when a victim needs help. Key elements of an effective response include knowing *how* to listen and *how* to respond with wisdom, as well as having a plan and programs in place. If you are a church member, you are to love and encourage the abused person as well as to confront and admonish when necessary. If you are a pastor, you have a dual responsibility as a *watchman,* who is entrusted with the safety of his people, and a *shepherd,* who is to guide and support them.

These roles may call for both the pastor and the parishioner to have keen eyes that watch for clues that may indicate abuse is taking place. Wife abuse thrives in a secret world of shame, and women are usually fearful of bringing what happens in the dark into the light. They feel disgraced and degraded—so much so they don't even want to say what is happening behind closed doors.

This is why it's vital for you to watch for signs of domestic violence, such as the repeated appearance of bruises and wounds, or a reluctance to talk about one's home life.

The Bible emphasizes the seriousness of your role:

> *"If the watchman sees the sword coming*
> *and does not blow the trumpet to warn the people*
> *and the sword comes and takes the life of one of them,*
> *that man will be taken away because of his sin,*
> *but I will hold the watchman accountable for his blood"*
> (EZEKIEL 33:6).

Practical Points for Pastors and Parishioners

Don't listen to an abused wife's story for only a brief time and then jump to a premature conclusion.

Do listen patiently and attentively with your head and your heart.

> *"Let the wise listen and add to their learning,*
> *and let the discerning get guidance"*
> (PROVERBS 1:5).

Don't require hearing the "other person's story" before being willing to believe what the abused wife is saying. This can put her in a potentially dangerous situation.

Do believe and support her. It takes tremendous courage for an abused wife to come forward and seek help.

> *"Do not withhold your mercy from me, O LORD;*
> *may your love and your truth always protect me"*
> (PSALM 40:11).

Don't place blame or guilt on the abused by inferring *she* may have done something to cause her husband to attack her. No one makes another person sin.

Do make supportive statements that encourage and validate her.

"This is what the LORD Almighty says:
'Administer true justice; show mercy and compassion to one another'"
(ZECHARIAH 7:9).

Don't react with disbelief and disgust over what an abused wife tells you.

Do listen responsively and compassionately.

"My dear brothers, take note of this:
Everyone should be quick to listen,
slow to speak and slow to become angry"
(JAMES 1:19).

Don't recommend marriage classes or counseling, for these will not address the immediate situation. Marriage counseling may be part of the long-term solution, but it's not the first step.

Do produce immediate and practical solutions that will meet the needs for safety and hope, procuring strength, and promoting empowerment.

"He gives strength to the weary
and increases the power of the weak"
(ISAIAH 40:29).

Don't do anything that will allow an abused wife to become overly dependent on you.

Do furnish her with resources to equip and empower her to provide safety and security for herself in the future as she trusts in the Lord.

"Some trust in chariots and some in horses,
but we trust in the name of the LORD our God"
(PSALM 20:7).

Don't try to "save" the situation on your own. Abusive people are complex and unpredictable. They often appear one way to their pastor yet are completely different at home.

Do consult with colleagues and experts in your community

who have expertise and wisdom as well as experience and resources to provide support for abused wives and to confront and hold accountable abusive husbands.

> *"He who walks with the wise grows wise"*
> (PROVERBS 13:20).

Don't play down the situation by suggesting an abused wife forgive the abuser and go back to him unless he has a repentant spirit and has made a radical change in behavior over an extended period of time.

Do proceed with wisdom and caution. Abusers may be sorry for what they have done and even make tearful apologies, asking for another chance. However, without the help of the transforming power of the Holy Spirit, the old behavior of the flesh will almost certainly return and repeat the abusive cycle.

> *"The way of a fool seems right to him,*
> *but a wise man listens to advice"*
> (PROVERBS 12:15).

Don't simply pray for an abused wife then share Scripture with her.

Do give her Scripture passages that she can pray to God— verses that express her heart, her hurt, and her hope for healing.

> *"I call with all my heart...I rise before dawn and cry for help;*
> *I have put my hope in your word...that I may meditate on your promises.*
> *Hear my voice in accordance with your love"*
> (PSALM 119:145,147-149).

Don't let an abused wife leave without having a plan of action to address the present crises or the ongoing abusive situation.

Do utilize whatever resources are available in the church or community to provide whatever physical and emotional protection the situation requires.

> *"Make plans by seeking advice…*
> *obtain guidance"*
> (Proverbs 20:18).

M. How to Promote Positive Action from the Pulpit

Sadly, the church has been silent for far too long on the widespread sin of domestic violence. Pastors can play a pivotal role by speaking out from the pulpit against all forms of domestic violence, initiating programs that address the needs of victims and even helping the victimizers receive help through qualified counselors.

The doors of churches and the hearts of church members must open wide to embrace the abused and to reach out to the abusers with the help they both so desperately need. *Transforming lives* is what true ministry is all about, and God's heart is to transform the lives of both victim and victimizer. The pulpit has served as a powerful venue for both spiritual and societal change in many areas of life; therefore, pastors can serve as the catalyst for powerful change in connection with this issue as well.

Jesus tells us that when we help victims, it is as though we are helping Him.

> *"Lord, when did we see you hungry and feed you,*
> *or thirsty and give you something to drink?*
> *When did we see you a stranger and invite you in,*
> *or needing clothes and clothe you?*
> *When did we see you sick or in prison and go to visit you?…*
> *'I tell you the truth,*
> *whatever you did for one of the least of these…you did for me'"*
> (Matthew 25:37-40).

Jesus also tells us that when we confront an abuser, we are helping save the sinner from death.

> *"If one of you should wander from the truth*
> *and someone should bring him back, remember this:*
> *Whoever turns a sinner from the error of his way will save him from death*
> *and cover over a multitude of sins"*
> (James 5:19-20).

Start Making a Difference

BE PROACTIVE

— Openly address from the pulpit and in other teaching venues the topic of domestic violence. Acknowledge that abuse takes place among people within the church.

— Present messages—sermons, courses, Bible studies, and seminars—on anger management, conflict resolution, confrontation, and boundaries within relationships.

— Invite domestic violence experts to make presentations on abuse issues.

— Establish a domestic violence committee to address abuse issues within the church.

— Require premarital counseling for couples who plan to marry, and specifically address domestic violence and how to handle disagreements, arguments, and control issues.

— Offer marriage counseling that includes a segment on domestic violence.

— Prepare separate programs for adolescents as well as for single adults that address dangerous dating.

— Require the women's and the men's ministries of the church to address abuse issues separately.

— Provide phone numbers for abuse hotlines or crisis lines.

— Designate an "abuse presentation" day, week, or month to educate and activate church members.

The Bible says,

> *"These are the things you are to do: Speak the truth to each other,
> and render true and sound judgment in your courts"*
> (ZECHARIAH 8:16).

BE REACTIVE

— Establish church procedures—"church discipline"—to hold abusers accountable.

— Confront abusers and offer help on how to handle conflicts and anger—both past and present—and how to love their wives as Christ loves the church.

— Train mentors who can help those struggling with abuse issues.

— Utilize counselors trained in domestic violence matters and lawyers who specialize in family law.

— Talk and pray with victims about the possibility of temporarily leaving their physically abusive partners if the violence continues.

— Provide a temporary safe place for victims and children who are living in danger.

— Provide counselors who have expertise in the area of domestic violence, and then arrange individual counseling sessions for abusers and for those they abuse (but *not* counseling for couples—the abused may feel too intimidated by such a setup).

— Offer support groups to victims of abuse and accountability groups for abusers.

— Give financial support to shelters and other agencies for abused wives and their children.

— Encourage testimonials in the church from survivors of abuse as well as from repentant abusers.

As a pastor, take to heart the biblical admonition to...

> *"Rescue those being led away to death;*
> *hold back those staggering toward slaughter.*
> *If you say, 'But we knew nothing about this,'*
> *does not he who weighs the heart perceive it?*
> *Does not he who guards your life know it?*
> *Will he not repay each person according to what he has done?"*
> (Proverbs 24:11-12).

N. How to Follow Do's and Don'ts as a Friend

If the abused is candid about being abused, remember, you're talking with a *victim*.

The person before you is wounded, emotionally fragile, and perhaps even traumatized. The tone and tenor of your words are essential to establishing a nurturing conversation that is conducive to her sharing her heart and your communicating hope from your heart. As in all cases of victimization, you must follow a definitive set of do's and don'ts to help ensure that your assistance will be positive.

Love, listen, and lend a helping hand. The Bible says,

> *"Defend the cause of the weak...*
> *maintain the rights of the poor and oppressed"*
> (Psalm 82:3).

Most victims choose to deny the severity of their situation by developing a strong defense mechanism. In addition to denying that anything is wrong, the abused tend to minimize or rationalize their abuser's behavior. If the abused woman is openly and honestly discussing the abusive situation, she is displaying significant courage. This effort in itself is quite an emotional ordeal. Be prepared to respond with love and patience when your friend begins to share the secrets of a broken heart. [44]

> *Don't* talk in generalities if you suspect abuse.
>> *Do* specifically ask whether there has been physical harm.

>> *"The purposes of a man's [or woman's] heart are deep waters,*
>> *but a man [or woman] of understanding draws them out"*
>> (Proverbs 20:5).

> *Don't* treat the problem lightly or minimize the abuse.
>> *Do* realize that violence can be a matter of life or death, and that wife abuse is against the civil law, the moral law, and God's law.

>> *"Keep me, O Lord, from the hands of the wicked;*
>> *protect me from men of violence who plan to trip my feet"*
>> (Psalm 140:4).

> *Don't* change the subject or act embarrassed when abuse is revealed.
>> *Do* encourage disclosure at any time about anything and be willing to listen.

> *"Listen carefully to my words;*
> *let this be the consolation you give me.*
> *Bear with me while I speak"*
> (Job 21:2-3).

Don't blame the victim for the abuse.

> *Do* help the victim see that no one can make another person sin. Abuse is solely the choice of the abuser, and the abuser is solely responsible to God.

> > *"God will bring every deed into judgment,*
> > *including every hidden thing,*
> > *whether it is good or evil"*
> > (Ecclesiastes 12:14).

Don't fear a strong display of emotions.

> *Do* allow the victim to express fear, shame, and anger, which are often avoided, denied, or wrongly perceived to *always* be sinful.

> > *"In your anger do not sin"*
> > (Psalm 4:4).

Don't advise your friend to preserve the family at all costs.

> *Do* affirm that moving the family out of harm's way—separating—is not the same as divorcing.

> > *"You will be secure, because there is hope;*
> > *you will look about you and take your rest in safety.*
> > *You will lie down, with no one to make you afraid"*
> > (Job 11:18-19).

Don't send the person home when physical abuse is likely to occur.

> *Do* provide temporary shelter and assist in discovering options.

> *"If anyone…sees his brother in need but has no pity on him,*

how can the love of God be in him?...
Let us not love with words or tongue but with actions and in truth"
(1 JOHN 3:17-18).

Don't accuse your friend of failing to be loving or submissive or long-suffering.

Do explain that it is not God's will for any wife to suffer abuse by her husband for any reason. The issue is neither submission nor lack of submission, love nor lack of love.

"You are not a God who takes pleasure in evil;
with you the wicked cannot dwell.
The arrogant cannot stand in your presence;
you hate all who do wrong"
(PSALM 5:4-5).

Don't merely tell the person to report injuries to a doctor or the police.

Do accompany your friend to the hospital and help fill out police reports.

"There is a friend who sticks closer than a brother"
(PROVERBS 18:24).

Don't allow the victim to stay all alone, paralyzed in fear of further abuse.

Do learn about legal options. Accompany your friend to court and help her get a restraining order.

"Submit yourselves for the Lord's sake
to every authority instituted among men:
whether to the king, as the supreme authority, or to governors,
who are sent by him to punish those who do wrong
and to commend those who do right"
(1 PETER 2:13-14).

Don't try to provide more counseling than you are trained to give.

Do show that you care and help find counseling from someone who has experience in working with victims of violence.

"He who guards his lips guards his life,
but he who speaks rashly will come to ruin"
(Proverbs 13:3).

Don't assume that your friend should know all the answers.

Do give assurance that God will guide and give wisdom every step of the way, especially when the way is unclear and the next step is unknown.

"The Lord is a refuge for the oppressed, a stronghold in times of trouble.
Those who know your name will trust in you,
for you, Lord, have never forsaken those who seek you"
(Psalm 9:9-10).

Is a husband's "headship" a license for wife abuse?
To the contrary! Does your head seek to hurt your hand?
Does your brain tell you to break your bone?
No, your head protects and provides for your body at all costs.
Likewise, the husband, as the God-ordained head
of the wife, is to protect her from harm, or else he forfeits his right
to headship. How significant that Christ, as the Head
of the church, not only loved her, but gave Himself up for her!

=== *Wife Abuse—Answers in God's Word* ===

Question: "Is it wrong to report a hot-tempered man who may have to pay a penalty?"

Answer: "A hot-tempered man must pay the penalty; if you rescue him, you will have to do it again" (Proverbs 19:19).

Question: "What is the attitude of the Lord toward those who love violence?"

Answer: "The Lord examines the righteous, but the wicked and those who love violence his soul hates" (Psalm 11:5).

QUESTION: "Is it wrong to ask others to confront an abuser and show him his fault?"

ANSWER: "If your brother sins against you, go and show him his fault, just between the two of you. If he listens to you, you have won your brother over. But if he will not listen, take one or two others along, so that 'every matter may be established by the testimony of two or three witnesses'" (Matthew 18:15-16).

QUESTION: "Should a wife report domestic violence to the governing authorities?"

ANSWER: "Everyone must submit himself to the governing authorities, for there is no authority except that which God has established. The authorities that exist have been established by God" (Romans 13:1).

QUESTION: "What should I do about someone in my life who is hot-tempered and easily angered?"

ANSWER: "Do not make friends with a hot-tempered man, do not associate with one easily angered" (Proverbs 22:24).

QUESTION: "If I feel I'm in danger, should I take refuge?"

ANSWER: "The prudent see danger and take refuge, but the simple keep going and suffer for it" (Proverbs 27:12).

QUESTION: "What should I do if I can't sleep in peace?"

ANSWER: "I will lie down and sleep in peace, for you alone, O LORD, make me dwell in safety" (Psalm 4:8).

QUESTION: "How can I win the approval of my husband when I've tried everything?"

ANSWER: "Am I now trying to win the approval of men, or of God? Or am I trying to please men? If I were still trying to please men, I would not be a servant of Christ" (Galatians 1:10).

QUESTION: "Who can I trust if I can't trust my own husband?"

ANSWER: "Your Maker is your husband—the LORD Almighty is his name" (Isaiah 54:5).

QUESTION: "Does the Bible say women should submit to or be protected from men of violence?"

ANSWER: "You must purge the evil from among you" (Deuteronomy 19:19).

HOPE FOR THE ABUSER
How to Break Free of Being Abusive

H ave you yourself been the victim of abusive treatment? Realize that if you were treated callously throughout childhood, you have probably developed a hard shell that does not allow sensitive emotions to come in or go out. And without empathy, a person is incapable of being sensitive to the emotional pain of someone else.[1]

"What a wretched man I am!
Who will rescue me from this body of death?
Thanks be to God—through Jesus Christ our Lord!"
(ROMANS 7:24-25).

In order for change to occur—for the relationship to experience healing—the loving work of God in the heart of the abuser is necessary and the abuser must be willing to meet certain criteria.

ABUSERS MUST HONESTLY ASSESS THEMSELVES

Are you aware that many abusers have no idea that they are abusive? Is it possible that you may have been abusive?

— Are you willing to consider that you may not be in touch with your own emotions because they have been buried for so long?

— Will you acknowledge that you tend to place all blame on another person and that you believe you are always right?

— Will you concede that you may be in denial about the seriousness of your behavior?

Remember:

> *"A truthful witness gives honest testimony,*
> *but a false witness tells lies"*
> (Proverbs 12:17).

Take the Honesty Test

____ Has a loved one ever said that you are emotionally insensitive or uncaring?

____ Has a loved one ever said your behavior is abusive or unreasonable?

____ Has a loved one ever said you act nicer when you are with others than when you are alone with that person?

____ Has a loved one ever said that you tend to overreact?

____ Do you avoid responding to questions you don't like?

____ Do you get angry when asked questions you don't like?

____ Do you refuse to acknowledge your past negative behaviors?

____ Do you have a short fuse that ignites anger?

____ Do you think your personal interactions with others could be destructive?

____ Have you previously had failed, unresolved relationships?

If you answered yes to at least three of the above questions, it is likely that you have been abusive.

> *"I know, my God, that you test the heart*
> *and are pleased with integrity"*
> (1 Chronicles 29:17).

Desire to Change Is the Uppermost Consideration

Change cannot take place unless you are willing for God to do His work in your life. Psalm 139:23-24 says, "Search me, O God, and know my heart; test me and know my thoughts. See if there is any offensive way in me, and lead me in the way everlasting."

===== *Do's and Don'ts—Take Responsibility for Your Abuse* =====

- *Don't* vent your pent-up anger on another person. Anger that is bottled up needs to be resolved and dissipated, not spewed out.
  - — *Do* understand that *feeling angry* is not a sin.
  - — *Do* recognize and admit that you may not know how to handle your anger.
- *Don't* say, "You're the reason I am so angry."
  - — *Do* realize that you may be using your anger to get your own way.
- *Don't* say, "I can never please you!"
  - — *Do* begin to see things from the other person's point of view.
- *Don't* say, "After all I do for you, it's never enough."
  - — *Do* recognize that courageous people are willing to admit their weaknesses.
- *Don't* use harsh, belittling, or sarcastic statements.
  - — *Do* realize that you can change. It's never too late.
- *Don't* withdraw emotionally.
  - — *Do* be willing to enlist friends and family members for accountability.

> *"A fool gives full vent to his anger,*
> *but a wise man keeps himself under control"*
> (PROVERBS 29:11).

REFLECTION IS BENEFICIAL

Some children grow up in abusive homes where they receive the brunt of excessive control and power. When a parent is severely dominating, a child's feelings are stepped on, and personal expression is stifled. This causes an atmosphere of fear to pervade the family, and these children grow up with a negative view of the offending person, vowing never to be like the father who always broke his promises or like the mother who was strict and unaffectionate. Although the children, when they grow up, might not behave in the same way as their offending parents, their negative views may cause them to develop the same attitudes of resentment and bitterness they so disliked in their parents. That is why the Bible says,

> *"See to it that no one misses the grace of God*
> *and that no bitter root grows up*
> *to cause trouble and defile many"*
> (HEBREWS 12:15).

=== *Points for the Abuser to Ponder* ===

___ When you were growing up, was there anyone in your family who was overly controlling of others?

___ Is there anyone in your past toward whom you still harbor resentment?

___ Do you bitterly vow that you will never exhibit the same behaviors your parents displayed toward you?

___ Do you have a negative view of one or both of your parents?

___ Do you still feel the need to talk about the negative behavior of your parent(s)?

___ Are you still angry over the way someone you love was treated by someone else who was abusive?

___ Have you learned to forgive the parents God gave you in spite of their faults and inabilities to communicate love?

> *"When you stand praying,*
> *if you hold anything against anyone,*
> *forgive him, so that your Father in heaven*
> *may forgive you your sins"*
> (MARK 11:25).

ANGER MANAGEMENT IS MANDATORY

When you have difficulty controlling your anger, you will express your anger in one of two ways. If you vent your anger at someone else, your anger is *explosive*, but if you keep your anger bottled up, your anger is *implosive*.

— *Explosive* anger is outwardly abusive.

— *Implosive* anger is inwardly abusive.

Both are damaging to relationships. God does not condemn our feelings of anger, but He does require that both kinds of anger be expressed appropriately.

> *"In your anger do not sin"*
> (Psalm 4:4).

Self-control Techniques Are Essential

Step #1: Discover Your Trigger Points

— Be aware of when you are feeling irritated or aggravated.

— Take note when a sudden feeling of anger explodes in your mind.

— Listen to yourself and realize when you are behaving badly, performing poorly, or snapping at those close to you.

— Stop! Take a few moments and give yourself time to discover the source of your anger.

> *"Get wisdom, get understanding"*
> (Proverbs 4:5).

Step #2: Be Aware of Your Early Family Background

— Read about and recall your early family dynamics.

— Did you discover that it was not safe to express anger?

— Did you learn that explosive anger was a means of control?

— Have you now learned to see your family through the eyes of an adult?

> *"When I was a child,*
> *I talked like a child, I thought like a child,*
> *I reasoned like a child. When I became a man,*
> *I put childish ways behind me"*
> (1 Corinthians 13:11).

Step #3: Restrain Angry Thoughts and Actions

— Turn your thoughts toward Christ: *Lord, may I have Your peace.*

— Count to ten before you respond.

— Walk away and then come back when your feelings are under control.

— Take a "time out" for 15 or 20 minutes, if necessary.

> *"Refrain from anger and turn from wrath;*
> *do not fret—it leads only to evil"*
> (PSALM 37:8).

Step #4: Choose the Right Time and Way to Express Your Feelings

— Train yourself to keep a lid on your anger until your agitation is calmed.

— Try to see the situation from the other person's point of view.

— If you are angry at another person, ask, "Is there a time when we could speak about something important to me?"

— If your anger has turned inward, talk with a friend and seek an objective view of the situation.

> *"An angry man stirs up dissension,*
> *and a hot-tempered one commits many sins"*
> (PROVERBS 29:22).

Step #5: Begin Absorbing Truth

— Pray for the Lord to reveal to you how He sees you—the person He created you to be before abuse marred and changed you. He will do this with love.

— Pray for the Lord to reveal His love for you.

— Acknowledge that you have God-given worth. Don't let others define who you are.

— Read through the book of Proverbs beginning at chapter 8. Write out all the verses pertaining to anger that are relevant to you.

"A gentle answer turns away wrath,
but a harsh word stirs up anger"
(PROVERBS 15:1).

Step #6: Come to Christ with a Sincere Heart

Confession: "I *admit* my behavior has been wrong and has hurt others."

"When a man or woman wrongs another in any way
and so is unfaithful to the LORD, that person is guilty
and must confess the sin he has committed"
(NUMBERS 5:6-7).

Repentance: "Relying on the strength of God, I will change my behavior because I truly desire to please God."

"He who conceals his sins does not prosper,
but whoever confesses and renounces them finds mercy"
(PROVERBS 28:13).

Forgiveness: "God, I thank You for Your willingness to forgive me in spite of my failure to honor You."

"I acknowledged my sin to you and did not cover up my iniquity.
I said, 'I will confess my transgressions to the LORD'—
and you forgave the guilt of my sin"
(PSALM 32:5).

Acceptance: "Jesus, I receive You as my Lord and Savior and give You control of my life. Thank You for being willing to adopt me into Your family."

"To all who received him, to those who believed in his name,
he gave the right to become children of God"
(JOHN 1:12).

Substitution: "I am willing to give up control of my life in exchange for a new heart and a new life in Christ."

> *"Rid yourselves of all the offenses you have committed,*
> *and get a new heart and a new spirit"*
> (EZEKIEL 18:31).

Restitution: "Lord, reveal the names of those to whom I owe a sincere apology. I will go to them and ask forgiveness for my inappropriate and hurtful behavior."

> *"If you are offering your gift at the altar*
> *and there remember that your brother has something against you,*
> *leave your gift there in front of the altar.*
> *First go and be reconciled to your brother;*
> *then come and offer your gift"*
> (MATTHEW 5:23-24).

Cleansing: "God, I thank You for Your promise to cleanse me and to *remove all my sins and unrighteousness.*"

> *"Wash away all my iniquity and cleanse me from my sin.*
> *For I know my transgressions, and my sin is always before me"*
> (PSALM 51:2-3).

RESPOND TO ABUSE GOD'S WAY

Living with a verbal and emotional abuser is like living with a rabid dog that is asleep in your own living room! Threatening...unpredictable...attacking...its presence should never be ignored. But think of what harm could be done if *no one* is willing to confront this boundaryless beast—for fear of inciting its wrath!

Yet all who enter will tiptoe carefully—trying to keep the peace, hoping to avoid a frightening confrontation. But it's important to remember: No matter how long you let "sleeping dogs lie," they eventually are bound to wake up.

Rather than spend the rest of your life permitting inexcusable attacks in "the living room of your life," decide today to respond God's way to all verbal and emotional abuse. Although your resolve will be tested, as you maintain a right spirit with firm boundaries, your life will begin to change—even if your abuser doesn't. What's more, your consistent, Christlike character could become the impetus that helps transform your emotional predator into "man's best friend"—one who becomes an encourager, one who brings glory to God.

"Such a change isn't possible," you say. As impossible as such a transformation may seem, Jesus offers this comforting hope:

"With man this is impossible,
but with God all things are possible"
(Matthew 19:26).

—— *From Death Row to Life Row:* ——
The Karla Faye Tucker Story

On a hot summer night in Houston, 23-year-old Karla Faye Tucker was swirling in a cesspool of drugs, sex, and violence. Karla's best friend Shawn was staying with her for a week—Shawn's biker husband, Jerry, had beaten her black and blue. Karla despised Jerry, and Jerry despised Karla. After a three-day binge, it's time to get revenge!

It was well after 2:00 a.m. when Karla and her boyfriend, Danny, snuck into Jerry Dean's apartment with a plan to steal his motorcycle (realize there's no greater insult to a biker than to steal his bike!). Jerry heard a noise and called out. In a fit of rage, Danny attacked Jerry in his bed, severely bashing his head with a hammer. Karla, who intensely hated Jerry, stood by as this happened.

Then Karla saw a woman in Jerry's bed who was trying to hide under the covers. This was her best friend's bed! Who was this woman hiding in bed with Shawn's husband? All of a sudden a powder keg of fiery emotions exploded within Karla. This was a lethal combination: a desire for revenge toward her best friend's husband, anger toward a strange woman in his bed, and the fact she was high on drugs.

Absolutely enraged, Karla grabbed a pickax lying on the floor and viciously...repeatedly...repeatedly...repeatedly attacked the woman until she was mush. No one could have imagined that Jerry's habit of keeping his work tools "handy" would be used to bring about his horrific demise. As for Deborah Thornton—the other victim of violence—she had known Jerry for only 12 hours. Her death epitomized what it means to be in the wrong place at the wrong time.

Before leaving the premises, Karla felt so empowered that she decided to finish Jerry off—with another 20 blows.

Karla and Danny were soon arrested for the 1983 double murder. As Karla awaited sentencing, she bore the trademark of a cold-blooded killer: that notorious blank stare, no expression on her face, no expression in her eyes.

Much in Karla's childhood led to her dead spirit: exposure to drugs before age 10, addiction by age 12, a prostitute mother teaching her "the tricks of the trade" at age 14.[2] When Karla attacked Jerry and Deborah that fateful night, a lifetime of anger, bitterness, and pain erupted from a volcanic core. But all the terrible inner turmoil came to an end in the corner of a dingy county jail cell prior to her trial. For it was here that Karla Faye Tucker got her first taste of *amazing grace*.

It all began with a puppet ministry at the jail, conducted by people Karla could see were once like her. She saw signs of hardness from a lifetime of crime, immorality, and drugs, but there was also a softness of spirit, a supernatural joy. What these strangers had, Karla knew she had to have. What these strangers had was Jesus.

Karla stole a Bible from them—unaware that she could have received one for free—and scurried back to her cell. It didn't take long for the Word of God to pierce deeply into Karla's spirit, convicting her of sin and causing her to cry out to God for forgiveness. God's unconditional love overwhelmed Karla when she learned that, despite her brutality, *she was loved*.

In an instant, in Karla's own words, God "reached down inside of me and ripped out that violence at the very roots and poured Himself in."[3]

After her conversion, Karla never looked back. Her spiritual hunger continually drew her into the Word of God, feeding her soul and filling her spirit with His presence. Although Karla was convicted for the infamous murders and spent 14 years on death row, there was never again a hint of the cold, calculating, cruel demeanor within her that had destroyed two lives.

While on death row, Karla literally helped save lives—physically, emotionally, and spiritually—by intervening to help suicidal women and leading other inmates to Christ. She taught Bible studies, led seminars, and discipled women. She commited her life to spreading hope to the hopeless by sharing the blessed hope of Christ. Karla even became good friends with the prison warden.

Through Karla, the light of Christ shone ever so brightly along the dark corridors of death row. Then came the news that Karla's execution date was set. Even the warden struggled to balance professionalism with her compassionate concern for Karla's date with death. When asked how Karla was' handling the news, the warden responded, "You know Karla, she asked *me*, 'How can I make this easier on you?'"[4]

News of an execution date sparked fiery rallies both for and against the execution of Karla Faye Tucker—cries for mercy meeting outcries for justice. Every time I saw Karla interviewed in media appearances, her loving, thoughtful demeanor expressed genuine repentance for the pain she had caused others and her gratitude to God for her changed life through Christ. Despite appeals all the way to the U.S. Supreme Court, a stay was denied, and Karla was ordered to pay the ultimate price for her crimes.

Those who had seen her changed life—the prisoners, guards, wardens, and thousands on the outside who knew of her transformation—felt a crushing weight of concern.[5] But the one they were so burdened for bore a spirit as light as a feather. Karla knew she was going "home," and after expressing her loving gratitude to family and friends, including the warden, Karla began to hum softly as the lethal injection filtered through her veins.

From her life on death row to her execution day, what can explain Karla's supernatural peace? Her words, written years before, reflect what had happened the night of her conversion: "Jesus delivered me that night from death to LIFE ROW!"[6]

EPILOGUE

Uplifting One Another

Haven't you been amazed at the sight…watching birds fly together in their V-shaped formation? We marvel at the sudden turns and dives—first heading one direction, then another—yet still maintaining their tight formation. Their fascinating flight patterns are a form of true beauty, and a necessity for their survival.

But how can birds travel hundreds of miles without tiring? If you watch them closely, you'll observe what makes this endurance possible. At certain intervals—depending on the strength of the headwind—the lead bird, who is doing most of the work by breaking the force of the wind for the flock, suddenly leaves its position and drops back to the end of the formation. Without missing a beat of the wings, another bird quickly moves into the lead position, taking on the task of meeting the wind head-on.

Ultimately, the V-formation is much more efficient than each bird flying separately. In fact, up to 60 percent less work is required! The unified flapping of all of their wings produces an *uplift of air* that enables the birds at the back to glide and soar on the created air currents—thus the birds formerly in the lead can recuperate by coasting on the current. In this way, the birds take turns "uplifting one another."

By working in formation together, migrating birds can travel hundreds of miles, *even thousands of miles* they could never travel on their own alone. Even the strongest birds could not cross large bodies of water without the help of the flock uplifting each other.

Similarly, when we uplift one another by encouraging and praying for one another—by caring and sharing in true heart-to-heart friendships—all of us in the "flock of God" can go further in our journey than we ever could by trying to find endurance on our own. By *uplifting* one another, we are helping one another.

Our God is a God who cares. Psalm 145:14 says, "The LORD upholds all those who fall and lifts up all who are bowed down." Your uplifting words can be used by God to give help to the helpless, to heal the brokenhearted, to give hope to the hurting.

Knowing how lost you once were, you can enjoy how free you are now! And realize that if we all *uplift one another*, we will all *rise above abuse*…and soar farther together than we ever could have gone on our own.

G od's heart is grieved when any one of His precious creations is abused. He loves you and knows how to set you free—physically, mentally, emotionally, and yes, even spiritually.

There are four spiritual truths you need to know.

RECOGNIZING THE FOUR POINTS OF GOD'S PLAN

1. God's Purpose for You Is *Salvation*

What was God's motive in sending Christ to earth? To express His love for you by saving you! The Bible says, "God so loved the world that he gave his one and only Son, that whoever believes in him shall not perish but have eternal life. For God did not send his Son into the world to condemn the world, but to save the world through him" (John 3:16-17)

What was Jesus' purpose in coming to earth? To forgive your sins, empower you to have victory over sin, and enable you to live a fulfilled life. Jesus said, "I have come that they may have life, and have it to the full" (John 10:10).

2. Your Problem Is *Sin*

What exactly is sin? Sin is living independently of God's standard—knowing what is right, but choosing what is wrong. The Bible says, "Anyone, then, who knows the good he ought to do and doesn't do it, sins" (James 4:17).

What is the major consequence of sin? Spiritual death, or eternal separation from God. Scripture states, "Your iniquities [sins] have separated you from your God…For the wages of sin is death, but the gift of God is eternal life in Christ Jesus our Lord" (Isaiah 59:2; Romans 6:23).

3. God's Provision for You Is the *Savior*

Can anything remove the penalty for sin? Yes! Jesus died on the cross to personally pay the penalty for your sins. "God demonstrates his own love for us in this: While we were still sinners, Christ died for us" (Romans 5:8).

What can keep you from being separated from God? Belief in (entrusting your life to) Jesus Christ as the only way to God the Father. Jesus says, "I am the way and the truth and the life. No one comes to the Father except through me" (John 14:6).

4. Your Part Is *Surrender*

Give Christ control of your life and entrust yourself to Him. "Jesus said to his disciples, 'If anyone would come after me, he must deny himself and take up his cross [die to his own self-rule] and follow me. For whoever wants to save his life will lose it, but whoever loses his life for me will find it. What good will it be for a man if he gains the whole world, yet forfeits his soul?'" (Matthew 16:24-26).

Place your faith in (rely on) Jesus Christ as your personal Lord and Savior and reject your good works as a means of earning God's approval. "It is by grace you have been saved, through faith—and this not from yourselves, it is the gift of God—not by works, so that no one can boast" (Ephesians 2:8-9).

Receiving Christ as Savior and Lord

The moment you choose to receive Jesus as your Savior and Lord and entrust your life to Him, He comes to live inside you. Then He gives you His power to live the fulfilled life God has planned for you, and He gives you His peace and brings healing from your hurts and trials. If you want to be fully forgiven by God and become the person God created you to be, you can tell Him in a simple, heartfelt prayer like this:

God, I want a real relationship with You.
I admit that many times I've chosen to go my own way instead of Your way.
Please forgive me for my sins.
Jesus, thank You for dying on the cross to pay the penalty for my sins.
Come into my life to be my Savior and my Lord.
Change me from the inside out and make me the person
You created me to be.
Heal the deep wounds I suffered as a result of being abused,
and cleanse me from all the unrighteous acts done to me.
In Your holy name I pray. Amen.

What Can You Expect Now?

If you sincerely prayed that prayer, you can embrace these words from the Bible!

"The LORD is close to the brokenhearted and
saves those who are crushed in spirit"
(PSALM 34:18).

NOTES

Introduction

1. John 14:27.
2. Matthew 5:9.
3. Romans 12:18.
4. Matthew 10:34.
5. John 8:32.
6. 2 Corinthians 1:3-4.
7. 1 Samuel 16:7.

Childhood Sexual Abuse: The Secret Storm

1. *Miss America,* lyrics and music by Wayne, Bernie, Command Music Co., Inc., 1955.
2. David Holthouse, "Crowning Achievement," *Denver Westword* (June 24, 2004).
3. Marilyn Van Derbur Atler, "The Darkest Secret," *People* (June 10, 1991).
4. Marilyn Van Derbur, *Miss America by Day: Lessons Learned from Ultimate Betrayals and Unconditional Love* (Denver, CO: Oak Hill Press, 2004), 57.
5. Van Derbur, *Miss America by Day,* 12.
6. Lenore Terr, *Unchained Memories: True Stories of Traumatic Memories, Lost and Found* (New York: BasicBooks, 1994), 121.
7. Van Derbur, *Miss America by Day*, 21.
8. Van Derbur, *Miss America by Day*, 21.
9. See *Merriam-Webster's Collegiate Dictionary*, electronic ed. (New York: Merriam-Webster, 2001), s.v. "Abuse."
10. James Strong, *The Exhaustive Concordance of the Bible,* electronic ed. (Ontario: Woodside Bible Fellowship, 1996), #H5953.
11. Maxine Hancock and Karen Burton Mains, *Child Sexual Abuse: Hope for Healing*, rev. ed. (Wheaton, IL: Harold Shaw, 1997), 22.
12. See Hancock and Mains, *Child Sexual Abuse*, 16-17.
13. Hancock and Mains, *Child Sexual Abuse*, 19.
14. Hancock and Mains, *Child Sexual Abuse*, 19.
15. Van Derbur, *Miss America by Day*, 23.
16. Van Derbur, *Miss America by Day*, 23.

17. See Grant L. Martin, *Counseling for Family Violence and Abuse*, ed. Gary R. Collins, vol. 6 (Dallas: Word, 1987), 151.

18. Van Derbur, *Miss America by Day*, 23.

19. Van Derbur, *Miss America by Day*, 25.

20. Van Derbur, *Miss America by Day*, 24.

21. Van Derbur, *Miss America by Day*, 22.

22. See *The Child Abuse Prevention and Treatment Act* as amended by *The Keeping Children and Families Safe Act of 2003* (Washington, D.C.: United States Department of Health and Human Services, June 25, 2003), sec. 111 42 US.C. 5106g, http://www.acf.hhs.gov/programs/cb/laws_policies/cblaws/capta03/capta_manual.pdf.

23. Van Derbur, *Miss America by Day*, 9.

24. Van Derbur, *Miss America by Day*, 9-10.

25. Hancock and Mains, *Child Sexual Abuse*, 122-24.

26. David Holthouse, "Crowning Achievement."

27. Van Derbur, *Miss America by Day*, 13.

28. Van Derbur, *Miss America by Day*, 18.

29. Van Derbur Atler, "The Darkest Secret."

30. For the sequence of events in abusive relationships see Martin, *Counseling for Family Violence and Abuse*, 165-71.

31. Van Derbur, *Miss America by Day*, 27.

32. Van Derbur, *Miss America by Day*, 27.

33. Van Derbur Atler, "The Darkest Secret."

34. Van Derbur Atler, "The Darkest Secret."

35. For further signs see Alice Huskey, *Stolen Childhood: What You Need to Know About Sexual Abuse* (Downer's Grove, IL: InterVarsity, 1990), 76-81.

36. Van Derbur, *Miss America by Day*, 30.

37. Van Derbur, *Miss America by Day*, 34-35.

38. Van Derbur, *Miss America by Day*, 66-67.

39. Van Derbur, *Miss America by Day*, 173, 185-87.

40. Van Derbur, *Miss America by Day*, 26.

41. Van Derbur, *Miss America by Day*, 26.

42. Van Derbur, *Miss America by Day*, 173.

43. Van Derbur, *Miss America by Day*, 106.

44. Van Derbur, *Miss America by Day*, 12.

45. See Hancock and Mains, *Child Sexual Abuse*, 96-99.

46. Van Derbur, *Miss America by Day*, 192.

47. Van Derbur Atler, "The Darkest Secret."

48. Van Derbur, *Miss America by Day*, 12-13.

49. See also Hancock and Mains, *Child Sexual Abuse*, 122-26.

50. See also Hancock and Mains, *Child Sexual Abuse*, 120-21.

51. Van Derbur, *Miss America by Day*, 387.

52. For characteristics of perpetrators see Hancock and Mains, *Child Sexual Abuse*, 122-27.

53. Van Derbur, *Miss America by Day*, 387.

54. Van Derbur, *Miss America by Day*, 387.

55. Van Derbur, *Miss America by Day*, 103.

56. Van Derbur, *Miss America by Day*, 103.

57. For reasons victims remain silent see Kay Marshall Strom, *Helping Women in Crisis: A Handbook for People Helpers* (Grand Rapids: Zondervan, 1986), 43.

58. Van Derbur, *Miss America by Day*, 528.

59. Van Derbur, *Miss America by Day*, 527.

60. On the three God-given inner needs, see Lawrence J. Crabb, Jr., *Understanding People: Deep Longings for Relationship* (Grand Rapids: Zondervan, 1987), 15-16; Robert S. McGee, *The Search for Significance*, 2nd ed. (Houston, TX: Rapha, 1990), 27-30.

61. Van Derbur, *Miss America by Day*, 315.

62. Van Derbur, *Miss America by Day*, 315.

63. Van Derbur, *Miss America by Day*, 314.

64. Van Derbur, *Miss America by Day*, 307.

65. For additional advice on responding to abusive situations see Grant Martin, *Please Don't Hurt Me* (Wheaton, IL: Victor, 1987), 52-60.

66. Van Derbur, *Miss America by Day*, 428.

67. Van Derbur, *Miss America by Day*, 324.

68. Van Derbur, *Miss America by Day*, 413.

69. Van Derbur, *Miss America by Day*, 413.

70. Van Derbur, *Miss America by Day*, 413.

71. See Martin, *Please Don't Hurt Me*, 51-59.

72. See Van Derbur, *Miss America by Day*, 423-24.

73. See Van Derbur, *Miss America by Day*, 207.

74. See Martin, *Please Don't Hurt Me*, 96.

75. For more preventative measures see Martin, *Please Don't Hurt Me*, 90-93.

76. For Jaycee Dugard's story see Alex Tresniowski, "Jaycee Dugard Captive No More," *People* (September 14, 2009); Alan B. Goldberg and Sarah Netter, "Jaycee Dugard Exclusive: 'It's Been a Long Haul,'" *ABC News* (March 5, 2010), at http://abcnews.go.com/2020/TheLaw/jaycee-dugard-home-video-kidnap-survivor-speaks-time/story?id=10009310&page=1; Jesse McKinley and Carol Pogash, "Kidnapping Victim Was Not Always Locked Away," *New York Times* (August 28, 2009), at http://www.nytimes.com/2009/08/29/us/29abduct.html?pagewanted=1&_r=2.

77. Alan B. Goldberg and Sarah Netter, "Jaycee Dugard Exclusive: 'It's Been a Long Haul,'" *ABC News* (March 5, 2010), at http://abcnews.go.com/2020/TheLaw/jaycee-dugard-home-video-kidnap-survivor-speaks-time/story?id=10009310&page=1.

78. *Abba* is an Aramaic term Jesus used to refer to God. It is a term of affection children would use to address their father, similar to saying, "Daddy." See Gerhard Kittel, Geoffrey William Bromiley, Gerhard Friedrich, *Theological Dictionary of the New Testament*, vol. 1, electronic ed. (Grand Rapids: Eerdmans, 1976), 5-6.

79. Van Derbur, *Miss America by Day,* 197-98.

80. Van Derbur, *Miss America by Day,* 252.

81. Van Derbur, *Miss America by Day,* 173.

Spiritual Abuse: Religion at Its Worst

1. Edward J. Cumella, "Religious Abuse," *The Remuda Review* (Spring 2005), 17.

2. David Johnson and Jeff VanVonderen, *The Subtle Power of Spiritual Abuse: Recognizing and Escaping Spiritual Manipulation and False Spiritual Authority Within the Church* (Minneapolis: Bethany House, 1991), 20.

3. See Ken Blue, *Healing Spiritual Abuse: How to Break Free from Bad Church Experiences* (Downers Grove, IL: InterVarsity, 1993), 44-48; Johnson and VanVonderen, *The Subtle Power of Spiritual Abuse,* 37-39.

4. *Merriam-Webster's Collegiate Dictionary*, electronic ed. (New York: Merriam-Webster, 2001), s.v. "Legal."

5. Charles C. Ryrie, *Balancing the Christian Life: Biblical Principles for Wholesome Living* (Chicago: Moody, 1969), 159.

6. Dr. Donald T. Atkinson, *Magic, Myth & Medicine* (New York: The World Publishing Company, 1956), 271-72.

7. Andrew White, *A History of the Warfare of Science with Theology in Christendom*, vol. 2 (New York: George Braziller, 1955), 63.

8. White, *A History of the Warfare of Science*, 125.

9. Bob George, *Discipleship Counseling Training Student Manual* (Dallas: Discipleship Counseling Services, n.d.).

10. See Cumella, "Religious Abuse," 17-18.

11. See also David A. Seamands, *Healing Grace* (Wheaton, IL: Victor, 1988), 18-19.

12. See also Seamands, *Healing Grace*, 100-06.

13. See Cumella, "Religious Abuse," 18.

14. See Cumella, "Religious Abuse," 18.

15. See Cumella, "Religious Abuse," 18.

16. See also Seamands, *Healing Grace*, 126-38.

17. See Cumella, "Religious Abuse," 18.

18. See also Seamands, *Healing Grace*, 12-14.

19. See also Cumella, "Religious Abuse," 19; Seamands, *Healing Grace*, 19.

20. David Schley Schaff, *John Huss: His Life, Teachings, and Death after Five Hundred Years* (New York: Charles Scribner's Sons, 1915), 249.

21. Schaff, *John Huss,* 255.

22. Schaff, *John Huss,* 257.

23. See also Seamands, *Healing Grace*, 12-19.

24. For further information on wrong thinking see Stephen Arterburn and Jack Felton, *Toxic Faith: Understanding and Overcoming Religious Addiction* (Nashville: Thomas Nelson, 1991), 265-314.

25. On the three God-given inner needs, see Lawrence J. Crabb, Jr., *Understanding People: Deep Longings for Relationship* (Grand Rapids: Zondervan, 1987), 15-16; Robert S. McGee, *The Search for Significance*, 2nd ed. (Houston, TX: Rapha, 1990), 27-30.

26. John Newton, "Amazing Grace" in *Olney Hymns* (London: W. Oliver, 1779).

27. See David R. Miller, *Breaking Free: Rescuing Families from the Clutches of Legalism* (Grand Rapids: Baker, 1992), 174-75.

28. See also Kevin A. Miller, "I Don't Feel Like a Very Good Christian: Why Does It Seem That You Can Never Quite Measure Up?" *Discipleship Journal* (September/October 1988), 9.

29. For teachings and practices of the FLDS see James Walker, "Watchman Profile: Fundamentalist Church of Jesus Christ of Latter Day Saints (FLDS)" (Arlington, TX: Watchman Fellowship, 2004), at http://www.watchman.org/old_wf/assets/files/flds_profile.pdf.

30. For information concerning Raymond Jessop and the 2008 raid in Eldorado, TX, see Edecio Martinez, "In Land of Fundamentalist Mormons, Can Texas Find Impartial Jury for Polygamist Raymond Jessop?" *CBS News* (October 27, 2009), at http://www.cbsnews.com/8301-504083_162-5129817-504083.html?tag=mncol;lst;1; "Polygamist Gets 10 Years for Marrying Teen" (Washington, D.C.: United Press International, November 11, 2009), at http://www.upi.com/Top_News/US/2009/11/11/Polygamist-gets-10-years-for-marrying-teen/UPI-28921257920937/.

31. Walker, "Watchman Profile: Fundamentalist Church of Jesus Christ of Latter Day Saints (FLDS)," at http://www.watchman.org/old_wf/assets/files/flds_profile.pdf.

32. Martinez, "In Land of Fundamentalist Mormons, Can Texas Find Impartial Jury for Polygamist Raymond Jessop?" http://www.cbsnews.com/8301-504083_162-5129817-504083.html?tag=mncol;lst;1.

33. W.E. Vine, Merrill F. Unger, and William White, *Vine's Complete Expository Dictionary of Biblical Words* (Nashville: Thomas Nelson, 1985), s.v. "Sabbath."

34. Kenneth O. Gangel, "Reexamining Biblical Worship," *Vital Christian Living Issues: Examining Crucial Concerns in the Spiritual Life*, ed. Roy B. Zuck (Grand Rapids: Kregel, 1997), 84.

35. Frederick Dale Bruner, *Matthew: A Commentary* (Grand Rapids: Eerdmans, 2004), 216.

36. Robert A. Baker and John M. Landers, *A Summary of Christian History* (Nashville: B&H Publishing Group, 2005), 15.

Verbal and Emotional Abuse: Victory over Verbal and Emotional Abuse

1. See Andre Bustanoby and Fay Bustanoby, *Just Talk to Me: The Principles and Practice of Communication in Marriage* (Grand Rapids: Zondervan, 1981), 148.

2. Charles R. Solomon, *The Ins and Outs of Rejection* (Littleton, CO: Heritage House, 1976), 13.

3. Solomon, *The Ins and Outs of Rejection*, 13, 18.

4. Francis Brown, Samual Rolles Driver, and Charles Augustus Briggs, eds., *Hebrew-Aramaic and English Lexicon of the Old Testament*, electronic ed. (Oak Harbor, WA: Logos Research Systems, 2000).

5. See *Merriam-Webster's Collegiate Dictionary*, electronic ed. (New York: Merriam-Webster, 2001), s.v. "Brainwashing."

6. Josh Mankiewicz, "Kidnapped Heiress: The Patty Hearst Story," *Dateline* transcript, July 25, 2009.

7. Mankiewicz, "Kidnapped Heiress: The Patty Hearst Story."

8. Mankiewicz, "Kidnapped Heiress: The Patty Hearst Story."

9. Frank Bolz, Kenneth J. Dudonis, David P. Schulz, *The Counterterrorism Handbook: Tactics, Procedures, and Techniques* (Boca Raton, FL: CRC Press, 2002), 209.

10. Mankiewicz, "Kidnapped Heiress: The Patty Hearst Story."

11. Mankiewicz, "Kidnapped Heiress: The Patty Hearst Story."

12. Mankiewicz, "Kidnapped Heiress: The Patty Hearst Story."

13. CNN Larry King Live, "Interview with Patty Hearst" (January 22, 2002), http://transcripts.cnn.com/TRANSCRIPTS/0201/22/lkl.00.html.

14. CNN Larry King Live, "Interview with Patty Hearst."

15. John 8:32.

16. For this section see also Robert Burney, "Emotional Abuse Is Heart and Soul Mutilation," Joy2MeU, http://www.joy2meu.com/emotional_abuse.html; Scott Wetzler, *Living with the Passive-Aggressive Man*, repr. ed. (1992; New York: Fireside, 1993), 35-37; Harold I. Kaplan and Benjamin J. Saddock, *Synopsis of Psychiatry: Behavioral Sciences/Clinical Psychiatry*, 8th ed. (Baltimore: Williams & Wilkins, 1997), 793-94; Michael Arndt and Clare Dacy, "Healing Emotional Abuse," *Designed Thinking*, at http:/www.designedthinking.com/Fear/Abuse/abuse.html.

17. For the three God-given inner needs, see Lawrence J. Crabb, Jr., *Understanding People: Deep Longings for Relationship* (Grand Rapids: Zondervan, 1987), 15-16; Robert S. McGee, *The Search for Significance*, 2nd ed. (Houston, TX: Rapha, 1990), 27-30.

18. See Crabb, *Understanding People*, 15-16; McGee, *The Search for Significance*, 27-30.

19. For suggestions on confronting parents see Susan Forward, *Toxic Parents: Overcoming Their Hurtful Legacy and Reclaiming Your Life* (New York: Bantam, 1989), 236-74.

20. Bustanoby and Bustanoby, *Just Talk to Me*, 159-60.

21. For additional advice on setting boundaries see Robert Burney, "Setting Personal Boundaries—Protecting Self," http://joy2meu.com/Personal_Boundaries.htm.

22. Chad J. Angotta, "Emotional Boundaries: To Be or Not to Be…Yourself," at http://www.psych-point.com/boundary.html.

23. Brown, Driver, and Briggs, eds., *Hebrew-Aramaic and English Lexicon of the Old Testament*.

24. See Crabb, *Understanding People*, 15-16; McGee, *The Search for Significance*, 27-30.

Victimization: Victory over the Victim Mentality

1. For this section see *Merriam-Webster's Collegiate Dictionary*, electronic ed. (New York: Merriam-Webster, 2001), s.v. "Victim."

2. James Strong, *Strong's Hebrew Lexicon*, electronic ed. (Winterbourne, Ontario: Timnathserah Inc., 2002).

3. "2 Arrested in Killing of U.S. Boy in Italy," *Wilmington Morning Star* (November 2, 1994), 6A.

4. Reg Green, "A Child's Legacy of Love," http://nicholasgreen.org/articles.html.

5. See http://www.nicholasgreen.org.

6. See http://www.nicholasgreen.org.

7. See http://www.nicholasgreen.org.

8. For this section see Malcolm Smith, *No Longer a Victim* (Tulsa, OK: Pillar, 1992), 9-10.

9. Stormie Omartian, *Stormie* (Eugene, OR: Harvest House, 1986), 43.

10. June Hunt, *June 1987 Stormie Omartian interview transcript*, 5.

11. June Hunt, *June 1987 Stormie Omartian interview transcript*, 4.

12. Omartian, *Stormie*, 60.

13. June Hunt, *June 1987 Stormie Omartian interview transcript*, 6.

14. Omartian, *Stormie*, 75-84.

15. Omartian, *Stormie*, 115.

16. Omartian, *Stormie,* 117.

17. Omartian, *Stormie,* 139.

18. Omartian, *Stormie,* 139-40.

19. Omartian, *Stormie,* 141.

20. Omartian, *Stormie,* 156.

21. See http://www.stormieomartian.com.

22. Harvest House Publishers, "Author Detail: Stormie Omartian," http://www.harvesthousepublish ers.com/books_authordetail.cfm?ED_ID=10277.

23. Candace Walters, *Invisible Wounds* (Portland, OR: Multnomah, 1987), 62.

24. One pound equals .454 kilograms. One hundred and fifty pounds equals 68.1 kilograms.

25. Ellen Bass and Laura Davis, *The Courage to Heal: A Guide for Women Survivors of Child Sexual Abuse* (New York: Harper & Row, 1988), 49.

26. For the three God-given inner needs, see Lawrence J. Crabb, Jr., *Understanding People: Deep Longings for Relationship* (Grand Rapids: Zondervan, 1987), 15-16; Robert S. McGee, *The Search for Significance,* 2nd ed. (Houston, TX: Rapha, 1990), 27-30.

27. Rich Buhler, *Pain and Pretending* (Nashville: Thomas Nelson, 1991), 65.

28. David A. Stoop, *Living with a Perfectionist* (Nashville: Oliver-Nelson, 1987), 44-45.

29. Stoop, *Living with a Perfectionist,* 36.

30. For this section see Bass and Davis, *The Courage to Heal,* 213, 217-219; Joyce Meyer, *Beauty for Ashes: Receiving Emotional Healing* (Tulsa, Okla.: Harrison House, 1994), 29-30.

31. See Carmen Renee Berry and Mark W. Baker, *Who's to Blame? Escape the Victim Trap & Gain Personal Power in Your Relationships* (Colorado Springs, CO: Piñon, 1996), 35-40, 52-58.

32. See Berry and Baker, *Who's to Blame,* 49-60; Lynda D. Elliott and Vicki L. Tanner, *My Father's Child: Help and Healing for the Victims of Emotional, Sexual, and Physical Abuse* (Brentwood, TN : Wolgemuth & Hyatt, 1988), 7-8.

33. Walters, *Invisible Wounds,* 62.

34. Buhler, *Pain and Pretending,* 65.

35. Elliott and Tanner, *My Father's Child,* 9-12.

36. Karen Randau, *Conquering Fear* (Dallas: Rapha, 1991), 44.

37. H. Norman Wright, *Anger* (Waco, TX: Word, 1980), audiocassette.

38. Wright, *Anger.*

39. See Crabb, *Understanding People,* 15-16; McGee, *The Search for Significance* 27-30.

40. Gary Jackson Oliver and H. Norman Wright, *When Anger Hits Home* (Chicago: Moody, 1992), 97.

41. Wright, *Anger.*

42. Crabb, *Understanding People,* 15-16; McGee, *The Search for Significance,* 27.

43. Wright, *Anger.*

44. Crabb, *Understanding People,* 15-16; McGee, *The Search for Significance,* 27.

45. Dan B. Allender, *The Wounded Heart* (Colorado Springs, CO: NavPress, 1990), 183-97.

46. Elliott and Tanner, *My Father's Child,* 109-24.

47. Allender, *The Wounded Heart,* 197.

48. Meyer, *Beauty for Ashes: Receiving Emotional Healing*, 52-53.

49. Bass and Davis, *The Courage to Heal*, 134-36.

50. Malcolm Smith, *No Longer a Victim* (Tulsa, OK: Pillar, 1992), 25-27.

51. Allender, *The Wounded Heart*, 227-29.

52. John Nieder and Thomas M. Thompson, *Forgive & Love Again: Healing Wounded Relationships* (Eugene, OR: Harvest House, 1991), 51-56.

53. David Augsburger, *The Freedom of Forgiveness*, rev. and exp. ed. (Chicago: Moody, 1988), 18.

54. Alexander Pope, *Essay on Criticism*, part 2, line 325.

55. Doris Van Stone and Erwin W. Lutzer, *No Place to Cry: The Hurt and Healing of Sexual Abuse* (Chicago: Moody, 1990), 90-92.

56. Laura L. Finley, *Encyclopedia of Juvenile Violence* (Santa Barbara, CA: Greenwood Publishing Group, 2006), 123.

57. Laura L. Finley, *Encyclopedia of Juvenile Violence,* 123.

58. Beth Nimmo, Darrell Scott, and Steve Rabey, *Rachel's Tears* (Nashville: Thomas Nelson, 2000), 90.

59. Nimmo, Scott, and Rabey, *Rachel's Tears*, 90.

60. Randy Patrick, "Thirteen Tears: A Columbine Legacy," *Newer World* (April 19, 2009), 2. See http://kyvoice.com/winchestersun/newerworld/?p=418.

61. David Van Biema, Julie Grace, and Emily Mitchell, "A Surge of Teen Spirit," *Time* (May 31, 1999).

62. See http://kyvoice.com/winchestersun/newerworld/?p=418, accessed March 19, 2010.

63. See http://kyvoice.com/winchestersun/newerworld/?p=418, entry by "Mark Francis" dated April 20, 2009 at 11:04 p.m., accessed March 19, 2010.

64. See http://kyvoice.com/winchestersun/newerworld/?p=418, entry by "Luis" dated November 21, 2009 at 2:33 a.m., accessed March 19, 2010.

65. See http://kyvoice.com/winchestersun/newerworld/?p=418, entry by "jeff walker" dated November 17, 2009 at 2:45 a.m., accessed March 19, 2010.

66. Smith, *No Longer a Victim*, 33-35.

67. David A. Seamands, *If Only* (Wheaton, IL: Victor, 1995), 59.

68. Ken Blue, *Healing Spiritual Abuse* (Downer's Grove, IL: InterVarsity, 1993), 120.

69. See the Hebrew dictionary entry in James Strong, *Strong's Exhaustive Concordance of the Bible* (Nashville: Abingdon, 1986), 17.

70. See Brent Curtis, *Guilt*, ed. Tom Varney (Colorado Springs, CO: NavPress, 1992), 17-29.

71. Doris Van Stone and Erwin Lutzer, *No Place to Cry: The Hurt and Healing of Sexual Abuse* (Chicago: Moody, 1990), 119.

Wife Abuse: Assault on a Woman's Worth

1. *What Every Congregation Needs to Know About Domestic Violence* (Seattle, WA: Center for the Prevention of Sexual and Domestic Violence, 1994), n.p.

2. Carol Forsloff, "Health Workers Facilitate Wife Beating," *Digital Journal* (February 1, 2009), http://www.digitaljournal.com/article/266301.

3. See *American Heritage Electronic Dictionary* (New York: Houghton Mifflin, 1992).

4. See *American Heritage Electronic Dictionary.*

5. See James Strong, *Strong's Hebrew Lexicon,* electronic ed. (Online Bible Millennium Ed. v. 1.13) (Timnathserah Inc., July 6, 2002).

6. Francis Brown, S.R. Driver, Charles Augustus Briggs, *Enhanced Brown-Driver-Briggs Hebrew and English Lexicon,* electronic ed. (Oak Harbor, WA: Logos Research Systems, 2000), 329.

7. See Kathy L. Cawthon, *Getting Out: An Escape Manual for Abused Women* (Lafayette, LA: Huntington House, 1996), 22-23; *Family Violence and Addiction: Implications for Treatment* (n.p.: Texas Department of Human Services, 1989).

8. *What Every Congregation Needs to Know About Domestic Violence,* n.p.

9. Ron Christenson, *Political Trials: Gordian Knots in the Law,* 2nd ed. (New Brunswick, NJ: Transaction Publishers, 1999), 109.

10. For information on the O.J. Simpson trial see Christenson, *Political Trials,* 107-10.

11. Raoul Felder and Barbara Victor, *Getting Away with Murder: Weapons for the War Against Domestic Violence* (New York: Simon & Schuster, 1996), 27.

12. J. David Woodard, *The America that Reagan Built* (Westport, CT: Praeger, 2006), 172.

13. Trudy Marshall, "Did OJ Simpson Get $3.5 Million for Book?" *Associated Content* (October 30, 2006), http://www.associatedcontent.com/article/76556/did_oj_simpson_get_35_million_for_book.htm.

14. Gavin De Becker, *The Gift of Fear* (New York: Dell, 1998), 190.

15. For different types of abuse see also Cawthon, *Getting Out,* 89-92.

16. For these characteristics see Mentor Research Institute, "About Domestic Violence Against Men" (May 20, 2007), http://www.oregoncounseling.org/Handouts/DomesticViolenceMen.htm.

17. Otto Weininger, *Sex and Character: An Investigation of Fundamental Principles,* trans. Ladislaus Lob, eds. Daniel Steuer and Laura Marcus (Bloomington, IN: Indiana University Press, 2005), 161, 163.

18. See *Merriam-Webster's Collegiate Dictionary,* electronic ed. (New York: Merriam-Webster, 2001).

19. See Margaret J. Rinck, *Christian Men Who Hate Women: Healing Hurting Relationships* (Grand Rapids: Zondervan, 1990), 17-18.

20. Elizabeth Dawn Keetley and John Charles Pettegrew, *Public Women, Public Words: A Documentary History of American Feminism* (Lanham, MD: Rowman & Littlefield, 2005), 172-73.

21. *Domestic Violence: The Facts* (Somerville, MA: Peace at Home, 2004), 4. See also http://www.better-man.org/dv-the-facts.pdf.

22. For cycles of abuse see Patricia Riddle Gaddis, *Battered but Not Broken: Help for Abused Wives and Their Church Families* (Valley Forge, PA: Judson, 1996), 27-29; Kay Marshall Strom, *In the Name of Submission: A Painful Look at Wife Battering* (Portland, OR: Multnomah, 1986), 44-46; Lenore E. Walker, *The Battered Woman* (New York: HarperPerennial, 1979), 55-70.

23. For research and statistics in this paragraph see Donald G. Dutton, "Witnessing Parental Violence as a Traumatic Experience Shaping the Abusive Personality" in Robert A. Geffner, Peter G. Jaffe, Marlies Sudermann, eds., *Children Exposed to Domestic Violence: Current Issues in Research, Intervention, Prevention, and Policy Development* (New York: The Haworth Maltreatment & Trauma Press, 2000), 61.

24. See also S.R. McDill and Linda McDill, *Shattered and Broken* (Old Tappan, NJ: Fleming H. Revell, 1991), 76-82; Ginny NiCarthy and Sue Davidson, *You Can Be Free: An Easy-to-Read Handbook for Abused Women* (Seattle, WA: Seal, 1989), 16-19; Strom, *In the Name of Submission,* 35-39.

25. See also Brent Curtis, *Guilt,* ed. Tom Varney (Colorado Springs, CO: NavPress, 1992), 14-29.

26. On the three God-given inner needs, see Lawrence J. Crabb, Jr., *Understanding People: Deep Longings for Relationship* (Grand Rapids: Zondervan, 1987), 15-16; Robert S. McGee, *The Search for Significance*, 2nd ed. (Houston, TX: Rapha, 1990), 27-30.

27. See also Marie M. Fortune, *Keeping the Faith: Questions and Answers for the Abused Woman* (San Francisco: HarperSanFrancisco, 1987), 28-29.

28. See also Strom, *In the Name of Submission*, 56-57.

29. See also Strom, *In the Name of Submission*, 56-58.

30. Sharon Ries, *My Husband My Maker* (Eugene, OR: Harvest House, 1989), 36.

31. *Hope for the Heart* transcript, "Surviving an Abusive Marriage," with Sharon Ries, April 23-27, 1990, 4.

32. See www.raulries.com

33. *Hope for the Heart* transcript, "Surviving an Abusive Marriage," 10.

34. Ries, *My Husband My Maker*, 98.

35. Raul Ries, *From Fury to Freedom* (Eugene, OR: Harvest House, 1986), 13.

36. Ries, *From Fury to Freedom*, 94.

37. Ries, *From Fury to Freedom*.

38. Ries, *From Fury to Freedom*, 97.

39. Ries, *From Fury to Freedom*, 102.

40. Ries, *From Fury to Freedom*.

41. Ries, *From Fury to Freedom*, 107.

42. Ries, *From Fury to Freedom*, 108.

43. For the following checklist, see Peace at Home, *Domestic Violence: The Facts*, (Somerville, MA: Peace at Home, 2004), 14-15, http://www.betterman.org/dv-the-facts.pdf.

44. For this section see Texas Young Lawyers Association, *Family Violence: Legal Choices for Victims of Domestic Violence* (Austin, TX: State Bar of Texas, 1996), http://www.texasbar.com/PrinterTemplate.cfm?Section=Home&CONTENTID=3881&TEMPLATE=/ContentManagement/ContentDis-play.cfm. Be sure to check the current laws in your area.

45. For the following section see also Strom, *In the Name of Submission*, 102-06.

Hope for the Abuser

1. See Patricia Evans, *The Verbally Abusive Relationship: How to Recognize It and How to Respond* (Holbrook, MA: Bob Adams, 1992), 164.

2. Linda Strom, *Karla Faye Tucker: Set Free* (Colorado Springs: Harold Shaw, 2000), 19.

3. Strom, *Karla Faye Tucker*, 49.

4. Strom, *Karla Faye Tucker*, 139

5. Strom, *Karla Faye Tucker*, 206.

6. Strom, *Karla Faye Tucker*, 52.

About the Author

June Hunt is an author, singer, speaker, and founder of Hope for the Heart, a worldwide biblical counseling ministry featuring the award-winning radio broadcast by the same name heard daily across America. In addition, *Hope in the Night* is June's live two-hour call-in counseling program that helps people untie their tangled problems with biblical hope and practical help. Hope for the Heart radio broadcasts currently air in more than 25 countries.

Early family pain was the catalyst that shaped June's compassionate heart. Later, as youth director for more than 600 teenagers, she became aware of the need for sound biblical counseling. Her work with young people and their parents led June to a life commitment of *providing God's truth for today's problems.*

After years of teaching and research, June began developing scripturally based counseling tools called *Biblical Counseling Keys,* which address definitions, characteristics, causes, and solutions for 100 topics (such as marriage and parenting, anger and abuse, guilt and grief). Recently these individual topics were compiled to create the landmark *Biblical Counseling Library.*

The *Counseling Keys* have become the foundation for the Hope Biblical Counseling Institute initiated by The Criswell College. Each monthly conference in the Dallas-based institute provides training to help spiritual leaders, counselors, and other caring Christians meet the very real needs of others.

June has served as a guest professor at colleges and seminaries, both nationally and internationally, teaching on topics such as crisis counseling, child abuse, wife abuse, homosexuality, forgiveness, singleness, and self-worth. Her works are currently available in 60 countries and more than 20 languages, including Russian, Romanian, Ukrainian, Spanish, Portuguese, German, Mandarin, Korean, Japanese, and Arabic.

She is the author of *How to Forgive... When You Don't Feel Like It, Seeing Yourself Through God's Eyes, Counseling Through Your Bible Handbook, How to Handle Your Emotions, Caring for a Loved One with Cancer,* and more than 40 topical HopeBooks. June is also a contributor to the *Soul Care Bible* and the *Women's Devotional Bible.*

As an accomplished musician, June has been a guest on numerous national television and radio programs, including the NBC *Today* show. She has toured overseas with the USO and been a guest soloist at Billy Graham crusades. Five recordings—*Songs of Surrender, Hymns of Hope, The Whisper of My Heart, The Shelter Under His Wings,* and *The Hope of Christmas*—all reflect her heart of hope.

Learn more about June and Hope for the Heart at...

Hope for the Heart, Inc.
2001 West Plano Parkway, Suite 1000
Plano, Texas 75075

1-972-212-9200
www.HopeForTheHeart.org

Other Harvest House Books
by June Hunt

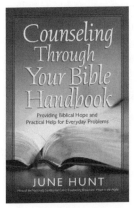

COUNSELING THROUGH
YOUR BIBLE HANDBOOK

No matter what the problem, God doesn't leave us without hope or help. The Bible is richly relevant when it comes to the difficult dilemmas we all face. Here you will find 50 chapters of spiritual wisdom and compassionate counsel on even the hardest issues, such as anger, adultery, depression, fear, guilt, grief, rejection, and self-worth.

HOW TO FORGIVE...
WHEN YOU DON'T FEEL LIKE IT

Though we know God has called us to forgive, we find ourselves asking hard questions: What if it hurts too much to forgive? What if the other person isn't sorry? How can I let someone off the hook for doing something so wrong? June speaks from experience as she offers biblical help and hope with heartfelt compassion. Here's how to find true freedom through forgiveness.

HOW TO HANDLE YOUR EMOTIONS

God created our hearts to be like a dashboard filled with dials—finely tuned controls to help process our full range of emotions in a healthy way. June helps you to better navigate your emotions as you come to understand their definitions, characteristics, causes, and the solutions that lead to emotional growth.

KEEPING YOUR COOL...
WHEN YOUR ANGER IS HOT!

The fiery emotion of anger often causes us to say and do things we later regret. And try as we might, it's an emotion that's tough to control. How can we prevail?

June explores the various causes and kinds of anger and the biblical steps toward resolution. You will learn how to identify the triggers of anger, ways of dealing with past angers buried deep in the heart, what the Bible says about righteous and unrighteous anger, and how to bring about real and lasting change.

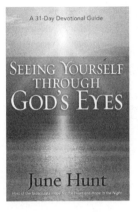

SEEING YOURSELF THROUGH GOD'S EYES

How you view yourself can have a profound effect on your everyday living. The key is to see yourself through God's eyes. After all, if you don't know who you are, you can't know God's plan and purpose for your life. Discover the great riches of your identity in Christ in the 31 devotions in this book.